Managing Behavior in Organizations

THIRD EDITION

Managing Behavior in Organizations

Jerald Greenberg
Fisher College of Business
The Ohio State University

Prentice
Hall

Upper Saddle River, New Jersey 07458

A 013183

Library of Congress Cataloging-in-Publication Data

Greenberg, Jerald.
    Managing behavior in organizations / Jerald Greenberg.—3rd ed.
        p. cm.
    Includes bibliographical references and index.
    ISBN 0-13-032824-3
        1. Organizational behavior. I. Title.

HD58.7 .G7176 2001
658.3—dc21

H F 102

2001021307

Acquisitions Editor: Melissa Steffens
Editor-in-Chief: Jeff Shelstad
Assistant Editor: Jessica Sabloff
Marketing Manager: Shannon Moore
Managing Editor (Production): Judy Leale
Production Editor: Keri Jean
Permissions Coordinator: Suzanne Grappi
Associate Director, Manufacturing: Vincent Scelta
Manufacturing Buyer: Diane Peirano
Design Manager: Pat Smythe
Designer: Michael Fruhbeis
Interior Design: Michael Fruhbeis
Cover Design: Michael Fruhbeis
Cover Illustration/Photo: John Douglas, "The Western Eye, © The Phoenix Art Group
Manager, Print Production: Christy Mahon
ETM Consultant: Ben Ko
ETM Assistant: Ina Kichen
Composition: Carlisle Communications
Full-Service Project Management: Ann Imhof
Printer/Binder: Hamilton

Credits and acknowledgments borrowed from other sources and reproduced,
with permission, in this textbook appear on appropriate page within text.

10 9 8 7 6 5 4 3 2 1
ISBN 0-13-032824-3

To my best pal, the center of the universe.
You know who you are . . .
JG

BRIEF CONTENTS

CONTENTS

PREFACE

As you hold this book in your hands, you can tell that it is not a traditional, full-featured organizational behavior (OB) text that covers all aspects of all topics. Its diminutive dimensions and paperback format suggest otherwise. Rather, you may consider it a tour of the scientific and practical highlights of OB housed in a succinct package. It gets "right to the point" by focusing on essential concepts and practices that students *really* must know. Fortunately, the thousands of students to whom I have taught this material over the years have done a fine job (albeit sometimes, with painful bluntness) of letting me know precisely what is wheat and what is chaff. It was with an eye toward answering their proverbial question "What's the most important stuff?" that I wrote this book.

For Whom Is This Book Written?

This book is aimed squarely at readers who have no special background or training in the social sciences. It is designed to be read by students taking their first class in management or organizational behavior. Specifically, these readers are as follows:

- Undergraduate students (in both two-year and four-year colleges)
- MBA students and those in related masters-level programs
- Practicing managers and executives in corporate training programs

Because this book is a stand-alone guide to the essentials of OB, in previous editions, it has been supplemented by additional materials such as cases, exercises, and readings that reflect instructors' particular approaches to teaching OB. In fact, rather than attempting to be an all-inclusive package that dictates precisely what and how to teach, this book offers instructors the ultimate in flexibility. Whether an instructor is teaching OB using the case method, an experiential approach, a seminar format, distance learning, or a traditional series of lectures, students must recognize, understand, and appreciate the essentials of OB as a practical and scientific field. Regardless of the mode of delivery (and previous editions have been used in all these ways), it is necessary to understand the basics of the field. And this, in a nutshell, is what this book offers.

A Balanced Approach to Theory and Practice

Many textbooks take a particularly narrow approach to whatever field they are describing. In the field of OB, some texts focus primarily on research and theory whereas others center mainly on managerial practice. In my opinion, these skewed orientations are misleading and do readers a disservice insofar as they fail to reflect the true nature of the field of OB. By its very nature, OB is a deliberate blend of the scientific and the practical—an applied science in the truest sense. And this carefully balanced orientation is reflected in this book. Accordingly, I have prepared this book so that readers will come away with a firm understanding of *what* should be done (and what currently is being done) to improve the functioning of organizations and the satisfaction of people who work in them, as well as the research and theory that accounts for *why* these practices are effective.

Although examples of this balanced approach to theory and practice may be found throughout this book, a few illustrations of this approach are in order. Take Chapter 4, on motivation. Here, my treatment of the various classic theories of motivation is framed in terms of the central practical question: How do you motivate employees? The same may be said for Chapter 12 on culture and creativity. Here, readers come away with a basic understanding of not only the concepts of culture and creativity but also the very practical matter of how to promote a culture in which creativity abounds. Virtually every chapter captures this dual allegiance to theory and practice.

Mission: Keeping Abreast of the Shifting Landscape

Keeping up with the ever-changing world of organizations is a full-time job. I know, because it's mine. As a researcher, consultant, educator, and author, I spend my working hours probing into the world of organizational behavior, which at cocktail parties I have been known to define as the field that explains "what makes people tick" on the job. In the three decades I have studied, taught, and written in this field, my standard cocktail-party line has not changed (much to the chagrin of my wife), although the field surely has. Several of the topics we once regarded as central while I watched the Watergate hearings have faded into the background as others have gained prominence. Research findings I took for granted when my hair covered my ears like headphones are seen in a new light today, when I consider myself lucky to have hair at all. And those organizations in which I applied my knowledge while wearing my best double-knit polyester slacks have undergone dramatic transformations—if, unlike those pants, they even still exist. Such core issues as what people do, how and why they do it, and even where they do it, cannot be understood from the lava lamp mentality of the 1970s.

Importantly, to truly understand the world of organizations today, we must seriously consider changes in organizational theory and practice that were made in only the three years since the previous edition of this book was published. Sweeping changes in Internet technology have revolutionized the functioning of organizations and the ways people work within them. Any reasonable effort to characterize the world of OB must reflect these rapid advances. Indeed, keeping abreast of such changes is both the challenge and the joy of writing textbooks in this field. Finding a sufficiently stable terrain about which to write amid an ever-shifting landscape is my ongoing mission in revising this book. It was with an eye toward chronicling the most current thinking about the state of the field of OB that I prepared this book. As a result, it contains topics that are completely new to this edition as well as material that was presented in different contexts or with different emphases in earlier editions.

These changes are not merely cosmetic, but reflect my objective—to present the most recent knowledge about the field of organizational behavior in a way that describes the field of OB as it is studied and practiced today. Specifically, here are just a few of the topics that are new to this edition of the book:

- Social identity theory (Chapter 2)
- The self-fulfilling prophecy (Chapter 2)
- Knowledge management (Chapter 2)
- Intellectual capital (Chapter 2)
- Emotional dissonance (Chapter 3)
- Emotional intelligence (Chapter 3)
- Mood congruence (Chapter 3)
- Procedural justice (Chapter 4)
- Concierge programs (Chapter 4)
- Myths about affirmative action (Chapter 5)
- Employee loyalty (Chapter 5)
- Social information processing model (Chapter 5)
- Dispositional model of job satisfaction (Chapter 5)
- Psychological contracts (Chapter 6)
- Deviant organizational behavior (Chapter 6)
- Career coaches (Chapter 7)
- Entrepreneurship (Chapter 7)
- Communicating in the global economy (Chapter 8)
- Communicating in a multilingual workforce (Chapter 8)
- Inspirational communication (Chapter 8)
- Law of telecosm (Chapter 9)
- Virtual teams (Chapter 9)
- Adaptive agents as decision aids (Chapter 10)
- Cultural differences in decision making (Chapter 10)
- Co-CEOs (Chapter 11)
- Grassroots leadership (Chapter 11)
- Leading in the digital age (Chapter 11)
- Divergent thinking (Chapter 12)
- Morphology (Chapter 12)
- Toxic organizational cultures (Chapter 12)
- The Internet and organizational culture (Chapter 12)
- Affiliate networks (Chapter 13)
- "Going virtual" (Chapter 13)
- Appreciative inquiry (Chapter 14)
- Strategic planning (Chapter 14)

I also included two new chapters, which include a blend of new and newly organized material. These are as follows:

- Chapter 3: Personality, Feelings, and Stress
- Chapter 6: Interpersonal Behavior in the Workplace

These additions reflect growing interest in these topics in recent years. They were guided by feedback from readers of the previous edition of this book, as well as my own assessment of what's happening in the field of OB. I resisted the temptation to include the latest fads. To have done otherwise would have triggered a departure from my mission of focusing on the essentials—in addition to dating the book prematurely and diminishing its usefulness for readers. As such, changes in content were made only where warranted.

Pedagogical Features

In addition to changes in coverage, I also added and enhanced the pedagogical features in this book.

CHAPTER-OPENING CASE: "MAKING THE CASE FOR . . . "

The most prominent change is the addition of a chapter-opening case that introduces and leads into the material. It is entitled "Making the Case for . . . " and is designed to do precisely what the name implies—describe a real organizational case that foreshadows and suggests the importance of the material in each chapter. Although such cases are more commonly found in full-featured OB texts than in brief ones, I added them here because they play the vital pedagogical function of establishing the relevance of the topic. And insofar as the true importance of OB may be found in the insight it provides into real organizational situations, these cases play a critical role in conveying the nature of the field.

HIGHLY DIVERSE COMPANY EXAMPLES

These cases—and all real company examples throughout the book, in fact—are selected to reflect the varied nature of organizations. Some describe giant multinational corporations, whereas others chronicle small, entrepreneurial-based businesses. Some of the organizations portrayed are government agencies, some are not-for-profits, and still others are for-profit companies in the private sector. And, of course, some examples illustrate the dynamics of today's faced-paced Internet-based businesses (dot-coms, as they are known), but I have not forgotten the traditional bricks-and-mortar businesses. This diversity in company examples is quite intentional. I wanted to illustrate that OB principles and practices are relevant to all types of organizations, not just some. And, insofar as readers are likely to work at a wide variety of organizations, I thought it was important for them to be able to relate to some of the examples and to learn about the others.

HIGHLIGHTING PRACTICAL APPLICATIONS:
"WINNING PRACTICES"

Highlighting my commitment to the interplay between the theoretical and the practical, each chapter contains a special boxed section entitled "Winning Practices." These sections contain all new material that calls readers' attention to currrent organizational practices that illustrate one or more key OB concepts from that chapter. In this sense, these sections are clear illustrations of practical applications of OB—the very kinds of material that convince students of the relevance of the field of OB. To get students thinking about the topics described in these sections, and to help make connections to the main text material, I have added three "questions for discussion" at the end of each. Whether used jointly in class, or by students individually, these questions are designed to stimulate reactions to the material.

ENHANCED TABLES AND ILLUSTRATIONS

This book is now more richly illustrated and full of descriptive tables than its predecessors. I have incorporated these features into the book because I am convinced that material presented in these formats helps many students understand and remember ideas that otherwise get camouflaged in the body of the text. Over the years, my students have always expressed their appreciation for interesting figures and tables, so I have gone out of my way to ensure that the ones in this book are as useful as possible.

RETURN OF POPULAR PEDAGOGICAL FEATURES

Back by popular demand are several of the most popular pedagogical features from the previous edition of this book. These features, found in each chapter, are as follows:

- *Learning Objectives.* At the beginning of each chapter, readers are provided a list of six specific things they should be able to do after reading that chapter. These all begin with verbs, such as define, describe, identify, and distinguish.
- *"Three Good Reasons Why You Should Care About. . . ."* Understandably, today's busy students may be prone to challenge the relevance of material, asking what value it has to them. Assuming that students are most receptive to learning about topics that have some recognizable benefits to themselves, these sections begin each chapter by indicating precisely why readers should care about the topic at hand.
- *You Be the Consultant.* These brief sections describe a hypothetical organizational problem and then challenge readers to draw on the material to find ways of solving them.
- *Summary: Have I Met the Learning Objectives?* The learning objectives are restated at the end of each chapter. Following each, I have provided summaries of the material bearing on that particular objective. These serve not only as chapter-end summaries, but they also provide valuable opportunities for self-testing of the chapters' major points.

Finally, I also have retained in each chapter the two skills-based exercises that were so popular in earlier editions of this book. These are as follows:

- *Self-Assessment Exercise.* These exercises are designed to provide readers with insight into key aspects of their own individual attitudes or relevant behavior.
- *Group Exercise.* These hands-on experiences require the joint efforts of small groups of students to help illustrate thinking about key phenomena described in the text.

These exercises can be an important part of students' learning experiences. They not only expose students to some of the phenomena described in the text on a firsthand basis, but they also stimulate critical thinking about those phenomena. Not unimportantly, they are fun.

Available Teaching and Learning Aids

This book is accompanied by a very helpful set of materials to aid both students and instructors. These teaching aids and instructional aids were prepared especially for this book.

FOR STUDENTS

Students reading this book will find a great deal of useful information available to them at the book's **companion Web site:** www.prenhall.com/greenberg. These include the following:

- Learning Objectives. Each chapter identifies six objectives students should be able to recognize and understand after reading the chapter.
- Interactive Study Guide. This consists of instantly-scored quizzes on each chapter that help students assess their mastery of the material.

FOR INSTRUCTORS

Available to professors adopting this book is a complete set of instructional aids consisting of the following items:

- *Instructor's Manual with Test Item File (print version).* Each chapter of the *Instructor's Manual* includes a chapter synopsis, lecture outline, and suggested answers to end-of-chapter questions. The Test Item File provides 25 multiple-choice questions, 25 true/false questions, and 5-7 short answer/essay questions for each chapter.
- *Prentice Hall Test Manager. Test Manager* is a comprehensive suite of tools for testing and assessment that contains all of the questions in the printed Test Item File.
- *PowerPoint Electronic Transparencies.* More than 100 slides, available on CD-ROM, illustrate key chapter material.
- *Downloads for Instructors.* The *Instructor's Manual* and PowerPoint slides also may be downloaded from a password-protected instructor's page on the book's companion Web site, www.prenhall.com/greenberg.

Instructors requesting these materials should contact their Prentice Hall sales representative.

Acknowledgments

In closing, I wish to acknowledge the many talented and hardworking individuals whose efforts have made this book possible. To begin, I thank my colleagues who have provided valuable suggestions and comments in response to various drafts of this and earlier editions of this book. These include:

- Richard Grover, *University of Southern Maine*
- Jeffrey Miles, *University of the Pacific*
- Michael Buckley, *University of Oklahoma*
- Suzyn Ornstein, *Suffolk University*
- Fabia Fernandes, *Boise State University*
- Pal A. Fadil, *Valdosta University*
- Greg Mathison, *GTE Communications Corp.*
- Robert Insley, *University of North Texas*
- Sally Riggs Fuller, *University of Washington*

Second, I wish to thank the editorial and production teams at Prentice Hall. My editors, John Sisson, Jennifer Glennon, Melissa Steffens, and Jessica Sabloff provided the steadfast guidance and support, along with the "gentle reminders," which have brought this book to fruition. On the production side, Judy Leale, Keri Jean, Nancy Marcello, and Michael Fruhbeis worked tirelessly at transforming my ramblings into the beautiful book you have before you. I am truly indebted to these kind professionals for lending their talents to this project.

Finally, I wish to acknowledge my many colleagues and students at the Fisher College of Business who somehow always can tell from my demeanor when I am writing a book. I shudder to think what the cues may be, but I thank them for sheltering me from this information. Most notably, I am grateful to my research assistants, Brian Dineen and Lai D'Bughe, for gathering much of the material that helped me prepare this book. And, as always, I wish to thank the family of the late Irving Abramowitz for their generous endowment to The Ohio State University, which provided invaluable support while I was preparing this book.

Jerald Greenberg
Columbus, Ohio

Managing Behavior in Organizations

1

What is organizational behavior?

understanding what the field is all about

LEARNING OBJECTIVES

After reading this chapter, you will be able to:

1. DEFINE organizational behavior (OB).
2. DESCRIBE the major characteristics of the field of OB.
3. DISTINGUISH between the Theory X and Theory Y philosophies of management.
4. IDENTIFY the fundamental assumptions of the field of OB.
5. DESCRIBE the historical roots of the field of OB.
6. CHARACTERIZE the nature of the field of OB today.

THREE GOOD REASONS WHY YOU SHOULD CARE ABOUT . . .

Organizational Behavior

You should care about organizational behavior because:

1. Understanding the dynamics of behavior in organizations is essential to achieving personal success as a manager, regardless of your area of specialization.
2. Principles of organizational behavior are involved in making employees both productive and happy.
3. To achieve success in today's rapidly changing environment, organizations must successfully address a wide variety of OB issues.

Making the Case for... Organizational Behavior

People: The Prescription for Success at Pharmacia

On April 3, 2000, the huge chemical bioengineering division of Monsanto merged with the multinational drug giant, Pharmacia & Upjohn (P&U), to create the Pharmacia Corporation—one of the world's fastest-growing pharmaceutical companies, with 60,000 employees in 60 countries. Prospects for the newly enlarged business were excellent, as Monsanto's top-selling arthritis drugs and contraceptives, combined with P&U's successes in antibiotics, all but ensured Pharmacia's dominance in the prescription drug business. Despite drug industry analysts' confidence in Pharmacia's success, Fred Hassan, the company's CEO, knew that a healthy bottom line was not automatic. The key, he realized, had to do with people. After all, he reasoned, for the new company to prosper, it had to keep on board the talented people who were responsible for success in the first place.

Hassan learned the hard way that this was easier said than done. When he became P&U's CEO in 1997, he took the reins of a newly merged company that until then was two multinational drug companies—Pharmacia AB, a Swedish company, and the Upjohn Company, based in Kalamazoo, Michigan. Complicating things further, P&U was completing the takeover of the Italian pharmaceutical company, Farmitalia. P&U's financial picture was bleak and morale was low, threatening to harm the company even further. Hassan realized, after talking to the employees, that the core of the problem was that they were highly anxious about what the future had in store for them. After all, mergers bring ambiguity, and employees who don't fully understand their company's goals—and even whether they will be keeping their jobs—can hardly be expected to be happy and productive.

To promote trust and acceptance within the workforce, Hassan met with the company's key people in Milan, Stockholm, and Kalamazoo, where he listened carefully to people's gripes and fears, and took careful notes on everything he heard. The biggest problem, he learned, had to do with culture clashes. Americans, for example, complained of having to work in Italian offices where people smoked, whereas Europeans complained about Americans' arrogance and poor language skills. As a result, employees from each country worked together, but routinely ignored their overseas colleagues. At this very time, when most CEOs would be inclined to focus exclusively on balance sheets, Hassan recognized the importance of focusing eye to eye with the very people responsible for those numbers.

Hassan knew the company's ultimate success required breaking up the dogfights that had developed between divisions in different countries. His unification plan involved creating a single mission, a strategy, and a set of values that could be shared throughout the company. The rallying point was a new product named Zyvox—the first new class of antibiotics to hit the market in 40 years. As top management got behind this product, pouring $100 million into its development, its success required the expertise of all the company's employees. Soon, it became clear that Zyvox was created not only by the Americans or the Swedes or the Italians. Rather, it was the result of cooperation by all Pharmacia's employees on both sides of the Atlantic. And, as ownership of this successful product fell over the entire company, employees began feeling more integrated with the company as a whole. The fights soon stopped, and people began working together. In short, an organization that once operated like several smaller companies was now functioning as a unified whole.

Although a clash between national cultures was not the issue when Monsanto joined P&U, Hassan recognized that insecurities were sure to run high following the merger. To reassure the most valued executives that their jobs were safe, he came up with a "Hate-to-Lose List," naming 100 valued employees at P&U and a like number at Monsanto. The pressures for financial success at the new Pharmacia Corporation are intense, Hassan admits. However, the key to success, he acknowledges, is the behavior and attitudes of its people—the one resource he manages most carefully. According to the company's Website, Pharmacia's goal is to become "the best managed company in the industry." Given Hassan's approach, it seems well on its way to achieving this lofty ambition.

What image comes to mind when you think of a huge pharmaceutical company like Pharmacia? Most likely, it's a huge building with miles of offices, laboratories containing the latest high-tech instruments, and a sprawling factory floor decked out with aisles of complicated-looking equipment. Although such facilities certainly are important when it comes to housing where work is done, what's missing from the picture is the one most important component of organizations themselves—*people*. This idea was not lost on Fred Hassan as he faced several huge mergers during the past few years.

Fortunately, he seems to have succeeded—and the key to his success was recognizing the importance of people. Specifically, Hassan carefully listened to his employees' concerns, he noted their low morale, he acknowledged their fears about the future, and he recognized the national differences that kept them from working together. More importantly, he did something to address these issues. In short, he recognized the importance of the human side of work, which happens to be the topic of this book. Indeed, this case highlights several key aspects of human behavior in organizations that will be explained fully in the chapters that follow.

Let's face it, there can be no organizations without people. So, no matter how sophisticated a company's equipment may be, or how healthy its bottom line, people problems can bring an organization down very quickly. By the same token, organizations in which people work happily and effectively can benefit greatly. Hence, it makes sense to realize that the human side of work is critical to the effective functioning—and basic existence—of organizations. It is this people-centered orientation that is taken in the field of *organizational behavior*—the topic of this book.

This chapter will introduce you to the field of organizational behavior—its characteristics, its history, and the tools it uses to learn about the behavior of people in organizations. I will begin by formally defining the field, describing exactly what it is and what it seeks to accomplish. Following this, I will summarize the history of the field of organizational behavior, tracing its roots from its origins to its emergence as a modern science.

What Is Organizational Behavior and Why Does It Matter?

Before going any further, it is necessary for you to understand exactly what we mean by organizational behavior, and why it is important to learn all about it.

ORGANIZATIONAL BEHAVIOR: A DEFINITION

As I have been alluding, the field of **organizational behavior** (or **OB**, as it is commonly called) deals with human behavior in organizations. Formally defined, organizational behavior is the multidisciplinary field that seeks knowledge of behavior in organizational settings by systematically studying individual, group, and organizational processes. This knowledge is used both by scientists interested in understanding human behavior and by practitioners interested in enhancing organizational effectiveness and individual well-being. Our orientation in this book will highlight both these purposes, focusing on how scientific knowledge has been—or may be—used for these practical purposes.

Having formally defined the field of OB, we are now ready to more closely examine some of its core characteristics.

CHARACTERISTICS OF THE FIELD OF OB

Our definition of OB highlights four central characteristics of the field. First, OB is firmly grounded in the scientific method. Second, OB studies individuals, groups, and organizations. Third, OB is interdisciplinary in nature. And fourth, OB is used as the basis for enhancing organizational effectiveness and individual well-being. I will now take a closer look at these four characteristics of the field.

OB applies the scientific method to practical managerial problems. Our definition of OB refers to seeking knowledge and to studying behavioral processes. Although it is neither as sophisticated as the study of physics or chemistry, nor is it as mature as these disciplines, the orientation of the field of OB is still scientific in nature. Thus, like other scientific fields, OB seeks to develop a base of knowledge by using an empirical, research-based approach. That is, it is based on systematic observation and measurement of the phenomena of interest. For an overview of some of the research techniques used in the field of organizational behavior, see Table 1.1.

Why is it so important to learn about behavior in organizational settings? To social scientists, learning about human behavior on the job—"what makes people tick" in organizations, so to speak—is valuable for its own sake. After all, scientists are interested in the generation of knowledge—in this case, insight into the effects of organizations on people and the effects of people on organizations. This is not to say, however, that such knowledge has no value outside of scientific circles. Far from it! OB specialists also apply knowledge from scientific studies, putting it to practical use. As they seek to improve organizational functioning and the quality of life of people working in organizations, they rely heavily on knowledge derived from OB research. Thus, there are both scientific and applied sides to the field of OB—facets that not only coexist, but that complement each other, as well. (Because we have all experienced OB phenomena, it sometimes seems commonsensical, leading us to wonder why the scientific approach is necessary. However, as you will see in the **Group Exercise** on p. 21, common sense is not always a reliable guide to the complexities of human behavior at work.)

OB focuses on three levels of analysis: Individuals, groups, and organizations. To best appreciate behavior in organizations, OB specialists cannot focus exclusively on individuals acting alone. After all, in organizational settings people frequently work together in groups and teams. Furthermore, people—alone and in groups—both influence and are

TABLE 1.1 Research Methods Used in OB: A Summary		

The field of OB is based on knowledge derived from scientific research. The major techniques used to conduct this research are summarized here.

Research Method	*Description*	*Comments*
Survey research	Questionnaires are developed and administered to people to measure how they feel about various aspects of themselves, their jobs, and their organizations. Responses to some questionnaires are compared to others, or to actual behaviors, to see how various concepts are interrelated.	This technique is the most popular one used in the field of OB.
Experimental research	Behavior is carefully studied—either in a controlled setting (a lab) or in an actual company (the field)—to see how a particular variable that is systematically varied affects other aspects of behavior.	This technique makes it possible to learn about cause–effect relationships.
Naturalistic observation	A nonempirical technique in which a scientist systematically records various events and behaviors observed in a work setting.	This technique is subject to the biases of the observer.
Case study	A thorough description of a series of events that occurred in a particular organization.	Findings from case studies may not be generalizable to other organizations.

> *The field of OB focuses on three distinct levels of analysis—individuals, groups, and organizations.*

influenced by their work environments. Considering this, it should not be surprising to learn that the field of OB focuses on three distinct levels of analysis—individuals, groups, and organizations.

The field of OB recognizes that all three levels of analysis must be considered to fully comprehend the complex dynamics of behavior in organizations. Careful attention to all three levels of analysis is a central theme in modern OB and will be fully reflected throughout this text. For example, I will be describing how OB specialists are concerned with individual perceptions, attitudes, and motives. I will also be describing how people communicate with each other and coordinate their activities between themselves in work groups. Finally, I will focus on organizations as a whole—the way they are structured and operate in their environments, and their effects on the individuals and groups within them.

OB is multidisciplinary in nature. When you consider the broad range of issues and approaches taken by the field of OB, it is easy to appreciate the fact that the field is multidisciplinary in nature. By this, I mean that it draws on a wide variety of social science disciplines. Rather than studying a topic from only one particular perspective, the field of OB is likely to consider a wide variety of approaches. These range from the

---

TABLE 1.2   The Multidisciplinary Roots of OB

Specialists in OB derive knowledge from a wide variety of social science disciplines to create a unique, multidisciplinary field. Some of the most important parent disciplines are listed here, along with some of the OB topics to which they are related (and the chapters in this book in which they are discussed).

Discipline	*Relevant OB Topics*
Psychology	Perception and learning (Chapter 2); personality, emotion, and stress (Chapter 3); attitudes (Chapter 4); decision making (Chapter 10)
Sociology	Group dynamics (Chapter 9); socialization (Chapter 7); communication (Chapter 8)
Anthropology	Organizational culture (Chapter 12); leadership (Chapter 11)
Political science	Interpersonal conflict (Chapter 6); organizational power (Chapter 11)
Economics	Decision making (Chapter 10); negotiation (Chapter 6); organizational power (Chapter 11)
Management science	Technology (Chapter 14); organizational quality and change (Chapter 14)

---

highly individual-oriented approach of psychology, through the more group-oriented approach of sociology, to issues in organizational quality studied by management scientists.

For a summary of some of the key fields from which the field of OB draws, see Table 1.2. If, as you read this book, you recognize some particular theory or approach as familiar, chances are good that you already learned something about it in another class. What makes OB so special is that it combines these various orientations together into a single—very broad and very exciting—field.

OB seeks to improve organizational effectiveness and the quality of life at work.   In the early part of the twentieth century, as railroads opened up the western portion of the United States and the nation's population rapidly grew (it doubled from 1880 to 1920!), the demand for manufactured products was great. New manufacturing plants were built, attracting waves of new immigrants in search of a living wage and laborers lured off farms by the employment prospects factory work offered. These men and women found that factories were gigantic, noisy, hot, and highly regimented—in short, brutal places in which to work. Bosses demanded more and more of their employees and treated them like disposable machines, replacing those who quit or who died from accidents with others who waited outside the factory gates.

Clearly, the managers of a century ago held very negative views of employees. They assumed that people were basically lazy and irresponsible, and treated them with disrespect. This very negativistic approach, which has been with us for many years, reflects the traditional view of management called a **Theory X** orientation. This philosophy of management assumes that people are basically lazy, dislike work, need direction, and will work hard only when they are pushed into performing.

Today, however, if you asked corporate officials to describe their views of human nature, you'd probably find some more optimistic beliefs. Although some of today's managers still think that people are basically lazy, many others would disagree, arguing that it's not that simple. They would claim that most individuals are just as capable of working hard as they are of "goofing off." If employees are recognized for their efforts (such as by being fairly paid) and are given an opportunity to succeed (such as by being well trained), they may be expected to work very hard without being pushed. Thus, employees may put forth a great deal of effort simply because they want to. Management's job, then, is to create those conditions that make people want to perform as desired.

The approach that assumes that people are not intrinsically lazy, but that they are willing to work hard when the right conditions prevail is known as the **Theory Y** orientation. This philosophy assumes that people have a psychological need to work and seek achievement and responsibility. In contrast to the Theory X philosophy of management, which essentially demonstrates distrust for people on the job, the Theory Y approach is strongly associated with improving the quality of people's work lives (for a summary of these differences, see Figure 1.1).

The Theory Y perspective prevails within the field of organizational behavior today. It assumes that people are highly responsive to their work environments, and that the ways they are treated will influence the ways they will act. In fact, OB scientists are very interested in learning exactly what conditions will lead people to behave most positively—that is, what makes work both productive for organizations and enjoyable for the people working in them. (Do your own assumptions about people at work more closely match a Theory X or Theory Y perspective? To find out, complete the **Self-Assessment Exercise** on p. 20.)

After reading this section you may find yourself wondering about productivity and profitability. After all, the primary reason why businesses exist is to make a profit.

FIGURE 1.1 Theory X versus Theory Y: A Summary

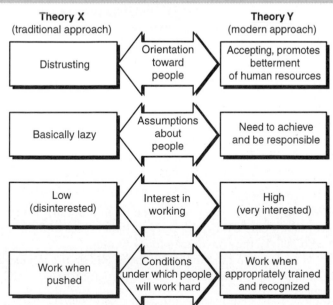

The traditional, *Theory X* orientation toward people is far more negativistic than the more contemporary, *Theory Y* approach, which is widely accepted today. Some of the key differences between these management philosophies are summarized here.

What does all this talk about people have to do with the bottom line? The answer is simple. Yes, OB is concerned about the profit of organizations. In fact, making organizations more profitable is one of the field's key objectives. However, the way OB goes about doing it differently than other areas of business. OB doesn't deal with the design of machines used in manufacturing; it doesn't address a company's accounting and marketing procedures; and it has nothing to say about the pricing strategies that help sell products and services. Instead, OB seeks to make organizations more profitable by addressing the treatment of people and the way work is done. As you read this book, you will see exactly how the field goes about meeting this objective.

WHY DOES OB MATTER?

Rather than keep you in suspense, however, I will give you a preview of things to come by showing you the importance of just a few of the ways in which the field of OB matters to people and companies. With this in mind, I pose a question that asks you to draw on your personal experiences: Have you ever had a job in which people don't get along, nobody knows what to do, everyone is goofing off, and your boss is—well, putting it politely—unpleasant? I can't imagine that you liked working in that company at all. Now, think of another position in which everyone is friendly, knowledgeable, hard-working, and very pleasant. Obviously, that's more to your liking. Such a situation is one in which you are likely to be interested in going to work, doing your best, and taking pride in what you do. What lies at the heart of these differences are all issues that are of great concern to OB scientists and practitioners—and, as a result, ones that will be covered in this book.

"Okay," you may be asking yourself, "in some companies things are nice and smooth, but in others, relationships are rocky—does it really matter?" As you will see throughout this book, the answer is a resounding *yes*! For now, here are just a few highlights of specific ways in which OB matters to people and the organizations in which they work.

- Companies whose managers accurately appraise the work of their subordinates enjoy lower costs and higher productivity than those that handle their appraisals less accurately.[1]
- People who are satisfied with the way they are treated on their jobs are generally more pleasant to their coworkers and bosses, and are less likely to quit than those who are dissatisfied with the way others treat them.[2]
- People who are carefully trained to work together in teams tend to be happier and more productive than those who are simply thrown together without any definite organizational support.[3]
- Employees who believe they have been treated unfairly on the job are likely to steal from their employers and to reject the policies of their organizations than those who believe they have been fairly treated.[4]
- People who are mistreated by their supervisors on the job experience more mental and physical illnesses than those who are treated with kindness, dignity, and respect.[5]
- Organizations that treat employees well with respect to pay, benefits, opportunities, job security, friendliness, fairness, and pride in company are, on average, twice as profitable as the Standard & Poor's 500 companies.[6]

- Companies that offer good employee benefits and that have friendly working conditions are more profitable than those that are less people-oriented.[7]

By now, you might be asking yourself: Why, if OB is so important, is there no one person in charge of it in an organization? After all, companies tend to have officials responsible for other basic areas, such as finance, accounting, marketing, and production. Why not OB? If you've never heard of a vice president of OB or a manager of organizational behavior, it's because organizations do not have any such formal posts. So then, back to the question: Who is responsible for organizational behavior? In a sense, the answer is everyone! Although OB is a separate field of study, it cuts across all areas of organizational functioning. Managers in all departments have to know such things as how to motivate their employees, how to keep people satisfied with their jobs, how to communicate fairly, how to make teams function effectively, and how to design jobs most effectively. In short, dealing with people at work is everybody's responsibility on the job. So, no matter what job you do in a company, knowing something about OB is sure to help you do it better. This is precisely why it's so vitally important for you to know the material in this book.

> *Who is responsible for organizational behavior? In a sense, the answer is everyone!*

What Are the Field's Fundamental Assumptions?

All fields are guided by a set of basic assumptions, and OB is no exception. I am referring to the fundamental ideas that are widely accepted by everyone who does scientific research on OB or who puts into practice the things we learn from those studies. For you to get the most out of this book, it is essential for you to understand the two central tenets of the field of OB that I will now describe.

OB RECOGNIZES THE DYNAMIC NATURE OF ORGANIZATIONS

Thus far, our characterization of the field of OB has focused more on behavior than on organizations. Nonetheless, it is important to point out that both OB scientists and practitioners do pay a great deal of attention to the nature of organizations themselves. Under what conditions will organizations change? How are organizations structured? How do organizations interact with their environments? Questions such as these are of major interest to specialists in OB. But, before I can consider them (as I will do in Chapter 13), I first must clarify exactly what I mean by an organization.

Formally, I define an **organization** as a structured social system consisting of groups and individuals working together to meet some agreed-upon objectives. In other words, organizations consist of structured social units, such as individuals or work groups, who strive to attain a common goal. Typically, we think of making a profit as the primary goal of an organization—and indeed, for most business organizations, it is. However, different organizations may be guided by different goals. For example, charitable organizations may focus on the objective of helping people in need, political parties may be interested in electing candidates with certain ideas, and religious organizations may strive to save souls. Regardless of the specific goals sought, the structured social units working together toward them may be considered organizations.

In studying organizations, OB scientists recognize that organizations are not static, but dynamic and ever-changing entities. In other words, they recognize that organizations are **open systems**—that is, self-sustaining systems that use energy to transform resources from the environment (such as raw materials) into some form of output (e.g., a finished product).[8] Figure 1.2 summarizes some of the key properties of open systems.

As this diagram indicates, organizations receive input from their environments and continuously transform it into output. This output gets transformed back to input, and the cyclical operation continues. Consider for example, how organizations may tap the human resources of the community by hiring and training people to do jobs. These individuals may work to provide a product in exchange for wages. They then spend these wages, putting money back into the community, allowing more people to afford the company's products. This, in turn, creates the need for still more employees, and so on. If you think about it this way, it's easy to realize that organizations are dynamic and constantly changing.

The dynamic nature of organizations can be likened to the operations of the human body. As people breathe, they take in oxygen and transform it into carbon dioxide. This, in turn, sustains the life of green plants, which in turn emit oxygen for people to breathe. The continuous nature of the open system characterizes not only human life, but the existence of organizations as well.

FIGURE 1.2 Organizations as Open Systems

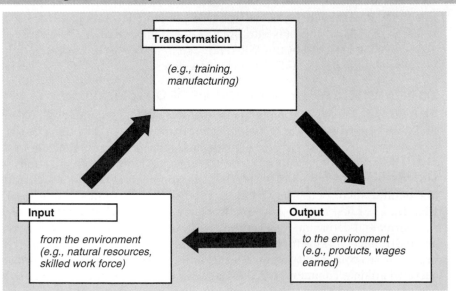

The *open systems* approach is characteristic of modern-day thinking in the field of OB. It assumes that organizations are self-sustaining—that is, that they transform inputs to outputs in a continuous fashion. (*Source:* Based on suggestions by Katz and Kahn, 1978, see Note 8.)

OB ASSUMES THERE IS NO "ONE BEST" APPROACH

What's the most effective way to motivate people? What style of leadership works best? Should groups of individuals be used to make important organizational decisions? Although these questions are quite reasonable, there is a basic problem with all of them. Namely, they all assume that there is a simple, unitary answer—that is, one best way to motivate, to lead, and to make decisions.

Specialists in the field of OB today agree that there is no one best approach when it comes to such complex phenomena. To assume otherwise is not only overly simplistic and naive, but, as you will see, grossly inaccurate. When it comes to studying human behavior in organizations, there are no simple answers. Instead, OB scholars embrace a **contingency approach**—an orientation that recognizes that behavior in work settings is the complex result of many interacting forces. This orientation is a hallmark of modern OB. Consider, for example, how an individual's personal characteristics (e.g., personal attitudes and beliefs) in conjunction with situational factors (e.g., an organization's climate, relations between coworkers) may all work together when it comes to influencing how a particular individual is likely to behave on the job.

Explaining OB phenomena often requires saying, "It depends." As our knowledge of work-related behavior becomes increasingly complex, it is difficult to give "straight answers." Rather, it is usually necessary to say that people will do certain things "under some conditions," or "when all other factors are equal." Such phrases provide a clear indication that the contingency approach is being used. In other words, a certain behavior occurs "contingent upon" the existence of certain conditions—hence, the name.

OB Then and Now: A Capsule History of the Field

The importance of understanding the behavior of people at work has not always been as recognized as widely as it is today. In fact, it was not until the early part of the twentieth century that the idea first developed, and only during the last few decades that it gained widespread acceptance. Now, in the twenty-first century, it is clear that the field has blossomed and matured. So that we can appreciate how the field of OB got to where it is today, I will now briefly outline its history and describe some of the most influential forces in its development.

SCIENTIFIC MANAGEMENT: THE ROOTS OF ORGANIZATIONAL BEHAVIOR

The earliest attempts to study behavior in organizations came out of a desire by industrial efficiency experts to improve worker productivity. Their central question was straightforward: What could be done to get people to do more work in less time? It's not particularly surprising that attempts to answer this question were made at the beginning of the twentieth century. After all, this was a period of rapid industrialization and technological change in the United States. As engineers attempted to make machines more efficient, it was a natural extension of their efforts to work on the human side of the equation—making people more productive, too. Given this history, it should not be too surprising that the earliest people we now credit for their contributions to OB were actually industrial engineers.

Frederick Winslow Taylor worked most of his life in steel mills, starting as a laborer and working his way up to the position of chief engineer. In the 1880s, while a foreman at Philadelphia's Midvale Steel Company, Taylor became aware of some of the inefficient practices of the employees.[9] Noticing, for example, that laborers wasted movements when shifting pig iron, Taylor studied the individual components of this task and identified a set of the most efficient motions needed to perform it. A few years later, while at Pittsburgh's Bethlehem Steel, Taylor similarly redesigned the job of loading and unloading railcars so it too could be done as efficiently as possible. On the heels of these experiences, Taylor published his groundbreaking book, *Scientific Management*. In this work, he argued that the objective of management is "to secure the maximum prosperity for the employer, coupled with the maximum prosperity of each employee."[10]

Beyond identifying ways in which manual labor jobs can be performed more efficiently, Taylor's **scientific management** approach was unique in its focus on the role of employees as individuals. Specifically, this approach emphasizes the importance of designing jobs as efficiently as possible. Taylor advocated two ideas that hardly seem special today, but were quite new at the beginning of the twentieth century. First, he recommended that employees be carefully selected and trained to perform their jobs. Second, he believed that increasing workers' wages would raise their motivation and make them more productive. Although this idea is unsophisticated by today's standards—and not completely accurate (as you will see in Chapter 4)—Taylor may be credited with recognizing the important role of motivation in job performance.

It was contributions like these that stimulated further study of behavior in organizations and created an intellectual climate that eventually paved the way for the development of the field of OB. Acknowledging these contributions, management theorist Peter Drucker has described Taylor as "the first man in history who did not take work for granted, but who looked at it and studied it."[11]

The publication of *Scientific Management* stimulated several other scientists to pick up on and expand Taylor's ideas. Among the most strongly influenced were the industrial psychologists Frank and Lillian Gilbreth. This husband-and-wife team pioneered an approach known as **time-and-motion study**, a type of applied research designed to classify and streamline the individual movements needed to perform jobs with the intent of finding "the one best way" to perform them. Although this approach appears to be highly mechanical and dehumanizing, the Gilbreths, parents of 12 children, practiced "Taylorism" with a human face in their personal lives. (If this sounds at all familiar, it may be because you recall the classic film *Cheaper by the Dozen*, which tells the story of how the Gilbreths applied the principles of scientific management to their own rather large household.)

THE HUMAN RELATIONS MOVEMENT AND THE HAWTHORNE STUDIES

Although scientific management did a good job of highlighting the importance of the efficient performance of work, it did not go far enough in directing our attention to the wide variety of factors that might influence work behavior. In fact, many experts rejected Taylorism, favoring instead an approach that focused on employees' own views and emphasized respect for individuals. At the forefront of this orientation was Elton W. Mayo, an organizational scientist and consultant widely regarded as the

TABLE 1.3 Scientific Management versus the Human Relations Movement: A Summary

Although both are early approaches to the study of behavior in organizations, *scientific management* and *the human relations movement* are different in several key ways summarized here.

Scientific Management	Human Relations Movement
Emphasis on human efficiency on the job	Emphasis on social conditions in organizations
Sought to improve productivity by minimizing wasted movements	Sought to improve productivity by developing good working relationships
Major proponent was Frederick Winslow Taylor	Major proponent was Elton Mayo

founder of what is called the **human relations movement**. This management philosophy rejects the primarily economic orientation of scientific management and focuses, instead, on the noneconomic, social factors operating in the workplace. Mayo and other proponents of the human relations movement recognized that task performance was greatly influenced by the social conditions that existed in organizations—that is, the way employees were treated by management, and the relationships they had with each other. For a comparison between scientific management and the human relations movement, see Table 1.3.

In 1927 a series of studies were conducted at the Western Electric's Hawthorne Works outside Chicago. The researchers were interested in determining several things, including the effects of illumination on work productivity. In other words, how brightly or dimly lit should the work environment be for people to produce at their maximum level? Two groups of female employees took part in the study. One group, the control room condition, did their jobs without any changes in lighting. The other group, the test room condition, worked while the lighting was systematically varied, sometimes getting brighter, and sometimes getting dimmer. The results were puzzling: Productivity increased in both locations. Just as surprising, there was no clear connection between illumination and performance. In fact, output in the test room remained high even when the level of illumination was so low that workers could barely see what they were doing!

In another study conducted at the company's Bank Wiring Room, male members of various work groups were observed during regular working conditions and were interviewed at length after work. In this investigation, no attempts were made to alter the work environment. What Mayo found here was also surprising: Instead of improving their performance, employees deliberately restricted their output. Not only did the researchers actually see the men stopping work long before quitting time, but in interviews, the men admitted that they easily could have done more if they desired.

Why did this occur? Eventually, Mayo and his associates recognized that the answer resided in the fact that organizations are social systems. How effectively people worked depended, in great part, not only on the physical aspects of the working conditions experienced, but also the social conditions encountered. In the Hawthorne studies, Mayo noted, productivity rose simply because people responded favorably to the special attention they received. Knowing they were being studied made them feel special and motivated them to do their best. Hence, it was these social factors, more than the physical factors, that had such profound effects on job performance.

The same explanation applied in the Bank Wiring Room study as well. Here, the employees feared that because they were being studied, the company would eventually raise the amount of work they were expected to do. So as to guard against the imposition of unreasonable standards (and, hopefully, to keep their jobs!), the men agreed among themselves to keep output low. In other words, informal rules (known as *norms*) were established about what constituted acceptable levels of job performance (this topic will be discussed more thoroughly in Chapter 9). These social forces at work in this setting proved to be much more potent determinants of job performance than the physical factors studied.

This conclusion, based on the surprising findings of the Hawthorne studies, is important because it ushered in a whole new way of thinking about behavior at work. It suggests that to understand behavior on the job, we must fully appreciate people's attitudes and the processes by which they communicate with each other. This way of thinking, so fundamental to modern OB, may be traced back to Elton Mayo's pioneering Hawthorne studies. Although the research was flawed in some important ways (e.g., conditions in the study rooms were not carefully controlled), what they revealed about the importance of human needs, attitudes, motives, and relationships in the workplace was quite influential—and novel for its time.

CLASSICAL ORGANIZATIONAL THEORY

During the same time that proponents of scientific management got people to begin thinking about the interrelationships between people and their jobs, another approach to managing people emerged. This perspective, known as **classical organizational theory**, focused on the efficient structuring of organizations. This is in contrast, of course, to scientific management, which sought to effectively organize the work of individuals.

Although several different theorists are identified with organizational theory, two of the most well known are Henri Fayol and Max Weber. Fayol was a French industrialist who attributed his managerial success to various principles he developed. Among these are the following:

- A *division of labor* should be used because it allows people to specialize, doing only what they do best.
- Managers should have *authority* over their subordinates, the right to order them to do what's necessary for the organization.
- Lines of authority should be uninterrupted; that is, a clear *chain of command* should connect top management to the lowest-level employees.
- There should exist a clearly defined *unity of command*, such that employees receive directions from only one other person so as to avoid confusion.
- Subordinates should be allowed to formulate and implement their own plans.

Although many of these principles are still well accepted today, it is widely recognized that they should not always be applied in exactly the same way. For example, whereas some organizations thrive on being structured according to a unity of command, still others require that some employees take directions from several different superiors.

TABLE 1.4 Characteristics of an Ideal Bureaucracy	

According to Max Weber, bureaucracies are the ideal organizational form. To function effectively, however, they must possess the characteristics identified here.

Characteristics	*Description*
Formal rules and regulations	Written guidelines are used to control all employees' behaviors.
Impersonal treatment	Favoritism is to be avoided, and all work relationships are to be based on objective standards.
Division of labor	All duties are divided into specialized tasks and are performed by individuals with the appropriate skills.
Hierarchical structure	Positions are ranked by authority level in clear fashion from lower-level to upper-level ones.
Authority structure	The making of decisions is determined by one's position in the hierarchy; higher-ranking people have authority over those in lower-ranking positions.
Lifelong career commitment	Employment is viewed as a permanent, lifelong obligation on the part of the organization and its employees.
Rationality	The organization is committed to achieving its ends (e.g., profitability) in the most efficient manner possible.

I will have more to say about this subject when we discuss various types of organizational designs in Chapter 13. For now, suffice it to say that current organizational theorists owe a debt of gratitude to Fayol for his pioneering and far-reaching ideas.

Probably the best-known classical organizational theorist is the German sociologist Max Weber. Among other things, Weber is well known for proposing a form of organizational structure well known today—the **bureaucracy**. Weber's idea was that the bureaucracy is the one best way to efficiently organize work in all organizations—much as proponents of scientific management searched for the ideal way to perform a job. The elements of an ideal bureaucracy are summarized in Table 1.4.

When you think about bureaucracies, negative images probably come to mind of lots of inflexible people getting bogged down in lots of red tape. Weber's "universal" view of bureaucratic structure lies in contrast to the more modern approaches to organizational design (see Chapter 13) in which it is recognized that different forms of organizational structure may be more or less appropriate under different situations. Although the bureaucracy may not have proven to be the perfect structure for organizing all work, many of Weber's ideas are still considered viable today.

Despite differences between Fayol's and Weber's principles for organizing work, both approaches assume that there is a single most effective way to structure organizations. Although, as noted earlier, such approaches seem simplistic by modern standards, we are indebted to Fayol, Weber, and other classical management theorists for calling our attention to the important effects that the design of organizations can have.

ORGANIZATIONAL BEHAVIOR IN THE MODERN ERA

The pioneering contributions noted thus far set the stage for the emergence of the modern science of organizational behavior. Although the first doctoral degrees in OB were granted in the 1940s, the field's early growth was uneven. It was not until the late 1950s and early 1960s that OB became an ongoing concern. By that time, active programs of research were going on, including investigations of such key processes as motivation and leadership, and the impact of organizational structure on productivity.

Stimulated by a report by the Ford Foundation in the 1960s, advocating that students trained in business receive firm grounding in the social sciences, the field of OB rapidly grew into one that borrowed heavily from other disciplines. In fact, the field of OB as we know it today may be characterized as a hybrid science that draws from many social science fields. For example, studies of motivation and work-related attitudes, dealing as they do with the processes of learning and perception, draw on psychology. Similarly, the study of group dynamics and leadership relies heavily on sociology. The topic of organizational communication, obviously, draws on research in the field of communication. And OB scientists look to the field of management science to understand the design of organizational hierarchies and other structural arrangements. Taken together, it is clear that modern OB has become a truly a multifaceted and interdisciplinary field.

> *The field of OB as we know it today may be characterized as a hybrid science that draws from many social science fields.*

ORGANIZATIONAL BEHAVIOR TODAY

Today, in the early part of the twenty-first century, the field of OB has added a few new characteristics worth noting. These reflect both changes that are occurring in the world as a whole and changes that have occurred as a result of advances in the science over the years. Although there are too many new developments to mention, a few current trends deserve to be pointed out.

- In keeping with the ever-growing globalization of business, the field of OB has been paying more increased attention than ever to the *cross-cultural aspects of behavior*, acknowledging that our understanding of organizational phenomena may not be universal. Today, research that considers the international generalizability of OB phenomena is considered key to understanding organizational competitiveness in a global society. Acknowledging this trend, you will find multicultural examples of OB throughout this book.

- The study of *unethical behavior in organizations* is considered more important than ever before. Indeed, OB scientists are fascinated by understanding the factors that lead people to make ethical or unethical decisions, and by their willingness to engage in such antisocial behaviors as lying, cheating, stealing, and acting violently. I will describe some of the factors that motivate people to behave unethically in Chapter 4—and you will also find examples of ethical and unethical behavior throughout this book. Importantly, ethics matters on the bottom line. In fact, research has shown that companies whose CEOs express a commitment to ethics in their annual reports perform better financially, on average, than those companies whose annual reports contain no such statements.[12]

- There can be no doubt that today's workforce is more *diverse* than ever before. Minority groups already comprise a quarter of the U.S. workforce, and their

Diverse employees help bring a wide variety of perspectives to the workplace that tends to improve the quality of organizational decisions.

numbers are growing so rapidly that it may soon be inaccurate to refer to such groups as minorities.[13] Fortunately, diverse employees help bring a wide variety of perspectives to the workplace that tends to improve the quality of organizational decisions. On the other hand, this benefit is too often threatened by prejudice and discrimination against such individuals. These issues are a major concern to today's OB specialists.

- The era of the employee who works from 9 to 5 and who stays with a single company all his or her life is rapidly fading. Today, many people are choosing to work part time and to change jobs many times over the course of their lives. These *alternative work arrangements* have important implications for the field of OB, as we will see in Chapters 3 and 7.

- *Advances in technology*, such as the Internet and wireless communication devices, have changed the nature of people's access to information. Employees who once had to be physically present in a room to receive the information needed to do their jobs can now do so from distant locations, paving the way for such trends as **telecommuting**—that is, using a computer to work while at home or any other remote location. Many people do different jobs, and perform them in different ways, than they did just a few years ago. Naturally, such developments are important to the field of OB, and we will discuss them more fully in Chapter 3.

- Organizations are facing *unrelenting change*—a fact that has not escaped the attention of OB scientists and practitioners. For example, e-business has changed the way people work. As you will see in Chapter 14, the field pays a great deal of attention to how people cope with change, and it seeks ways of encouraging people to accept change. After all, unless people roll with the changes, their organizations will find it difficult to thrive—or even to survive.

As you read this book you will learn more about not only the traditional issues of concern in OB but also these rapidly developing topics. One thing that makes the field of OB so interesting is that these trends, and many others, are all operating at once, making organizations highly concerned about a wide variety of OB principles and practices. For an example of how one company has made good use of OB principles in its day-to-day operations, see the **Winning Practices** section on p. 18.

What Lies Ahead in This Book?

Now that you have a solid idea what the field of OB is all about, you are in a good position to appreciate what to expect as you continue reading this book. In the chapters ahead, you will learn about a wide variety of organizational behavior phenomena. Our orientation will reflect the dual purposes of the field of OB—understanding and practical application. In other words, the focus will be on both basic processes as well as ways these can be applied to organizational practice. And, just to eliminate doubt about whether this material really matters in organizations, I will share lots of

The Hallmark of Success in the Greeting Card Business

Mention greeting cards, and most of us think of Hallmark. With recent annual sales totaling $4.2 billion, and a strong dominance in the greeting cards business, that's hardly surprising. But, to Hallmark Cards' 21,000 employees, the Kansas City–based company is more than just a big business; it's a very friendly place to work—indeed, it's downright homey. Offering six-month family leaves for new mothers or new adoptive parents, $5,000 in adoption aid, and free health insurance, Hallmark Cards ranks highly in *Fortune* magazine's list of the 100 Best Companies to Work for in America.[14]

In an era in which many companies are finding it difficult to attract and retain talented employees, Hallmark Cards isn't having too many problems. A key reason is that the company cares for its employees. As an illustration, in 1990 it established a Work and Family Services Department that focuses on offering family care assistance (e.g., various plans to help employees whose children are ill), education programs (e.g., seminars on how to best use their company benefits), and alternative work arrangements (e.g., working part time by sharing jobs with others).[15] Why does the company do all these things? The idea is simple: By helping employees achieve peace of mind, they are freed to concentrate on their work.

But it's more than just a family-friendly atmosphere that keeps Hallmark Cards at the top of its game. The company also does a great job of keeping lines of communication open with its employees. With this in mind, for over 40 years, it has published a daily employee newsletter. But the communication is not only one way. Ten times a year, CEO Irvine Hockaday holds CEO Forums in which he meets with groups of 50 employees to discuss whatever is on their minds. And at quarterly Corporate Town Hall meetings, top executives hold three meetings a day, each with groups of 400 employees. Ideas from these open discussions are taken back to the executive suite, where they are taken very seriously in making decisions about how the company is run.

Since 1992, Hallmark Cards has had a Diversity Department. It not only trains employees in various ways to promote tolerance between people of different cultures, but the department also provides mentoring to minority employees and ensures that no groups are systematically excluded from the company's activities. Any employee who has an idea about how to promote diversity can apply for a Diversity Grant to help bring it to fruition.

Finally, just when you're thinking that Hallmark Cards would be a great place to work, consider this: At no time in its history has it ever laid off an employee! Not too many other companies can say this. Then again, not too many companies have treated their employees as well as Hallmark has.

Questions for Discussion

1. What principles of OB does Hallmark Cards appear to have put into practice? You will have to look through this book to answer this question (but that's quite intentional!).
2. Based on what was said here, how would you feel about working at Hallmark Cards? What advantages or disadvantages does it appear to offer relative to other companies with which you are familiar?
3. Besides what's mentioned here, what other practices do you think Hallmark Cards should put into practice to help improve the lives of its employees?

current examples to illustrate how OB principles actually have been followed within them.

The book is organized around the three units of analysis described in this chapter—individuals, groups, and organizations. Specifically, Part II consists of Chapters 2 to 5, focusing on individual behavior. Part III, consisting of Chapters 6 to 10, examines group behavior. And finally, in Part IV, with Chapters 11 to 14, attention will be paid to organizational-level processes. In a sense, these distinctions are artificial insofar as anything that happens in an organization is a blend of forces stemming from all three sources. With this in mind, you can expect to see several important connections between topics as you go through this book. These connections are indeed real and reflect the complexities of the field of OB as well as its multidisciplinary nature. Rather than finding them frustrating, I think you will come to appreciate the fascination they hold. After all, the field of OB can be no more straightforward than people themselves—and, as you know, we are not all that simple to understand! So with all this in mind, I hope you enjoy your tour of the field of OB presented in the next 13 chapters.

SUMMARY: HAVE I MET THE LEARNING OBJECTIVES?

You can be certain that you have met the learning objectives for this chapter found on page 1 if you understand the following:

1. **DEFINE organizational behavior (OB).** Organizational behavior (OB) is the multidisciplinary field that seeks knowledge of behavior in organizational settings by systematically studying individual, group, and organizational processes.
2. **DESCRIBE the major characteristics of the field of OB.** The field of OB applies the scientific method (such as in surveys and experiments) to understanding practical organizational issues. It also may be characterized as focusing on three levels of analysis—individuals, groups, and organizations—and as being multidisciplinary in nature (i.e., drawing upon a variety of social science disciplines). Its primary objective is to improve both organizational effectiveness and people's quality of life at work.
3. **DISTINGUISH between the Theory X and Theory Y philosophies of management.** Traditionally, management practitioners favored a *Theory X* philosophy, assuming that people are disinterested in working hard and will do so only when goaded into performing. However, contemporary theorists and practitioners adopt a *Theory Y* approach, believing instead that people are interested in working hard and that they will do so under the right conditions.
4. **IDENTIFY the fundamental assumptions of the field of OB.** Scientists and practitioners in the field of OB recognize the dynamic nature of organizations—that they are ever-changing systems. Specialists in the field also acknowledge that there is no "one best" approach to doing things in organizations. Instead, what works best depends on a wide variety of individual, group, and organizational factors all taken into account together.
5. **DESCRIBE the historical roots of the field of OB.** The earliest approach to OB was Taylor's *scientific management*, which focused on ways of doing work as efficiently as possible. Rejecting this approach as overly mechanical, Mayo advanced the *human relations movement*. This approach acknowledged that job performance is influenced by the social conditions existing within organizations.

Classical organizational theory, including Weber's concept of *bureaucracy*, advanced a single best way of designing organizations (e.g., having rigid rules and a strict division of labor). By contrast, modern OB recognizes that there may be many effective ways to design the way work is done in organizations.

6. **CHARACTERIZE the nature of the field of OB today.** Today, OB is a dynamic field that is sensitive to the realities of modern life in organizations. For example, it pays considerable attention to the cross-cultural aspects of behavior, as well as the growing diversity of the workforce. Considerable attention is also paid to changing work arrangements that make it possible for people to enjoy their personal lives along with their work lives. OB scientists are also interested in understanding—and attempting to eliminate—the unethical things people do (e.g., stealing from their employers and behaving aggressively on the job). Finally, the field of OB is also paying great attention to the way work is changing due to advances in technology, competition, and other forces for change.

You Be the Consultant

You are taking a course on organizational behavior, for which your company is paying. However, your boss is skeptical because he doesn't quite understand what the field is all about and how it will benefit the company for you to know anything about it. Answer the following questions relevant to this situation based on the material in this chapter.

1. How would you describe the course to your boss?
2. How would you respond if he replies by saying, "yeah, but it's all just common sense"?
3. What benefits to the company would you tell your boss he might see as a result of following the principles and practices described in this course?

SELF-ASSESSMENT EXERCISE

Testing Your Assumptions About People at Work: Theory X or Theory Y?

What assumptions do you make about human nature? Are you inclined to think of people as primarily lazy and disinterested in working (a *Theory X* approach) or that they are willing to work hard under the right conditions (a *Theory Y* approach)? This exercise is designed to give you some insight into this question.

Directions

For each of the eight pairs of statements below, select the one that best reflects your feelings by marking the letter that corresponds to it.

1. (a) If you give people what they need to do their jobs, they will act very responsibly.
   (b) Giving people more information then they need will lead them to misuse it.

2. (c) People naturally want to get away with doing as little as work possible.
    (d) When people avoid working, it's probably because the work itself has been stripped of its meaning.
3. (e) It's not surprising to find that employees don't demonstrate much creativity on the job because people tend not to have much of it to begin with.
    (f) Although many people are, by nature, very creative, they don't show it on the job because they aren't given a chance.
4. (g) It doesn't pay to ask employees for their ideas because their perspective is generally too limited to be of value.
    (h) When you ask employees for ideas, you are likely to get some useful suggestions.
5. (i) The more information people have about their jobs, the more closely their supervisors have to keep them in line.
    (j) The more information people have about their jobs, the less closely they have to be supervised.
6. (k) Once people are paid enough, they tend to care less about being recognized for a job well done.
    (l) The more interesting work people do, the less likely they care about their pay.
7. (m) Supervisors lose prestige when they admit that their subordinates may have been right, while they were wrong.
    (n) Supervisors gain prestige when they admit that their subordinates may have been right, while they were wrong.
8. (o) When people are held accountable for their mistakes, they raise their standards.
    (p) Unless people are punished for their mistakes, they will lower their standards.

Scoring

1. Give yourself 1 point for having selected b, c, e, g, i, k, m, and p. The sum of these points is your Theory X score.
2. Give yourself 1 point for having selected a, d, f, h, j, l, n, and o. The sum of these points is your Theory Y score.

Questions for Discussion

1. Which perspective did this questionnaire indicate that you more strongly endorsed, Theory X or Theory Y? Is this consistent with your own intuitive conclusion?
2. Do you tend to manage others in ways consistent with Theory X or Theory Y ideas?
3. Can you recall any experiences that may have been crucial in defining or reinforcing your Theory X or Theory Y philosophy?

(**GROUP EXERCISE**)

Putting Your Common Sense About OB to the Test

Even if you already have a good intuitive sense about behavior in organizations, some of what you think may be inconsistent with established research findings (many of which are noted in this book). So that you don't have to rely on your own judgments (which may be idiosyncratic), working with others in this exercise will give you a good sense of what our collective common sense has to say about behavior in organizations. You just may be enlightened.

Directions
Divide the class into groups of about five. Then within these groups, discuss the following statements, reaching a consensus as to whether each is true or false. Spend approximately 30 minutes on the entire discussion.

1. People who are satisfied with one job tend to be satisfied with other jobs too.
2. Because "two heads are better than one," groups make better decisions than do individuals.
3. The best leaders always act the same, regardless of the situations they face.
4. Specific goals make people nervous; people work better when asked to do their best.
5. People get bored easily, leading them to welcome organizational change.
6. Money is the best motivator.
7. Interpersonal conflict is likely in a highly diverse workforce.
8. People generally shy away from challenges on the job.

Scoring
Give your group one point for each item you scored as follows: 1 = True, 2 = False, 3 = False, 4 = False, 5 = False, 6 = False, 7 = False, and 8 = False. (Should you have questions about these answers, information bearing on them appears in this book as follows: 1 = Chapter 5, 2 = Chapter 9, 3 = Chapter 11, 4 = Chapter 4, 5 = Chapter 14, 6 = Chapter 4, 7 = Chapter 6, and 8 = Chapter 4.)

Questions for Discussion
1. How well did your group do? Were you stumped on a few?
2. Comparing your experiences to those of other groups, did you find that there were some questions that proved trickier than others (i.e., ones where the scientific findings were more counterintuitive)? If you did poorly, don't be frustrated. These statements are a bit simplistic and need to be qualified to be fully understood. Have your instructor explain the statements that the class found most challenging.
3. Did this exercise give you a better understanding of the sometimes surprising (and complex) nature of behavior in organizations?

NOTES

Case Notes
Griffith, V. (2000). The people factor in post-merger integration. *Strategy & Business*, issue 20 (third quarter), pp. 82-90. Koberstein, W. (2000). The mergers, miracles, madness, or mayhem? *Pharmaceutical Executive, 20*(3), 48-68. Langreth, R. (1999, December 20). Monsanto merger is just latest of bold moves by Pharmacia CEO, *Wall Street Journal*, pp. 1, 3. Pharmacia Web site: www.pharmacia.com.

Chapter Notes
[1] Risher, H. (1999). *Aligning pay and results*. New York: AMACOM.
[2] Judge, T. A., & Church, A. H. (2000). Job satisfaction: Research and practice. In C. A. Cooper & E. A. Locke (Eds.), *Industrial and organizational psychology: Linking theory to practice* (pp. 166–198). Malden, MA: Blackwell.

[3] Hackman, J. R., Wageman, R., Ruddy, T. M., & Ray, C. L. (2000). Team effectiveness in theory and in practice. In C. Cooper & E. A. Locke (Eds.), *Industrial and organizational psychology: Linking theory to practice* (pp. 109-129). Malden, MA: Blackwell.

[4] Greenberg, J. (2001). Promote procedural justice to enhance acceptance of work outcomes. In E. A. Locke (Ed.), *A handbook of principles of organizational behavior*. Malden, MA: Blackwell.

[5] Benavides, F. G., Benach, J., Diez-Roux, A. V., & Roman, C. (2000). How do types of employment relate to health indicators? Findings from the Second European Survey on working conditions. *Journal of Epidemiology & Community Health, 54,* 494–501. Roberts, S. (2000, June 26). Integrating EAPs, work/life programs holds advantages. *Business Insurance, 34*(36), 3, 18–19. Vahtera, J., Kivimaeki, M., Pentti, J., & Theorell, T. (2000). Effect of change on the psychosocial work environment on sickness absence: A seven year follow up of initially healthy employees. *Journal of Epidemiology & Community Health, 54,* 484–493.

[6] The Corporate Research Foundation UK. (2000). *Britain's best employers: A guide to the 100 most attractive companies to work for*. New York: McGraw-Hill.

[7] Bollinger, D. (1996). *Aiming higher: 25 stories of how companies prosper by combining sound management and social vision*. New York: AMACOM.

[8] Katz, D., & Kahn, R. (1978). *The social psychology of organizations*. New York: John Wiley.

[9] Kanigel, R. (1997). *The one best way*. New York: Viking.

[10] Taylor, F. W. (1947). *Scientific management*. New York: Harper & Row.

[11] Drucker, P. F. (1974). *Management: Tasks, responsibilities, practices*. New York: Harper & Row.

[12] Verschoor, C. C. (1998). A study of the link between a corporation's financial performance and its commitment to ethics. *Journal of Business Ethics, 17,* 1509–1516.

[13] Retrieved in 2000 from the Bureau of Labor Statistics, on the World Wide Web: http://www.bls.gov.

[14] Levering, R., & Moscowitz, M. (1998, January 12). 100 best companies to work for in America. *Fortune*, pp. 84–90, 92, 94, 96.

[15] Rosenbluth, H. F., & Peters, D. F. (1998). *Good company: Caring as fiercely as you compete*. Reading, MA: Perseus Books.

2

Social perception and learning

LEARNING OBJECTIVES

After reading this chapter, you will be able to:

1. DEFINE social perception and EXPLAIN the processes by which people come to make judgments about what others are like.

2. DESCRIBE social identity theory and Kelley's theory of causal attribution.

3. DESCRIBE the various types of biases that make the social perception process imperfect.

4. DEFINE learning and DESCRIBE the two basic kinds of learning that occur in organizations.

5. DISTINGUISH between the four main contingencies of reinforcement.

6. IDENTIFY various organizational activities that actively involve principles of learning.

THREE GOOD REASONS WHY YOU SHOULD CARE ABOUT . . .

Social Perception and Learning

You should care about social perception and learning because:

1. The process by which we perceive others is fundamental to a wide variety of organizational activities.
2. Principles of learning are key to effective training in organizations.
3. Effectively managing and disciplining employees requires knowing the basic principles of learning.

Making the Case for... Social Perception and Learning

Preparing Sales Reps for the "Real Whirled"

What do you get when you put eight young people in their twenties together in a beach house for two months during the summer of 1999? The answer is not the latest reality-based TV show, but the basis for what home appliance giant Whirlpool claims is one of its most effective sales tools. Dubbed "Real Whirled," after the MTV show, *Real World,* that inspired it, its goal is straightforward: to get sales reps to know the company's products by giving them personal experiences with these appliances as consumers.

That's precisely what happened. The six women and two men who lived together in a small house in St. Joseph, Michigan, washed their clothes, prepared their meals, and cleaned their house using only Whirlpool products, and spent the rest of their time talking to each other about what they learned. After leaving the house, they then passed along their newfound wisdom to salespeople at Whirlpool retailers, who in turn, shared these experiences with prospective customers, frequently turning them into actual customers.

Although the residents didn't vote one another out of the house, they faced the scrutiny of a much more demanding audience—hungry executives from company headquarters in nearby Benton Harbor who dropped by for meals. Serving undercooked chicken or wearing dirty clothes not only made residents look incompetent to their bosses but also left them unsatisfied and uncomfortable in their daily lives. To avoid this fate, they carefully studied the features of the appliances they used and taught each other various tips and tricks they learned along the way.

Until his Real Whirled experience, for example, Dan Fitzgerald, a 26-year-old college graduate and new hire, hardly knew how to cook for himself, let alone how to make a blueberry crisp in the microwave. Today, however, if you inquire about a Whirlpool microwave oven at Home Depot or Sears, the salesperson is very likely to tell you how you can use it to prepare Dan's delicious blueberry crisp, and how he came about developing it that summer in the house.

Stories such as these are precisely what Whirlpool's former director of sales operations, Josh Gitlin, claims makes the Real Whirled experience so valuable. Before reps were able to talk firsthand about their experiences with Whirlpool appliances, all they could do was share statistics touting their quality. But numbers go only so far when it comes to telling why one should buy a particular appliance. A more compelling story comes from recreating a consumer's problem and showing him or her how to use a product to solve it. This is precisely what those eight residents learned that summer—and, what makes today's Whirlpool sales reps so professional and effective. As Gitlin put it, "I don't know how we survived before this program."

Do you think you would enjoy going through an experience like Real Whirled? Whether you personally would be comfortable with such an intensive encounter, it's clear that Whirlpool officials are pleased with the program's success. From an OB perspective, there are two reasons why its effectiveness is not particularly surprising. First, the session was an effective way of getting the sales reps to learn what they needed to know about the products they sell. And *learning,* as you might imagine, is a vital process when it comes to getting people to perform effectively on the job. Second, it is apparent that the eight participants were interested in developing their new cooking and cleaning skills so as to avoid suggesting to their housemates and their bosses that they were not particularly adept at these things. Selling household appliances for a living, it was important for them to convince others that they knew all about using these products. In other words, they were concerned about the way other people perceived them, a key part of the process known as *social perception*.

Because social perception and learning are so fundamental to the way people behave in organizations, I devote this chapter to describing them in detail. Specifically, I begin by discussing the various processes that are responsible for social perception, and discuss the specific ways they operate in organizations. Then, I move on to the topic of learning. Here too, I review both the basic principles that are responsible for successful learning, as well as specific applications of these principles on the job. After reading this chapter, you will come away with a good understanding of some of the basic psychological processes that contributed to the success of the Real Whirled program—processes that will help you understand how to be successful yourself.

Social Perception: Understanding and Judging Others

What do the following organizational situations have in common?

- You are interviewing a prospective employee for a new position in your company.
- You apologize profusely after spilling a cup of coffee on your boss.
- You complete a form asking you to rate the strengths and weaknesses of your subordinates.

If you don't immediately see the connection, it's probably because these situations all involve a phenomenon that is so automatic that you probably never have thought about it before. The answer is that they all involve understanding and evaluating others—in other words, figuring out what they are like. In our example, you judge the applicant's qualifications, you make sure your boss's opinion of you is not negative, and you assess the extent to which your employees are doing their jobs properly. In each of these instances, you are engaging in **social perception**—the process of integrating and interpreting information about others so as to accurately understand them. As these examples illustrate, social perception is a very important process in a wide variety of organizational situations.[1] To better understand social perception, we will examine several different ways in which the process works.

SOCIAL IDENTITY THEORY: ANSWERING THE QUESTION "WHO ARE YOU?"

How would you answer if someone asked, "Who are you?" There are many things you might say. For example, you could focus on individual characteristics, such as your appearance, your personality, and your special skills and interests—that is, your **personal identity**. You could also answer in terms of the various groups to which you belong, saying, for example, that you are a student in a particular organizational behavior class, an employee of a certain company, or a citizen of a certain country—that is, your **social identity**. The conceptualization known as **social identity theory** recognizes that the way we perceive others and ourselves is based on both our unique characteristics

FIGURE 2.1 Social Identity Theory: An Overview

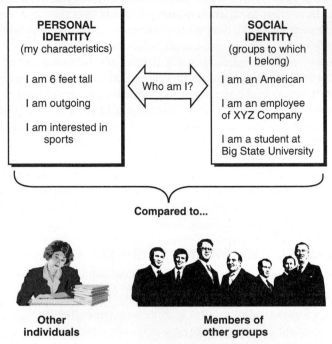

According to *social identity theory*, people identify themselves in terms of their individual character-istics and their group memberships. They then compare themselves to other individuals and groups to help define who they are, both to themselves and others.

(i.e., personal identity) and our membership in various groups (i.e., social identity).[2] For an overview of this approach, see Figure 2.1.

Social identity theory claims that the way we identify ourselves is likely to be based on our uniqueness in a group. Say, for example, that you are the only business major in an English class. In this situation, you will be likely to identify yourself as "the business major," and so too will others come to recognize you as such. In other words, that will become your identity in this particular situation. Because we belong to many groups, we are likely to have several unique aspects of ourselves to use as the basis for estab-lishing our identities (e.g., you may be the only left-handed person, the only one to have graduated college, or even the only one to have committed a crime). How do we know which particular bases for defining our personal identities people will choose?

Given the natural desire to per-ceive ourselves positively and to get others to see us positively as well, we are likely to identify ourselves with groups we believe to be per-

> *Given the natural desire to perceive ourselves positively and to get others to see us positively as well, we are likely to identify ourselves with groups we believe to be perceived positively by others.*

ceived positively by others. We know, for example, that people in highly regarded professions, such as doctors, are more inclined to identify themselves with their profession than are those who have lower-status jobs.[3] Likewise, people tend to identify themselves with winning sports teams by wearing the colors and logos of those teams. In fact, the tendency to wear clothing that identifies oneself as a fan of a certain team depends on how successful that team has been: The better a team has performed, the more likely its fans are to sport apparel that publicly identifies themselves with that team.[4]

In addition to explaining how we perceive ourselves, social identity theory also explains how we come to perceive others. Specifically, the theory explains that we focus on the differences between ourselves and other individuals as well as members of other groups (see the lower portion of Figure 2.1). In so doing, we tend to simplify things by assuming that people in different groups share certain qualities that make them different from ourselves—even if they really are not so different after all.

Not only do we perceive others as different from ourselves, but different in negative ways. This is particularly so when we are competing against them (see Chapter 6). Take athletic competitions, for example. If you ever have heard the negative things that students from one college or university say about those from other schools that they are competing against in various sports, then you know quite well the phenomenon I am describing here. Although such perceptions tend to be exaggerations—and inaccurate, as a result—most of us stick with these perceptions, nevertheless. The reason why is simple. Making such categorizations helps bring order to the world. After all, distinguishing between "the good guys" and "the bad guys" makes otherwise complex judgments quite simple. And, after all, bringing simplicity to a complex world is what social perception is all about.

ATTRIBUTION: JUDGING WHAT PEOPLE ARE LIKE
AND WHY THEY DO WHAT THEY DO

A question we often ask about others is "why?" Why did the manager use the wrong data in his report? Why did the chief executive develop the policy she did? When we ask such questions, we're attempting to get at two different types of information: (1) What is someone really like? and (2) What made the person behave as he or she did? People attempt to answer these questions in different ways.

Making correspondent inferences: Using acts to judge dispositions. Situations frequently arise in organizations in which we want to know what someone is like. Is your new boss likely to be tough or kindhearted? Are your coworkers prone to be punctual or late? The more you know about what people are like, the better equipped you are to know what to expect and how to deal with them. How, then, do we go about identifying another's traits?

Generally speaking, the answer is that we infer others' traits based on what we are able to observe of their behavior. The judgments we make about what people are like based on what we have seen them do are known as correspondent inferences. Simply put, **correspondent inferences** are judgments about people's dispositions—their traits and characteristics—that correspond to what we have observed of their actions.

At first glance, this process seems deceptively simple. A person with a disorganized desk may be thought of as sloppy. Someone who slips on the shop floor may be considered clumsy. Such judgments might be accurate, but not necessarily! After all, the messy desk actually may be the result of a coworker rummaging through it to find some important documents. Similarly, the person who slipped could have encountered oily conditions under which anyone, even the least clumsy individual, would have fallen. In other words, it is important to recognize that the judgments we make about someone may be inaccurate because there are many possible causes of behavior. For this reason, correspondent inferences may not always be accurate.

Another reason why correspondent inferences may be misleading is that people frequently conceal some of their traits—especially when these may be viewed as negative. So, for example, a sloppy individual may work hard in public to appear to be organized. Likewise, the unprincipled person may talk a good show about the importance of being ethical. In other words, people often do their best to disguise some of their basic traits. Not surprisingly, this makes the business of forming correspondent inferences risky, at best.

Causal attribution of responsibility: Answering the question "why?"   Imagine finding out that your boss just fired one of your fellow employees. Naturally, you'd ask yourself, "why did he do that?" Was it because your coworker violated the company's code of conduct? Or, was it because the boss is a cruel and heartless person? These two answers to the question "why?" represent two major classes of explanations for the causes of someone's behavior: *internal* causes, explanations based on actions for which the individual is responsible, and *external* causes, explanations based on situations over which the individual has no control. In this case, the internal cause would be the person's violation of the rules, and the external cause would be the boss's cruel and arbitrary behavior.

Generally speaking, it is very important to be able to determine whether an internal or an external cause was responsible for someone's behavior. Knowing why something happened to someone else might better help you prepare for what might happen to you. For example, in this case, if you believe that your colleague was fired because of something for which she was responsible herself, such as violating a company rule, then you might not feel as vulnerable as you would if you thought she was fired because of the arbitrary, spiteful nature of your boss. In the later case, you might decide to take some precautionary actions, to do something to protect yourself from your boss, such as staying on his good side, or even giving up and finding a new job—before you are forced to. The key question of interest to social scientists is this: How do people go about judging whether someone's actions were caused by internal or external causes?

An answer to this question is provided by **Kelley's theory of causal attribution**. According to this conceptualization, we base our judgments of internal and external causality on three types of information. These are as follows:

- *Consensus*—The extent to which other people behave in the same manner as the person we're judging. If others do behave similarly, consensus is considered high; if they do not, consensus is considered low.
- *Consistency*—The extent to which the person we're judging acts the same way at other times. If the person does act the same at other times, consistency is high; if he or she does not, then consistency is low.
- *Distinctiveness*—The extent to which this person behaves in the same manner in other contexts. If he or she behaves the same way in other situations, distinctiveness is low; if he or she behaves differently, distinctiveness is high.

According to the theory, after learning about these three factors, we combine this information to make our attributions of causality. Here's how. If we learn that other people act like this one (consensus is high), this person behaves in the same manner at other times (consistency is high), and this person does not act in the same manner in other situations (distinctiveness is high), we are likely to conclude that this person's behavior stemmed from *external* causes. In contrast, imagine learning that other people do not act like this one (consensus is low), this person behaves in the same manner at other times (consistency is high), and this person acts in the same manner in other situations (distinctiveness is low). In this case, we will probably conclude that this person's behavior stemmed from *internal* causes.

Because this explanation is highly abstract, let's consider an example to illustrate how the process works. Imagine that you're at a business lunch with several of your company's sales representatives when the sales manager makes some critical remarks about the restaurant's food and service. Further imagine that no one else in your party acts this way (consensus is low), you have heard her say the same things during other visits to the restaurant (consistency is high), and you have seen her acting critically in other settings, such as the regional sales meeting (distinctiveness is low). What would you conclude in this situation? You would probably say that her behavior stems from internal causes. In other words, she is a "picky" person, someone who is difficult to please.

Now, imagine the same setting, but with different observations. Suppose that in addition to the sales manager, several other members of your group also complain about the restaurant (consensus is high), you have seen this person complain in the same restaurant at other times (consistency is high), but you have never seen her complain about anything else before (distinctiveness is high). By contrast, in this case, you probably would conclude that the sales manager's behavior stems from external causes: The restaurant really *is* inferior. For a summary of these contrasting conclusions, see Figure 2.2.

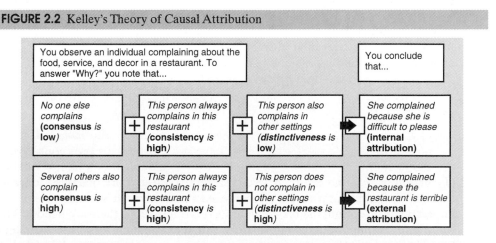

FIGURE 2.2 Kelley's Theory of Causal Attribution

In determining whether another's behavior stems mainly from internal or external causes, we rely on the three types of information identified here *consensus, consistency*, and *distinctivenees*.

THE BIASED NATURE OF SOCIAL PERCEPTION

As you might imagine, people are far from perfect when it comes to making judgments of others. In fact, researchers have noted that there are several important types of biases that interfere with making completely accurate judgments of others.

The fundamental attribution error.   Despite what Kelley's theory says, people are *not* equally predisposed to reach judgments regarding internal and external causality. Rather, they are more likely to explain others' actions in terms of internal rather than external causes. In other words, we are prone to assume that others' behavior is due to the way they are, their traits and dispositions (e.g., "she's that kind of person"). So, for example, we are more likely to assume that someone who shows up for work late does so because she is lazy rather than because she got caught in traffic. This tendency is so strong that it is known as the **fundamental attribution error**.

   This phenomenon stems from the fact that it is far easier to explain someone's actions in terms of his or her traits than to recognize the complex pattern of situational factors that may have affected their actions. As you might imagine, this tendency can be quite damaging in organizations. Specifically, it leads us to prematurely assume that people are responsible for the negative things that happen to them (e.g., "he wrecked the company car because he is careless"), without considering external alternatives, ones that may be less damning (e.g., "another driver hit the car"). And this can lead to inaccurate judgments about people.

Stereotypes: Fitting others into categories.   Inaccurate judgments about people also can stem from the preconceived ideas we hold about certain groups. Here, we are referring to **stereotypes**—beliefs that all members of specific groups share similar traits and behaviors. Expressions of stereotypes usually take this form: "People from group *X* possess characteristic *Y*." For example, what comes to mind when you think about people who wear glasses? Are they studious? Eggheads? Although there is no evidence of such a connection, it is interesting that for many people, such an image lingers in their minds.

   Deep down inside many of us know, and can articulate, that not all people from a specific group possess the characteristics—either negative or positive—with which we associate them. In other words, most of us accept that the stereotypes we use are at least partially inaccurate. After all, not *all X*s are *Y*; there are exceptions (maybe even quite a few). If so, then why are stereotypes so prevalent? Why do we use them?

People tend to do as little cognitive work as possible when it comes to thinking about others. That is, we tend to rely on mental shortcuts.

To a great extent, the answer lies in the fact that people tend to do as little cognitive work as possible when it comes to thinking about others. That is, we tend to rely on mental shortcuts. If assigning people to groups allows us to assume that we know what they are like and how they may act, then we can save the tedious work of having to learn about them as individuals. After all, we come into contact with so many people that it's impractical—if not impossible—to learn everything about them we need to know. So, we rely on readily available information—such as someone's age, race, gender, or job type—as the basis for organizing our perceptions in a coherent way. If you believe that members of group *X* tend to have trait *Y*, then simply observing that someone belongs to group X becomes the basis for your believing something about that individual (in this case, that he or she possesses trait Y). To the extent that the stereotype applies in this case, then the perception will be accurate. But, in that case, we are just lucky. More likely than not, such mental shortcuts will lead us to judgments about people that are inaccurate—the price we pay for using stereotypes.

It is easy to imagine how the use of stereotypes can have powerful effects on the kinds of judgments people make in organizations. For example, if a personnel officer believes that members of certain groups are lazy, then he purposely may avoid hiring anyone belonging to those groups. The personnel officer may firmly believe that he is using good judgment—gathering all the necessary information and listening to the candidate carefully. Still, without being aware of it, the stereotypes he holds may influence the way he judges people. The result, of course, is that the fate of the individual in question is sealed in advance—not necessarily because of anything he or she may have done or said, but by the mere fact that he or she belongs to a certain group. In other words, even people who are not being intentionally bigoted still may be influenced by the stereotypes they hold. The effects of stereotypes may be quite subtle and unintentional. (To give you a feel for some of the stereotypes people hold toward members of certain occupational groups, complete the **Group Exercise** on p. 48.)

OVERCOMING BIAS IN SOCIAL PERCEPTION: SOME GUIDELINES

In most cases, people's biased perceptions of others are not the result of any malicious intent to inflict harm. Instead, biases in social perception tend to occur because we, as perceivers, are imperfect processors of information. We assume that people are internally responsible for their behavior because we cannot be aware of all the possible situational factors that may be involved—hence, we make the fundamental attribution error. Further, it is highly impractical to be able to learn everything about someone that may guide our reactions—hence, we use stereotypes. This does not mean, however, that we cannot minimize the impact of these biases. Indeed, there are several steps that can be taken to help promote the accurate perception of others in the workplace. For an overview of several such suggestions see Table 2.1.

We recognize that many of these tactics are far easier to say than to do. However, to the extent that you conscientiously attempt to apply these suggestions to your everyday interaction with others in the workplace, you will stand a good chance of perceiving people more accurately. And this, of course, is a fundamental ingredient in the recipe for managerial success.

SELF-FULFILLING PROPHECIES: THE PYGMALION EFFECT AND THE GOLEM EFFECT

In case it already isn't apparent just how important perceptions are in the workplace, consider the fact that the way we perceive others actually can dictate how effectively people will work. Put differently, perceptions can influence reality! This is the idea behind what is known as the **self-fulfilling prophecy**—the tendency for someone's expectations about another to cause that individual to behave in a manner consistent with those expectations.

Self-fulfilling prophecies can take both positive and negative forms. In the positive case, holding high expectations of another tends to improve that individual's performance. This is known as the **Pygmalion effect**. This effect was demonstrated in a study of

TABLE 2.1   Guidelines for Overcoming Perceptual Biases

Although perceptual biases are inevitable, the suggestions outlined here may be useful ways of reducing their impact.

Recommendation	*Explanation*
Do not overlook external causes of others' behavior.	Ask yourself if anyone else may have performed just as poorly under the same conditions. If the answer is yes, then you should not automatically assume that the poor performer is to blame. Good managers need to make such judgments accurately so that they can decide whether to focus their efforts on developing employees or changing work conditions.
Identify and confront your stereotypes.	Although it is natural to rely on stereotypes, erroneous perceptions are bound to result—and quite possibly, at the expense of someone else. For this reason, it's good to identify the stereotypes you hold. Doing so will help you become more aware of them, taking a giant step toward minimizing their impact on your behavior. (You will find the **Group Exercise** on p. 48 useful in this regard.)
Evaluate people based on objective factors.	The more objective the information you use to judge others, the less your judgments will be subjected to perceptual distortion.
Avoid making rash judgments.	It is human nature to jump to conclusions about what people are like, even when we know very little about them. Take the time to get to know people better before convincing yourself that you already know all you need to know about them. What you learn may make a big difference in the opinion you form.

Israeli soldiers who were taking a combat command course.[5] The four instructors who taught the course were told that certain trainees had high potential for success, whereas the others had either normal potential or an unknown amount of potential. In reality, the trainees identified as belonging to each of these categories were assigned to that condition at random. Despite this, trainees who were believed to have high potential were found at the end of the training session to be more successful (e.g., they had higher test scores). This demonstrates the Pygmalion effect: Instructors who expected their trainees to do well actually saw them perform well.

Researchers also have found that the self-fulfilling prophecy works in the negative direction—that is, low expectations of success lead to poor performance. This is known as the **Golem effect**. Illustrating the Golem effect, researchers have found that paratroopers whose instructors expected them to perform poorly in their training class did, in fact, perform worse than those about whom instructors had no advance expectations.[6] Clearly, this effect can be quite devastating, but fortunately, it can be overcome.

A recent study compared the performance of female military recruits enrolled in a special training program for Israeli soldiers whose limited schooling and mental test scores put them at risk for poor success in the military.[7] Platoon leaders in the experimental group were told, "You will be training recruits whose average ability is significantly higher than usual for special recruits" and that "you can expect better than average achievement from the recruits in your platoon." Leaders of the control group

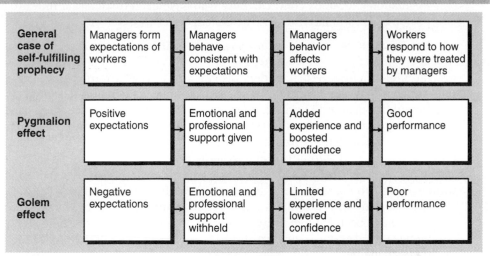

FIGURE 2.3 The Self-Fulfilling Prophecy: A Summary

The processes underlying the *self-fulfilling prophecy* are summarized here. As indicated, its effects may produce positive results (the *Pygmalion effect*) or negative results (the *Golem effect*).

were not given any such information, and their recruits showed the Golem effect. However, no such effect was found in the experimental group, suggesting that even those who are expected to perform poorly can be kept from doing so by being led to believe that success is possible.

Why do self-fulfilling prophecies occur, both the Pygmalion effect and the Golem effect? Research into the underlying processes responsible for self-fulfilling prophecies suggest that both types of self-fulfilling prophecies operate according to the four steps illustrated in Figure 2.3.[8]

1. *People form expectations of others.* Whether accurate or inaccurate, we judge others and form expectations about what they will be like. These can be either positive or negative.
2. *We behave toward others consistent with our expectations of them.* The higher our expectations, the more supportive we will be both emotionally and professionally. Most supervisors would likely be so pleased with individuals expected to succeed that they would give them better training and more opportunities to show what they can do. By contrast, those who are expected not to succeed will be perceived as poor investments and will be denied opportunities.
3. *Our behavior, in turn, affects employees.* Not only will those treated positively benefit by the special opportunities they are given, but they also are likely to benefit psychologically insofar as receiving such special treatment will boost their confidence in their abilities, which in turn will lead them to work harder. (I will describe this belief, referred to as *self-efficacy*, more thoroughly in Chapter 3.) Of course, those treated negatively will lose confidence for being singled out in such an unflattering manner.
4. *People behave in ways following from how they are treated.* As you might expect, people who have benefited from special treatment and who have confidence in

their abilities are likely to display particularly high levels of performance (the Pygmalion effect). By contrast, those who have been treated as if they are expected to fail will likely do so (the Golem effect).

The lesson to be learned from research on self-fulfilling prophecies is very clear: Managers should take concrete steps to promote the Pygmalion effect and to discourage the Golem effect. When leaders display enthusiasm toward people and express optimism about each person's potential, such positive expectations become contagious and spread throughout the organization. As a case in point, consider the great enthusiasm and support that Gordon Bethune showed toward employees of Continental Airlines in 1995 when he took over as that bankrupt company's CEO.[9] It would have been easy for him to be unsupportive and to show his disappointment with the workforce, but he did just the opposite. Only a few years after Bethune was at the helm, the airline turned around to become one of the most successful carriers in the sky. Although the changes he made to the airline's systems and equipment helped, these things alone would not have been enough if the employees had felt like failures. Indeed, Bethune's acceptance of and enthusiasm toward members of Continental's workforce contributed greatly to giving the encouragement needed to bring the airline "from worst to first."

Learning: Adapting to the World of Work

Question: What process is so broad and fundamental to human behavior that it may be said to occur in organizations—and throughout life in general—continuously? The answer: *learning*. This process is so basic to our lives that you probably have a good sense of what learning is—but, you may find it difficult to define. So, to make sure that we clarify exactly what it is, we formally define **learning** as a relatively permanent change in behavior occurring as a result of experience.

Several aspects of this definition bear pointing out. First, it's clear that learning requires that some kind of change occur. Second, this change must be more than just temporary. Finally, it must be the result of experience—that is, continued contact with the world around us. Given this definition, we cannot say that short-lived performance changes on the job, such as those due to illness or fatigue, are the result of learning. Learning is a difficult concept for scientists to study because it cannot be directly observed. Instead, it must be inferred on the basis of relatively permanent changes in behavior. We will now consider two of the most prevalent forms of learning that occur in organizations—*operant conditioning* and *observational learning*.

OPERANT CONDITIONING: LEARNING THROUGH REWARDS AND PUNISHMENTS

Imagine you are a chef working at a catering company where you are planning a special menu for a fussy client. If your dinner menu is accepted and the meal is a hit, the company stands a good chance of adding a huge new account. You work hard at doing the best job possible and present your culinary creation to the skeptical client. Now, how does the story end? If the client loves your meal, your grateful boss gives you a huge raise and a promotion. However, if the client hates it, your boss asks you to turn in your chef's hat. Regardless of which of these outcomes occurs, one thing is certain: Whatever you did in this situation, you will be sure to do it again *if* it were successful or to avoid doing it again *if* it failed.

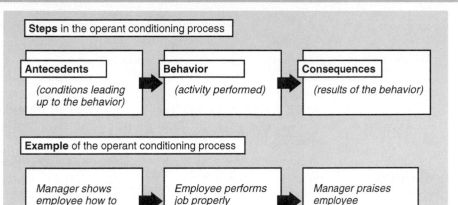

FIGURE 2.4 The Operant Conditioning Process

The basic premise of operant conditioning is that people learn by associating the consequences of their behavior with the behavior itself. In this example, the manager's praise increases the subordinate's tendency to perform the job properly in the future.

This situation nicely illustrates an important principle of **operant conditioning** (also known as **instrumental conditioning**)—namely, that our behavior produces consequences and that how we behave in the future will depend on what those consequences are. If our actions have pleasant effects, then we will be more likely to repeat them in the future. If, however, our actions have unpleasant effects, we are less likely to repeat them in the future. This phenomenon, known as the **Law of Effect**, is fundamental to operant conditioning. Our knowledge of this phenomenon comes from the work of the famous social scientist B. F. Skinner.[10] Skinner's pioneering research has shown us that it is through the connections between our actions and their consequences that we learn to behave in certain ways. I summarize this process in Figure 2.4.

The various relationships between a person's behavior and the consequences resulting from it are known collectively as **contingencies of reinforcement**. We may identify four different kinds of contingencies, each of which describes the conditions under which rewards and punishments are either given or taken away. These are *positive reinforcement*, *negative reinforcement*, *punishment*, and *extinction*. As we discuss each of these below, you may find it useful to refer to the summary in Table 2.2.

Positive reinforcement. A great deal of behavior is learned because of the pleasurable outcomes that we associate with it. In organizations, for example, people usually find it pleasant and desirable to receive monetary bonuses, paid vacations, and various forms of recognition. The process by which people learn to perform acts leading to such desirable outcomes is known as **positive reinforcement**. Whatever behaviors led to the positive outcomes are likely to occur again, thereby strengthening those behaviors. For a reward to serve as a positive reinforcer, it must be made contingent on the specific behavior sought. So, for example, if a sales representative is given a bonus after landing a huge account, that bonus will only reinforce the person's actions *if* he

TABLE 2.2   Contingencies of Reinforcement

The four reinforcement contingencies may be defined in terms of the presentation or withdrawal of a pleasant or unpleasant stimulus. Positively or negatively reinforced behaviors are strengthened; punished or extinguished behaviors are weakened.

Stimulus Presented or Withdrawn	*Desirability of Stimulus*	*Name of Contingency*	*Strength of Response*	*Example*
Presented	Pleasant	Positive reinforcement	Increases	Praise from a supervisor encourages continuing the praised behavior.
	Unpleasant	Punishment	Decreases	Criticism from a supervisor discourages enacting the punished behavior.
Withdrawn	Pleasant	Extinction	Decreases	Failing to praise a helpful act reduces the odds of helping in the future.
	Unpleasant	Negative reinforcement	Increases	Future criticism is avoided by doing whatever the supervisor wants.

or she associates it with the landing of the account. When this occurs, the individual will be more inclined in the future to do whatever it was that helped get the account.

Negative reinforcement.   Sometimes we also learn to perform acts because they permit us to avoid undesirable consequences. Unpleasant events, such as reprimands, rejection, probation, and termination, are some of the consequences faced for certain negative actions in the workplace. The process by which people learn to perform acts leading to the avoidance of such undesirable consequences is known as **negative reinforcement**, or **avoidance**. Whatever response led to the termination of these undesirable events is likely to occur again, thereby strengthening that response. For example, you may stay late at the office one evening to revise a sales presentation because you believe that the boss will "chew you out" if it's not ready in the morning. You learned how to avoid this type of aversive situation and behave accordingly.

Punishment.   Thus far, we have identified responses that are strengthened—because they lead to either positive consequences or the termination of negative consequences. However, the connection between a behavior and its consequences is not always strengthened; such links also may be weakened. This is what happens in the case of **punishment**. Punishment involves presenting an undesirable or aversive consequence in response to an unwanted behavior. A behavior accompanied by an undesirable outcome is less likely to reoccur if the person associates the negative consequences with the behavior. For example, if you are chastised by your boss for taking excessively long coffee breaks, you are considered punished for this action. As a result, you will be less likely to take long breaks again in the future.

Extinction.   The link between a behavior and its consequences also may be weakened by withholding reward—a process known as **extinction**. When a response that was once rewarded is no longer rewarded, it tends to weaken and eventually die out—or be *extinguished*. Let's consider an example. Suppose for many months you brought boxes of donuts to your weekly staff meetings. Your colleagues always thanked you as they gobbled them down. You were positively reinforced by their approval, so you continued bringing the donuts. Now, after several months of eating donuts, your colleagues have begun dieting. So, although tempting, your donuts go uneaten. After several months of no longer being praised for your generosity, you will be unlikely to continue bringing donuts. Your once-rewarded behavior will die out; it will be extinguished.

OBSERVATIONAL LEARNING: LEARNING BY IMITATING OTHERS

Although operant conditioning is based on the idea that we engage in behaviors for which we are directly reinforced, many of the things we learn on the job are *not* directly reinforced. Suppose, for example, on your new job you see many of your coworkers complimenting your boss on his attire. Each time someone says something flattering, the boss stops at his or her desk, smiles, and acts friendly. By complimenting the boss, they are reinforced by being granted his social approval. Chances are, after observing this several times, you too eventually will learn to say something nice to the boss. Although you may not have directly experienced the boss' approval, you would expect to receive it based on what you have observed from others. This is an example of a kind of learning known as **observational learning**, or **modeling**. It occurs when someone acquires new knowledge *vicariously*—that is, by observing what happens to others.

A great deal of what is learned about how to behave in organizations can be explained as the result of the process of observational learning. On the job, observational learning is a key part of many formal job instruction training programs. As I will explain in the next section, trainees given a chance to observe experts doing their jobs, followed by an opportunity to practice the desired skills, and given feedback on their work, tend to learn new job skills quite effectively. Observational learning also occurs in a very informal, uncalculated manner. For example, people who experience the norms and traditions of their organizations and who subsequently incorporate these into their own behavior may be regarded as having learned through observation.

Finally, it is important to note that people learn not only what to do by observing others but also what *not* to do. Specifically, research has shown that people observing their coworkers getting punished for behaving inappropriately on the job tend to refrain from engaging in those same actions themselves. As you might imagine, this is a very effective way for people to learn how to behave—and without ever experiencing any displeasure themselves.

APPLICATIONS OF LEARNING IN ORGANIZATIONS

The principles of learning we have discussed thus far are used in organizations in many different ways. We will now discuss four systematic approaches to incorporating learning in organizations: *training*, *organizational behavior management*, *discipline*, and *knowledge management*.

Training: Learning and developing job skills.   Probably the most obvious use to which principles of learning may be applied in organizations is **training**—that is, the process through which people systematically acquire and improve the skills and abilities needed to better their job performance. Just as students learn basic educational skills in the classroom, employees must learn their job skills. Training is used not only to prepare newly hired employees to meet the challenges of the jobs they will face, but

According to the American Society for Training and Development, American companies spend over $44 billion on training annually.

also to upgrade and refine the skills of existing employees. In fact, according to the American Society for Training and Development, American companies spend over $44 billion on training annually. For a summary of some of the most inventive training practices in use today, see Table 2.3.[11]

In view of this staggering investment, it is important to consider ways of enhancing the effectiveness of employee training. Four major principles may be identified.

1. **Participation**. People not only learn more quickly, but also retain the skills longer when they have actively participated in the learning process. This applies to the learning of both motor tasks as well as cognitive skills. For example, when learning to swim, there's no substitute for actually getting in the water and moving your arms and legs. In the classroom, students who listen attentively to lectures, think about the material, and get involved in discussions tend to be learn more effectively than those who just sit passively.

2. **Repetition**. If you know the old adage "practice makes perfect," you are already aware of the benefits of repetition on learning. Perhaps you learned the multiplication tables or a poem or a foreign language phrase by going over it repeat-

---

TABLE 2.3   Training: What Are Today's Companies Doing?

As summarized here, some of today's companies are investing considerable resources in training efforts and reaping huge dividends as a result. (*Sources:* Based on information in Ewing, 1999, and Meister, 1998; see Note 11.)

Company	*Training Effort*	*Result*
Motorola	"Motorola University" trains over 100,000 employees each year in work-related skills	Each dollar spent on training brings in $30 in increased productivity every three years.
Corning	For up to two years, apprentices are trained the equivalent of one day per week in becoming specialists in Celcor (a product used in catalytic converters).	Product defects dropped by 38 percent.
Harley-Davidson	A variety of courses are offered to Dealers ("Dealer Operations Training") to help them become more effective.	Market share and profitability have risen steadily since training began.
Sears	Sears aims to train virtually all employees at "Sears University" to help make the company a better place at which to work and to shop.	Salespeople have become more knowledgeable, helping close more sales.
Siemens	In Munich, Germany, Siemens uses its own analysts and engineers to train other employees in the kinds of business challenges the company faces.	The program pays for itself and saved the company $11 million in 1999 alone.

edly. Scientists not only have established the benefits of repetition on learning but also have shown that these effects are even greater when practice is spread out over time than when it is lumped together. After all, when practice periods are too long, learning can suffer from fatigue, whereas learning a little bit at a time allows the material to sink in.

3. **Transfer of training**. As you might imagine, for training to be most effective, what is learned during training must be applied to the job. In general, the more closely a training program matches the demands of a job, the more effective the training will be. A good example is the elaborate simulation devices used to train pilots and astronauts. At a more down-to-earth level is the equipment used in many technical schools for people to learn skilled trades such as welding, computer repair, and radiation technology.

4. **Feedback**. It is extremely difficult for learning to occur in the absence of feedback—that is, knowledge of the results of one's actions. Feedback provides information about the effectiveness of one's training.[12] Of course, unless you learn what you already are doing well and what behaviors you need to correct, you probably will be unable to improve your skills. For example, it is critical for people being trained as word processing operators to know exactly how many words they correctly entered per minute for them to gauge their improvement.

In sum, these four principles—participation, repetition, transfer of training, and feedback—are the key to the effectiveness of any training program. The most effective training programs are those that incorporate as many of these principles as possible. This is often far easier said than done, especially when it comes to training those individuals who lack basic work skills. For a look at how some of today's companies are addressing this challenge, please see the **Winning Practices** section on p. 42.

Organizational behavior management: Positively reinforcing desirable organizational behaviors.   Earlier, in describing operant conditioning, I noted that the consequences of our behavior determine whether we repeat it or abandon it. Behaviors that are rewarded tend to be strengthened, repeated in the future. With this in mind, it is possible to administer rewards selectively to help reinforce behaviors that we wish repeated in the future. This is the basic principle behind **organizational behavior management** (also known as **organizational behavior modification**, or more simply, **OB Mod**). Organizational behavior management may be defined as the systematic application of positive reinforcement principles in organizational settings for the purpose of raising the incidence of desirable organizational behaviors.

Organizational behavior management programs have been used successfully to stimulate a variety of behaviors in many different organizations.[14] For example, a particularly interesting and effective program has been used in recent years at Diamond International, the Palmer, Massachusetts, company of 325 employees that manufactures Styrofoam egg cartons. In response to sluggish productivity, a simple but elegant reinforcement was put into place. Any employee working for a full year without an industrial accident is given 20 points. Perfect attendance is given 25 points. Once a year, the points are totaled. When employees reach 100 points, they get a blue nylon jacket with the company's logo on it and a patch identifying their membership in the "100 Club." Those earning still more points receive extra awards. For example, at 500 points,

WINNING PRACTICES

Training Employees Who Lack Basic Skills

As recently as a decade ago, companies that needed new employees had little difficulty attracting applicants who were at least somewhat qualified. Back then, training often involved little more than teaching new employees the highly specialized skills required to perform their new jobs. Today, however, with unemployment at record low levels, the pool of available employees—let alone qualified ones—has grown so small that many companies, out of desperation, are tapping a new source of employees: people lacking basic work skills. This may include people who have never worked at all, who have been out of the workforce for a long time, or who are so poorly educated that their employment options are severely limited. As you might imagine, companies tapping into this reserve have found it necessary to go to great lengths to bring such individuals up to speed so they are capable of filling their positions.[13]

Sometimes, this means not only training people how to perform their jobs, but helping them develop basic life skills as well. Burger King, for example, trains new employees in such fundamental skills as how to balance a checkbook and the importance of getting to work on time. Ecolab, Inc., the Wisconsin-based maker of cleaning products, has found it almost impossible to find employees with the skills needed to advance to jobs beyond the most basic entry-level positions. Rather than searching for new recruits, who are almost impossible to find in a state with unemployment hovering just over 3 percent, company execs have taken to training existing employees in the skills needed to advance, such as math, basic physics, and blueprint reading. Its "if you can't hire them, train them—no matter how basic it is" approach is catching on.

Several companies have partnered with various community groups and local government agencies to tackle the problem. Ecolab, for example, has hired several employees from organizations that specialize in removing people from welfare rolls and putting them onto payrolls. Marriott Hotels, which has enrolled its new employees in basic training programs since 1991, has paved the way for some of its most needy employees to take jobs by working with local agencies that subsidize child-care expenses. One small moving company in Cleveland even has gone so far as to hire people with substance abuse problems and to refer them to Alcoholics Anonymous.

Although these tactics don't work in all cases, they have been successful in turning around the lives of many people who would not have been employed otherwise. Until such individuals develop positive images of themselves and internalize the value of working at a steady job, which comes in time, employers often have to put up with chronic lateness and absenteeism. Still, many find dealing with these problems far better than leaving jobs vacant altogether. As many of these individuals are receiving training, they are getting off welfare, slowly chipping away at the myth that all welfare recipients are lazy. Indeed, by seeking out such individuals and training them to work—even if it means showing them how to do things you think they already should know—many of today's employers are learning that this assumption is far from true. Moreover, companies are becoming more productive by filling positions that would have remained vacant otherwise.

Questions for Discussion

1. What indications of training in basic life skills have you seen in the companies you know?
2. What benefits and risks do you believe will result from hiring people known to have substance abuse problems? How can these risks be overcome?
3. How long lasting do you believe the effects will be of training new employees in basic life skills? What problems are likely to interfere with its effectiveness over time?

employees can select any of a number of small household appliances. These inexpensive prizes go a long way toward symbolizing to employees the company's appreciation for their good work.

This program has helped improve productivity dramatically at Diamond International. Compared to before the OB Mod program began, output improved 16.5 percent, quality-related errors dropped 40 percent, grievances decreased 72 percent, and time lost due to accidents was lowered by 43.7 percent. The result of all of this has been over $1 million in gross financial benefits for the company—and a much happier workforce. Needless to say, this has been a very simple and effective organizational behavior management program. Although not all such programs are equally successful, evidence suggests that they are generally quite beneficial.

Discipline: Eliminating undesirable organizational behaviors Just as organizations may use rewards systematically to encourage desirable behavior, they also may use punishment to discourage undesirable behavior. Problems such as absenteeism, lateness, theft, and substance abuse cost companies vast sums of money, situations many companies attempt to manage by using **discipline**—the systematic administration of punishment.

By administering an unpleasant outcome (e.g., suspension without pay) in response to an undesirable behavior (e.g., excessive tardiness), companies seek to minimize the undesirable behavior. In one form or another, using discipline is a relatively common practice. Survey research has shown, in fact, that 83 percent of companies use some form of discipline, or at least the threat of discipline, in response to undesirable behaviors. But, as you might imagine, disciplinary actions taken in organizations vary greatly. At one

> *83 percent of companies use some form of discipline, or at least the threat of discipline, in response to undesirable behaviors.*

extreme, they may be very formal, such as written warnings that become part of the employee's permanent record. At the other extreme, they may be informal and low-key, such as friendly reminders and off-the-record discussions between supervisors and their problem subordinates.

The trick to disciplining effectively is to know how to administer punishment in a way that is considered fair and reasonable. Fortunately, research and theory have pointed to some effective principles that may be followed to maximize the effectiveness of discipline in organizations. We will now consider several of these.

1. *Deliver punishment immediately after the undesirable response occurs.* The less time that passes between the occurrence of an undesirable behavior and the administration of a negative consequence, the more strongly people will make the connection between them. When people make this association, the consequence is likely to serve as a punishment, thereby reducing the probability of the unwanted behavior. Thus, it is best for managers to talk to their subordinates about their undesirable behaviors immediately after committing them. Expressing disapproval after several days or weeks have gone by will be less effective because the passage of time will weaken the mental association between behavior and its consequences.

2. *Give moderate levels of punishment—nothing too high or too low.* If the consequences for performing an undesirable action are not very severe (e.g., rolling one's eyes as a show of disapproval), then it is unlikely to serve as a punishment. After all, it is quite easy to live with such a mild response. In contrast, consequences that are overly severe might be perceived as unfair and inhumane. When this occurs, not only might the individual resign, but also a strong signal will be sent to others about the unreasonableness of the company's actions.

3. *Punish the undesirable behavior, not the person.* Effective punishment is impersonal in nature and focuses on the individual's actions rather than on his or her personality. So, for example, when addressing an employee who is repeatedly caught taking excessively long breaks, it is unwise to say, "You're lazy and have a bad attitude." Instead, it would be better to say, "By not being at your desk when expected, you're making it more difficult for all of us to get our work done on time." Responding in this manner will be less humiliating for the individual. Additionally, focusing on exactly what people can do to avoid such disapproval (taking shorter breaks, in this case) increases the likelihood that they will attempt to alter their behavior in the desired fashion. By contrast, the person who feels personally attacked might not only "tune out" the message but also not know exactly how to improve.

4. *Use punishment consistently—all the time, for all employees.* Sometimes, managers attempting to be lenient turn a blind eye to infractions of company rules. Doing this may cause more harm than good insofar as it inadvertently reinforces the undesirable behavior (by demonstrating that one can get away with breaking the rules). As a result, it is considered most effective to administer punishment after each occurrence of an undesirable behavior. Similarly, it is important to show consistency in the treatment of all employees. In other words, everyone who commits the same infraction should be punished the same way, regardless of the person administering the punishment. When this occurs, supervisors are unlikely to be accused of showing favoritism.

5. *Clearly communicate the reasons for the punishment given.* Making clear exactly what behaviors lead to what disciplinary actions greatly facilitates the effectiveness of punishment. Clearly communicated expectations help strengthen the perceived connection between behavior and its consequences. Wise managers use their opportunities to communicate with subordinates to make clear that the punishment being given does not constitute revenge, but an attempt to eliminate an unwanted behavior (which, of course, it is).

If, after reading all this, you are thinking that it is truly difficult to properly administer rewards and punishments in organizations, you have reached the same conclusion as experts in the field of organizational behavior. Indeed, one of the key skills that make some managers so effective is their ability to influence others by properly administering rewards and punishments (to practice this skill, see the **Self-Assessment Exercise** on p. 47).

KNOWLEDGE MANAGEMENT: SHARING WHAT IS KNOWN

Thus far, our discussion of learning has focused on individuals. One by one, employees learn what they need to know and develop areas of expertise that are called upon when needed to perform certain jobs. However, there are occasions in which somebody, somewhere in an organization is doing something that requires special expertise, but doesn't know how to find it within the company. When this occurs, the company may waste time and money by "reinventing the wheel," developing expertise that already exists (if they only knew where to find it!). In other cases, if the necessary expertise is not tapped or new expertise is not developed, then either something will not get done properly, or it will not get done at all.

Acknowledging this situation, in recent years many companies have instituted what are known as *knowledge management* programs. **Knowledge management** is defined as the process of gathering, organizing, and sharing a company's information and knowledge assets. Typically, knowledge management programs involve using technology to establish repository databases and retrieval systems. These are ways of using computers to sort through and identify the areas of expertise represented in the company—that is, its **intellectual capital**.

This is done, for example, at British Petroleum (BP), where an employee-driven database available on the company's intranet contains information about the expertise of some 10,000 employees, making it a simple task to determine "who knows what."[15] BP also employs **knowledge managers**—individuals who are specifically charged with organizing the wealth of corporate knowledge represented by its people and ensuring that this information gets used effectively. Knowledge managers at BP actively seek out and summarize the lessons learned in various business units and distill the main points over the intranet. Harnessing knowledge in this way has led to considerable savings in the cost of construction and increased efficiency in the drilling of oil fields.

Knowledge management has also helped companies improve their customer service efforts. If you have a Dell computer and have ever called its service center regarding a problem, for example, you probably know that its technicians consult a huge knowledge base that advises them what questions to ask and what steps to take to repair problems. By providing a repository of knowledge in this manner, the company makes it possible for its service representatives to better solve your problems. These days, companies such as Dell and Microsoft, and others that provide highly technical services to consumers, have put their knowledge bases online, for customers to access via the Internet. In this fashion, customers can help themselves directly, often without having to consult anyone in the company.

Making it easy to find out whose brains to pick in an organization has proven very successful for many different companies. Indeed, some highly impressive results of implementing knowledge management programs have been reported. At IBM, for example, the sharing of information has made it possible for consultants to reduce the average time it takes to prepare a proposal from 200 hours down to 30 hours. Using "Eureka," a database compiled by Xerox technicians, has made it possible for that company's service representatives to slash in half the average amount of time required to repair one of its copy machines. Although setting up and operating a knowledge management program is no easy task (nor is doing so

> *At IBM, for example, the sharing of information has made it possible for consultants to reduce the average time it takes to prepare a proposal from 200 hours down to 30 hours.*

inexpensive!), results like these are encouraging a growing numbers of companies that do not have such programs in place to implement them in the near future. In fact, a recent survey reveals that only about a third of all companies already have some type of knowledge management system in place, although most others expect to implement such a program in the near future.[16]

SUMMARY: HAVE I MET THE LEARNING OBJECTIVES?

You can be certain that you have met the learning objectives for this chapter found on p. 25 if you understand the following:

1. **DEFINE social perception and EXPLAIN the processes by which people come to make judgments about what others are like.** Social perception is the process of integrating and interpreting information about others so as to accurately understand them. By observing others' behavior, people make judgments about the characteristics those individuals possess. Such judgments are known as correspondent inferences.

2. **DESCRIBE social identity theory and Kelley's theory of causal attribution.** Social identity theory recognizes that the way people perceive others and themselves is based on both their unique characteristics (i.e., personal identity) and their membership in various groups (i.e., social identity). People tend to view themselves in terms of their membership in various groups, exaggerating the differences between themselves and other groups such that they perceive their own group more positively than those in other groups. Kelley's theory of causal attribution recognizes that judgments about the underlying causes behind people's behavior may be based on either internal reasons (e.g., one's own characteristics) or external reasons (e.g., the situation). The extent to which we attribute the causes of people's behavior to internal or external causes is said to depend on three types of information: consensus (whether others act in a similar manner), consistency (whether the individual previously acted in this way in the same situation), and distinctiveness (whether this person acted similarly in different situations).

3. **DESCRIBE the various types of biases that make the social perception process imperfect.** People tend to explain others' behavior in terms of internal explanations rather than external ones. This is known as the fundamental attribution error. Our judgments of others are also biased by stereotypes—beliefs that all members of specific groups share similar traits.

4. **DEFINE learning and DESCRIBE the two basic kinds of learning that occur in organizations.** Learning is a relatively permanent change in behavior occurring as a result of experience. Much learning in organizations occurs as a result of operant conditioning, which is learning based on the association between behavior and its consequences. Learning also occurs indirectly, through observing what happens to others and imitating their behavior. This is known as observational learning.

5. **DISTINGUISH between the four main contingencies of reinforcement.** Behavior is repeated when it is associated with desirable outcomes (positive reinforcement) or the removal of undesirable outcomes (negative reinforcement). Behavior is not repeated when it is associated with undesirable outcomes (punishment) or the removal of positive outcomes (extinction).

6. **IDENTIFY various organizational activities that actively involve principles of learning.**   Principles of learning are actively involved in training, organizational behavior management, disciplinary practices, and knowledge management.

You Be the Consultant

In your capacity as the human resources manager of a large broadcasting company, you are responsible for training current employees and appraising their job performance. Answer the following questions based on the material in this chapter.

1. What types of biases and inaccuracies may be expected in the process of appraising employees' job performance? What can be done to minimize the impact of these factors?
2. Given that the company invests a great deal of money in its training program, you are interested in seeing that it works as effectively as possible. What specific steps can you take to ensure that learning of job skills occurs at a high level?
3. How can knowledge management and organizational management be used to improve performance?

SELF-ASSESSMENT EXERCISE

Disciplining a Generally Good Employee

Even the best employees sometimes behave inappropriately. When this occurs, managers confront a special challenge: How can they address the problem behavior without offending or turning off the employee in question? The following exercise will get you to think about handling this difficult, but not uncommon, type of dilemma.

Directions

Read the following scenario. Then describe what you would do to handle the situation.

Michael M. has been a laborer with your home construction company for almost four years, during which time he has amassed an excellent record. He has been an outstanding craftsman who always does meticulous work and completes his projects ahead of schedule. Michael has always gotten along well with his coworkers, and even customers have praised him for his kind and professional manner. Employees like Michael are hard to find, making you very interested in keeping him happy so that he will continue to work for you. There has been one recurrent problem, however. Because he knows he is so good and that you are reluctant to fire him, Michael has been taking advantage of you by showing up for work late—sometimes by as much as an hour. When you have spoken to him about this, he admits to being late quite often, but says that this sometimes is necessary because he has to help send his children to school in the morning. Besides, he claims that he works so quickly that he makes up for being late, so it shouldn't matter. However, your company has a strict rule against being late ("three strikes and you're out"), and you are concerned that by turning a blind eye to Michael, you are sending the message to the other employees that Michael is "above the law" and that you are "playing favorites" with him. You do not want to threaten your credibility by ignoring the problem, but you also don't want risk making Michael quit.

Following the guidelines for discipline described on pp. 43–44, describe three specific things you would do to handle this situation.

1. _____
2. _____
3. _____

Questions for Discussion

1. What do you believe are the main strengths and weaknesses of your suggestions? Are they practical? Do you believe they would work?
2. How were you affected, if at all, by the fact that Michael's lateness resulted from the need to take care of his children? Did this matter? If so, how, and what would you do about it?
3. Discuss your three solutions with others in your class. How did your suggestions differ from theirs?

(GROUP EXERCISE)

Identifying Occupational Stereotypes

Although we usually reserve our concern over stereotypes to women and members of racial and ethnic minorities, the simple truth is that people can hold stereotypes toward members of just about *any* group. And, in organizations, people are likely to hold stereotypes about people based on a variable whose importance cannot be downplayed—the occupational groups to which they belong. What we expect of people, and the way we treat them, is likely to be affected by stereotypes about their professions. This exercise will help you better understand this phenomenon.

Directions

Divide the class into groups of approximately five to eight students, and gather each group in a circle. Then, working together, rate each of the following occupational groups with respect to how much of the characteristics listed they tend to show. Record your opinions using the following scale:

1 = not at all
2 = a slight amount
3 = a moderate amount
4 = a great amount
5 = an extremely great amount

Accountants	Professors	Lawyers
_____ interesting	_____ interesting	_____ interesting
_____ generous	_____ generous	_____ generous
_____ intelligent	_____ intelligent	_____ intelligent
_____ conservative	_____ conservative	_____ conservative

Clergy	Physicians	Plumbers
_____ interesting	_____ interesting	_____ interesting
_____ generous	_____ generous	_____ generous
_____ intelligent	_____ intelligent	_____ intelligent
_____ conservative	_____ conservative	_____ conservative

Questions for Discussion

1. How easy was it for your group to form a consensus? Did members of your group generally agree or disagree on the ratings?
2. What professions were generally easiest to rate? Which were most difficult?
3. Did the various groups agree or disagree with each other? In other words, how strongly held were the stereotypes overall?
4. To what extent were your group's responses based on specific people that group members knew? How did knowledge, or lack of knowledge, of members of the various occupational groups influence your group's ratings?
5. To what extent do you believe that exposing these stereotypes will: (a) perpetuate them, or (b) help you refrain from behaving in accord with them?

NOTES

Case Note

Balu, R. (1999, December). Whirlpool gets real with customers. *Fast Company,* pp. 74, 76.

Chapter Notes

[1] Forgas, J. P. (2000). *Handbook of affect and social cognition.* Mahwah, NJ: Lawrence Erlbaum Associates.

[2] Ashforth, B. E., & Mael, F. (1989). Social identity theory and the organization. *Academy of Management Review, 14,* 20–29.

[3] LaTendresse, D. (2000). Social identity and intergroup relations within the hospital. *Journal of Social Distress and the Homeless, 9,* 51–69.

[4] Cialdini, R. B., Borden, R. J., Thorne, A., Walker, M. R., Freeman, S., & Sloan, L. R. (1999). Basking in reflected glory: Three (football) field studies. In R. F. Baumeister (Ed.), *The self in social psychology* (pp. 436–445). Philadelphia: Psychology Press/Taylor & Francis.

[5] Eden, D., & Shani, A. B. (1982). Pygmalion goes to boot camp: Expectancy, leadership, and trainee performance. *Journal of Applied Psychology, 67,* 194–199.

[6] Oz, S., & Eden, D. (1994). Restraining the Golem: Boosting performance by changing the interpretation of low scores. *Journal of Applied Psychology, 79,* 744–754.

[7] Davidson, O. B., & Eden, D. (2000). Remedial self-fulfilling prophecy: Two field experiments to prevent Golem effects among disadvantaged women. *Journal of Applied Psychology, 85,* 386–398.

[8] Eden, D. (1997). Leadership and expectations: Pygmalion effects and other self-fulfilling prophecies in organizations. In R. Vecchio (Ed.), *Leadership: Understanding the dynamics of power and influence in organizations* (pp. 177–193). Notre Dame, IN: University of Notre Dame Press.

[9] Bethune, G. (1999). *From worst to first: Behind the scenes of Continental's remarkable comeback.* New York: John Wiley.

[10] Nye, R. D. (1992). *The legacy of B. F. Skinner: Concepts and perspectives, controversies and misunderstandings.* Belmont, CA: Brooks/Cole.

[11] Ewing, J. (1999, November 15). Siemens: Building a "B-school" in its own backyard. *Business Week*, pp. 281–282. Meister, J. C. (1998). *Corporate universities.* New York: McGraw-Hill.

[12] Ilgen, D. R., & Moore, C. F. (1987). Types and choices of performance feedback. *Journal of Applied Psychology, 72*, 401–406.

[13] Leonhardt, D., & Cohn, L. (1999, April 26). Business takes up the challenge of training its rawest recruits. *Business Week*, pp. 30–32.

[14] Frederiksen, L. W. (1982). *Handbook of organizational behavior management.* New York: John Wiley.

[15] McCune, J. C. (1999, April). Thirst for knowledge. *Management Review*, pp. 10–12.

[16] Wah, L. (1999, April). Behind the buzz. *Management Review*, pp. 17–26.

3

Personality, feelings and stress

LEARNING OBJECTIVES

After reading this chapter, you will be able to:

1. DEFINE personality.

2. DESCRIBE various personality dimensions that are responsible for individual differences in organizational behavior.

3. DISTINGUISH between emotions and moods.

4. DESCRIBE the effects of emotions and moods on behavior in organizations.

5. IDENTIFY the major causes and consequences of stress.

6. IDENTIFY steps that can be taken, both personally and by organizations, to control stress.

THREE GOOD REASONS WHY YOU SHOULD CARE ABOUT . . .

Personality, Feelings, and Stress

You should care about personality, feelings, and stress in organizations because:

1. Understanding people's personalities helps us know what to expect of them, and understanding our own personalities provides valuable insight into our own behavior.

2. Recognizing others' moods and emotions helps us appreciate how to interact with them effectively on the job.

3. Knowing the signs of stress and how to manage your own stress not only can help you work effectively on your job but also can contribute to having a healthy, happy life.

Making the Case for... Personality, Feelings, and Stress

Seph Barnard: An Entrepreneur, "Tired and True"

If you need an occasional blank cassette tape for your personal camcorder, audiotape deck, or VCR, you probably pick it up at your nearest discount store or supermarket. But where do radio and TV stations and professional video production companies shop for the miles and miles of high-quality tape they use? For about a decade, many have been purchasing such products from Tape Resources, Inc., the Virginia Beach, Virginia–based supplier of audio and videotape to the industry.

Although this company now has 13 full-time employees and does $5.3 million in annual sales, it wasn't always thriving. In fact, when Seph Barnard, the president of the company, first bought it in 1993, the firm was in deep financial trouble. Tape Resources needed Barnard's full-time attention, and he proved he was up to the task of turning it around. Acknowledging "the thing that gives me enjoyment in life is the challenge," Barnard transformed the company into one of the 500 fastest-growing companies in the United States.

The company's strategy is straightforward: It doesn't compete with larger companies on price, but instead, offers great service—free, same-day shipping of any of the 250 brands and lengths of blank tapes and disks kept in stock. To ensure high-quality customer service, Barnard kept close tabs on all business operations himself. Not content to rest on the company's success, he worked tirelessly on everything from sending out checks and examining invoices, to even assembling the shelves in the company's warehouse. If there was something to be done, he did it. With 18-hour days and no vacations, the company consumed his life. And there was no escaping it when he got home, either. Barnard's wife, Dawn-Marie, was in charge of Tape Resources' human resource department. Barnard characterized himself as being "really focused." To say the least! You might even say he was driven—if not obsessed—with success.

Unfortunately, Barnard's relentless schedule took its toll on him. He never had a moment's rest. Even while eating dinner, he'd be mulling things over in his mind. He had no hobbies and virtually no social life. No matter where he was physically, mentally he was at work. Exhausted, he became remote—so much so that he began working at home, where Dawn-Marie often fielded his phone calls. Things needed to change, and they did one day when Barnard received a letter from a prominent investment-banking firm indicating that a large office supply company was interested in buying his business.

This could have been "the out" that many would have taken in this situation—especially considering the $2 million it would have put in Barnard's pocket. But, he didn't take it. Although selling the company would have solved some of his personal worries, it probably would have meant destroying much of what he worked so hard to create. He couldn't bring himself to do this. Instead, he chose to hand over the reins of the company to David Durovy, the company's sales manager, and empowered the other employees to make their own decisions. This frees him to take a sabbatical, traveling for six months or so, allowing him to come back to Virginia Beach refreshed and renewed.

So, what will he do when he comes back? He plans to check in on Tape Resources only occasionally. "I'm starting to recognize there's a time to hand a company over and stand back," he says, acknowledging that this time has come. What then? Barnard freely admits that he'll probably do what he really likes most—starting up another company (or two, or three)!

You may find yourself remarking how special Mr. Barnard is. After all, it isn't everyone who would work so hard to make his company so successful. Indeed, he is unique. But then again, we are all unique in our own ways. Like Seph Barnard, we all have our own special combination of characteristics that make us distinct from others. It is this distinct pattern of traits that defines one's *personality,* the first topic we will examine in this chapter. Clearly, one of Barnard's most special qualities is his capacity to express his emotions toward other things and people—whether it's his feelings toward Tape Resources as an entity or the loyal employees who have stuck with him over the years. The nature of people's *feelings,* as reflected in their emotions and mood, is the second topic covered in this chapter.

Finally, the case reveals that Barnard worked so hard that he gave up everything else in his life, which he knew wasn't healthy. After a few years of this, he decided not to sell the company, but to change his role in it, leaving daily operations in the hands of his sales manager and decision making in the hands of the employees themselves. This was Barnard's way of keeping his sanity in the face of the high level of stress that pervaded his daily life. Given its relevance to personality and emotions, *stress* is the third topic we will consider in this chapter and one about which Barnard knows only too well.

Personality: The Unique Differences Between Us

If our experience with other people tells us anything, it is that they are all in some way *unique*, and at least to a degree, they are all *consistent*. That is, we each possess a distinct pattern of traits and characteristics not fully duplicated in any other person, and these are generally stable over time. Thus, if you know someone who is courteous and outgoing today, he or she probably showed these traits in the past and is likely to continue showing them in the future. Moreover, this person will tend to show them in many different situations over time.

Together, these two facts form the basis for a useful working definition of **personality**—the unique and relatively stable pattern of behavior, thoughts, and emotions shown by individuals. In short, personality refers to the lasting ways in which any one person is different from all others. And, as you might imagine, personality characteristics can be very important on the job. With this in mind, I will review several key personality dimensions that are most relevant to OB.

THE "BIG FIVE" DIMENSIONS OF PERSONALITY

Although there are many different dimensions of personality that can be used to describe people, some are more important than others. One group of variables that scientists have found to be especially important is referred to as the **big five dimensions of personality**.[1] For a summary of these vital aspects of personality, see Table 3.1.

As you might imagine, the big five dimensions of personality play an important role in organizational behavior.[2] For example, research has shown that employees who are highly conscientious tend to perform better than those who are not so conscientious. Organizational scientists also have found that people who are highly extraverted tend to succeed in managerial and sales jobs—much as the stereotype suggests.[3] However, not all research findings are as easily explained. For example, neither agreeableness nor emotional stability have been linked to success in various kinds of jobs. This

Table 3.1	The Big Five Dimensions of Personality

A cluster of personality traits known as the *big five dimensions of personality* have been found to account for important differences in the way people behave in organizations. Those characteristics of which the big five is composed are described here.

Component of the Big Five	*Description*
Conscientiousness	The degree to which someone is hardworking, organized, dependable, and persevering (high in conscientiousness), as opposed to lazy, disorganized, and unreliable (low in conscientiousness)
Extraversion–introversion	The degree to which someone is gregarious, assertive, and sociable (extraverted), as opposed to reserved, timid, and quiet (introverted)
Agreeableness	The degree to which someone is cooperative and warm (highly agreeable), as opposed to belligerent and cold (highly disagreeable)
Emotional stability	The degree to which someone is insecure, anxious, and depressed (emotionally unstable), as opposed to secure, calm, and happy (emotionally stable)
Openness to experience	The extent to which someone is creative, curious, and cultured (open to experience), as opposed to practical and having narrow interests (closed to experience)

Personality plays an important—but often unpredictable—role when it comes to understanding behavior in organizations.

may well be because large numbers of disagreeable and unstable people leave their jobs early. As a result, those who are left behind, and whose performance is measured by the researchers, tend to be relatively agreeable and stable. Clearly, as you can see, personality plays an important—but often unpredictable—role when it comes to understanding behavior in organizations.

THE TYPE A AND TYPE B BEHAVIOR PATTERNS

Think about the people you know. Can you identify someone who always seems to be in a hurry, is extremely competitive, and is often irritable? Now, name someone who shows the opposite pattern—a person who is relaxed, not very competitive, and easygoing. The people you have in mind represent extremes on one key dimension of personality. The first individual would be labeled *Type A* and the second, *Type B*. People categorized as **Type A** personalities show high levels of competitiveness, irritability, and time urgency (i.e., they are always in a hurry). In addition, they demonstrate certain stylistic patterns, such as loud and exaggerated speech, and a tendency to respond very quickly in many contexts. For example, during conversations they often begin speaking before others are through. People classified as having the **Type B** personality show the opposite pattern; they are calmer and more relaxed.

Do people who are Type A's and Type B's differ with respect to job performance? Given their high level of competitiveness, it seems reasonable to expect that Type A's will work harder at various tasks than will Type B's and, as a result, will perform at higher levels. In fact, however, the situation turns out to be more complex than this. On the one hand, Type A's *do* tend to work faster on many tasks than do Type B's, even when no pressure or deadline is involved. Similarly, they are able to get more done in the presence of distractions. In addition, Type A's often seek more challenges in their work than do Type B's (e.g., given a choice, they tend to select more difficult tasks).

Despite these differences, Type A's do not *always* perform better than Type B's. For example, Type A's frequently do poorly on tasks requiring patience or careful, considered judgment. For the most part, they are simply in too much of a hurry to complete such work in an effective manner. A study comparing Type A and Type B nurses suggests why this may be so. Although Type A's were significantly more involved in their jobs and invested greater effort, they also were more overloaded (i.e., they took on too much to do) and experienced more conflict with respect to the various aspects of the job required of them. It is easy to understand how differences such as these may well interfere with any possible improvements in performance that may derive from effort alone.

These and other findings suggest that neither pattern has the overall edge when it comes to task performance. Although Type A's may excel on tasks involving time pressure or solitary work, Type B's have the advantage when it comes to tasks involving complex judgments and accuracy, as opposed to speed.

SELF-EFFICACY: THE "CAN DO" FACET OF PERSONALITY

Suppose that two individuals are assigned the same task by their supervisor, and that one is confident of her ability to carry it out successfully, whereas the other has some serious doubts on this score. Which person is more likely to succeed? Assuming that all other factors (e.g., differences in their ability and motivation) are held constant, it is reasonable to predict that the first will do better. Such an individual is higher in a personality variable known as **self-efficacy**—one's belief in his or her own capacity to perform a task. When considered in the context of a given task, self-efficacy is not, strictly speaking, an aspect of personality. However, based on direct experiences and vicarious experiences, people acquire general expectations about their ability to perform a wide range of tasks in many different contexts. Such generalized beliefs about self-efficacy are stable over time, and these can be viewed as a personality variable.

Self-efficacy is a good predictor of people's work behavior. For example, in a study of university professors, it was found that self-efficacy was positively correlated with research productivity—that is, productivity increased as self-efficacy increased. In addition, it has been found that unemployed people who are trained in ways of enhancing their self-efficacy perceptions are more likely to look for jobs, and therefore, more likely to find jobs.[4]

> *Unemployed people who are trained in ways of enhancing their self-efficacy perceptions are more likely to look for jobs, and therefore, more likely to find jobs.*

We also know that women who have taken physical self-defense training classes not only tend to be confident in their ability to defend themselves but also tend to be assertive on the job.[5] Clearly, when it comes to a wide variety of behavior in organizations, self-efficacy is an important aspect of personality.

SELF-ESTEEM: THE IMPORTANCE OF SELF-EVALUATIONS

Beliefs about one's ability to perform specific tasks are an important part of the *self-concept*—individuals' conceptions of their own abilities, traits, and skills. Yet, they are only a small part. Another important aspect involves **self-esteem**—the extent to which people hold positive or negative views about themselves. People high in self-esteem evaluate themselves favorably, believing they possess many desirable traits and qualities. In contrast, people low in self-esteem evaluate themselves unfavorably, believing they are lacking in important respects and that they have characteristics that others consider unappealing. (To get a sense of your own self-esteem, complete the **Self-Assessment Exercise** on p. 77.)

Considerable evidence suggests that self-esteem is very important when it comes to a wide variety of organizational behavior.[6] For example, people who are low in self-esteem tend to be less successful in their job searches than those who are high in self-esteem. In addition, when people with low self-esteem are eventually employed, they are attracted to positions in larger organizations, where they are unlikely to be noticed and to call attention to themselves.

Once on the job, what can be expected of people who are low in self-esteem? The lower an employee's self-esteem, the less likely he or she is to take any active steps to solve problems confronted on the job (e.g., spending insufficient time to do a job). As a result, his or her performance tends to suffer. By contrast, employees with high levels of self-esteem are inclined to actively attempt to acquire the resources needed to cope with work problems, and to use their skills and abilities to their fullest—and, as a result, perform at higher levels.[7] Interestingly, people with low self-esteem tend to be aware of their tendency to perform poorly. They are predisposed to evaluate themselves quite negatively (especially when ambiguity exists concerning their performance) and to believe that they are inherently responsible for their poor performance.

Although my comments thus far sound discouraging with respect to the fate of people with low self-esteem, I can conclude on a more positive note that low self-esteem can be boosted. Although formal approaches are available, techniques that require the skills of a trained professional to implement (such as psychiatrists or clinical psychologists) can be very time-consuming. Fortunately, there are things that you can do on an everyday basis in organizations to minimize other people's feelings of low self-esteem. For an overview of some of these practices, see Table 3.2.

ACHIEVEMENT MOTIVATION: STRIVING FOR SUCCESS

You probably know some people who yearn for and focus on success, concentrating on doing what it takes to achieve it. Tape Resources' Seph Barnard, described in this chapter's opening case, is a clear example. Others, as you know, are far less concerned about success. If it comes, fine, but if not, that's okay, too. These individuals may be said to differ with respect to an important dimension of personality known as **achievement motivation** (sometimes termed the **need for achievement**). This may be defined as the strength of an individual's desire to excel—to succeed at difficult tasks and to do them better than anyone else.

People high in achievement motivation may be characterized as having a highly task-oriented outlook. That is, they are more concerned with getting things done than they are with having good relationships with others. Also, because they are so inter-

| Table 3.2   Boosting Low Self-Esteem: Some Suggestions |

Although it is difficult to completely change key aspects of a personality, such as self-esteem, without intensive psychological help, there are several things that organizations can do to boost and maintain the self-esteem of their employees.

Suggestion	*Description*
• Make people feel uniquely valuable.	Create opportunities for people to feel accepted by finding ways to make use of their unique skills and experiences.
• Make people feel competent.	Recognize the good things that people do and praise them accordingly. That is, "catch someone in the act of doing something right."
• Make people feel secure.	Employees' self-esteem will be enhanced when managers make their expectations clear and are forthright with them.
• Make people feel empowered.	People given opportunities to decide how to do their jobs feel good about themselves and their work.

ested in achieving success, people who have a high amount of achievement motivation tend to seek tasks that are moderately difficult and challenging. After all, a too difficult task is likely to lead to failure, and a too easy task doesn't offer sufficient challenge to suit them. The opposite pattern describes people who are low on achievement motivation. These individuals strongly prefer extremely difficult or extremely easy tasks. This is because success is almost guaranteed if the task is easy enough, and failure can readily be justified by attributing it to external sources (i.e., the extreme difficulty of the task) if the task is difficult (see Figure 3.1).[8]

As you might imagine, people who are high in achievement motivation strongly desire feedback on their performance. This allows them to adjust their aspirations (i.e., to shoot for easier or more difficult goals) and to determine when they have succeeded, allowing them to attain the good feelings about their accomplishments that they crave. As part of this tendency, people who differ with respect to achievement motivation are attracted to different kinds of jobs. People high in need achievement prefer jobs in which they receive feedback that tells them how well they are doing, whereas those low in need achievement have little such interest. Not surprisingly, it has been found that people high in achievement motivation prefer jobs in which pay is based on merit, whereas those low in achievement motivation prefer jobs in which pay is based on seniority.

Given their strong desire to excel, you may expect that people who are high in achievement motivation will have highly successful careers. To some extent, this is true. Such individuals tend to gain promotions more rapidly than those who are low in motivation, at least early in their careers. However, people who are high in achievement motivation are not necessarily superior managers. In part, this is because people who are high in achievement motivation tend to create situations in which they can receive credit for their performance while carefully monitoring others. As we will see later in this book (Chapter 13), however, such ways of structuring organizations are not always conducive to high performance.

FIGURE 3.1 Achievement Motivation and Attraction to Tasks

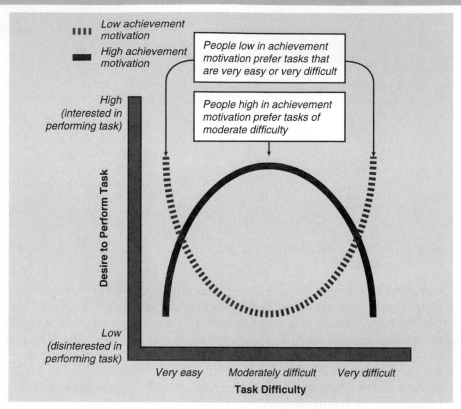

People who are high in achievement motivation are attracted to tasks of moderate difficulty, whereas people who are low in achievement motivation are attracted to tasks that are very easy or very difficult.

Feelings: The Importance of Emotions and Mood at Work

Just as stable aspects of ourselves—that is, our personalities—influence behavior in organizations, so too do more temporary feelings, such as our emotional states and our moods. If emotions and moods seem like they may be trivial, it's simply because their effects are so widespread that we take them for granted. However, their effects on the way we work can be considerable. Consider, for example, the following.

- It was a beautiful, sunny day—the kind that inspired Helen to come up with lots of new ideas for her clients.
- Janet was so upset about not making any progress on her sales report that she left her desk and went to the gym to work out.
- It was a special day for Martin. He was so pleased that Brooke agreed to marry him that he made his way through his delivery route in half the usual time—and with a lively spring in his step.

Not only do scientists acknowledge that people's feelings at any given time are important, they also recognize that two different kinds of feelings are involved—*emotions* and *mood*. Although you certainly have experienced different emotional states and different moods in your life, and have seen them in others, you shouldn't assume that you know exactly how they influence behavior in organizations. As you will see, each of these states is far more complex than you might imagine.

EMOTIONS: WHAT ARE THEY AND HOW DO THEY AFFECT US?

By definition, **emotions** are overt reactions that express feelings about events. You get angry when a colleague takes advantage of you. You become sad when your best friend leaves to take a new job. And, you become afraid of what the future holds when a larger firm merges with the company in which you've worked for 15 years. These are all examples of emotional reactions. The key thing to remember about emotions is that they have an object—that is, something or someone triggers them. Although it may seem that people have an infinite number of emotions, these all fit into the six basic categories shown in Table 3.3.[9]

We are interested in emotions in the field of OB because they are involved in three key aspects of how we work. We will review each of these here.

Emotional dissonance. As you know, people sometimes are required to display emotions on the job that are inconsistent with how they actually feel. This phenomenon, known as **emotional dissonance**, can be a significant source of work-related stress (the major topic that will be discussed later in this chapter).[10]

You probably can think of several good examples of what may well be emotional dissonance. Imagine a flight crew of a major airliner whose members are both tired and annoyed at the rude passengers they have encountered on a long flight. These individuals do not have the option of expressing how they really feel—or even expressing nothing at all. Instead, they are expected to act as if everything is okay, thanking the passengers for choosing their airline, and cheerfully saying good-bye (more like "buh-bye") to them as they exit the plane. The conflict between the emotions they may be really feeling (anger) and those they are required to express (happiness) is considered a source of stress that eventually may take its toll on these individuals' well-being.

Table 3.3 Major Categories of Emotion and their Associated Subcategories

Scientists have found it useful to categorize people's emotions into the six major categories (and several associated subcategories) identified here.

Category of Emotion	Subcategories
Anger	Disgust, envy, exasperation, irritation, rage, torment
Fear	Alarm, anxiety
Joy	Cheerfulness, contentment, enthrallment, optimism, pride, relief, zest
Love	Affection, longing, lust
Sadness	Disappointment, neglect, sadness, shame, suffering, sympathy
Surprise	(No subcatergories)

Emotional intelligence. Emotions also are important on the job insofar as people who are good at "reading" and understanding emotions in others, and who are able to regulate their own emotions, tend to have an edge when it comes to dealing with others. Recently, experts have come to recognize the importance of what is called **emotional intelligence**—that is, a cluster of skills related to the emotional aspects of life, such as the ability to monitor one's own and others' emotions, to discriminate among emotions, and to use such information to direct our thoughts and actions.[11] Specifically, people who are considered to have high emotional intelligence (those said to have a high *EQ*) demonstrate four key characteristics:

- *Skill in regulating one's own emotions.* People with high EQ's are good at self-regulation—that is, they are aware of their own feelings and display the most appropriate emotions. For example, if you know people who are especially good at calmly talking about their feelings instead of yelling at others at whom they are angry, chances are good that they have a high degree of emotional intelligence.
- *Ability to monitor others' emotions.* People with high EQ's are very good at judging how they are affecting other people and behave accordingly. For example, such an individual would refrain from sharing bad news with a colleague who already is very upset about something in his or her life. Instead, he or she would be inclined to wait for a more appropriate time.
- *Interest in motivating oneself.* There are times when many of us feel frustrated and lack interest in whatever we are doing and want to quit. This is not the case for people with high EQ's. Rather, such individuals are able to motivate themselves to sustain their performance, directing their emotions toward personal goals, and resisting the temptation to quit.
- *Highly developed social skills.* People with high EQ's are also very good at keeping a great number of relationships going over long periods of time. If you know people like this, you may realize that being this way is no accident. Such individuals are not only good at forming networks of relationships, but they are able to carefully coordinate their efforts with people and are good at working out ways of getting along with others, even during difficult periods.

> *In the world of work people who have highly developed emotional intelligence have an edge in many different ways.*

As you might imagine, in the world of work people who have highly developed emotional intelligence have an edge in many different ways. Consider entrepreneurs, for example. To be successful, such individuals have to be able to judge accurately what other people are like and to get along with others well enough to craft successful business deals. Not surprisingly, several aspects of emotional intelligence are related to the financial success of entrepreneurs.[12] Likewise, scientists who are well accepted by their colleagues and who, as a result, are well networked, tend to be up on the latest advances and, as a result, tend to be more productive. Clearly, having high levels of emotional intelligence is a real plus when it comes to one's success on the job.

With this in mind, some organizations, such as the U.S. Air Force, are considering candidates' emotional intelligence when making key placement decisions.[13] Some other organizations, such as Hong Kong Telecom, are training employees in ways of increasing their emotional intelligence. Although emotional intelligence is a new concept, it clearly holds a great deal of promise when it comes to understanding behavior in organizations.

Job performance. Emotions play an important role on the job insofar as they can interfere with job performance.[14] Will you work at your best when you are in a highly emotional state? Probably not. Someone who is excited because she is about to go on vacation or attend a big sporting event the next day might not be focusing on the job as completely as she otherwise might while in a less emotional state.

The negative impact of emotional states is even greater in the case of negative emotions. Consider, for example, an employee who is unhappy and upset because he received an unsatisfactory performance rating. This individual may be expected to be so distraught that he will lose the capacity to pay attention and become distracted from his work. Not only is this likely to impede task performance, but it also is likely to interfere with the potentially useful feedback that this individual might receive from the supervisor giving the evaluation. For this reason, successful managers recommend not even trying to get messages across to people while they are upset. In the case of the poorly performing employee, it may be best to wait until another time when the employee can be better focused to help him or her learn ways of improving.

MOOD: SUBTLE FEELINGS WITH BIG IMPACT

In contrast to emotions, which are highly specific and intense, we also have feelings that are more diffuse in scope, known as *moods*. Scientists define **mood** as an unfocused, relatively mild feeling that exists as background to our daily experiences. Whereas we are sure to recognize the emotions we are feeling, moods are more subtle and difficult to detect. For example, you may say that you are in a good mood or a bad mood, but what you are expressing isn't as focused as saying that you are experiencing a certain emotion, such as anger or sadness.

Moods, as we all know, fluctuate rapidly, sometimes widely, during the course of a day. Whereas favorable feedback from our bosses may make us feel good, harsh criticism may put us in a bad mood. Such temporary shifts in feeling *states*—short-term differences in the way we feel—are only partly responsible for the mood that people demonstrate. Superimposed over these passing conditions are also more stable personality *traits*—consistent differences between people's predispositions toward experiencing positive or negative affect. Mood, in other words, is a combination of both who we are personality-wise and the conditions we face.[15]

Not surprisingly, then, the moods we experience can be based on our individual experiences (e.g., receiving a raise), as well as the general characteristics of our work groups or organizations (e.g., the extent to which they are upbeat, energetic, and enthusiastic). For example, the importance of having fun at work is emphasized at such companies as Southwest Airlines and Ben & Jerry's Homemade Ice Cream.[16] No wonder people working for these companies are generally in a good mood.

Positive and negative affectivity. As you might imagine, scientists are far more specific about classifying people's moods than saying that they are simply good or bad. A particularly popular way of doing so is by distinguishing between *positive and negative affectivity*. Some people, as you know, are generally energetic, exhilarated, and have a real zest for life. You know them to be "up" all the time. Such individuals may be said

FIGURE 3.2 Positive and Negative Affectivity

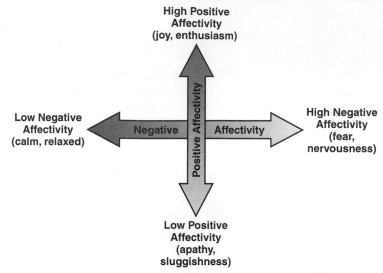

Scientists conceive of positive affectivity and negative affectivity as two different dimensions. The mood states associated with high and low levels of each are shown here. (*Source*: Based on suggestions by Weiss and Cropanzano, 1996; see Note 9.)

to be high in **positive affectivity**. By contrast, people who are low in positive affectivity are generally apathetic and listless.

Another dimension of mood is known as **negative affectivity**. It is characterized at the high end by people who are generally angry, nervous, and anxious, and at the low end, by those who feel calm and relaxed most of the time. As indicated in Figure 3.2, positive affectivity and negative affectivity are not the opposite of each other, but rather, two separate dimensions.

It probably comes as no surprise that differences in people's characteristic levels of mood play an important role in organizational behavior. For example, research comparing the performance of MBA students making various simulated managerial decisions found that people showing high positive affectivity were superior to those showing high negative affectivity. They made decisions that were more accurate, more important to the group's effectiveness, and had greater managerial potential.

Mood and behavior. Research has shown that our moods influence the way we behave on the job in several important respects. First, researchers have shown that mood is related to memory. Specifically, we know that being in a positive mood helps people recall positive things, and being in a negative mood helps people recall negative things.[17] This idea is known as **mood congruence**. For example, if you go to work while you're in a good mood, chances are that this will help you remember those things on the job that also put you in a good mood, such as the friendly relationships you have with your coworkers. Likewise, someone who is in a bad mood is likely to recall negative things associated with work, such as a recent fight with one's boss.

Mood also biases the way we evaluate people and things. For example, people report greater satisfaction with their jobs while they are in a good mood than while they are in a bad mood.[18] Being in a good mood also leads people to judge others' work more positively. The practical advice is clear: Make sure your boss is in a good mood before he or she conducts your annual performance evaluation. It just may make a difference!

Finally, it is important to note that mood strongly affects the extent to which people help each other, cooperate with each other, and refrain from behaving aggressively (forms of behavior we will discuss in more detail in Chapter 6). People who are in a good mood also tend to be more generous and are inclined to help their fellow workers who may need their assistance. So, if you need help with an important project on the job, it may be in your best interest to approach someone who is in a good mood. People who are in a good mood are also inclined to work carefully with others to resolve conflicts with them, whereas people in a bad mood are likely to keep those conflicts brewing. As a result, if someone is in a bad mood, this might not be the best time to sit down with her to discuss ways of settling an argument she is having with you. Let it rest for now—or, better yet, help put that person in a good mood before approaching this issue.

Stress in Organizations

Stress is an all-too-common part of life today, something few individuals can avoid. In fact, a nationwide survey conducted by a large life insurance company showed that nearly 46 percent of American workers believe their jobs are highly stressful.[19] For 27 percent, work was the single greatest source of stress in their lives. And growing evidence suggests that high levels of stress adversely affect physical health, psychological well-being, and many aspects of task performance.[20] Such evidence makes a strong case for understanding organizational stress. In this final section of the chapter, I will review the major causes and effects of stress, as well as ways of effectively managing stress so as to reduce its negative impact. Before doing this, however, I will define stress more carefully and distinguish it from other concepts with which it is related.

> *A nationwide survey conducted by a large life insurance company showed that nearly 46 percent of American workers believe their jobs are highly stressful.*

WHAT IS STRESS?

What do each of the following situations have in common?

- You are fired the day before you become eligible to receive your retirement pension.
- You find out that your company is about to eliminate your department.
- Your boss tells you that you will not be getting a raise this year.
- Your spouse is diagnosed with a serious illness.

The answer, besides that they are all awful situations, is that each situation involves external events (i.e., ones beyond our own control) that create extreme demands on us.

Stimuli of this type are known as **stressors**, formally defined as any demands, either physical or psychological in nature, encountered during the course of living.

When we encounter stressors, our bodies (in particular, our sympathetic nervous systems and endocrine systems) are mobilized into action, such as through elevated heart rate, blood pressure, and respiration.[21] Arousal rises quickly to high levels, and many physiological changes take place. If the stressors persist, the body's resources eventually may become depleted, at which point people's ability to cope (at least physically) decreases sharply, and severe biological damage may result. It is these patterns of responses that we have in mind when we talk about stress. Specifically, scientists define **stress** as the pattern of emotional states and physiological reactions occurring in response to demands from within or outside organizations (i.e., stressors).

The mechanisms by which stressors lead to stress reactions are not direct and mechanical in nature. Specifically, stress involves people's *cognitive appraisal* of the potential stressors they face. In simple terms, for stress to occur people must perceive that (1) the situation they face is somehow threatening to them; and (2) they will be unable to cope with these potential dangers or demands—that the situation, in essence, is beyond their control. In short, stress does not simply shape our thoughts; it also derives from them and is strongly affected by them.

To the extent that people appraise various situations as stressors, they are likely to have stress reactions. And often, these can have damaging behavioral, psychological, or psychological effects. Indeed, physiological and psychological stress reactions can be so great that eventually they take their toll on the body and mind, resulting in such maladies as insomnia, cardiovascular disease, and depression. Such reactions are referred to as **strain**, defined as deviations from normal states of human function resulting from exposure to stressful events. Prolonged exposure to strain can result in a syndrome known as *burnout*, a constellation of symptoms that we will describe later in this chapter. For a summary of the relationship between stressors, stress, strain, and burnout, refer to Figure 3.3. (As you probably have seen in dealing with different people in your

FIGURE 3.3 Stressors, Stress, Strain, and Burnout

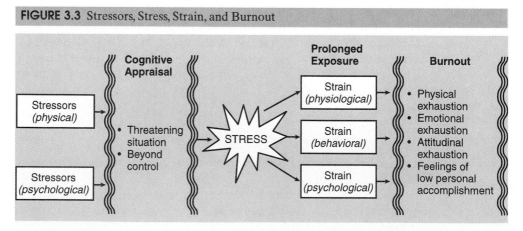

Stimuli known as *stressors* lead to *stress* reactions when they are cognitively appraised as threatening and beyond one's control. The deviations from normal states resulting from stress are known as *strain*. Prolonged stressful experiences can lead to *burnout*.

own lives, some individuals are far tougher than others. That is, they have the mental toughness to focus their minds and manage their emotions under stressful conditions.[22] To see how well you and your fellow team members fare in this regard, complete the **Group Exercise** on p. 78.)

CAUSES OF STRESS

What causes stress in work settings? Unfortunately, as you will see, the list is quite long; many different factors play a role in creating stress in the workplace.

Occupational demands.   Some jobs, such as emergency room physician, police officer, firefighter, and airline pilot, expose the people who hold them to high levels of stress. Others, such as a college professor, janitor, and librarian, do not. This basic fact—that some jobs are much more stressful than others—has been confirmed by the results of a survey involving more than 130 different occupations.[23] For a listing of some of the most stressful jobs, see Table 3.4.

What, precisely, makes some jobs more stressful than others? Research has shown that several features of jobs determine the levels of stress they generate. Specifically, people experience greater stress the more their jobs require (1) making decisions, (2) constantly monitoring devices or materials, (3) repeatedly exchanging information with

Table 3.4   What Jobs Are Most—and Least—Stressful?

Using a variety of standards, scientists rated 250 different jobs regarding how stressful they are. Shown here are the rankings and stress scores for selected occupations. (Higher scores reflect greater levels of stress encountered.) (*Source:* Reprinted by permission of the *Wall Street Journal;* © 1997 Dow Jones & Company, Inc. All rights reserved worldwide.)

Rank Score	Stress Score	Rank Score	Stress Score
1. U.S. president	176.6	47. Auto salesperson	56.3
2. Firefighter	110.9	50. College professor	54.2
3. Senior executive	108.6	60. School principal	51.7
6. Surgeon	99.5	103. Market research	
10. Air traffic controller	83.1	analyst	42.1
12. Public relations		104. Personnel recruiter	41.8
executive	78.5	113. Hospital	
16. Advertising account		administrator	39.6
executive	74.6	119. Economist	38.7
17. Real estate agent	73.1	122. Mechanical engineer	38.3
20. Stockbroker	71.7	124. Chiropractor	37.9
22. Pilot	68.7	132. Technical writer	36.5
25. Architect	66.9	149. Retail salesperson	34.9
31. Lawyer	64.3	173. Accountant	31.1
33. General physician	64.0	193. Purchasing agent	28.9
35. Insurance agent	63.3	229. Broadcast technician	24.2
42. Advertising		245. Actuary	20.2
salesperson	59.9		

others, (4) working in unpleasant physical conditions, and (5) performing unstructured rather than structured tasks. The greater the extent to which a job possesses these characteristics, the higher the level of stress that job produces among individuals holding it. Nurses and long-distance bus drivers perform jobs that match this profile—and, not surprisingly, people doing these jobs tend to show many of the adverse signs of stress.

Conflict between work and nonwork. If you've ever known anyone who has had to face the demands of working while at the same time trying to raise a family, you are probably well aware of how difficult this situation can be. Not only must you confront the usual pressures to spend time at work while concentrating on what you're doing, but you also must pay attention to the demands placed on you by members of your family (e.g., to spend time with them). When people confront such incompatibilities in the various sets of obligations they have, they are said to experience **role conflict**. As you might expect, when we experience conflicts between our work and nonwork lives, something has to give. Not surprisingly, the more time people devote to their jobs, the more events in their nonwork lives (e.g., personal errands) adversely affect their jobs (e.g., not being able to get the job done on time).

The stressful nature of role conflicts is particularly apparent among people who are expected to rapidly switch back and forth between the demands of work and family—a source of stress known as *role juggling*. This is an especially potent source of stress among one very large segment of the population—parents. Indeed, the more that people, such as working mothers and fathers, are forced to juggle the various roles in their lives, the less fulfilling they find those roles to be, and the more stress they suffer in their lives.[24]

Role ambiguity: Stress from uncertainty. Even if individuals are able to avoid the stress associated with role conflict, they still may encounter an even more common source of job-related stress: **role ambiguity**. This occurs when people are uncertain about several aspects of their jobs (e.g., the scope of their responsibilities, what's expected of them, how to divide their time between various duties). Most people dislike such uncertainty and find it quite stressful, but it is difficult to avoid. In fact, role ambiguity is quite common: Thirty-five to 60 percent of employees surveyed report experiencing it to some degree.[25] Clearly, managers who are interested in promoting a stress-free workplace should go out of their way to help employees understand precisely what they are expected to do. As obvious as this may sound, such advice is all too frequently ignored in actual practice.

> *Role ambiguity is quite common: thirty-five to 60 percent of employees surveyed report experiencing it to some degree.*

Overload and underload. When the phrase *work-related stress* is mentioned, most people envision scenes in which employees are asked to do more work than they possibly can handle. Such an image is indeed quite legitimate, for such *overload* is an important cause of stress in many work settings. In fact, in today's business environment, where many companies are trimming staff size (the phenomenon known as *downsizing*, which I will discuss in Chapter 14), fewer employees are required to do more work than ever before. A distinction needs to be made, however, between

quantitative overload—the belief that one is required to do more work than possibly can be completed in a specific period—and **qualitative overload**—the belief that one lacks the required skills or abilities to perform a given job.

Overload is only part of the total picture when it comes to stress. Although being asked to do too much can be stressful, so too can being asked to do too little. In fact, there seems to be considerable truth in the following statement: "The hardest job in the world is doing nothing—you can't take a break." *Underload* leads to boredom and monotony. Because these reactions are quite unpleasant, underload, too, can be stressful. Again, there is a distinction between the *quantitative* and *qualitative* aspects. **Quantitative underload** refers to the boredom that results when employees have so little to do that they find themselves sitting around much of the time. In contrast, **qualitative underload** refers to the lack of mental stimulation that accompanies many routine, repetitive jobs. Both quantitative and qualitative overload and underload are unpleasant, and researchers have linked them to high levels of stress. For a summary of how the concepts of overload and underload relate to stress, see Figure 3.4.

FIGURE 3.4 Overload and Underload: Important Sources of Stress

The belief that one is expected to do more than is possible

Quantitative Overload

The belief that one lacks the required skills or abilities

Qualitative Overload

Having too little work to do

Quantitative Underload

Lack of mental stimulation from the job

Qualitative Underload

As summarized here, stress can stem from both *overload* and *underload*—each of which has quantitative and qualitative forms.

Responsibility for others: A heavy burden. By virtue of differences in their jobs, some people (such as managers and supervisors) tend to deal more with people than do others. And people, as you probably suspect, can be a major source of stress. In general, individuals who are responsible for other people experience higher levels of stress than those who have no such responsibility. Such individuals are more likely to report feelings of tension and anxiety, and are actually more likely to show overt symptoms of stress such as ulcers or hypertension, than their counterparts in nonsupervisory positions. In this connection, it also is important to note that managers who deal with people ineffectively—such as those who communicate poorly and who treat people unfairly—add stress to the lives of those they supervise. As you surely know from your own experiences, a poor manager can be quite a significant source of stress. That said, it is clear that knowing and effectively practicing what you have learned about OB in this book can help alleviate stress in the workplace.

> *Managers who deal with people ineffectively—such as those who communicate poorly and who treat people unfairly—add stress to the lives of those they supervise.*

Lack of social support: The costs of isolation. According to an old saying, "Misery loves company." With respect to stress, this statement implies that if we have to face stressful conditions, it's better to do so along with others (and with their support) rather than alone. Does this strategy actually work? In general, the answer seems to be "yes." Research has shown that when individuals believe they have the friendship and support of others at work, their ability to resist the adverse effects of stress increases. For example, a recent study found that police officers who felt they could talk to their colleagues about their reactions to a traumatic event (such as a shooting) experienced less stressful reactions than those who lacked such support.[26] Clearly, social support can be an important buffer against the effects of stress.[27]

Sexual harassment: A pervasive problem in work settings. There can be no doubt that a particularly troublesome source of stress in today's workplace is **sexual harassment**—unwanted contact or communication of a sexual nature, usually against women. The stressful effects of sexual harassment stem from both the direct affront to the victim's personal dignity and the harasser's interference with the victim's capacity to do the job. After all, it's certainly difficult to pay attention to what you're doing on your job when you have to concentrate on ways to ward off someone's unwanted attentions! Not surprisingly, sexual harassment has caused some people to experience many severe symptoms of illness, including various forms of physical illness, and voluntary turnover.[28]

Unfortunately, this particular source of work-related stress is shockingly common. Indeed, when asked in a *New York Times*–CBS News poll whether they had ever been the object of sexual advances, propositions, or unwanted sexual discussions from men who supervise them, 30 percent of the women surveyed answered "yes." And this is not a one-sided perception: When asked if they had ever said or done something at work that could be construed by a female colleague as harassment, 50 percent of the men polled indicated that they had done so.[29] The good news is that many companies are training employees in how to avoid sexual harassment, and such efforts are helping people become aware of ways they are behaving that may be considered inappropriate.

MAJOR EFFECTS OF ORGANIZATIONAL STRESS

By now, I'm sure you are probably convinced that stress stems from many sources, and that it exerts important effects on the people who experience it. What may not yet be apparent, though, is just how powerful and far-reaching such effects can be. In fact, so widespread are the detrimental effects of stress (i.e., strain) that it has been estimated that its annual costs exceed 10 percent of the U.S. gross national product![30] For some other alarming statistics about stress, see Table 3.5.[31]

Stress and task performance. The most current evidence available suggests that stress exerts mainly negative effects on task performance. In other words, performance can be disrupted even by relatively low levels of stress: The greater the stress people encounter on the job, the more adversely affected their job performance tends to be.[32]

As tempting as it may be to accept this idea, it does not always apply. For example, some individuals seem to "rise to the occasion" and turn in exceptional performances at times of high stress. This may result from the fact that they are truly expert in the tasks being performed, making them so confident in what they are doing that they appraise a potentially stressful situation as a challenge rather than a threat. People also differ widely with respect to the impact of stress on task performance. Whereas some

---

Table 3.5   Some Alarming Statistics About Stress Today

Recent statistics tell a sobering story about the effects of stress today. In general, people are aware of the effects of stress in their lives, but are still doing things that promote stress, creating dramatic costs in the workplace. (*Sources:* Based on data reported by Niemann, 1999, and Wah, 2000; see Note 31.)

People feel the effects of stress:

- 36 percent feel used up at the end of the workday.
- 28 percent work so hard they do not have time or energy to spend with their families.
- 26 percent feel emotionally drained by their work.

People are contributing to their own stress levels:

- 83 percent of people would prefer to have a $10,000 per year raise than an extra hour per day at home.
- 71 percent of people are unwilling to make trade-offs between home and work.
- 49 percent of people indicate that they are not in control of how many hours they work.

Stress is costly:

- Unscheduled absences due to stress have tripled from 1995 to 1999, and cost companies $602 per year for each employee.
- Among the industrialized nations, Americans work more but produce less than those in many other countries, making the cost of labor highly inefficient.
- On average, companies spend a quarter of their after-tax profits on medical bills.

people seem to thrive on stress, finding it exhilarating and a boost to improve their performance, others seek to avoid high levels of stress, finding it upsetting and a source of interference with job performance.

Stress as a source of desk rage.   A particularly unsettling manifestation of stress on the job that has become all too prevalent in recent years is known as **desk rage**—the lashing out at others in response to stressful encounters on the job. Just as angered drivers have been known to express their negative reactions to others in dangerous ways (commonly referred to as *road rage*), so too have office workers been known to behave violently toward others when stressed-out by long hours and difficult working conditions. What makes desk rage so frightening is how extremely widespread it is and, as a recent survey indicates, the many different forms it takes (see Figure 3.5).

Burnout: Stress and psychological adjustment.   Most jobs involve some degree of stress. Yet, somehow, the people performing them manage to cope. That is, they continue to function despite their daily encounters with various stressors. Others, however, are not so fortunate, and over time, find themselves worn down by chronic levels of stress.[33] Such people are often described as suffering from **burnout**—a syndrome of emotional, physical, and mental exhaustion coupled with feelings of low self-esteem or low self-efficacy, resulting from prolonged exposure to intense stress, and the strain reactions following from them (see Figure 3.3). Fortunately, some of the signs of burnout are clear, if you know what to look for. The distinct characteristics of burnout are as follows:

FIGURE 3.5 Common Forms of Desk Rage

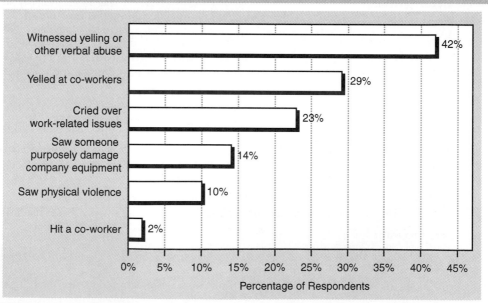

Adults completing a survey were asked to indicate the negative signs of stress they either experienced directly or witnessed in the workplace. As summarized here, their responses indicated that *desk rage* took many different forms. (*Sources*: Based on data collected by Integra Reality Resources, reported in <u>Business Week</u>, November 27, 2000; see Note 33.)

1. *Physical exhaustion.* Victims of burnout have low energy and feel tired much of the time. In addition, they report many symptoms of physical strain, such as frequent headaches, nausea, poor sleep, and changes in eating habits (e.g., loss of appetite).
2. *Emotional exhaustion.* Depression, feelings of helplessness, and feelings of being trapped in one's job are all part of burnout.
3. *Depersonalization.* People suffering from burnout often demonstrate a pattern of attitudinal exhaustion known as **depersonalization**. Specifically, they become cynical about others, tend to treat them as objects rather than as people, and hold negative attitudes toward them. In addition, they tend to derogate themselves, their jobs, their organizations, and even life in general. To put it simply, they come to view the world around them through dark gray rather than rose-colored glasses.
4. *Feelings of low personal accomplishment.* People suffering from burnout conclude that they haven't been able to accomplish much in the past and assume that they probably won't succeed in the future, either.

Stress and health: The silent killer.   How strong is the link between stress and personal health? The answer, say medical experts, is "very strong, indeed." In other words, physiological strain reactions can be quite severe. In fact, some authorities estimate that stress plays a role in anywhere from 50 to 70 percent of all forms of physical illness.[34] Moreover, included in these figures are some of the most serious and life-threatening ailments known to medical science. A list of some of the more common ones is shown in Table 3.6. Even the most cursory look at this list must leave you with the conclusion that the health-related effects of stress are not only quite widespread but also extremely serious.

WHAT ARE COMPANIES DOING TO REDUCE EMPLOYEES' STRESS?

Stress stems from so many different factors and conditions that to eliminate it entirely from our lives is impossible. However, there still are many things that companies can

Table 3.6   Health-Related Consequences of Stress

Stress causes a variety of different health problems, including medical, behavioral, and psychological problems. Listed here are some of the major consequences within each category. (*Sources:* Based on material reported by Quick and Quick, 1984, and Frese, 1985; see Note 35.)

Medical Consequences	*Behavioral Consequences*	*Psychological Consequences*
Heart disease and stroke	Smoking	Family conflict
Backache and arthritis	Drug and alcohol abuse	Sleep disturbances
Ulcers	Accident proneness	Sexual dysfunction
Headaches	Violence	Depression
Cancer	Appetite disorders	
Diabetes		
Cirrhosis of the liver		
Lung disease		

do reduce the intensity of stress on employees and to minimize its harmful effects when it occurs. Fortunately, several good strategies exist for attaining these goals.[35] To ensure that these tactics are followed, many companies have introduced systematic programs designed to help employees reduce or prevent stress. The underlying assumption of these programs is that by minimizing employees' adverse reactions to stress, they will be healthier, less likely to be absent, and consequently, more productive on the job—which, in turn, has beneficial effects on the bottom line.

Employee assistance programs. A recent survey of major companies found that nearly two-thirds have **employee assistance programs** (**EAPs**) in place.[36] These are plans that provide employees with assistance for various personal problems (e.g., substance abuse, career planning, financial and legal problems). The Metropolitan Life Insurance Company (MetLife), for example, has one of the most extensive EAPs in use today. It offers toll-free telephone consultation for employees who wish to talk about their problems, as well as on-site access to medical and psychological professionals. As is always the case in such programs, anonymity is important. Employees seeking help are assured that nobody in their company will be able to learn that they have sought the services of the EAP.

Wellness programs. About 56 percent of today's larger companies have **wellness programs**. These involve training employees in a variety of things they can do to promote healthy lifestyles. Very broad-based wellness programs usually consist of workshops in which employees can learn many things to reduce stress and maintain their health. Exercise, nutrition, and weight-management counseling are among the most popular areas covered. Companies that have used such programs have found that they pay off handsomely. For example, at its industrial sites that offer wellness programs, DuPont has found that absenteeism is less than half of what it is at sites that do not offer such programs. Companies such as The Travelers Corporation and the Union Pacific Railroad have enjoyed consistently high returns for each dollar they invest in employee wellness.

Absence control programs. Acknowledging that employees sometimes need to take time off the job to relieve stress, a few companies are offering **absence control programs**—procedures that give employees flexibility in when they will be taking time off work. Typically, employees take time off work when they are suffering problems caused by stress, but absence control programs allow employees to take time off before these problems develop (hopefully, requiring less time off).[37] Importantly, they recognize that such absences are important and should not be considered grounds for discipline. For example, some companies offer employees a predetermined number of days known as a "paid-leave bank," from which they can draw for any reason without having to call in sick. In a variation of this, the clothing retailer Eddie Bauer offers what it calls "balance days"—that is, days employees can take off to help juggle their work and personal demands. Whenever possible, the company asks for advance notice before granting balance days so that the employee's work group can plan accordingly and not be left in a lurch.

Stress management programs. Systematic efforts known as **stress management programs** involve training employees in a variety of techniques (e.g., meditation and relaxation) that they can use to become less adversely affected by stress. (I describe many of these techniques on the following page.) These are used by about 21 percent of companies. Among them is the Equitable Life Insurance Company. Its "Emotional Health Program" offers training in a variety of ways that employees can learn to relax, including napping. Although some managers might not like the idea of seeing their employees asleep on the job, others recognize that brief naps can, in fact, help their employees recharge and combat the negative effects of stress. This isn't even the most unusual approach that companies are taking to combat the effects of stress among employees. For a look at some of the most novel approaches that today's companies are taking to win the war against stress, see the **Winning Practices** section on p. 74.

HOW CAN YOU MANAGE YOUR OWN STRESS?

Even if your own company does not have a formal program in place to manage stress, there still are several things you can do by yourself to help control the stress in your life.

Eat a healthy diet and be physically fit. Growing evidence indicates that reduced intake of salt and saturated fats, and increased consumption of fiber- and vitamin-rich fruits and vegetables are steps that can greatly increase the body's ability to cope with the physiological effects of stress.[39] Regular exercise also helps. People who exercise regularly tend to be resistant to the adverse effects of stress.

> *People who exercise regularly tend to be resistant to the adverse effects of stress.*

For example, fitness reduces both the incidence of cardiovascular illness and the death rate from such diseases. Similarly, physical fitness lowers blood pressure, an important factor in many aspects of personal health.

With this in mind, it is not surprising that growing numbers of companies are taking steps to ensure that their employees engage in regular exercise. Will Smith III, for example, the CEO of the Denver-based Ensicon, a provider of technical consultants to biomedical and engineering companies, recognizes that his 30 corporate employees are likely to experience high amounts of stress as they struggle to keep up with the long hours they face.[40] To keep them healthy and focused on the job, he offers them 90-minute lunch hours and pays their initiation fee to a local health club. And, if they keep exercising for a year, he also pays half their dues.

Relax and meditate. When you think of successful executives at work, what picture comes to mind? Most of us would probably conjure up an image of someone on three phones at once, surrounded by important papers in a whirlwind of activity. Probably the farthest thing from your mind would be the image of someone resting calmly in a serene setting. Yet, for a growing number of today's employees, this picture is quite common. What's going on in these companies *is* designed to help people become more productive, not in the traditional, stress-inducing way, but by helping them cope more effectively with stress. One technique used in this regard is **meditation**, the process of learning to clear one's mind of external thoughts, often by repeating a single syllable (known as a *mantra*) over and over again. Those who follow this systematic way of relaxing claim that it helps a great deal in relieving the many sources of stress in their lives.

Relaxing doesn't have to mean sitting still and meditating. In fact, it can also mean quite the opposite—even playing drums in a rock band. This is the path taken by Tom

Fighting the Battle Against Stress

Although many companies are doing things to help their employees reduce the effects of stress, some are being particularly creative.[38] Given how successful they've been, it is worthwhile to know about some of these novel practices.

You've heard of teachers taking sabbaticals—time off, so they can recharge or learn new skills. What you might not know is that growing numbers of companies are offering sabbaticals to their employees as well. Take Arrow Electronics, for example, the Melville, New York, company specializing in distributing electronic components and computer products to industrial and commercial customers. After working for seven years, employees are allowed to take a 10-week paid sabbatical during which they can do whatever they want. Company officials claim that the 1,400 employees who have taken advantage of this benefit return to their jobs refreshed and with greater appreciation for their work.

A quite different approach has been in use at Burmah Castrol, the multinational distributor of specialty lubricants and chemicals to business based in the United Kingdom. Here, Tony Yardley-Jones serves as "chief medical adviser," a post requiring him to provide strategic vision and advice on matters of occupational health. For example, when many of the company's top executives were asked to do more work in less time, they began showing signs of stress-related illness. To alleviate these problems, he conducted workshops in which employees were trained in various biomedical techniques that helped them recognize signs of stress (e.g., adrenaline rushes and increased heartbeat) and showed them how to control these reactions by using various concentration techniques (i.e., "mind over matter").

Other companies take a far simpler approach. They help manage stress on a one-on-one basis by having employees look for signs that their colleagues may be suffering the adverse effects of stress. For example, in the restaurant business, where very long hours are the rule, employees of Hard Rock Café International are encouraged to do whatever it takes to help their fellow employees avoid stress. Case in point: When the wife of the general manager of the Hard Rock in San Diego went into labor the same time as the restaurant's opening night, executives told him to join his wife instead of staying for the festivities. Although his presence was critical to the event, execs realized that people are the company's top asset and released him from his obligations so as to enhance his personal well-being at this important time in his life. This program appears to be working: Hard Rock has one of the lowest turnover rates in the restaurant industry today—about half the national average.

As you might imagine, stress can be particularly acute for entrepreneurs who run their own small businesses. After all, they are expected to be everywhere at once. This was the problem faced by Cynthia Guiang, who cofounded the Townsend Agency, an advertising and public relations agency in San Diego. A few years after founding the business, she had her first two children, making time together with the family necessary, but difficult to find. Rather boldly, she started saying something that many entrepreneurs learn only after it's too late—"no." Now, at the end of the day, she simply leaves her work behind and goes home instead of staying long hours at the office. Rather than causing the business to crumble, as she feared, her improved mood created such harmony in her life that it caused her to be far more kind and supportive of people than she used to be, encouraging her associates to work at their peak performance. Taking steps to reduce the stress in her life not only promoted her own health, but the health of her company's bottom line as well.

Questions for Discussion

1. How exactly would taking a sabbatical help you avoid the effects of stress on your own job?
2. In what ways can you and your coworkers look for signs of stress in each other? Do you already do this? If so, what forms has it taken?
3. What special challenges do entrepreneurs face when it comes to managing stress in their lives? What obstacles do you think Cynthia Guiang had to overcome before the people in her agency learned to operate effectively without her constant attention?

Melaragno, the CEO of Compri Consulting, a Denver-based information technology consulting firm.[41] By delegating much of his work to others, Melaragno has carved out time to spend with his family and to devote every other Wednesday night rehearsing with his group, the Orphan Boys, and occasionally playing local gigs. Refusing to risk his health and to jeopardize his family, Melaragno is convinced that his approach to relieving stress—by taking time to play—helps keep him on track.

Avoid inappropriate self-talk. This involves telling ourselves over and over how horrible and unbearable it will be if we fail, if we are not perfect, or if everyone we meet does not like us. Such thoughts seem ludicrous when spelled out in the pages of a book, but the fact is that most people entertain them at least occasionally. Unfortunately, such thoughts can add to personal levels of stress, as individuals *awfulize* or *catastrophize* in their own minds the horrors of not being successful, perfect, or loved. Fortunately, such thinking can be readily modified. For many people, merely recognizing that they have implicitly accepted such irrational and self-defeating beliefs is sufficient to produce beneficial change and increased resistance to stress.

Control your reactions. When faced with stressful events, people often protect themselves from the rising tide of anxiety by adopting actions that are *incompatible* with such feelings. For example, instead of allowing our speech to become increasingly rapid and intense as we become upset, we can consciously modulate this aspect of our behavior. A reduction in arousal and tension is likely to result. People who practice this skill report great success. In other words, practice acting calmly, and you just may find yourself getting calmer.

When confronted with rising tension, people may find it useful to consciously choose to insert a brief period of delay known as a **time-out**. This can involve taking a short break, going to the nearest rest room to splash cold water on one's face, or any other action that yields a few moments of breathing space. Such actions interrupt the cycle of ever-rising tension that accompanies stress and can help to restore equilibrium and the feeling of being at least partly in control of ongoing events.

SUMMARY: HAVE I MET THE LEARNING OBJECTIVES?

You can be certain that you have met the learning objectives for this chapter found on p. 51 if you understand the following.

1. **DEFINE personality.** Personality is the unique and relatively stable pattern of behaviors, thoughts, and emotions shown by individuals.

2. **DESCRIBE various personality dimensions that are responsible for individual differences in organizational behavior.** A cluster of personality traits known as the *big five dimensions of personality* influences behavior in organizations. This consists of conscientiousness, extraversion, agreeableness, emotional stability, and openness to experience. Another key personality variable is the *Type A* and *Type B* behavior patterns. Type A's are frenzied, highly competitive, and always in a hurry, whereas Type B's are calmer and more relaxed. Three additional characteristics involve performance in one way or another. *Self-efficacy* is one's belief in his or her own capacity to perform a specific task, whereas *self-esteem* refers to the extent to which people hold positive or negative views about themselves in general. Finally, *achievement motivation* refers to the strength of an individual's desire to excel at some task.

3. **DISTINGUISH between emotions and moods.** Whereas *emotions* are overt reactions that express people's feelings about a specific event, moods are more general. *Moods* are unfocused, relatively mild feelings that exist as background to our daily experiences.

4. **DESCRIBE the effects of emotions and moods on behavior in organizations.** Emotions affect behavior in organizations in three distinct ways. First, when people are required to display emotions on the job that conflict with those they really feel, *emotional dissonance* results, which is a source of stress. Second, people differ in terms of *emotional intelligence*—a cluster of skills that involve their ability to monitor their own and others' emotions, to discriminate among emotions, and to use such information to guide their thoughts and actions. High degrees of each of these skills contribute to success on the job. Third, extreme emotions, especially negative ones, interfere with concentration, hence job performance. Moods also influence job behavior in three ways. Specifically, compared to those who are in a bad mood, people in a good mood tend to (1) remember things associated with being in a good mood at other times in the past (they display *mood congruence*), (2) give more positive evaluations to others, and (3) show greater generosity and helpfulness toward others.

5. **IDENTIFY the major causes and consequences of stress.** Stress is caused by many different factors, including: occupational demands, conflicts between the work and nonwork aspects of one's life (i.e., *role conflict*), not knowing what one is expected to do on the job (i.e., *role ambiguity*), overload and underload, having responsibility for other people, not having social support, and experiencing sexual harassment. In general, stress adversely affects task performance, leads to *burnout* (emotional, physical, and mental exhaustion), and a wide range of medical and psychological problems.

6. **IDENTIFY steps that can be taken, both personally and by organizations, to control stress.** To help reduce employees' stress, companies are doing such things as using *employee assistance programs*, *wellness programs*, *absence con-*

trol programs, and *stress management programs*. As individuals, we can also control the stress we face in our lives by eating a healthy diet and being physically fit, relaxing and meditating, avoiding inappropriate self-talk, and taking control over our reactions.

You Be the Consultant

As the managing director of a large e-tail sales company, you are becoming alarmed about the growing levels of turnover your company has been experiencing lately. It already has passed the industry average, and you are growing concerned about the company's capacity to staff the call center and the warehouse during the busy holiday period. In conducting exit interviews, you learn that the employees who are leaving generally like their work and the pay they are receiving. However, they are displeased with the way their managers are treating them, and this is creating stress in their lives. They are quitting to take less stressful positions in other companies. Answer the following questions based on material in this chapter.

1. What personality differences do you suspect would be found between the people who quit and those who choose to remain on their jobs?
2. Assuming that the employees' emotions and moods are negative, what problems would you expect to find in the way they are working?
3. How should the company's supervisors behave differently so as to get their subordinates to experience less stress on the job (or, at least, to get them to react less negatively)?

SELF-ASSESSMENT EXERCISE

How Much Self-Esteem Do You Have?

To objectively measure self-esteem (and most other personality variables), scientists rely on paper-and-pencil questionnaires. This scale, adapted from one actually used to measure self-esteem, should give you some good insight into this important aspect of your personality.[42] Although this measure is not definitive, you should find it interesting to see what the scale tells you about yourself.

Directions
For each of the following items, indicate whether you *strongly disagree (SD), disagree (D), agree (A), or strongly agree (SA)* by marking the space provided.

_____ 1. I believe I am a worthwhile person, who is as good as others.
_____ 2. I have several positive qualities.
_____ 3. For the most part, I consider myself a failure.
_____ 4. Generally speaking, I can do things as well as others.
_____ 5. I cannot be proud of too many things about myself.
_____ 6. My feelings about myself are quite positive.
_____ 7. In general, I am very pleased with myself.
_____ 8. I really don't have a lot of self-respect.

_____ 9. There are times when I feel useless.
_____ 10. Sometimes I don't think I'm very good at all.

Scoring
1. For items 1, 2, 4, 6, and 7, assign points as follows: $SD = 1$; $D = 2$; $A = 3$; $SA = 4$.
2. For items 3, 5, 8, 9, and 10, assign points as follows: $SD = 4$; $D = 3$; $A = 2$; $SA = 1$.
3. Add the number of points in 1 and 2. This should range from 10 to 40. Higher scores reflect greater degrees of self-esteem.

Questions for Discussion
1. Does your score make sense to you? In other words, does the questionnaire tell you something you already believed about yourself, or has it provided new insight?
2. Why do you think items 1, 2, 4, 6, and 7 are scored opposite from items 3, 5, 8, 9, and 10?
3. Do you think the techniques outlined in Table 3.2 on p. 57 may help raise your self-esteem?

(**GROUP EXERCISE**)

Are You Tough Enough to Endure Stress?

A test known as the Attentional and Interpersonal Style (TAIS) inventory has been used in recent years to identify the extent to which a person can stay focused and keep his or her emotions under control—the core elements of performing well under high-pressure conditions (see Note 23). Completing this exercise (which is based on questions similar to those actually used by such groups as Olympic athletes and U.S. Navy Seals) will help you understand your own strengths and limitations in this regard. And, by discussing these scores with your teammates, you will come away with a good feel for the extent to which those with whom you work differ along this dimension as well.

Directions
1. Gather in groups of three or four people whom you know fairly well. If you are part of an intact group, such as a work team, or a team of students working on a class project, meet with these individuals.
2. Individually, complete the following questionnaire by responding to each question as follows: *never, rarely, sometimes, frequently,* or *always.*
   _____ 1. When time is running out on an important project, I am the person who should be called upon to take control of things.
   _____ 2. When listening to a piece of music, I can pick out a specific voice or instrument.
   _____ 3. The people who know me think of me as being "serious."
   _____ 4. It is important to me to get a job completely right in every detail, even if it means being late.
   _____ 5. When approaching a busy intersection, I easily get confused.
   _____ 6. Just by looking at someone, I can figure out what he or she is like.
   _____ 7. I am comfortable arguing with people.
   _____ 8. At a cocktail party, I have no difficulty keeping track of several different conversations at once.

3. Discuss your answers with everyone else in your group. Item by item, consider what each person's response to each question indicates about his or her ability to focus.

Questions for Discussion
1. What questions were easiest to interpret? Which were most difficult?
2. How did each individual's responses compare with the way you would assess his or her ability to focus under stress?
3. For what jobs is the ability to concentrate under stress particularly important? For what jobs is it not especially important? How important is this ability for the work you do?

NOTES

Case Note
Solomon, S. D. (1999, October 12). Fit to be tired. *Inc. 500*, pp. 89–90, 92, 95, 98. Tape Resources Web site: www.tapesources.com

Chapter Notes
[1] Mount, M. K., & Barrick, M. R. (1998). Five reasons why the "Big Five" article has been frequently cited. *Personnel Psychology, 51*, 849–857.
[2] Le Pine, J. A., Colquitt, J. A., & Erez, A. (2000). Adaptability to changing task contexts: Effects of general cognitive ability, conscientiousness, and openness to experience. *Personnel Psychology, 54*, 563–593.
[3] Barrick, M. R., & Mount, M. K. (1993). Autonomy as a moderator of the relationships between the big five personality dimensions and job performance. *Journal of Applied Psychology, 78*, 111–118.
[4] Eden, D., & Aviram, A. (1993). Self-efficacy training to speed reemployment: Helping people to help themselves. *Journal of Applied Psychology, 78*, 352–360.
[5] Weielauf, J. C., Smith, R. E., & Cervone, D. (2000). Generalization effects of coping-skills training: Influence of self-defense training on women's efficacy beliefs, assertiveness, and aggression. *Journal of Applied Psychology, 85*, 625–633.
[6] Wiesenfeld, B. M., Brockner, J., & Thibault, V. (2000). Procedural fairness, managers' self-esteem, and managerial behaviors following a layoff. *Organizational Behavior and Human Decision Processes, 83*, 1–32.
[7] Richman, E. L., & Shaffer, D. R., (2000). "If you let me play sports:" How might sport participation influence the self-esteem of adolescent females? *Psychology of Women Quarterly, 24*, 189–199.
[8] McClelland, D. C. (1985). *Human motivation*. Glenview, IL: Scott, Foresman.
[9] Weiss, H. M., & Cropanzano, R. (1996). Affective events theory: A theoretical discussion of the structure, causes, and consequences of affective experiences at work. In B. M. Staw and L. L. Cummings (Eds.), *Research in organizational behavior* (Vol. 18, pp. 1–74). Greenwich, CT: JAI Press.
[10] Morris, J. A., & Feldman, D. C. (1997). Managing emotions in the workplace. *Journal of Managerial Issues, 9*, 257–274.
[11] Goleman, D. (1998). *Working with emotional intelligence*. New York: Bantam.
[12] Baron, R. A., & Markam, G. (in press). Social competence and entrepreneurs' financial success. *Journal of Applied Psychology*.
[13] Unconventional smarts. (1998, January). *Across the Board*, pp. 22–23.
[14] See Note 9.
[15] George, J. M., & Brief, A. P. (1996). Motivational agendas in the workplace: The effects of feelings on focus of attention and work motivation. In B. M. Staw and L. L. Cummings (Eds.), *Research in organizational behavior* (Vol. 18, pp. 75–119). Greenwich, CT: JAI Press.

[16] Freiberg, K., Freiberg, J., & Peters, T. (1998). *Nuts!: Southwest Airlines' crazy recipe for business and personal success*. New York: Bantam Doubleday. Cohen, B., Greenfield, J., and Mann, M. (1998). *Ben & Jerry's double dip: How to run a values-led business and make money, too*. New York: Fireside.

[17] Clore, G. L., Schwartz, N., & Conway, M. (1994). Affective causes and consequences of social information processing. In R. S. Wyer Jr. and T. K. Srull (Eds.), *Handbook of social cognition* (Vol. 1, pp. 323–417). Hillsdale, NJ: Lawrence Erlbaum Associates.

[18] Brief, A. P., Butcher, A. B., & Roberson, L. (1995). Cookies, disposition, and job attitudes: The effects of positive mood-inducing agents and negative affectivity on job satisfaction in a field experiment. *Organizational Behavior and Human Decision Processes, 62*, 55–62.

[19] Northwestern National Life Insurance Company. (1991). *Employee burnout: America's newest epidemic*. Minneapolis, MN: Author.

[20] Quick, J. C., Murphy, L. R., & Hurrell, J. J., Jr. (1992). *Stress and well-being at work*. Washington, DC: American Psychological Association.

[21] Selye, H. (1976). *Stress in health and disease*. Boston: Butterworths.

[22] Kane, K. (1997, October–November). Can you perform under pressure? *Fast Company*, pp. 54, 56. Enhanced Performance Web site: www.enhanced-performance.com.

[23] See Note 20. Stress at work. (1997, April 15). *Wall Street Journal*, p. A12.

[24] Fenn, D. (1999, November). Domestic policy. *Inc.*, pp. 38–42, 44–45. Hammonds, K. H., & Palmer, A. T. (1998, September 21). The daddy trap. *Business Week*, pp. 56–58, 60, 62, 64.

[25] McGrath, J. E. (1976). Stress and behavior in organizations. In M. D. Dunnette (Ed.), *Handbook of industrial and organizational psychology* (pp. 1351–1398). Chicago: Rand McNally.

[26] Stephens, C., & Long, N. (2000). Communication with police supervisors and peers as a buffer of work-related traumatic stress. *Journal of Organizational Behavior, 21*, 407–424.

[27] Beehr, T. A., Jex, S. M., Stacy, B. A., & Murray, M. A. (2000). Work stressors and coworker support as predictors of individual strain and job performance. *Journal of Organizational Behavior, 21*, 391–405.

[28] Fisher, A. B. (1993, August 23). Sexual harassment: What to do. *Fortune*, pp. 84–86, 88.

[29] Kolbert, E. (1991, October 10). Sexual harassment at work is pervasive. *New York Times*, pp. A1, A17.

[30] Sullivan, S. E., & Bhagat, R. S. (1992). Organizational stress, job satisfaction, and job performance: Where do we go from here? *Journal of Management, 18*, 353–374.

[31] Nieman, C. (1999, July–August). How much is enough? *Fast Company*, pp. 108–116. Wah, L. (2000, January). The emotional tightrope. *Management Review*, pp. 38–43.

[32] Motowidlo, S. J., Packard, J. S., & Manning, M. R. (1986). Occupational stress: Its causes and consequences for job performance. *Journal of Applied Psychology, 71*, 618–629.

[33] Bakker, A. B., Schaufeli, W. B., Sixma, H. J., Bosveld, W., & Van Dierendonck, D. (2000). Patient demands, lack of reciprocity, and burnout: A five-year longitudinal study among general practitioners. *Journal of Organizational Behavior, 21*, 425–441.

[34] Frese, M. (1985). Stress at work and psychosomatic complaints: A causal interpretation. *Journal of Applied Psychology, 70*, 314–328. Quick, J. C., & Quick, J. D. (1984). *Organizational stress and preventive management*. New York: McGraw-Hill.

[35] Latack, J. C., & Havlovic, S. J. (1992). Coping with job stress: A conceptual evaluation framework for coping measures. *Journal of Organizational Behavior, 13*, 479–508.

[36] Wah, L. (2000, January). The emotional tightrope. *Management Review*, pp. 38–43.

[37] See Note 35.

[38] See Note 35.

[39] See Note 35.

[40] Singer, T. (2000, October 17). The balance of power. *Inc. 500*, pp. 105–108, 110.

[41] See Note 40.

[42] Rosenberg, M. (1965). *Society and the adolescent self-image*. Princeton, NJ: Princeton University Press.

4

What motivates people to work?

LEARNING OBJECTIVES

After reading this chapter, you will be able to:

1. DEFINE motivation.

2. EXPLAIN need hierarchy theory and how it applies in organizations.

3. DESCRIBE equity theory's approach to motivation in the workplace.

4. OUTLINE the basic assumptions of expectancy theory and its implications in organizations.

5. EXPLAIN how goals can be set to motivate high levels of job performance.

6. DESCRIBE ways in which jobs can be designed so as to enhance motivation.

THREE GOOD REASONS WHY YOU SHOULD CARE ABOUT . . .

Motivation in Organizations

You should care about motivation in organizations because:

1. Managers typically have a variety of opportunities to motivate employees by virtue of how they treat them.

2. In many different ways, motivated individuals tend to be better employees.

3. Jobs can be designed in such a manner as to make them inherently interesting to the individuals who perform them.

Making the Case for. . . Motivation in Organizations

Paula Lawlor: Not Your Ordinary CEO

Helping hospitals maintain patient records and organize documents for accreditation is probably not the most glamorous business, especially when housed in a nondescript facility in King of Prussia, Pennsylvania. Yet, none of the 175 employees of Medi-Health Outsourcing considers his or her job boring. Most are so highly charged, in fact, that they can hardly wait to get to work. Strange? Maybe so, but Medi-Health has a secret weapon—CEO Paula Lawlor.

It isn't your ordinary CEO who storms headquarters wearing track pants and running shoes, admonishing everyone to get up and exercise. And, it certainly isn't any ordinary CEO who disrupts office routine with sidesplitting personal stories. Then again, there's nothing ordinary about Paula Lawlor. Described by her sisters, both of whom work at the company, as "a tornado," Lawlor is considered charming, but demanding. Goof off, and you're out the door, but do well, and you can go very far. Indeed, the sky's the limit for employees of Medi-Health, where salaried managers are encouraged to run their divisions as they see fit, and hourly employees are treated more like independent consultants.

At Medi-Health, nobody has to get bored. All employees are free to move around the company until they find a job that best suits them, no matter what it takes to train them! No one can have any excuse for failing to get his or her work done. If it means working from home, that's fine, and if it means arranging schedules around family obligations, that's acceptable as well. You even can take a three-month leave of absence without risking your job. As chaotic as things seem, there's a method to Lawlor's madness: She doesn't care when or how you work, so long as you get the job done. Employees are free to manage their work and their lives as they see fit without discussion. However, if you fail to meet your goals, you'll have to answer to Lawlor, who can be just as unforgiving about what you didn't do as she is accepting of how you do it!

Responsibility is the flip side of flexibility, and both are key to Medi-Health's operations. Some employees have adjusted their schedules to attend their kids' soccer games, even if it means working into the wee hours of the morning. For a while, financial analyst Gabe Urban took off every Friday to train for the Ironman Triathlon, but nobody minded because he got all his work done by Thursday. For most, the target numbers are clear: Meet the required goal—in one department, abstracting 100 medical records per week with 95 percent accuracy—and the rest of the time is yours.

At the executive level, each of the four departments is run as a separate business. Each senior manager drafts a mini business plan. Then, with Lawlor's approval, he or she is given a budget to bring it to fruition. How much everyone makes depends on the company's performance in satisfying that plan, as well as each individual's success in hitting targets along the way. Because everyone's pay is tied to the company's success, there's a great deal of peer pressure to perform, and everyone pitches in to make things work. Those who don't relish the responsibility tend to leave the company right away. Lawlor admits, "It's a hard place to work because we expect people to manage their lives." But, those who welcome the responsibility are given whatever tools they need to succeed—and that they do. Not one of the company's top managers has ever left his or her position. With profit consistently running at 15 percent annually, what's working out so well for the employees is also showing up on the company's bottom line.

Paula Lawlor surely knows what it takes to light a fire under her employees. She gives them responsibility over what they do, she holds them to target goals, and she pays them based on how well they perform. As you will see in this chapter, these are some of the key things it takes to motivate employees. We will discuss these and several other related ways of motivating employees in this chapter—identifying not only what you can do to motivate people, but precisely what makes various motivational techniques successful.

The question of exactly what it takes to motivate workers has received a great deal of attention by both practicing managers and organizational scientists. In addressing this question, I examine five different approaches. Specifically, I will focus on motivating by: (1) meeting basic human needs, (2) treating people fairly, (3) enhancing beliefs that desired rewards can be attained, (4) setting goals, and (5) designing jobs so as to make them more desirable. Before turning attention to these specific orientations I first must consider a very basic matter—namely, what exactly is meant by the term *motivation*.

What Is Motivation? A Definition

Scientists have defined **motivation** as the process of arousing, directing, and maintaining behavior toward a goal. As this definition suggests, motivation involves three components. The first component, *arousal,* has to do with the drive or energy behind our actions. For example, when we are hungry we are driven to seek food. The *direction* component involves the choice of behavior made. A hungry person may make many different choices—eat an apple, have a pizza delivered, go out for a burger, and so on. The third component, *maintenance,* is concerned with people's persistence, their willingness to continue to exert effort until a goal is met. The longer you would continue to search for food when hungry, the more persistent you would be.

Putting it all together, it may help to think of motivation by using the analogy of driving a car. In this manner, arousal may be likened to the energy generated by the car's engine and fuel system. The direction it takes is dictated by the driver's manipulation of the steering wheel. Finally, maintenance may be thought of as the driver's determination to stay on course until the final destination is reached.

Despite this simple analogy, motivation is a highly complex concept. This is reflected by the fact that people often are motivated by many things at once, sometimes causing conflicts. For example, a factory worker may be motivated to make a positive impression on his supervisor by doing a good job, but at the same time, he may be motivated to maintain friendly relations with his coworkers by not making them look bad. This example has to do with job performance, and indeed, motivation is a key determinant of performance. However, it is important to note that *motivation is not synonymous with performance.* In fact, as I will explain later, even the most highly motivated employee may fall short of achieving success on the job—especially if he or she lacks the required skills or works under unfavorable conditions. Clearly, although motivation does not completely account for job performance, it surely is one important

> *Even the most highly motivated employee may fall short of achieving success on the job—especially if he or she lacks the required skills or works under unfavorable conditions.*

factor in bringing it about. Moreover, it is something about which managers can do something. With this in mind, you are now prepared to understand the different approaches to motivating people on the job.

Motivating by Meeting Basic Human Needs

As the definition suggests, people are motivated to fulfill their needs—whether it's a need for food, as in our example, or other needs, such as the need for social approval. Companies that help their employees in this quest are certain to reap the benefits. In fact, companies that actively strive to meet the needs of their employees attract the best people and motivate them to do excellent work.[1]

Some insight into how this may come about is provided by Maslow's **need hierarchy theory**.[2] Maslow's basic idea is simple: People will not be healthy and well adjusted unless they have their needs met. This idea applies whether we're talking about becoming a functioning member of society, Maslow's original focus, or a productive employee of an organization, a later application of his work. Specifically, Maslow identified five different types of needs, which, he claimed, are activated in a specific order. These start at the lowest, most basic needs and work upward to higher-level needs (which is what makes it a hierarchy). Furthermore, these needs are not aroused all at once or in random fashion. Rather, each need is triggered only after the one beneath it in the hierarchy has been satisfied. The specific needs, and the hierarchical order in which they are arranged, are summarized in Figure 4.1. You may find it useful to refer to this overview as I describe each of Maslow's five categories of needs.

FIGURE 4.1 Need Hierarchy Theory

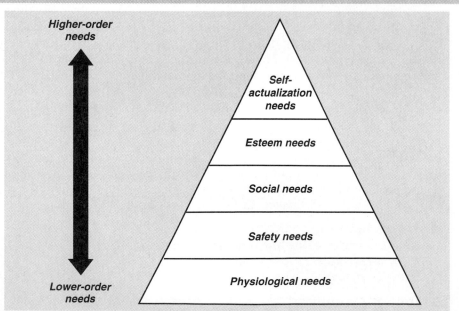

Maslow's need hierarchy specifies that the five needs shown here are activated in order, from lowest to highest. Each need is triggered after the one immediately below it in the hierarchy is satisfied.

PHYSIOLOGICAL NEEDS

The lowest-order needs involve satisfying fundamental biological drives, such as the needs for air, food, water, and shelter. These **physiological needs**, as they are called, are surely the most basic needs, because unless they are met people will become ill and suffer. For this reason, they are depicted at the base of the triangle in Figure 4.1.

There are many things that companies do to help meet their employees' basic physiological needs. Probably the simplest involves paying them a living wage, money that can be exchanged for food and shelter. But, there's more to satisfying physiological needs than giving employees a paycheck. There are also coffee breaks and opportunities to rest. Even the cruelest, slave-driving bosses know the importance of giving workers time to relax and recharge their systems.

Staying physically healthy involves more than just resting; it also requires exercise, something that the sedentary nature of many of today's technologically advanced jobs does not permit. With this in mind, thousands of companies are providing exercise facilities for their employees. In fact, a recent survey found that the perk most desired by managers seeking new jobs is membership in a health club.[3] This makes perfectly good business sense. By keeping the workforce healthy and fit, companies are paving the way for people to become productive. Some, such as Southern California Edison and Hershey Foods, have taken this thinking to the extreme. They offer insurance rebates to employees who live healthy lifestyles (e.g., physically fit nonsmokers) and raise the premiums of those at greater risk for illness. In this manner, not only are the insurance burdens distributed fairly, but the incentives encourage wellness activities that promise to benefit both employers and employees.

SAFETY NEEDS

After physiological needs have been satisfied, the next level of needs is triggered— **safety needs**. These are concerned with the need to operate in an environment that is physically and psychologically safe and secure, one free from threats of harm.

Organizations help satisfy their employees' safety needs in several ways. For example, they protect shop workers from hazards in the environment by providing such basic services as security and fire prevention, and by fitting them with goggles and hard hats. Even seemingly safe work settings, such as offices, can be riddled with safety hazards. This is why efforts are made to spare office workers from eyestrain, wrist injuries (such as the increasingly prevalent carpal tunnel syndrome), and back pain, by using ergonomically designed computer keyboards, desks, and chairs.

Psychological safety is important as well. By offering health and disability insurance, companies are promoting their employees' psychological well-being by assuring them that they will not be harmed financially in the event of illness. Although almost all companies offer health insurance benefits, a select few have taken psychological security to the extreme by having no-layoff policies. For over 60 years, Lincoln Electric Company of Cleveland, Ohio, for example, has not laid off a single worker.[4] When times are bad, it simply reassigns its employees to other jobs. Knowing that your job will always be there regardless of economic conditions is surely a source of psychological reassurance.

SOCIAL NEEDS

Once people's physiological and safety needs have been satisfied, Maslow claims, **social needs** are activated. These refer to the need to be affiliative—that is, to be liked and accepted by others. As social animals we want to be with others and to have them approve of us.

Organizations do much to satisfy these needs when they sponsor social events such as office parties and company picnics. For example, by holding its annual "Family Day" picnic near its Armonk, New York, headquarters, IBM employees enjoy good opportunities to socialize with their coworkers and their families. Similarly, joining a company's bowling team or softball team also provides good opportunities to meet social needs within an organization. In discussing physiological needs I noted that many companies provide health club facilities for their employees. Besides keeping employees healthy, it's easy to see how such opportunities also help satisfy social needs. "Playing hard" with those with whom we also "work hard" provides good opportunities to fulfill social needs on the job.

> *"Playing hard" with those with whom we also "work hard" provides good opportunities to fulfill social needs on the job.*

ESTEEM NEEDS

Not only do we need to be liked by others socially, but we also need to gain their respect and approval. In other words, we have a **need for self-esteem**—that is, to achieve success and have others recognize our accomplishments. Consider, for example, reserved parking spots or plaques honoring the "employee of the month." Both are ways of demonstrating esteem for employees. So too are awards banquets at which worthy staff members' contributions are recognized.[5] The same thing is frequently done in print by recognizing one's organizational contributions on the pages of a corporate newsletter. For example, employees of the large pharmaceutical company Merck enjoyed the recognition they received for developing Proscar (a highly successful drug treatment for prostate enlargement) when they saw their pictures in the company newsletter. In fact, it meant more to Merck employees to have their colleagues learn of their success than it did to have their accomplishments touted widely, but to an anonymous audience, on the pages of the *New York Times*.

The practice of awarding bonuses to people making suggestions for improvement is another highly successful way to meet employees' esteem needs. Companies have used a variety of different rewards in this regard. For example, small prizes, such as VCRs and computers, are used routinely by companies such as Shell Oil, Campbell Soup, AT&T, and American Airlines to reward a wide range of special contributions. However, few companies have taken the practice of rewarding contributions to the same high art as has Mary Kay Cosmetics. Not only are lavish banquets staged to recognize modest contributions to this company's bottom line, but top performers are awarded the most coveted prize of all—a pink Cadillac. As founder Mary Kay Ash put it, "There are two things people want more than sex and money . . . recognition and praise."[6] Companies that cannot afford such lavish gifts needn't be concerned about failing to satisfy their employees' self-esteem needs. After all, sometimes the best recognition is nothing more than a heartfelt "thank you." Or, as Mark Twain put it, "I can live for two months on a good compliment."

SELF-ACTUALIZATION NEEDS

What happens after all an employee's lower-order needs are met? According to Maslow, people will strive for **self-actualization**—that is, they will work to become all they are capable of being. When people are self-actualized, they perform at their maximum level of creativity and become extremely valuable assets to their organizations. For this reason, companies are interested in paving the way for their employees to self-actualize by meeting their lower-order needs.

As this discussion clearly suggests, Maslow's theory provides excellent guidance with respect to the needs that workers are motivated to achieve. Indeed, many organizations have taken actions that are directly suggested by the theory and have found them to be successful. For this reason, the theory remains popular with organizational practitioners. Scientists, however, have noted that specific elements of the theory—notably, the assertion that there are only five needs and that they are activated in a specific order—have not been supported. Despite this shortcoming, the insight that Maslow's theory provides into the importance of meeting human needs in the workplace makes it a valuable approach to motivation.

Motivating by Being Fair

There can be little doubt about the importance of money as a motivator on the job. However, it would be overly simplistic and misleading to say that people only want to earn as much money as possible. Even the highest-paid executives, sports figures, and celebrities sometimes complain about their pay despite their multimillion-dollar salaries.[7] Are they being greedy? Not necessarily. Often, the issue is not the actual amount of pay received, but rather pay fairness.

Not surprisingly, people are very concerned about maintaining fairness on the job. In fact, workers frequently rebel when they believe they are operating under a pay system that treats them unfairly. This is precisely what happened in August 1997 when 185,000 members of the Teamsters Union went on strike against UPS, the world's largest package distribution company. Among the union's claims was that the company hired large numbers of part-time workers, whom they paid less than full-time workers who did the same exact work. After a 16-day strike that cost UPS millions of dollars in lost revenue, and that crippled package shipments throughout the world, a settlement was reached that the Teamsters believed would result in more equitable payment for its members. Although not all such reactions to inequitable treatment are as extreme, it is safe to say that just about everyone who works is concerned about being fairly rewarded for the work he or she does.

Organizational scientists have been actively interested in the difficult task of explaining exactly what constitutes fairness on the job and how people respond when they believe they have been unfairly treated. Two major approaches to these issues are *equity theory* and *procedural justice*.[8]

EQUITY THEORY: BALANCING OUTCOMES AND INPUTS

Equity theory proposes that people are motivated to maintain fair, or equitable, relationships between themselves and others, and to avoid those relationships that are unfair, or inequitable. To make judgments of equity, people compare themselves to others by focusing on two variables: outcomes—what we get out of our jobs (e.g., pay, fringe benefits, prestige)—and inputs—the contributions made (e.g., time worked, effort exerted, units produced). It helps to think of these judgments in the form of ratios—that is, the outcomes received relative to the inputs contributed (e.g., $500 per week in exchange for working 40 hours). It is important to note that equity theory deals with outcomes and inputs as they are perceived by people, not necessarily objective standards. As you might imagine, well-intentioned people sometimes disagree about what constitutes equitable treatment.

According to equity theory people make equity judgments by comparing their own outcome-input ratios to the outcome-input ratios of others. This so-called "other" may be someone else in one's work group, another employee in the organization, an individual working in the same field, or even oneself at an earlier point in time—in short, almost anyone against whom we compare ourselves. As shown in Figure 4.2, these comparisons can result in any of three different states: *overpayment inequity,* *underpayment inequity,* or *equitable payment.*

FIGURE 4.2 Equity Theory: A Summary and Example

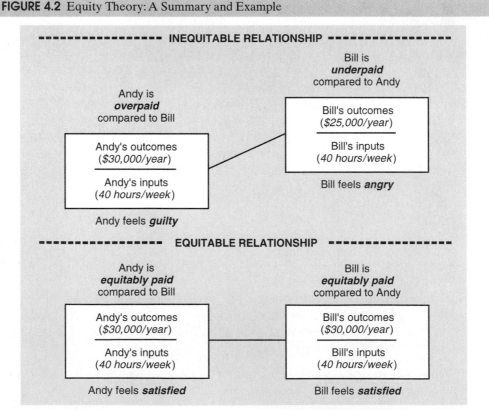

People make judgments of equity or inequity by comparing the ratios of their outcomes-inputs to the corresponding ratios of others. People are motivated to change inequitable relationships (such as the one shown on top) to equitable ones (such as the one shown on the bottom).

Let's consider an example. Imagine that Andy and Bill work together as copywriters in an advertising firm. Both men have equal amounts of experience, training, and education, and work equally long and hard at their jobs. In other words, their inputs are equivalent. But, suppose Andy is paid an annual salary of $30,000 while Bill is paid only $25,000. In this case, Andy's ratio of outcomes-inputs is higher than Bill's, creating a state of *overpayment inequity* for Andy (because the ratio of his outcomes-inputs is higher), but *underpayment inequity* for Bill (because the ratio of his outcomes-inputs is lower). According to equity theory, Andy, realizing that he is paid more than an equally qualified person doing the same work, will feel *guilty* in response to his *overpayment*. By contrast, Bill, realizing that he is paid less than an equally qualified person for doing the same work, will feel *angry* in response to his *underpayment*. Guilt and anger are negative emotional states that people are motivated to change. As a result, they will seek to create a state of *equitable payment* in which their outcome/input ratios are equal, leading them to feel *satisfied*.

Creating equity.   How can inequitable states be turned into equitable ones? The answer lies in adjusting the balance of outcomes to inputs. Among people who are underpaid, equity can be created by lowering one's outcomes or raising one's inputs. Likewise, those who are overpaid may either raise their inputs or lower their outcomes. In both cases, either action would effectively make the two outcome-input ratios equivalent. For example, the underpaid person, Bill, might lower his inputs such as by slacking off, arriving at work late, leaving early, taking longer breaks, doing less work, or doing lower quality-work—or, in an extreme case, quit his job. He also may attempt to raise his outcomes, such as by asking for a raise or even taking home company property, such as tools or office supplies. By contrast, the overpaid person, Andy, may do the opposite—raise his inputs or lower his outcomes. For example, he might put forth much more effort, work longer hours, and try to make a greater contribution to the company. He also might lower his outcomes, such as by working while on a paid vacation, or not taking advantage of fringe benefits the company offers.

These are all specific *behavioral* reactions to inequitable conditions—that is, things people can *do* to turn inequitable states into equitable ones. However, people may be unwilling to do some of the things necessary to respond behaviorally to inequities. In particular, they may be reluctant to steal from their employers or unwilling to restrict their productivity, for fear of getting caught "goofing off." In such cases, people may attempt to resolve inequity *cognitively,* by changing the way they think about the situation. As noted earlier, because equity theory deals with perceptions, inequitable states may be redressed by altering the thinking about one's own, and others', outcomes and inputs. For example, underpaid people may rationalize that others' inputs are really higher than their own (e.g., "I suppose she really *is* more qualified than I am"), thereby convincing themselves that their higher outcomes are justified. Similarly, overpaid people may convince themselves that they really *are* better and deserve their relatively higher pay. So, by changing the way they see things, people can come to perceive inequitable situations as equitable, thereby effectively relieving their feelings of guilt and anger, and transforming them into feelings of satisfaction.

Responding to inequities on the job.   There is a great deal of evidence to suggest that people are motivated to redress inequities at work and that they respond much as equity theory suggests. Consider two examples from the world of sports. Research has shown that professional basketball players who are underpaid (i.e., ones who are paid less than others who perform as well or better) score fewer points than those who are equitably paid.[9] Similarly, among baseball players, those paid less than others who play comparably well tend to change teams or even leave the sport when they are unsuccessful at negotiating higher pay. Cast in terms of equity theory, the underpaid players may be said to have lowered their inputs.

We also know that underpaid workers attempt to raise their outcomes. For example, in an organization studied by the author, workers at two manufacturing plants suffered an underpayment created by the introduction of a temporary pay cut of 15 percent.[10] During the 10-week period under which workers received lower pay, company officials noticed that theft of company property increased dramatically, approximately 250 percent. However, in another factory in which comparable work was done by workers paid at their normal rates, the theft rate remained low. This pattern suggests that employees may have stolen property from their company in order to compensate for their reduced pay. Consistent with this possibility, it was found that when the normal rate of pay was reinstated in the two factories, the theft rate returned to its usual, low level. These findings suggest that companies that seek to save money by lowering pay may merely be encouraging their employees to find other ways of making up for what they believe is rightfully theirs—such as stealing company property.

> *Companies that seek to save money by lowering pay may merely be encouraging their employees to find other ways of making up for what they believe is rightfully theirs—such as stealing company property.*

In closing this section, consider the examples I've given. First, UPS drivers went on strike when the company hired temporary workers to do the same work as permanent employees, but paid them considerably less. Second, professional athletes performed worse, or even quit, when they received salaries that were not commensurate with their performance. Third, factory workers stole from their employers while they received lower pay than usual. Together, these examples clearly illustrate a key point explained by equity theory—namely, that people are highly motivated to seek equity and to redress the inequities they face on the job.

PROCEDURAL JUSTICE: MAKING DECISIONS FAIRLY

Thus far, our discussion of fairness on the job has focused on the outcomes people receive (i.e., *what* and *how much* they get). However, we have ignored another important aspect of fairness—namely, how decisions leading to these outcomes are made in the first place. If you were evaluating the fairness of a legal decision, for example, you surely wouldn't limit yourself to considering only the court's verdicts. You also would want to know how those verdicts came about. Did the judge carefully consider each side's argument? Did the attorneys represent their client's interests? Is there an appeals procedure in place that allows judgments to be overturned if it is clear that errors have been made? These are all questions about the nature of the procedures used to make decisions. The perception people have of the fairness of the procedures used to make decisions is known as **procedural justice**.

TABLE 4.1 Tips for Promoting Procedural Justice on the Job	

Procedural justice has to do with people's perceptions of the fairness of the policies and the procedures used to make decisions in organizations. Such perceptions may be enhanced by following the suggestions identified here.

Suggestion	*Comment*
1. Give people a voice in how decisions are made.	The more people have a say in how the organization operates, the more fair they will believe it to be.
2. Provide an opportunity for errors to be corrected.	Like the appeals procedure in the courtroom or the replay rule in professional football, procedures that correct wrong decisions are believed to be fair.
3. Apply policies consistently and in an unbiased manner.	Playing favorites is a sure way to get people to believe that you are being unfair.
4. Explain how decisions are made.	Even people who are harmed by certain decisions perceive them as fair to the extent that these have been explained in a detailed fashion.
5. Treat people with dignity and respect.	People who believe they have been shown the dignity and respect they deserve are likely to believe they are treated fairly, even if they don't like the decisions that were made.

As you might imagine, procedural justice is very important in organizations. After all, any manager who is suspected of not making decisions fairly is unlikely to be accepted. Indeed, research has shown that people who believe that their managers (or the entire organization) use unfair procedures are likely to respond negatively, such as by failing to follow organizational policies and resigning. We even know that among people who have been laid off, the more strongly they believe their organizations have used unfair procedures, the more likely they are to bring lawsuits against their former employers.[11] Procedural fairness is even involved in the game of football. The instant replay rule, which has officials review the accuracy of the calls made on the field, is used to ensure that the game is played fairly.[12]

That said, we may ask what can be done to promote procedural justice in the workplace. Fortunately, several useful suggestions have been offered by researchers in this area. For a summary of some of the most effective ways of promoting procedural justice, see Table 4.1.

Expectancy Theory: Believing You Can Get What You Want

Beyond seeking fair treatment on the job, people are also motivated by the belief that they can expect to achieve certain desired rewards by working hard to attain them. If you've ever put in long hours studying in the hopes of receiving an "A" in one of your classes, then you know what I mean. Believing that there may be a carrot dangling at the end of the stick, and that it may be attained by putting forth the appropriate effort, can be a very effective motivator. This is one of the basic ideas behind the popularity of pay systems known as *merit pay plans,* or *pay-for-performance plans,* which formally establish links between job performance and rewards. However, a recent survey found that only 25 percent of employees see a clear link between good job performance and their pay raises. Clearly, companies are not doing all that they can to take advantage of this form of motivation. To better understand this process, let's take a look at a popular theory of motivation that addresses this issue—**expectancy theory**.

THREE COMPONENTS OF MOTIVATION

Expectancy theory claims that people will be motivated to exert effort on the job when they believe that doing so will help them achieve the things they want.[13] It assumes that people are rational beings who think about what they have to do to be rewarded and how much the reward means to them before they perform their jobs. Specifically, expectancy theory views motivation as the result of three different types of beliefs that people have. These are **expectancy**—the belief that one's effort will affect performance, **instrumentality**—the belief that one's performance will be rewarded, and **valence**—the perceived value of the expected rewards. For a summary of these components and their role in the overall theory, see Figure 4.3.

Expectancy. Sometimes people believe that putting forth a great deal of effort will help them get a lot accomplished. However, in other cases, people do not expect that their efforts will have much effect on how well they do. For example, an employee operating a faulty piece of equipment may have a very low *expectancy* that his or her efforts will lead to high levels of performance. Someone working under such condi-

FIGURE 4.3 Overview of Expectancy Theory

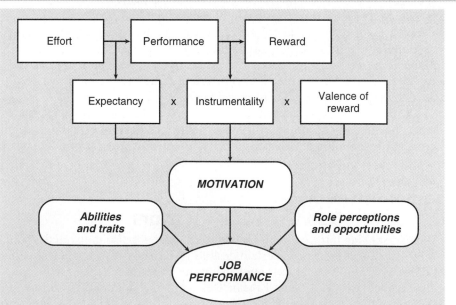

Expectancy theory claims that motivation is the combined result of the three components identified here—expectancy, instrumentality, and valence of reward. It also recognizes that motivation is only one of several determinants of job performance.

tions probably would not continue to exert much effort. After all, there is no good reason to go on trying to fill a bucket riddled with holes. Accordingly, good managers will do things that help their subordinates believe that their hard work will lead them to do their jobs better. With this in mind, training employees to do their jobs better can be very effective in helping enhance expectancy beliefs (recall our discussion of training in Chapter 2). Indeed, a large part of working more effectively involves making sure that one's efforts will pay off.

Some companies have taken a more direct approach by soliciting and following their employees' suggestions about ways to improve their work efficiency. For example, United Electric Controls (a manufacturer of industrial temperature and pressure controls located in Watertown, Massachusetts) routinely asks its employees for ways to do their jobs more effectively. Since instituting this approach, not only have individual employees become more effective, but so too has the company. In fact, key indicators revealed that the company's performance improved dramatically after it began following its employees' suggestions (e.g., on-time deliveries rose from 65 percent to 95 percent).

Instrumentality.   Even if an employee performs at a high level, his or her motivation may suffer if that performance is not appropriately rewarded—that is, if the performance is not perceived as *instrumental* in bringing about the rewards. So, for example, an extremely productive employee may be poorly motivated if he or she has already reached the top level of pay given by the company. Recognizing this possibility, several organizations have crafted pay systems that explicitly link desired performance to rewards.

Consider, for example, the pay plan instituted for IBM's 30,000 sales representatives. Previously, most of the pay these reps received was based on flat salary; their compensation was not linked to how well they did. Now, however, their pay is carefully tied to two factors that are essential to the company's success—profitability and customer satisfaction. So, instead of receiving commissions on the amount of the sale, as so many salespeople do, 60 percent of IBMers' commissions are tied to the company's profit on that sale. As a result, the more the company makes, the more the reps make. And, to make sure that the reps don't push only high-profit items that customers might not need, the remaining 40 percent of their commissions are based on customer satisfaction. Checking on this, customers are regularly surveyed about the extent to which their sales representatives helped them meet their business objectives. The better the reps have done in this regard, the greater their commissions. Since introducing this plan a few years ago, IBM has been effective in reversing its unprofitable trend. Although there are certainly many factors responsible for this turnaround, experts are confident that this practice of clearly linking desired performance to individual rewards is a key factor.

Valence.   Thus far, we have been assuming something that needs to be made explicit—namely, that the rewards the organization offers in exchange for desired performance are themselves desirable. In other words, using terminology from expectancy theory, they should have a positive *valence*. This is no trivial point if you consider that rewards are not equally desirable to everyone. For example, whereas a bonus of $200 may not be seen like much of a reward to a multimillionaire CEO, it may be quite valuable to a minimum-wage employee struggling to make ends meet. Valence is not just a matter of the amount of reward received, but what that reward means to the person receiving it. (To help recognize those sources of reward that are currently most valuable to you personally, complete the **Self-Assessment Exercise** on p. 107.)

These days, with a highly diverse workforce, it would be erroneous to assume that employees are equally attracted to the same rewards. Some (e.g., single, young employees) might recognize the incentive value of a pay raise, whereas others (e.g., those taking care of families) might prefer additional vacation days, improved insurance benefits, and day care, or elder-care, facilities. So, how can an organization find out what its employees want? Some companies have found a simple answer—asking them. For example, executives at PKF-Mark III (a construction company in Newton, Pennsylvania) have recently done just this. They put together a committee of employees representing a broad cross section of the company and allowed them to select exactly what fringe benefits they wanted most. This led to a package of fringe benefits that was highly desirable to the employees.

Many more companies have taken a completely individualized approach, introducing **cafeteria-style benefit plans**—incentive systems allowing employees to select their fringe benefits from a menu of available alternatives.[14] Given that fringe benefits represent almost 40 percent of payroll costs, more and more companies are recognizing the value of administering them flexibly. In fact, a recent survey found that such plans are in place in as many as half of all large companies (those employing over 5,000) and 22 percent of smaller companies (those with under 1,000 employees). For example, Primerica has had a flexible benefit plan in use since 1978—one that almost all of the employees believe is extremely beneficial to them. (Many of today's companies are doing highly creative things to ensure that their employees can achieve rewards that have value to them. For a summary of some of these practices, see the **Winning Practices** section on p. 95.)

THE ROLE OF MOTIVATION IN PERFORMANCE

Thus far, we have discussed the three components of motivation identified by expectancy theory. However, expectancy theory views motivation as just one of several determinants of job performance. As shown at the bottom of Figure 4.3, motivation combines with a person's skills and abilities, role perceptions, and opportunities to influence job performance.

It's no secret that the unique characteristics, special skills, and abilities of some people predispose them to perform their jobs better than others. For example, a tall, strong, well-coordinated person is likely to make a better professional basketball player than a very short, weak, uncoordinated one—even if the shorter person is highly motivated to succeed. Recognizing this, it would be a mistake to assume automatically that someone performing below par is poorly motivated. Instead, some poor performers may be very highly motivated, but lacking the knowledge or skills needed to succeed. With this in mind, companies often make big investments in training employees so as to ensure that they have what it takes to succeed (see Chapter 2), regardless of their levels of motivation.

Expectancy theory also recognizes that job performance will be influenced by people's *role perceptions*—that is, what they believe is expected of them on the job. To the extent that there are uncertainties about what one's job duties may be, performance may suffer. For example, a shop foreman who believes his primary job duty is to teach

WINNING PRACTICES

Going "Beyond the Fringe" in Benefits: Especially Creative Reward Practices

Traditionally, someone who gets a new job receives not only a salary but also a standard set of fringe benefits, such as health insurance, life insurance, a paid vacation, and a retirement plan. These days, however, these basic benefits are not enough to bring job prospects through the door. The incentives that motivate today's employees are far more varied—and, in many cases, truly lavish.[15]

Suppose, for example, you work at the Framingham, Massachusetts, corporate headquarters of the office supply chain Staples, and that you have children who need to be cared for while you are at work. No problem. You simply drop them off at the company's brand-new, $1.4 million, 8,000-square-foot child-care center near your office. Although there is a great need for on-site child-care facilities, only 11 percent of today's companies, such as Staples, offer them. This benefit makes it possible for Staples employees to concentrate on their work without having to worry about who's taking care of their children.

If you work at Staples, you also have available to you a wonderful concierge service, which runs all kinds of errands for busy employees (e.g., picking up dry cleaning, washing their cars), making their lives far easier. Staples isn't alone in offering concierge services. In fact, several companies have come into being in the past few years that offer concierge services to companies that seek them for their employees. For example, the San Francisco-based firm LesConcierges provides this service to employees of several well-known companies, including America Online and its sister company, CompuServe.

Some companies offer even more lavish benefits. For example, to attract employees to its out-of-the-way location in rural Wisconsin, Quad/Graphics, the printer, offers its employees rental apartments in its new $5 million complex. During its annual slow period, Rhino Foods (in Burlington, Vermont) helps its employees find jobs at other local businesses. Getting holidays off isn't so special; everyone gets them, right? Well, they might not be exactly the ones that you want to celebrate. This isn't a problem for employees of the Stamford, Connecticut, marketing firm Marquardt & Roche. This firm allows its employees to select any 11 out of 24 possible holidays.

Finally, some companies are even offering such benefits as pet insurance, auto financing, Internet access, home security systems, prepaid legal services, and even personal loans to their employees. Clearly, the days of finding so-called "standard" fringe benefits are over. What passes for standard today is anybody's guess.

Questions for Discussion

1. What is the most unusual fringe benefit of which you are aware?
2. Of the many unusual fringe benefits noted here, which one would be of greatest value to you?
3. What do you see as the downside of offering lavish fringe benefits?

new employees how to use the equipment may find that his performance is downgraded by a supervisor who believes he should be spending more time doing routine paperwork instead. In this case, the foreman's performance wouldn't suffer due to any deficit in motivation, but because of misunderstandings regarding what the job entails.

Finally, expectancy theory also recognizes the role of *opportunities to perform* one's job. Even the best employees may perform at low levels if their opportunities are limited. This may occur, for example, if there is an economic downturn in a salesperson's territory, or if the company's available inventory is insufficient to meet sales demand.

In conclusion, expectancy has done a good job of sensitizing managers to several key determinants of motivation, variables that frequently can be controlled. Beyond this, the theory clarifies the important—but not unique—role that motivation plays in determining job performance.

Goal Setting: Taking Aim at Performance Targets

Suppose that you are a word processing operator. You are performing quite well, but your boss believes that you can do even better. She asks you to try to type 70 words per minute (wpm) from now on instead of the 60 wpm you've been doing all along. Would you work hard to meet this goal, or would you simply give up? Organizational scientists have found that under certain conditions **goal setting** can lead to marked improvements in performance.[16] Specifically, it has been found that improvements result under three conditions—when goals are (1) specific; (2) difficult, but reasonable; and (3) accompanied by feedback.

ASSIGN SPECIFIC GOALS

In our word processing example, the supervisor set a goal that was very specific (70 wpm) and also somewhat difficult to attain (10 wpm faster than current performance). Would you perform better under these conditions than if the supervisor merely said something general, such as "Do your best to improve"? Decades of research on goal setting suggest that the answer is "yes."

Indeed, we know that people perform at higher levels when asked to meet specific high-performance goals than when they are directed simply to "do your best" or when no goal at all is assigned. People tend to find specific goals quite challenging and are motivated to try to meet them—not only to fulfill management's expectations but also to convince themselves that they have performed well. Scientists have explained that attaining goals enhances employees' beliefs in their *self-efficacy,* which I noted in Chapter 3 refers to people's assessments of themselves as being competent and successful. And, when people believe that they can, in fact, succeed at a task, they will be motivated to work hard at it. For this reason people will be motivated to pursue specific goals, ones that readily enable them to define their accomplishments, enhancing their self-efficacy beliefs.

To demonstrate this principle, let's consider a classic study conducted at an Oklahoma lumber camp owned by Weyerhauser, a major producer of paper products.[17] The initial step in the papermaking process involves cutting down trees and hauling them to the sawmill, where they are ground into pulp. For some time, the company was

FIGURE 4.4 Goal Setting at a Logging Camp: An Impressive Demonstration

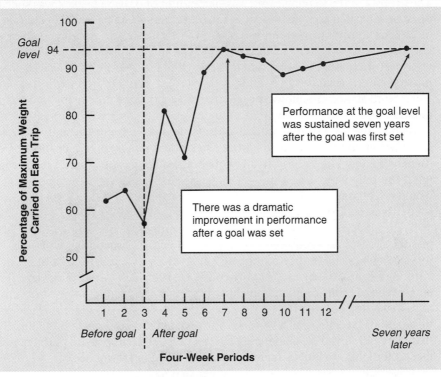

After a specific goal was set, loggers did a better job of loading trucks to their maximum limits before returning to the mill. (*Source:* Adapted from Latham and Baldes, 1975; see Note 17.)

plagued by a problem: The loggers were loading the trucks to only about 60 percent of their maximum capacity. This resulted in wasted trips, adding considerable cost. To help solve this problem, a goal-setting program was introduced. A specific goal was set: The loggers were challenged to load the trucks to 94 percent of their capacity before returning to the mill.

How effective was this goal in raising performance? The results, summarized in Figure 4.4, show that the goal was extremely effective. In fact, not only was the specific goal effective in raising performance to the goal level in just a few weeks, but the effects were long lasting as well. In fact, the loggers were found to sustain this level of performance as long as seven years later! The resulting savings logged in (pun intended) by the company has been considerable, a classic goal-setting success story.

Importantly, these dramatic effects are not unusual, nor are they limited to this special setting. Rather, this study is just one of many that highlight the effectiveness of setting specific, challenging performance goals in a variety of organizational contexts. For example, specific goals also have been used to help improve many other kinds of organizational behaviors, such as reducing absenteeism and lowering the occurrence of industrial accidents.

ASSIGN DIFFICULT, BUT ACCEPTABLE, PERFORMANCE GOALS

The goal set at the logging camp was successful not only because it was specific but also because it pushed crew members to a higher standard. Obviously, a goal that is too easy to attain will *not* bring about the desired increments in performance. For example, if you already type at 60 wpm, a goal of 50 wpm, although specific, would probably *lower* your performance. The key point is that a goal must be difficult, as well as specific, for it to raise performance.

At the same time, however, people will work hard to reach challenging goals so long as these are within the limits of their capability. As goals become too difficult, performance suffers because people reject them as unrealistic and unattainable. For example, you may work much harder as a student in a class that challenges your ability than in one that is very easy. In all likelihood, however, you would probably give up trying if the only way of passing was to get perfect scores on all exams—a standard you would reject as being unacceptable. In short, specific goals are most effective if they are set neither too low nor too high.

The same phenomenon occurs in organizations. For example, Bell Canada's telephone operators are required to handle calls within 23 seconds, and Fed Ex's customer service agents are expected to answer customers' questions within 140 seconds. Although both goals were initially considered difficult when they were imposed, the employees of both companies eventually met—or exceeded—these goals, and enjoyed the satisfaction of knowing they succeeded at this task. At a General Electric manufacturing plant, specific goals were set for productivity and cost reduction. Those goals that were perceived as challenging but possible led to improved performance, whereas those thought to be unattainable led to decreased performance.

How should goals be set in a manner that strengthens employees' commitment to them? One obvious way of enhancing goal acceptance is to involve employees in the goal-setting process. Research on workers' participation in goal setting has demonstrated that people better accept goals that they have been involved in setting than goals that have been assigned by their supervisors—and, they work harder as a result.[18]

People better accept goals that they have been involved in setting than goals that have been assigned by their supervisors—and, they work harder as a result.

Participation in the goal-setting process may have these beneficial effects for several reasons. For one, people are more likely to better understand and appreciate goals they had a hand in setting themselves than those that are merely presented to them. In addition, employees are likely to be committed to attaining such goals, in large part because they must psychologically rationalize their decisions to set those goals. (After all, one can hardly justify setting a specific goal and then not work to attain it.) Finally, because workers often have more direct knowledge about what it takes to do a job than their supervisors, they are in a good position to come up with goals that are acceptably high, but not unreasonable. Further capitalizing on workers' experiences, executives generally agree that it is a good idea to let employees figure out the best way to meet new goals. In the words of John Snow, CEO of the large railroad company, CSX, "It's people in the field who find the right path."[19] This sentiment is echoed by Bob Freese, CEO of Alphatronix Inc., in Research Triangle Park, North Carolina: "We let employees tell us when they can accomplish a project and what resources they need," he says. "Virtually always they set higher goals than we would ever set for them."[20]

PROVIDE FEEDBACK CONCERNING GOAL ATTAINMENT

The final condition for setting effective goals appears to be glaringly obvious, although it is not followed in practice as often as you might expect: Provide feedback about the extent to which goals have been met. Just as golfers can improve their games when they learn where their balls have landed, so too do workers benefit by feedback about how closely they are approaching their performance goals. Extending our golf analogy, when it comes to setting work goals effectively, "hooks" and "slices" need to be corrected.

A study of the performance of work crews in the U.S. Air Force illustrates the importance of using feedback in conjunction with goal setting.[21] A standardized index of job performance was used to measure five different groups repeatedly over a two-year period. During the first nine months, a baseline measure of effectiveness was taken that was used to compare the relative impact of feedback and goal setting. The groups then received feedback for five months (reports detailing how well they performed on various performance measures). Following this, the goal-setting phase of the study was begun. During this period, the crew members set goals for themselves with respect to their performance on various measures. Then, for the final five months, in addition to the feedback and goal setting, an incentive (time off from work) was made available to crew members who met their goals.

It was found that feedback and goal setting dramatically increased group effectiveness. Group feedback improved performance approximately 50 percent over the baseline level. The addition of group goal setting improved it 75 percent over baseline. These findings show that the combination of goal setting and feedback helps raise the effectiveness of group performance. Groups that know how well they're doing and have a target goal tend to perform very well. Providing incentives, however, improved performance only negligibly. The real incentive seems to be meeting the challenge of performing up to the level of the goal.

In sum, goal setting is a very effective tool managers can use to motivate people. Setting a specific, acceptably difficult goal and providing feedback about progress toward attaining it greatly enhance job performance. To demonstrate the effectiveness of goal setting in your own behavior, complete the **Group Exercise** on p. 107.

Designing Jobs That Motivate

As you may recall from Chapter 1, Frederick W. Taylor's approach to stimulating work performance was to design jobs so that people worked as efficiently as possible. No wasted movements and no wasted time added up to efficient performance, or so Taylor believed. However, Taylor failed to consider one important thing: The repetitive machine-like movements required of his workers were highly routine and monotonous. And, not surprisingly, people became bored with such jobs and frequently quit. Fortunately, organizational scientists have found several ways of designing jobs that not only can be performed very efficiently but also are highly pleasant and enjoyable.

This is the basic principle behind **job design**, the process of creating jobs that people desire to perform because they are so inherently appealing.

JOB ENLARGEMENT: DOING MORE OF THE SAME KIND OF WORK

If you've ever purchased a greeting card, chances are good that you've picked up at least one made by American Greetings, one of the United States' largest greeting card companies. What you might not know is that this Cleveland, Ohio-based organization recently redesigned some 400 jobs in its creative division. Now, rather than always working exclusively on, say, Christmas cards, employees will be able to move back and forth between different teams, such as those working on birthday ribbons, humorous mugs, and Valentine's Day gift bags. Similarly, employees at the Blue Ridge, Georgia, plant of Levi-Strauss & Company used to perform the same task all day on the assembly line, but now they have been trained to handle three different jobs. Employees at American Greetings and Levi-Strauss reportedly enjoy the variety, as do those at RJR Nabisco, Corning, and Eastman Kodak, other companies that recently have allowed employees to make such lateral moves.

Scientists have referred to what these companies are doing as **job enlargement**—the practice of giving employees more tasks to perform at the same level. There's no higher responsibility involved, nor any greater skills, just a wider variety of the same types of tasks. The idea behind job enlargement is simple: You can decrease boredom by giving people a greater variety of jobs to do.

Do job enlargement programs work? To answer this question, consider the results of a study comparing the job performance of people doing enlarged and unenlarged jobs.[22] In the unenlarged jobs different employees performed separate paperwork tasks such as preparing, sorting, coding, and keypunching various forms. The enlarged jobs combined these various functions into larger jobs performed by the same people. Although it was more difficult and expensive to train people to perform the enlarged jobs than the separate jobs, important benefits resulted. In particular, employees expressed greater job satisfaction and less boredom. And, because one person followed the whole job all the way through, greater opportunities to correct errors existed. Not surprisingly, customers were more satisfied with the result.

In a follow-up investigation of the same company conducted two years later, however, it was found that not all the beneficial effects continued.[23] Notably, employee satisfaction leveled off, and the rate of errors went up, suggesting that as employees got used to their enlarged jobs they found them less interesting and stopped paying attention to all the details. Hence, although job enlargement may help improve job performance, its effects may be short lived. It appears that the problem with enlarging jobs is that people eventually get bored with them, and they need to be enlarged still further.

> *The problem with enlarging jobs is that people eventually get bored with them, and they need to be enlarged still further.*

Because it is impractical to continue enlarging jobs all the time, the value of this approach is rather limited.

JOB ENRICHMENT: INCREASING REQUIRED SKILLS AND RESPONSIBILITIES

As an alternative, consider another approach taken to redesign jobs. For many years, Procter & Gamble (P&G) manufactured detergent by having large numbers of people perform a series of narrow tasks. Then, in the early 1960s, realizing that this rigid approach did little to utilize the full range of skills and abilities of employees, P&G executive David Swanson introduced a new way to make detergent in the company's Augusta, Georgia, plant. The technicians worked together in teams (see Chapter 9) to take control over large parts of the production process. They set production schedules, hired new coworkers, and took responsibility over evaluating each others' performance, including the process of deciding who was going to get raises. In short, they not only performed more tasks, but ones at higher levels of skill and responsibility. The general name given to this approach is **job enrichment**.

One of the best-known job enrichment programs was the one developed by Volvo, the Swedish auto manufacturer. In response to serious dissension among its workforce in the late 1960s, the company's then-president, Pehr Gyllenhammar, introduced job enrichment in its Kalmar assembly plant. Cars were assembled by 25 groups of approximately 20 workers who each were responsible for one part of the car's assembly (e.g., engine, electrical system). In contrast to the usual assembly-line method of manufacturing cars used in Detroit, Volvo's work groups are set up so they can freely plan, organize, and inspect their own work. In time, workers become more satisfied with their jobs and the plant experienced a significant reduction in turnover and absenteeism.

Although job enrichment programs also have been successful at other organizations, several factors limit their popularity. First, there is the difficulty of implementation. Redesigning existing facilities so that jobs can be enriched is often prohibitively expensive. Besides, the technology needed to perform certain jobs makes it impractical for them to be redesigned. Another impediment is the lack of universal employee acceptance. Although many relish it, some people do *not* desire the additional responsibility associated with performing enriched jobs. In fact, when a group of American auto workers was sent to Sweden to work in a Saab engine assembly plant where jobs were highly enriched, five out of six indicated that they preferred their traditional assembly-line jobs. As one union leader put it, "If you want to enrich the job, enrich the paycheck."[24] Clearly, enriched jobs are not for everyone.

THE JOB CHARACTERISTICS MODEL

Thus far, I have failed to specify precisely *how* to enrich a job. What elements of a job need to be enriched for it to be effective? An attempt to expand the idea of job enrichment, known as the **job characteristics model**, provides an answer to this important question.[25]

Basic elements of the job characteristics model.   This approach assumes that jobs can be designed so as to help people get enjoyment out of their jobs and care about the work they do. The model identifies how jobs can be designed to help people feel that they are doing meaningful and valuable work. In particular, it specifies that enriching certain elements of jobs alters people's psychological states in a manner that enhances

FIGURE 4.5 The Job Characteristics Model

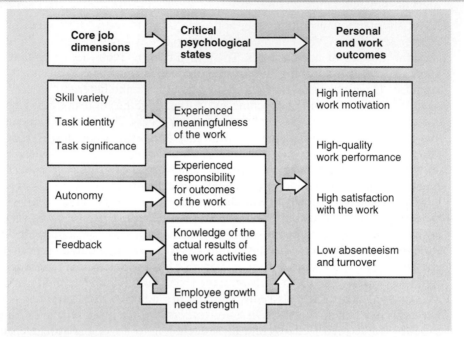

According to the job characteristics model, the five core job dimensions listed create three critical psychological states, which in turn influence the personal and work outcomes shown. The model also acknowledges that these relationships are strongest among those individuals highest in growth need strength. (*Source:* Adapted from Hackman and Oldman, 1980; see Note 25.)

their work effectiveness. Specifically, the model identifies five *core job dimensions* that help create three *critical psychological states*, leading, in turn, to several beneficial *personal and work outcomes* (see Figure 4.5).

The five critical job dimensions are *skill variety, task identity, task significance, autonomy,* and *feedback.* Let's take a closer look at these:

- *Skill variety* is the extent to which a job requires using several different skills and talents that an employee has. For example, a restaurant manager with high skill variety will perform many different tasks (e.g., maintaining sales records, handling customer complaints, scheduling staff, supervising repair work, and the like).
- *Task identity* is the degree to which a job requires doing a whole task from beginning to end. For example, tailors will have high task identity if they do everything associated with making an entire suit (e.g., measuring the client, selecting the fabric, cutting and sewing it, and altering it to fit).
- *Task significance* is the amount of impact a job is believed to have on others. For example, medical researchers working on a cure for a deadly disease surely recognize the importance of their work to the world at large. Even more modest contributions to the company can be recognized as being significant to the extent that employees understand the role of their jobs in the overall mission of the organization.

- *Autonomy* is the extent to which employees have the freedom and discretion to plan, schedule, and carry out their jobs as desired. For example, in 1991 a team of Procter & Gamble employees was put in charge of making all the arrangements necessary for the building of a new $5 million facility for making concentrated Downy fabric softener.
- *Feedback* is the extent to which the job allows people to have information about the effectiveness of their performance. For example, telemarketing representatives regularly receive information about how many calls they make per day and the monetary values of the sales made.

The job characteristics model specifies that these various job dimensions have important effects on certain associated critical psychological states. Specifically, skill variety, task identity, and task significance jointly contribute to a task's *experienced meaningfulness.* A task is considered meaningful insofar as it is experienced as being highly important, valuable, and worthwhile. Jobs that provide a great deal of autonomy are said to make people feel *personally responsible and accountable for their work.* When they are free to decide what to do and how to do it, they feel more responsible for the results, whether good or bad. Finally, effective feedback is said to give employees *knowledge of the results of their work.* When a job is designed to provide people with information about the effects of their actions, they are better able to develop an understanding of how effectively they have performed—and, such knowledge improves their performance.

The job characteristics model specifies that the three critical psychological states affect various personal and work outcomes—namely: people's feelings of motivation, the quality of work performed, satisfaction with work, absenteeism, and turnover. The higher the experienced meaningfulness of work, responsibility for the work performed, and knowledge of results, the more positive the personal and work benefits will be. When they perform jobs that incorporate high levels of the five core job dimensions, people should feel highly motivated, perform high-quality work, be highly satisfied with their jobs, be absent infrequently, and be unlikely to resign from their jobs.

I should also note that the model is theorized to be especially effective in describing the behavior of individuals who are high in *growth need strength*—that is, people who have a high need for personal growth and development. People not particularly interested in improving themselves on the job are not expected to experience the theorized psychological reactions to the core job dimensions, nor consequently, to enjoy the beneficial personal and work outcomes predicted by the model. By introducing this variable, the job characteristics model recognizes the important limitation of job enrichment noted earlier—not everyone wants and benefits from enriched jobs.

Assessing the motivating potential of jobs. Based on the proposed relationship between the core job dimensions and their associated psychological reactions, the model claims that job motivation will be highest when the jobs performed rate high on the various dimensions. To assess this, a questionnaire known as the Job Diagnostic Survey (JDS) has been developed to measure the degree to which various job characteristics are present in a particular job. Based on responses to the JDS, we can make predictions about the degree to which a job motivates people who perform it.

The job characteristics model has been the focus of many empirical tests, most of which are supportive of many aspects of the model. One study conducted among a group of South African clerical workers found particularly strong support.[26] The jobs of employees in some of the offices in this company were enriched in accordance with techniques specified by the job characteristics model. Specifically, employees performing the enriched jobs were given opportunities to choose the kinds of tasks they perform (high skill variety), do the entire job (high task identity), receive instructions regarding how their job fit into the organization as a whole (high task significance), freely set their own schedules and inspect their own work (high autonomy), and keep records of their daily productivity (high feedback). Another group of employees, equivalent in all respects except that their jobs were not enriched, served as a control group.

After employees performed the newly designed jobs for six months, comparisons were made between them and their counterparts in the control group. With respect to most of the outcomes specified by the model, individuals performing redesigned jobs showed superior results. Specifically, they reported feeling more internally motivated and more satisfied with their jobs. There also were lower rates of absenteeism and turnover among employees performing the enriched jobs. The only outcome predicted by the model that was not found to differ was actual work performance; people performed equally well in enriched and unenriched jobs. Considering the many factors that are responsible for job performance (as discussed in connection with expectancy theory), this finding should not be too surprising.

Suggestions for enhancing the motivating potential of jobs.   The job characteristics model specifies several ways in which jobs can be designed to enhance their motivating potential. For example, instead of using several workers, each of whom performs a separate part of a whole job, it would be better to have each person perform the entire job. Doing so helps provide greater skill variety and task identity. For example, Corning Glass Works in Medford, Massachusetts, redesigned jobs so that people who assembled laboratory hot plates put together entire units instead of contributing a single part to the assembly process.

The job characteristics model also suggests that jobs should be set up so that the person performing a service (such as an auto mechanic) comes into contact with the recipient of the service (such as the car owner). Jobs designed in this manner will help the employee by not only providing feedback but also enhancing skill variety (e.g., talking to customers in addition to fixing cars) and building autonomy (by giving people the freedom to manage their own relationships with clients). This suggestion has been implemented at Sea-Land Service, the large containerized ocean-shipping company. After this company's mechanics, clerks, and crane operators started meeting with customers, they became much more productive. Having faces to associate with the once-abstract jobs they did clearly helped them take the jobs more seriously.

Jobs should be designed so as to give employees as much feedback as possible. The more people know how well they're doing (be it from customers, supervisors, or coworkers), the better equipped they are to take appropriate corrective action.

Another implication of the job characteristics model is that jobs should be designed so as to give employees as much feedback as possible. The more people know how well they're doing (be it from customers, supervisors, or coworkers), the better equipped they are to take appropriate corrective action (recall our discussion in Chapter 2 about the importance of feedback in training). As a case in point, Childress Buick Company, a Phoenix, Arizona, auto dealership, once suffered serious customer dissatisfaction and employee retention problems before owner Rusty Childress began encouraging his employees to rely upon feedback from customers and fellow employees to discover ways of doing their jobs better.

SUMMARY: HAVE I MET THE LEARNING OBJECTIVES?

You can be certain that you have met the learning objectives for this chapter found on p. 81 if you understand the following:

1. **DEFINE motivation**. Motivation is the process of arousing, directing, and maintaining behavior toward a goal.
2. **EXPLAIN need hierarchy theory and how it applies in organizations**. Need hierarchy theory specifies that people are motivated to fulfill a series of needs, arranged in hierarchical fashion from the lowest to the highest. Most basic are physiological needs, which employers can help meet by paying workers enough to satisfy their basic needs for food and shelter. The next level, safety needs, can be met by providing workplaces that are free from both physical and psychological harm. Social needs are often met by giving employees opportunities to socialize with each other, such as by engaging in athletic pursuits. Programs honoring special contributions, such as "employee of the month" awards, are useful in helping satisfy esteem needs. When all of these needs have been met, the theory says, people will strive to self-actualize—that is, to become all they are capable of being. Insofar as self-actualized employees work at their maximum creative potential, they are valued employees of the organizations in which they work.
3. **DESCRIBE equity theory's approach to motivation in the workplace**. The basic premise of equity theory is that people are motivated to redress inequities in the workplace, both overpayment and underpayment, and to establish equitable relationships with others. This involves making sure that people are paid the same as others doing comparable work. When people believe that this is not the case, they frequently attempt to change conditions—working less hard or seeking higher pay—to help restore equity. Insofar as employees who feel inequitably treated have been known to respond in extreme ways, such as by going on strike and stealing from their employers, managers should work hard to make sure that employees believe that they are being treated fairly.
4. **OUTLINE the basic assumptions of expectancy theory and its implications in organizations**. Expectancy theory specifies that people will be motivated to work hard when they believe that their efforts will lead them to perform well, that their performance will be suitably rewarded, and that the rewards they receive are valued. As such, it is considered useful to make sure that workers are trained well enough to have their efforts pay off, are rewarded in a manner commensurate with their performance (e.g., a merit pay system), and receive rewards that they truly value (such as by allowing them to select fringe benefits from a list of options). Expectancy theory recognizes that motivation is necessary but not sufficient for good performance to result. Employees also must have the skills and abilities needed to succeed (such as those provided by

training and natural talent) as well as opportunities to succeed (e.g., the necessary sales tools and customer base).

5. **EXPLAIN how goals can be set to motivate high levels of job performance**. The process of goal setting has been used to stimulate high levels of performance. To be successful, goals must meet three characteristics. First, they must be highly specific, identifying exactly the level of performance that is expected. Second, they must be difficult, but not impossible to attain. Finally, feedback helps people understand the adjustments in their behavior needed to reach their goals.

6. **DESCRIBE ways in which jobs can be designed so as to enhance motivation**. Workers' motivation can be enhanced by the process of job design—making jobs so inherently appealing that people will be motivated to do them. One major approach has been job enlargement, giving people more jobs to do at the same level. Although this works temporarily, people soon become bored with their jobs, requiring even more enlargement. Job enrichment is considered a more successful approach. This involves giving people not only more jobs, but ones with greater levels of responsibility. The job characteristics model specifies that jobs should be enriched by adding to the number of skills required, allowing people to perform entire tasks, helping them understand the significance of their work, giving them the freedom and discretion to do their jobs as they wish, and regularly sharing information about the effectiveness of their work.

You Be the Consultant

Suppose that you were just hired by a large manufacturing company to help resolve problems of poor morale that have been plaguing the workforce. Turnover and absenteeism are high, and performance is at an all-time low. Answer the following questions relevant to this situation based on the material in this chapter.

1. Suppose, after interviewing the workers, you found that they believed that no one cared how well they were doing. What theories could help explain this problem? Applying these approaches, what would you recommend the company do to resolve this situation?

2. Company officials tell you that the employees are well paid, adding to their surprise about the low morale. However, your interviews reveal that the employees themselves feel otherwise. Why is this a problem? What could be done to help?

3. "I'm bored with my job," an employee tells you, and you believe he speaks for many within the company. What could be done to make the jobs more interesting to those who perform them? What are the limitations of your plan? Would it work equally well for all employees?

What Rewards Do You Value?

According to expectancy theory, one thing companies can do to motivate employees is to give rewards that have positive valence to them. What work-related rewards have the greatest value to you? Completing this questionnaire will help you answer this question.

Directions
Below are 10 work-related rewards. For each, circle the number that best describes the value that particular reward has for you personally. Use the following scale to express your feelings: 1 = no value at all, 2 = slight value, 3 = moderate value, 4 = great value, 5 = extremely great value.

Reward	*Personal Value*			
Good pay	1	2	3	4	5
Prestigious title	1	2	3	4	5
Vacation time	1	2	3	4	5
Job security	1	2	3	4	5
Recognition	1	2	3	4	5
Interesting work	1	2	3	4	5
Pleasant conditions	1	2	3	4	5
Chances to advance	1	2	3	4	5
Flexible schedule	1	2	3	4	5
Friendly coworkers	1	2	3	4	5

Questions to Ask Yourself
1. Based on your answers, which rewards do you value most? Which do you value least? Do you think these preferences will change as you get older and perform different jobs? If so, how?
2. To what extent do you believe that you will be able to attain each of these rewards on your job? Do you expect that the chances of receiving these rewards will improve in the future? Why or why not?
3. Do you believe that the rewards you value most are also the ones valued by other people? Are these reward preferences likely to be the same for all people everywhere, or at least for all workers performing the same job in the same company?

Demonstrating the Effectiveness of Goal Setting

The tendency for specific, difficult goals to enhance task performance is very well established. The following exercise is designed to help you demonstrate this effect yourself. All you need is a class of students willing to participate and a few simple supplies.

Directions

1. Select a page of text from a book and make several photocopies. Then, carefully count the words, and number each word on one of the copies. This will be your score sheet.
2. Find another class of 30 or more students who don't know anything about goal setting. (We don't want their knowledge of the phenomenon to bias the results.) On a random basis, divide the students into three equal-size groups.
3. Ask the students in the first group ("baseline" group) to copy as much of the text as they can onto another piece of paper, giving them exactly one minute to do so. Direct them to work at a fast pace. Using the score sheet created in step 1, identify the highest number of words counted by any one of the students. Then, multiply this number by 2. This will be the specific, difficult goal level.
4. Ask the students in another group ("specific goal" group) to count the number of words on the same printed page for exactly one minute. Tell them to try to reach the specific goal number identified in step 3.
5. Repeat this process with the third group ("do your best" group) but instead of giving them a specific goal, direct them to "try to do your best at this task."
6. Compute the average number of words copied in the "difficult goal" group and the "do your best" group. Have your instructor compute the appropriate statistical test (a *t*-test, in this case) to determine the statistical significance of the difference between the performance levels of the two groups.

Questions for Discussion

1. Was there, in fact, a statistically significant difference between the performance levels of the two groups? If so, did students in the "specific goal" group outperform those in the "do your best" group, as expected? What does this reveal about the effectiveness of goal setting?
2. If the predicted findings were not supported, why do you suppose this happened? What was it about the procedure that may have led to this failure? Was the specific goal (twice the fastest speed in the "baseline" group) too high, making the goal unreachable? Or, was it too low, making the specific goal too easy?
3. What do you think would happen if the goal were lowered, making it easier, or raised, making it more difficult?
4. Do you think it would have helped to provide feedback about goal attainment (e.g., someone counting the number of words copied and calling this out to the performers as they worked)?
5. For what other kinds of tasks do you believe goal setting may be effective? Specifically, do you believe that you can use goal setting to improve your own performance on something you do? Explain this possibility.

NOTES

Case Note

Fenn, D. (2000, February). Personnel best. *Inc.* pp. 75-76, 78, 81, 83.

Chapter Notes

[1] Waterman, R. H., Jr. (1994). *What America does right: Learning from companies that put people first.* New York: W.W. Norton.

[2] Maslow, A. H. (1970). *Motivation and personality (2nd ed.)*. New York: Harper & Row.

[3] Where's my Stairmaster? (1999, October). *Across the Board*, p. 5.

[4] Against the grain. (1999, May). *Across the Board*, p. 1.

[5] Klubnik, J. P. (1995). *Rewarding and recognizing employees*. Chicago: Richard D. Irwin. Leverence, J. (1997). *And the winner is...*. Santa Monica, CA: Merritt Publishing.

[6] Shepherd, M. D. (1993, February). Staff motivation. *U.S. Pharmacist*, pp. 82, 85, 89-93 (quote, p. 91).

[7] Light, L. (1999, April 19). Executive pay. *Business Week*, pp. 72-75.

[8] Adams, J. S. (1965). Inequity in social exchange. In L. Berkowitz (Ed.), *Advances in experimental social psychology* (Vol. 2, pp. 267-299). New York: Academic Press.

[9] Harder, J. W. (1992). Play for pay: Effects of inequity in a pay-for-performance context. *Administrative Science Quarterly. 37*, 321-335.

[10] Greenberg, J. (1993). Stealing in the name of justice: Informational and interpersonal moderators of theft reactions to underpayment inequity. *Organizational Behavior and Human Decision Processes, 54*, 81-103.

[11] Lind, E. A., Greenberg, J., Scott, K. S., & Welchans, T. D. (2000). The winding road from employee to complainant: Situational and psychological determinants of wrongful termination claims. *Administrative Science Quarterly, 45*, 557-590.

[12] Greenberg, J. (2000). Promote procedural justice to enhance acceptance of work outcomes. In E. A. Locke (Ed.), *A handbook of principles of organizational behavior*. Oxford, England: Blackwell.

[13] Porter, L. W., & Lawler, E. E., III. (1968). *Managerial attitudes and performance*. Homewood, IL: Irwin.

[14] Schrage, M. (2000, April 3). Cafeteria benefits? Ha, you deserve a richer banquet. *Fortune*, p. 274.

[15] Boreman, A. M. (1999, October 19). Clean my house, and I'm yours forever. *Inc.*, p. 214. Emerging optional benefits. (1998, December), Management Review, p. 8. Hickins, M. (1999, April). Creative "get-a-life" benefits. *Management Review*, p. 7. Nelson, B. (1994). *1001 ways to reward employees*. New York: Waterman. Palmer, A. T. (1999, April 26). Who's minding the baby? The company. *Business Week*, p. 32.

[16] Locke, E. A., & Latham, G. P. (1990). *A theory of goal setting and task performance*. Upper Saddle River, NJ: Prentice-Hall.

[17] Latham, G., & Baldes, J. (1975). The practical significance of Locke's theory of goal setting. *Journal of Applied Psychology, 60*, 122-124.

[18] Latham, G. P., Erez, M., & Locke, E. A. (1988). Resolving scientific disputes by the joint design of crucial experiments by the antagonists: Application to the Erez-Latham dispute regarding participation in goal setting. *Journal of Applied Psychology, 73*, 754–772.

[19] See Note 16 (quote, p. 148).

[20] Finegan, J. (1993, July). People power. *Inc.*, pp. 62-63 (quote, p. 63).

[21] Pritchard, R. D., Jones, S. D., Roth, P. L., Stuebing, K. K., & Ekberg, S. E. (1988). Effects of group feedback, goal setting, and incentives on organizational productivity. *Journal of Applied Psychology, 73*, 337-358.

[22] Campion, M. A., & McClelland, C. L. (1991). Interdisciplinary examination of the costs and benefits of enlarged jobs: A job design quasi-experiment. *Journal of Applied Psychology, 76*, 186-198.

[23] Campion, M. A., & McClelland, C. L. (1993). Follow-up and extension of the interdisciplinary costs and benefits of enlarged jobs. *Journal of Applied Psychology, 78*, 339-351.

[24] Winpisinger, W. (1973, February). Job satisfaction: A union response. *AFL-CIO American Federationist*, pp. 8-10 (quote, p. 9).

[25] Hackman, J. R., & Oldham, G. R. (1980). *Work redesign*. Reading, MA: Addison-Wesley.

[26] Orpen, C. (1979). The effects of job enrichment on employee satisfaction, motivation, involvement, and performance: A field experiment. *Human Relations 32*, 189-217.

5

Work-related attitudes:
prejudice, job satisfaction, and organizational commitment

LEARNING OBJECTIVES

After reading this chapter, you will be able to:

1. DISTINGUISH between prejudice, stereotypes, and discrimination.

2. DISTINGUISH between affirmative action plans and diversity management programs.

3. DESCRIBE four theories of job satisfaction.

4. IDENTIFY the consequences of having dissatisfied employees and DESCRIBE ways of boosting job satisfaction.

5. DISTINGUISH between three forms of organizational commitment.

6. IDENTIFY the benefits of having a committed workforce and DESCRIBE ways of developing organizational commitment.

THREE GOOD REASONS WHY YOU SHOULD CARE ABOUT . . .

Work-Related Attitudes

You should care about work-related attitudes because:

1. We are all potential victims of prejudice and discrimination on the job.

2. The more people are satisfied with their jobs and committed to their organizations, the less likely they are to be absent and to voluntarily resign.

3. Changing attitudes is not impossible. There are specific things that can be done to enhance the work-related attitudes of employees.

111

Making the Case for... Work-Related Attitudes

Texaco: Today, Only the Oil Is Crude

One fall day in 1996, while Texaco was in the midst of defending itself against legal charges of discrimination brought by 1,400 African American employees, a few top executives met to decide how to proceed. Secret tape recordings of that meeting revealed not only that these officials discussed destroying some incriminating documents, but worse yet, they freely used racial epithets in the course of doing so. After these tapes were shared with the plaintiffs' attorneys and the *New York Times*, Texaco found itself in the midst of a public relations nightmare. In the days that followed, the company's stock dropped so much that it lost nearly $1 billion in value.

Shortly thereafter, Texaco's chairman and CEO, Peter I. Bijur, settled the lawsuit, paying $140 million in damages and back pay to minority employees, and setting aside another $35 million for a task force to monitor the company's treatment of women and minorities for the next five years. In doing so, Texaco's goal, according to Bijur, was to become "a model of workplace opportunity for all men and women." Has Texaco met this goal? Observers note that although Texaco is still not among the most hospitable companies for members of minority groups, it has made considerable strides.

Statistics tell the story. In recent years, over 40 percent of recent hires and about a quarter of all newly promoted employees have come from minority ranks. Also, over $1 billion—approximately 15 percent of the company's spending—has been directed at businesses owned by women and members of minority groups. And, although 80 percent of the company's top executives are still white men, growing numbers are coming from minority ranks. "Now," Bijur remarks, "we treat all people with the utmost respect—and that is a real achievement."

Because Texaco is under careful scrutiny—from both the courts and the public—with respect to its treatment of women and minorities, it doesn't have much choice in the matter. Still, the company has shown that it is quite serious. By completely overhauling the way Texaco went about hiring and treating people, Bijur took several steps to show that he would not tolerate disrespect. Rather than simply talking about promoting equality and respect for everyone, he set meaningful goals and timetables to help advance women and minorities. So serious are these goals that a portion of all top executives' and managers' annual evaluations is based on how effectively they meet them. Importantly, the company has prospered financially as it has strived toward these goals.

Clearly, changes have resulted: Corporate attorneys who used to spend time defending against discrimination lawsuits have found that virtually no such complaints have reached their desks in recent years. Even Bari-Ellen Roberts, the woman who initiated the lawsuit against Texaco, is optimistic that the company will continue its efforts to improve the treatment of women and minorities in the years ahead. "Then again," she said, "they had to—things could not remain the same."

———————————

Although rather inelegantly, it is clear that Texaco has learned a lesson that many companies knew all along: By hiring and retaining ethnically diverse employees and giving them opportunities that they once may have been denied, the company stands to benefit. Indeed, Texaco now can draw on its human capital to help improve performance—and, ultimately, the bottom line. After all, the company has little or no chance of keeping employees on the job who are made to feel unwelcome. And, without people, there can be no company.

That said, how do you feel about your job? Is it pleasant or pure drudgery? How about your organization? Do you want to stay there, or are you considering quitting? What do you think of your coworkers? Do they know what they're doing, or would the company be better off without them? And, unlike the Texaco of a few years ago, do they respect and value you as an individual? Such questions are likely to elicit strong opinions. Indeed, people often have definite feelings about everything related to their jobs, whether it's the work itself, superiors, coworkers, subordinates, or even the food in the company cafeteria. Feelings such as these are referred to as **work-related attitudes**, the topic of this chapter.

As you might imagine, these attitudes can be very important in organizations. Not only do we want to feel good about our work for its own sake, but also such feelings may have important effects on how we do our jobs and the functioning of organizations. Our examination of work-related attitudes will focus on three major targets— attitudes toward others (including a special kind of negative attitude known as *prejudice*), attitudes toward the job (known as *job satisfaction*), attitudes toward the organization (known as *organizational commitment*).

Prejudice: Negative Attitudes Toward Others

How do you feel about your associate in the next cubicle? How about your boss or accountants in general? Our attitudes toward other people are obviously very important when it comes to understanding behavior in organizations. Such attitudes are highly problematic when they are negative, especially when these feelings are based on misguided beliefs that prompt harmful behavior. *Prejudice* is the term used to refer to attitudes of this type. Specifically, **prejudice** may be defined as negative feelings about people belonging to certain groups. Members of racial or ethnic groups, for example, are victims of prejudice when they are believed to be lazy, disinterested in working, or inferior in one way or another. Prejudicial attitudes often hold people back, creating an invisible barrier to success commonly known as the *glass ceiling* (we will discuss this topic more fully in Chapter 7, in the context of careers).

At the root of prejudicial feelings is the fact that people tend to be uncomfortable with those who are different from themselves. Today, ethnic differences between people in the workplace are not the exception, but the rule. For example, not so long ago the American workforce was composed predominantly of white

Today, ethnic differences between people in the workplace are not the exception, but the rule.

males. But that has been changing. White men now represent less than half of the current American workforce, and this figure is rapidly dropping. By 2008, 70 percent of new entrants to the workforce are expected to be women and people of color.[1] This is due to three key trends. First, there have been unequal shifts in the birth rate. Presently, three-quarters of the growth in the U.S. population is coming from African Americans, Hispanic Americans, and Asian Americans.[2] Second, growing numbers of foreign nationals are entering the American workforce, making it more ethnically diverse than ever before. Finally, we now see gender parity in the workforce.[3] About half of today's workforce is composed of women, and well over half of all adult American women work outside the home.

What do these demographic changes mean for organizations? Clearly, they bring with them several important challenges. White males, for example, must recognize that their era of dominance in the workplace is over. In fact, many white men, so used to being in the majority, are highly threatened by the prospect of losing this status.[4] For females and members of ethnic minority groups, old barriers to success must be broken, and acceptance by others must be gained as old stereotypes and prejudicial attitudes fade away only slowly. As you probably already know, this is not an easy thing to do.

Because prejudicial attitudes can have devastating effects on both people and organizations, I will examine them closely in this section of the chapter. To give you a feel for how serious prejudices can be, I describe specific targets of prejudice in the workplace and the special nature of the problems they confront. I will then follow up on this by describing various strategies that have been used to overcome prejudice in the workplace. Before doing this, however, I will take a closer look at the concept of prejudice and distinguish it from related concepts.

ANATOMY OF PREJUDICE: SOME BASIC DISTINCTIONS

When people are prejudiced, they rely on beliefs about others based on the groups to which they belong. So, to the extent that we believe that people from certain groups possess certain characteristics, knowing that someone belongs to that group will lead us to believe certain things about him or her. Beliefs of this type are referred to as **stereotypes.**

Stereotypes. As you surely realize, stereotypes, whether positive or negative, are generally inaccurate. If we knew more about someone than whatever we assumed based on his or her membership in various groups, we probably would make more accurate judgments. However, to the extent that we often find it difficult or inconvenient to learn everything we need to know about someone, we frequently rely on stereotypes as a kind of mental shortcut. So, for example, if you believe that individuals belonging to group X are lazy, and you meet person A, who belongs to group X, you likely would believe that person A is lazy too. Although this may be logical, engaging in such stereotyping runs the risk of misjudging person A. He or she might not be lazy at all, despite the fact that you assumed so based on the stereotype.

Nonetheless, assume you believe person A to be lazy. How do you feel about lazy people? Chances are that you don't like them—that is, your evaluation of person A would be negative. Would you want to hire a lazy individual, such as A, for your company? Probably not. Thus, you would be predisposed against hiring A. Your prejudice toward person A is clear.

Discrimination. Prejudicial attitudes are particularly harmful when they translate into actual behaviors. In such instances, people become the victims of others' prejudices—

FIGURE 5.1 Prejudice versus Discrimination

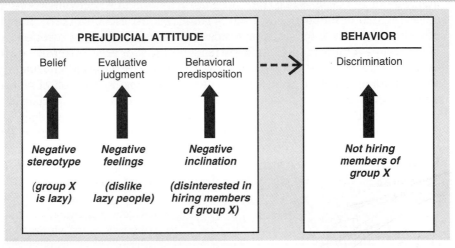

Prejudice is an attitude consisting of negative beliefs known as *stereotypes,* negative feelings about those beliefs, and negative predispositions toward people described by those stereotypes. These attitudes often lead to behavior consistent with it—that is, *discrimination.*

that is, **discrimination.** In other words, as summarized in Figure 5.1, prejudice is an attitude, whereas discrimination is a form of behavior consistent with that attitude.

Completing our example, you might refrain from hiring person *A* or giving him or her a positive recommendation. By acting this way, you would be behaving consistent with your attitude. Although this might be logical, it certainly is not in the best interest of the individual involved. After all, your behavior may be based on an attitude formed on the basis of inaccurate stereotypes. For this reason, it is important to identify ways of overcoming the natural tendency to base our attitudes on stereotypes and to unfairly discriminate between people on this basis. Later in this chapter I will outline some strategies shown to be effective in this regard. Before doing so, however, it would be useful to give you a feel for the seriousness of prejudicial attitudes in organizations today.

EVERYBODY IS A VICTIM OF PREJUDICE!

Unfortunate as it may be, we are all potential victims of prejudicial attitudes. Indeed, no matter what personal characteristics we may have, there may very well be people out there who are prejudiced against us. This is not surprising if you consider that people hold stereotypes about many different things. Whatever you look like, wherever you're from, whatever your interests, chances are good that at least some people will approach you with predisposed beliefs about what you're like. Sadly, for many groups of people, these beliefs have negative connotations, leading to discriminatory behavior. Here, I will describe some of the most prevalent targets of discrimination in American society today.

Prejudice based on age.   As people are living longer and the birth rate is holding steady, the median age of Americans is rising all the time. Despite this trend—often referred to as the "graying of America"—prejudice against older people is all too common. Although U.S. laws (e.g., the Age Discrimination in Employment Act) have done much to counter employment discrimination against older workers, prejudices continue to exist.[5] Part of the problem resides in stereotypes that older workers are too set in their ways to train and that they will tend to be sick or accident-prone. As in the case of many attitudes, these prejudices are not founded on accurate information. In fact, survey findings paint just the opposite picture: A Yankelovich poll of 400 companies found that older workers are considered very good or excellent, especially in such critical areas as punctuality, commitment to quality, and practical knowledge.

It is not just older workers who find themselves victims of prejudice, but younger ones as well. For them, part of the problem is that as the average age of the workforce advances (from an average of 29 in 1976 to 39 today), there develops a gap in expectations between the more experienced older workers who are in charge and the younger employees just entering the workforce.[6] Specifically, compared to older workers, who grew up in a different time, today's under-thirty employees view the world differently. They are more prone to question the way things are done, not to see the government as an ally, and not to expect loyalty. They are likely to consider self-development to be their main interest and are willing to learn whatever skills are necessary to make them marketable. These differing perspectives may lead older employees, who are likely to be their superiors, to feel uncomfortable with their younger colleagues.

> *Compared to older workers, who grew up in a different time, today's under-thirty employees view the world differently. They are more prone to question the way things are done, not to see the government as an ally, and not to expect loyalty.*

Prejudice based on physical condition. There are currently some 43 million Americans with disabilities, 14.6 million of whom are of working age, between 16 and 65. However, less than 30 percent of these individuals are working—and among these, most work only part time or irregularly. Clearly, there exist barriers that are keeping millions of potentially productive people from gainful employment. Often, the most formidable barriers are not physical, but attitudinal. Most people who are not physically challenged don't know how to treat and what to expect from those who are. Experts advise that people with disabilities don't want to be pitied, but respected for the skills and commitment to work they bring to their jobs. That is, they wish to be recognized as whole people who just happen to have a disabling condition, rather than a special class of "handicapped people."

Legal remedies have been enacted to help break down these barriers. For example, in the early 1990s, legislation known as the Americans with Disabilities Act (ADA) was enacted in the United States to protect the rights of people with physical and mental disabilities. Its rationale is straightforward: Simply because an employee is limited in some way, it does not mean that accommodations cannot be made to help the individual perform his or her job.[7] Companies that do not comply are subject to legal damages, and recent violators have paid dearly. However, probably the most important reason to refrain from discriminating against people with disabilities is not simply to avoid fines, but to tap into a pool of people who are capable of making valuable contributions if given an opportunity.

Prejudice against women. There can be no mistaking the widespread—and ever-growing—presence of women in today's workforce. Although 47 percent of all American workers are women, only about one large company in nine is headed by a woman.[8] Is this likely to change? Eighty-two percent of executives completing a recent *Business Week–Harris* poll indicated that it was not likely that their company would have a female CEO in the next 10 years. Thus, it appears that "women populate corporations, but they rarely run them."[9] For some recent data on the percentage of women holding top organizational positions, see Figure 5.2.[10] Equality for women in the workplace is improving, although it is a slow victory, to be sure.

Why is this the case? Although sufficient time may not have passed to allow more women to work their way into the top echelons of organizations, there appear to be more formidable barriers. Most notably, it is clear that powerful *sex role stereotypes* persist, narrow-minded beliefs about the kinds of tasks for which women are most appropriately suited. For example, 8 percent of the respondents to the *Business Week–Harris* poll indicated that females are not aggressive or determined enough to make it to the top. Although this number is small, it provides good evidence of the persistence of a nagging—and highly limiting—stereotype. The existence of this problem has led growing numbers of women to venture out on their own. In fact, twice as many women than men are starting their own small businesses. As they do so, they may be expected to hire other women, potentially breaking the pattern of prejudicial behavior that has been so prevalent for so long.

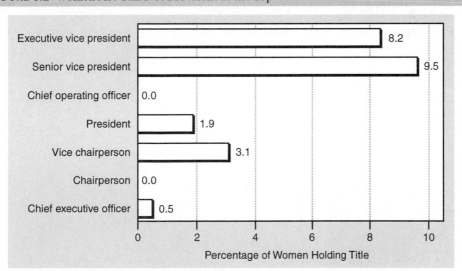

FIGURE 5.2 Women Are Still Not Prevalent at the Top

Although women and men are almost equally represented in today's workforce, very few women have worked their way up to top positions in large organizations. As of March 31, 1999, the percentage of executives holding the most powerful titles who are women is still quite small. (*Source:* Catalyst, 2000; see Note 11.)

Prejudice based on sexual orientation.   Unlike people with physical disabilities, who are protected from discrimination by federal law, no such protection exists (yet, at least!) for another group whose members are frequently victims of prejudice—gay men and lesbian women. (However, several states and over 100 municipal laws have been enacted to protect the rights of gays and lesbians in the workplace.) Unfortunately, although more people than ever are tolerant of nontraditional sexual orienta-

> *Unlike people with physical disabilities, who are protected from discrimination by federal law, no such protection exists (yet, at least!) for another group whose members are frequently victims of prejudice—gay men and lesbian women.*

tions, antihomosexual prejudice still exists in the workplace.[11] Indeed, about two-thirds of CEOs from major companies admit their reluctance to put a homosexual on a top management committee. Not surprisingly, without the law to protect them, and widespread prejudices against them, many gays and lesbians are reluctant to make their sexual orientations known openly.

Fears of being "discovered," exposed as a homosexual, represent a considerable source of stress among such individuals. For example, a gay vice president of a large office-equipment manufacturer admitted in a magazine interview that he'd like to become the company's CEO, but fears that his chances would be ruined if his sexual orientation were to become known. If the pressure of going through working life with a disguised identity is disruptive, imagine the cumulative effect of such efforts on organizations in which several employees are homosexual. Such misdirection of energy can become quite a serious threat to productivity. In the words of consultant Mark Kaplan, "gay and lesbian employees use a lot of time and stress trying to conceal a big part of their identity."[12] To work in an organization with a homophobic culture, to have to endure jokes slurring gays and lesbians, can easily distract even the most highly focused employees.

To help avoid these problems—and, out of respect for diverse sexual orientations—many organizations have adopted internal fair employment policies that include sexual orientation. In addition, some companies are actively working to prohibit discrimination on the basis of sexual orientation. Extending this idea, still other companies are now extending fringe benefits, which traditionally have been offered exclusively to opposite-sex partners, to same-sex domestic partners as well. For example, companies such as Ben & Jerry's Homemade, Inc. (in Waterbury, Vermont), MCA, Inc. (in Universal City, California), and Beth Israel Medical Center (in New York) extend fringe benefits to their employees' partners regardless of whether they are of the same sex or the opposite sex. Clearly, although some companies are passively discouraging diversity with respect to sexual orientation, others encourage it, much to their own—and their employees'—advantages.

Prejudice based on race and national origin.   The history of the United States is marked by struggles over acceptance for people of various racial and ethnic groups. Although the American workplace is now more racially diverse than ever, it is clear that prejudice lingers on.

Not only do members of various minority groups believe they are the victims of prejudice and discrimination, they are also taking action. For example, the number of complaints of discrimination based on national origin filed at the Equal Employment Opportunity Commission (EEOC) has been increasing steadily in recent years. Moreover, discrimination victims have been winning such cases. For example, in 1993 the Supreme Court of the state of Washington upheld a $389,000 judgment against a Seattle bank brought by a Cambodian American employee fired because of his accent.

Outside the courtroom, companies that discriminate pay in other ways as well—notably in lost talent and productivity. According to EEOC Commissioner Joy Cherian, employees who feel victimized "may not take the initiative to introduce inventions and other innovations," adding, "every day, American employers are losing millions of dollars because these talents are frozen."[13] Some companies are taking concrete steps to help minimize these problems. For example, AT&T Bell Labs in Murray Hill, New Jersey, is working with managers to find ways of helping the company's many ethnic minority employees get promoted more rapidly. Similarly, Hughes Aircraft Company of Los Angeles has been assigning mentors to minority group employees to help teach them about the company's culture and the skills needed to succeed. Although both examples are only modest steps, they represent very encouraging trends intended to help reduce a long-standing problem.

STRATEGIES FOR OVERCOMING WORKPLACE PREJUDICE: MANAGING A DIVERSE WORKFORCE

It's one thing to identify prejudicial attitudes and quite another to eliminate them. Two major approaches have been taken toward doing precisely this—*affirmative action plans* and *diversity management programs*.

Affirmative action plans.   Traditionally, in the United States, **affirmative action plans** have been used to promote the ethical treatment of women and members of minority groups in organizations. Derived from civil rights initiatives of the 1960s, these generally involve efforts to give employment opportunities to qualified individuals belonging to groups that traditionally have been disadvantaged. The rationale is quite reasonable: By encouraging the hiring of qualified women and minority group members into positions in which they traditionally have been underrepresented, more people will be exposed to them, forcing them to see that their negative stereotypes were misguided. Then, as these stereotypes begin to crumble, prejudice will be reduced, along with the discrimination on which it is based.

After almost 40 years of experience with affirmative action programs, it is clear that there have been major gains in the opportunities that have become available to women and minority groups. Yet, they are not always well accepted.[14] Not surprisingly, several myths about affirmative action programs have developed over the years.[15] For a summary of these, and the facts that refute them, see Table 5.1.

Diversity management programs.   In recent years, organizations have become increasingly proactive in their attempts to eliminate prejudice and have taken it upon themselves to go beyond affirmative action requirements. Their approach is not just to hire a broader group of people than usual, but to create an atmosphere in which

| TABLE 5.1 | Affirmative Action: Myth versus Fact |

Throughout the years, various myths about the ineffectiveness of affirmative action programs have become popular. However, as summarized here, these don't square with the facts. (*Source:* Based on information from Polus, 1996; see Note 16.)

Myth	*Fact*
Affirmative action has not led to increased representation of women and minorities in the workplace.	Gains have been substantial. Affirmative action programs have helped 5 million minority group members and 6 million white and minority women rise to higher positions.
Affirmative action programs reduce the self-esteem of women and racial minorities.	The opposite is true. By providing women and minority group members opportunities to succeed, their self-esteem actually increases.
Affirmative action will cause white workers to lose jobs.	Even if every unemployed African American worker (2 million) replaced a white worker (100 million), hardly any whites would be affected at all.
Affirmative action plans bring unqualified people into the workplace.	Affirmative action programs specify that only qualified women and minority group members be hired.
The public no longer supports affirmative action programs.	This is overstated. Eighty percent of Americans currently believe that some sort of affirmative action is a good idea.
Although affirmative action programs may have been useful in the 1960s, they are less beneficial today.	The playing field is still far from level. For every dollar earned by men, women earn 74 cents, African American women earn 63 cents, and Hispanic women earn only 57 cents.

diverse groups can flourish. They are not merely trying to obey the law or attempting to be socially responsible (although they surely have these concerns), but recognize that diversity is a business issue. As one consultant put it, "A corporation's success will increasingly be determined by its managers' ability to naturally tap the full potential of a diverse workforce."[16] Indeed, research has established that there is, in fact, an advantage to having a diverse workforce. A recent study of the financial success of banks that actively pursued a growth strategy (i.e., those that were getting larger rather than smaller in size) found that the more highly diverse their workforce, the better they performed financially.[17] This, in turn, added value to these banks, giving them advantages over their competitors. Clearly, promoting diversity is a wise business strategy.

It is with this in mind that three-quarters of American organizations are adopting **diversity management programs**—efforts to celebrate diversity by creating supportive, not just neutral, work environments for women and minorities. Simply put, the underlying philosophy of diversity management programs is that cracking the glass ceiling requires that women and minorities be not just tolerated, but valued. This sentiment was expressed nicely by Darlene Siedschlaw, the director of diversity for U.S. West (the Denver-based telecommunications firm), when she said, "Tapping all available human resources is the key to our corporate survival."[18]

Diversity management programs consist of various efforts not only to create opportunities for diverse groups of people within organizations but also to train people

> *Xerox's "Step-Up" program, in existence for over 35 years, has been one of the most thorough and sustained efforts to hire minority group members and train them to succeed.*

to embrace differences between them. For example, Xerox's "Step-Up" program, in existence for over 35 years, has been one of the most thorough and sustained efforts to hire minority group members and train them to succeed. Similarly, Pacific Bell and U.S. West also have made great strides at reaching out to minority group members (e.g., through internship programs), creating jobs for them in positions that have broad opportunities for advancement. Digital Equipment Corporation (DEC) has extended such initiatives in its "Valuing Differences" program, an approach that focuses on not just giving people opportunities to succeed, but valuing them *because* of their differences. DEC officials rationalize that the broader the spectrum of differences in the workplace, the richer the depth of ideas upon which the organization can draw—hopefully, leading it to be more productive. Many different companies have been actively involved in a wide variety of diversity management activities.[19] For a small sampling of these, see Table 5.2, and for a close-up look at one particularly successful program, see the **Winning Practices** section on the next page.

Although most companies have been pleased with the ways their diversity management efforts have promoted harmony between employees, such programs are not

TABLE 5.2 Diversity Management: Some Current Practices

Many of today's companies are taking proactive steps to celebrate the diverse backgrounds of their employees. Summarized here are just a few illustrative practices. (*Source:* Based on information from Gingold, 2000, and Rosen, 1991; see Note 20.)

Company	Name of Program	Description
Pitney Bowes	Pitney Bowes Celebrates Diversity Around the World	Held a weeklong outreach program consisting of over 100 events in which employees, customers, and community neighbors in 40 states and 11 countries recognized everyone else's ethnic backgrounds
DaimlerChrysler	Minority Dealer Program	Actively develops dealerships owned by members of the ethnic communities the company serves
Tellabs	You've Got ConneXions	Offers lavish rewards to employees for referring talented members of ethnic minorities
AT&T	Gay and Lesbian Awareness Week	Designates one week in which gay and lesbian issues are discussed and celebrated
Pace Food	Bilingual Operations	Presents all staff meetings and company publications in both English and Spanish
DuPont Corp.	Committee to Achieve Cultural Diversity	Holds focus groups that lead to career development programs for minority group members

WINNING PRACTICES

Diversity as a Competitive Weapon at Allstate

Although many companies have diversity management programs, the Allstate Insurance Company uses its program to create a strategic advantage. The idea is straightforward: By reflecting the racial and ethnic diversity of its customers, Allstate employees are more specific to needs that otherwise may go unrecognized, and therefore, unfulfilled, by a more homogeneous group of employees. According to Joan Crockett, Allstate's senior vice president of human resources, diversity training isn't inspired solely by the company's social conscience. Rather, "it's a compelling business strategy."[20]

Allstate's diversity management program takes a broad perspective. Not limited to only gender and ethnicity, it also pays attention to diversity with respect to age, religion, sexual orientation, and religion. Specifically, it promotes diversity along three major fronts:

- Allstate recruiters visit historically black colleges and universities to attract members of the African American community. It also recruits from schools in Puerto Rico in an effort to expand its Hispanic customer base. From the many awards it has received for its efforts in these areas (e.g., the "1999 Best Companies for Hispanics to Work"), such initiatives appear to be working. And the more such recognition the company receives, the easier it is for it to attract more individuals from these groups.

- Attracting recruits is half the battle, but retaining them is far trickier. With this in mind, Allstate carefully trains all its employees that they are expected to show no bias toward others. It also goes out of its way to encourage minority candidates by showing them the route to promotion within the company. In fact, minority candidates are considered seriously when it comes time to planning for succession up the ranks.

- Within his or her first six months on the job, each new Allstate employee receives diversity training (about three-quarters of a million person-hours have been spent thus far). This consists of classroom training that encourages people to recognize the way they see themselves and others as well as ways of sustaining a trusting environment among people who are different. Refresher courses also are given to managers from time to time.

Because it is an insurance company, it probably comes as no surprise to you that Allstate keeps careful statistical records of its diversity efforts and the company's financial success. Twice a year, the company's 53,000 employees complete a questionnaire known as the Diversity Index asking them to indicate, among other things, the extent to which they witness insensitive or inappropriate behavior at work, the amount of dignity and respect they are shown, and their beliefs about the company's commitment to delivering services to customers regardless of their ethnic background. Interestingly, the higher the overall score on the Diversity Index, the more managers are successful in promoting a diverse work environment, and the more satisfied they are. And the company's statistics show that when this happens, Allstate does a better job of satisfying and retaining its customers. Indeed, Allstate is the top insurer of lives and automobiles among African Americans and also ranks as the top insurer of homes and lives among Hispanic Americans. Clearly, at Allstate, promoting diversity is a highly successful business strategy.

Questions for Discussion

1. How might Allstate's approach, or one like it, be used in the company in which you work?
2. What problems do you believe Allstate might encounter while implementing its diversity management programs? How might they be overcome?
3. Do you believe that Allstate's programs will change attitudes (i.e., how employees really feel) as well as behavior (i.e., how they actually behave)?

automatically successful. For diversity management activities to be successful, experts caution that they must focus on accepting a range of differences between people. That is, they should not treat someone as special because he or she is a member of a certain group, but because of the unique skills or abilities he or she brings to the job. To the extent that managers are trained to seek, recognize, and develop the talents of their employees without regard to the groups to which they belong, they will help break down the stereotypes on which prejudices are based. This, in turn, will bring down the barriers that made diversity training necessary in the first place. (One of the most difficult steps in eliminating prejudicial attitudes involves recognizing the sometimes subtle ways that these have infiltrated the culture of an organization. The **Group Exercise** on p. 137 presents a useful way to help identify these negative attitudes.)

Job Satisfaction: Attitudes Toward One's Job

Do people generally like their jobs? Despite what you may hear in the news about dissatisfied workers going on strike or even acting violently toward their supervisors, overall, people are quite satisfied with their jobs. In fact, surveys have found that the percentage of people reporting satisfaction with their jobs averages between 80 and 90 percent.[21] These feelings, reflecting attitudes toward one's job, are known as **job satisfaction.** Insofar as job satisfaction plays an important role in organizations, it makes sense to ask: What factors contribute to job satisfaction? As I will point out, a great deal of research, theory, and practical application bears upon this question.

THEORIES OF JOB SATISFACTION AND THEIR IMPLICATIONS

Although there are many different approaches to understanding job satisfaction, four particular ones stand out as providing our best insight into this very important attitude—the *two-factor theory of job satisfaction, value theory,* the *social information processing model,* and the *dispositional model.*

Two-factor theory of job satisfaction. There is no more direct way to find out what causes people's satisfaction and dissatisfaction with their jobs than to ask them. Some 40 years ago, an organizational scientist assembled a group of accountants and engineers and asked them to recall incidents that made them feel especially satisfied and especially dissatisfied with their jobs.[22] His results were surprising: Different factors accounted for satisfaction and dissatisfaction. Rather than finding that the presence of certain variables made people feel satisfied and that their absence made them feel dissatisfied, as you might expect, he found that satisfaction and dissatisfaction stemmed from two different sources. For this reason, this approach is widely referred to as the **two-factor theory of job satisfaction.**

What are the two factors? In general, people were satisfied with aspects of their jobs that had to do with the work itself or to outcomes directly resulting from it. These included things such as chances for promotion, opportunities for personal growth, recognition, responsibility, and achievement. Because these variables are associated with high levels of satisfaction, these are referred to as *motivators*. However, dissatisfaction was associated with conditions surrounding the job, such as working conditions, pay, security, relations with others, and so on, rather than the work itself. Because these variables prevent dissatisfaction when present, they are referred to as *hygiene factors* (or *maintenance factors*).

Rather than conceiving of job satisfaction as falling along a single continuum anchored at one end by satisfaction and at the other by dissatisfaction, this approach conceives of satisfaction and dissatisfaction as separate variables. Motivators, when present at high levels, contribute to job satisfaction, but when absent, do not lead to job dissatisfaction—just less satisfaction. Likewise, hygiene factors contribute only to dissatisfaction when present, but not to satisfaction when absent. You may find the diagram in Figure 5.3 helpful in summarizing these ideas.

Two-factor theory has important implications for managing organizations. Specifically, managers would be well advised to focus their attention on factors known to promote job satisfaction, such as opportunities for personal growth. Indeed, several of today's companies have realized that satisfaction within their workforces is enhanced when they provide opportunities for their employees to develop their repertoire of professional skills on the job. For example, front-line service workers at Marriott

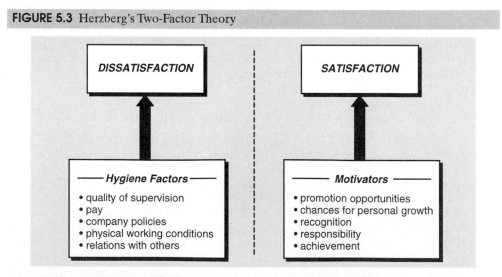

FIGURE 5.3 Herzberg's Two-Factor Theory

According to Herzberg's *two-factor theory,* job satisfaction and dissatisfaction are not opposite ends of the same continuum but independent dimensions. Some examples of *hygiene factors,* which lead to dissatisfaction, and *motivators,* which lead to satisfaction, are presented here.

Hotels, known as "guest services associates," are hired to perform a variety of tasks, including checking guests in and out, carrying their bags, and so on. Instead of doing just one job, this approach enables Marriott employees to call upon and develop many of their talents, thereby adding to their level of job satisfaction. (If you are thinking that this sounds like an example of *job enrichment,* described in Chapter 4, you are correct. Indeed, two-factor theory was greatly responsible for the development of the job enrichment approach to motivation.)

Two-factor theory also implies that steps should be taken to create conditions that help avoid dissatisfaction—and, it specifies the kinds of variables required to do so (i.e., hygiene factors). For example, creating pleasant working conditions may be quite helpful in getting people to avoid being dissatisfied with their jobs. Specifically, research has shown that dissatisfaction is great under conditions that are highly overcrowded, dark, noisy and that have extreme temperatures and poor air quality. These factors, associated with the conditions under which work is performed, but not directly linked to the work itself, contribute much to the levels of job dissatisfaction encountered.

Value theory.   Another approach to job satisfaction, known as **value theory,** takes a broader look at the question of what makes people satisfied. This theory argues that almost any factor can be a source of job satisfaction so long as it is something that people value. The less people have of some aspect of the job (e.g., pay, learning opportunities) relative to the amount they want, the more dissatisfied they will be—especially for those facets of the job that are highly valued. Thus, value theory focuses on discrepancies between what people have and what they want: The greater those discrepancies, the more dissatisfied they will be.

This approach to job satisfaction implies that an effective way to satisfy workers is to find out what they want and, to the extent possible, give it to them. Believe it or not, this is sometimes easier said than done. In fact, organizations sometimes go through great pains to find out how to satisfy their employees. With this in mind, a growing number of companies, particularly big ones, have been systematically surveying their employees. For example, FedEx is so interested in tracking the attitudes of its employees that it has started using a fully automated online survey. The company relies on information gained from surveys of its 68,000 U.S.-based employees as the key to identifying sources of dissatisfaction and testing possible remedies.

Social information processing model.   It's your first day on a new job. You arrive at the office excited about what you will be doing, but you soon discover that your coworkers are far less enthusiastic. "This job stinks," they all say, and you hear all the details when you hang out with them during lunch. Soon, your own satisfaction with the job begins to fade. What once seemed exciting now seems boring, and your boss who once seemed so pleasant, now looks more like an ogre. Your attitudes changed not because of any objective changes in the job or your boss, but because you changed your outlook based on the messages you received from your coworkers.

The idea that people's attitudes toward their jobs is based on information they get from other people is inherent in the **social information processing model.** This approach specifies that people adopt attitudes and behaviors in keeping with the cues provided by others with whom they come into contact.[23] The social information processing model is important insofar as it suggests that job satisfaction can be affected by such subtle things as the offhand comments others make. With this in mind, it makes

A few well-chosen remarks may go a long way toward raising employees' job satisfaction. By the same token, a few offhand slips of the tongue may go a long way toward lowering morale.

sense for managers to pay careful attention to what workers are thinking and feeling about their jobs. These things can be as important as actual characteristics of the jobs themselves when it comes to how people feel about them. This approach also suggests that managers should be very careful about what they say. A few well-chosen remarks may go a long way toward raising employees' job satisfaction. By the same token, a few offhand slips of the tongue may go a long way toward lowering morale.

Dispositional model of job satisfaction. Do you know some people who always seem to like their jobs, no matter what they are doing, and others who are always grumbling about their jobs? If so, you are aware of the basic premise underlying what is known as the **dispositional model of job satisfaction.** This approach says that job satisfaction is a relative stable characteristic that stays with people over various situations.[24] According to this conceptualization, people who like the jobs they are doing at one time also tend to like the jobs they may be doing at another time, even if the jobs are different (see Figure 5.4).

Supporting this approach, researchers have found that people are consistent in liking or disliking their jobs over as long as a 10-year period, although they have had several different jobs during that time. Such evidence is in keeping with the idea that job

FIGURE 5.4 The Dispositional Model of Job Satisfaction

According to the *dispositional model of job satisfaction,* some people are consistently more satisfied with their jobs than others, even when they hold different jobs throughout their lives.

satisfaction operates much like the stable dispositions toward positive and negative affect described in Chapter 3.

CONSEQUENCES OF JOB DISSATISFACTION

Thus far, I have been alluding to the negative effects of job dissatisfaction, but without specifying exactly what these are. Specifically, what consequences may be expected among workers who are dissatisfied with their jobs? Several effects have been well documented.

Employee withdrawal: Voluntary turnover and absenteeism. As you might expect, people who are dissatisfied with their jobs want little to do with them—that is, they withdraw. An extreme form of employee withdrawal is quitting, formally referred to as *voluntary turnover*. Withdrawal also may take the form of *absenteeism*.

Organizations are highly concerned about these behaviors insofar as they are very costly. The expenses involved in selecting and training employees to replace those who have resigned can be considerable. Even unscheduled absences can be expensive—averaging between $247 and $534 annually per employee, by one estimate. Although voluntary turnover is permanent, whereas absenteeism is a short-term reaction, both are effective ways of withdrawing from dissatisfying jobs.

As an example, consider the reactions of the highly dissatisfied bakery workers at the Safeway market in Clackamas, Oregon. So upset with their jobs (particularly the treatment they received from management) were the bakery's 130 employees, that they frequently were absent, quit their jobs, and had on-the-job accidents. And these were no minor problems. In one year alone, accidents resulted in 1,740 lost workdays—a very expensive problem. Accidents only occurred, of course, when employees showed up. At unpopular times, such as Saturday nights, it was not unusual for as many as 8 percent of the workers to call in sick. Almost no one stayed for more than a year.

Consistent with this incident, research has shown that the more dissatisfied people are with their jobs, the more likely they are to be absent and to resign. However, we also know that these relationships are not especially strong. In other words, job satisfaction is only modestly correlated with voluntary turnover and absenteeism. The reason for this is simple: Job dissatisfaction is likely to be only one of many factors responsible for someone's decision to resign or to stay off the job. For example, a dissatisfied employee may show up for work despite feeling dissatisfied if she believes that it is critical for her to perform certain tasks. However, still others may care so little that they would not bother to show up anyway. Thus, job satisfaction is not a particularly strong predictor of absenteeism.

The same may be said with respect to turnover. Whether people will quit their jobs is likely to depend on several factors. Among them is likely to be the availability of other jobs. So, if conditions are such that alternative positions are available, people may be expected to resign in response to dissatisfaction. However, when such options are limited, voluntary turnover may be a less viable option. Hence, knowing that one is dissatisfied with his or her job does not automatically suggest that he or she will be inclined to quit. Indeed, many people stay on jobs that they dislike.

Job performance: Are dissatisfied employees poor workers? How about those dissatisfied employees who remain on their jobs? Does their performance suffer? As in the case of withdrawal behaviors, the link between job performance and satisfaction is also quite modest. One key reason for this is that performance on some jobs is so carefully regulated (e.g., by the machinery required to do the work) that people may have little leeway to raise or lower their performance even if they wanted to. The weak negative association between job satisfaction and employee withdrawal, and the weak positive association between job satisfaction and performance are good examples of the fact that attitudes are not perfect predictors of behavior. Indeed, the important work-related attitude, job satisfaction, has been found to be only modestly related, at best, to important aspects of job behavior.

> *The weak negative association between job satisfaction and employee withdrawal, and the weak positive association between job satisfaction and performance are good examples of the fact that attitudes are not perfect predictors of behavior.*

The weak association between job satisfaction and performance appears to hold for most standard measures of performance, such as quantity or quality of work. However, when it comes to completely voluntary forms of work behavior, such as helping one's coworkers or tolerating temporary inconveniences without complaint, the connection to job satisfaction is much stronger. Such activities, which enhance social relationships and cooperation with the organization but go beyond the formal job requirements, are referred to as **organizational citizenship behaviors.** These forms of behavior, although not reflected in standard performance measures (e.g., sales figures), contribute greatly to the smooth functioning of organizations. The topic of organizational citizenship will be discussed more completely in Chapter 6. For now, I will say only that workers who feel satisfied with their jobs may be willing to help their organizations and others who have contributed to those good feelings by engaging in acts of good organizational citizenship. In fact, research has shown that the more people are satisfied with their jobs, the greater the good citizenship contributions they tend to make.

TIPS FOR PROMOTING JOB SATISFACTION

In view of the negative consequences of dissatisfaction, it makes sense to consider ways of raising satisfaction on the job. Although an employee's dissatisfaction might not account for all aspects of his or her performance, it is important to try to promote satisfaction if for no other reason than to make people happy. After all, satisfaction is a desirable end in itself. With this in mind, what can be done to promote job satisfaction? Based on the available research, I can offer several suggestions.

1. *Pay people fairly*. People who believe that their organizations' pay systems are inherently unfair tend to be dissatisfied with their jobs. (Recall our discussion of pay fairness in Chapter 4.) This applies not only to salary and hourly pay but also to fringe benefits. In fact, when people are given opportunities to select the fringe benefits they desire most, their job satisfaction tends to rise. This idea is consistent with value theory. After all, given the opportunity to receive the fringe benefits they most desire, employees may have little or no discrepancies between those they want and those they actually have.

2. *Improve the quality of supervision.* It has been shown that satisfaction is highest among employees who believe that their supervisors are competent, treat them with respect, and have their best interests in mind. Similarly, job satisfaction is enhanced when employees believe that they have open lines of communication with their superiors.

For example, in response to the dissatisfaction problems that plagued the Safeway bakery employees described earlier, company officials responded by completely changing their management style. Traditionally, they were highly intimidating and controlling, leaving employees feeling powerless and discouraged. Realizing the problems caused by this iron-fisted style, they began loosening their highly autocratic ways, replacing them with a new openness and freedom. Employees were allowed to work together toward solving problems of sanitation and safety, and were encouraged to make suggestions about ways to improve things. The results were dramatic: Workdays lost to accidents dropped from 1,740 a year down to two, absenteeism fell from 8 percent to 0.2 percent, and voluntary turnover was reduced from almost 100 percent annually to less than 10 percent. Clearly, improving the quality of supervision went a long way toward reversing the negative effects of satisfaction at this Safeway bakery.

3. *Decentralize organizational power.* Although I will present the concept of *decentralization* more fully later in this book (e.g., in Chapters 8 and 13), it is worth introducing here. **Decentralization** is the degree to which the capacity to make decisions resides in several people, as opposed to one or just a handful. When power is decentralized, people are allowed to participate freely in the process of decision making. This arrangement contributes to their feelings of satisfaction because it leads them to believe that they can have some important effects on their organizations. By contrast, when the power to make decisions is concentrated in the hands of just a few, employees are likely to feel powerless and ineffective, thereby contributing to their feelings of dissatisfaction.

The changes in supervision made at the Safeway bakery provide a good illustration of moving from a highly centralized style to a highly decentralized style. The power to make certain important decisions was shifted into the hands of those who were most affected by them. Because decentralizing power gives people greater opportunities to control aspects of the workplace that affect them, it makes it possible for workers to receive the outcomes they most desire, thereby enhancing their satisfaction. This dynamic appears to be at work in many of today's organizations. For example, at the Blue Ridge, Georgia, plant of Levi-Strauss, the sewing machine operators run the factory themselves. In a less extreme example, a committee of employees meets monthly with the CEO of Palms West Hospital (in Palm Beach County, Florida) to make important decisions concerning the hospital's operation. High satisfaction in these facilities can be traced in large part to the decentralized nature of decision-making power.

4. *Match people to jobs that fit their interests.* People have many interests, and these are only sometimes satisfied on the job. However, the more people find that they are able to fulfill their interests while on the job, the more satisfied they will be with those jobs.

For example, a recent study found that college graduates were more satisfied with their jobs when these were consistent with their college majors than when these fell outside their fields of interest. It is, no doubt, with this in mind that career counselors

> *AT&T, IBM, Ford Motor Company, Shell Oil, and Kodak systematically test and counsel their employees so they can effectively match their skills and interests to those positions to which they are best suited.*

frequently find it useful to identify people's nonvocational interests. For example, several companies, such as AT&T, IBM, Ford Motor Company, Shell Oil, and Kodak systematically test and counsel their employees so they can effectively match their skills and interests to those positions to which they are best suited. Some, including Coca-Cola and Disneyland, go so far as to offer individualized counseling to employees so that their personal and professional interests can be identified and matched.

Organizational Commitment: Attitudes Toward Companies

Thus far, our discussion has centered around people's attitudes toward their jobs. However, to fully understand work-related attitudes we also must focus on people's attitudes toward the organizations in which they work—that is, their **organizational commitment.** The concept of organizational commitment is concerned with the degree to which people are involved with their organizations and are interested in remaining within them. A generation or two ago, most workers remained loyal to their companies throughout their working lives. However, as a whole, today's workers are generally willing to move from job to job to advance their careers. For a look at some interesting statistics indicative of this trend, see Table 5.3.[25]

It is important to note that organizational commitment may be unrelated to job satisfaction. For example, a nurse may really like the kind of work she does, but dislike the hospital in which she works, leading her to seek a similar job elsewhere. By the same token, a waiter may have positive feelings about the restaurant in which he works, but may dislike waiting on tables. These complexities illustrate the importance of studying organizational commitment. Our presentation of this topic will begin by examining the different dimensions of organizational commitment. I will then review

---

TABLE 5.3   Whatever Happened to Employee Loyalty?

Recent statistics tell a sobering tale about the low levels of employee commitment among members of today's workforce. Here are just a few. (*Source:* See Note 25.)

- From August 1999 through January 2000, 66 percent of CEOs from the computer industry voluntarily resigned, as did 52 percent from the field of finance.
- A quarter of all employees indicate that they would leave their current job for a pay raise of only 10 percent. Fully half would leave for a 20 percent raise.
- Only 19 percent of new MBAs expect to stay with their first employer for more than five years. Half expect to remain for three to five years.
- Among employees who are satisfied with their company's training programs, only 12 percent plan to leave within the next year, compared to 41 percent who are dissatisfied with the training they receive.

the impact of organizational commitment on organizational functioning and conclude by presenting ways of enhancing commitment.

VARIETIES OF ORGANIZATIONAL COMMITMENT

Being committed to an organization is not only a matter of "yes or no?" or even "how much?" Distinctions also can be made with respect to "what kind?" of commitment. Specifically, scientists have distinguished between three distinct forms of commitment, which I will review here (see summary in Figure 5.5).[26]

Continuance commitment. Have you ever stayed on a job because you just don't want to bother to find a new one? If so, you are already familiar with the concept of **continuance commitment.** This refers to the strength of a person's desire to remain working for an organization due to his or her belief that it may be costly to leave. The longer people remain in their organizations, the more they stand to lose what they have invested in the organizations over the years (e.g., retirement plans, close friendships). Many people are committed to staying on their jobs simply because they are unwilling to risk losing these things. Such individuals may be said to have a high degree of continuance commitment.

Signs suggest that continuance commitment is not as high today as it used to be. Traditionally, people sought jobs that would offer them lifetime employment. Many employees would stay on their jobs their whole working lives, starting at the bottom and working their way up to the top. But today, that scenario is not readily found; the unspoken pact of job security in exchange for loyalty has all but faded from the organizational scene. In the words of a young project manager working at a New Jersey location of Prudential, "If the economy picked up, I'd consider a job elsewhere much sooner than before. I wouldn't bat an eye."[27] This expression of the willingness to leave one's job reflects a low degree of continuance commitment.

FIGURE 5.5 Three Kinds of Organizational Commitment

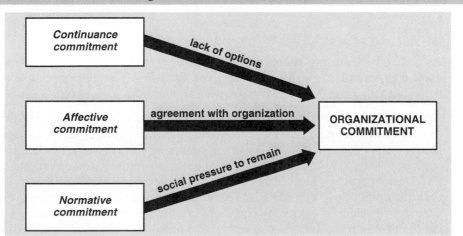

Scientists have distinguished between the three different types of organizational commitment summarized here.

Affective commitment.   A second type of organizational commitment is **affective commitment**—the strength of people's desires to continue working for an organization because they agree with its underlying goals and values. People feeling high degrees of affective commitment desire to remain in their organizations because they endorse what the organization stands for and are willing to help it in its mission. Sometimes, particularly when an organization is undergoing change, employees may wonder whether their personal values continue to be in line with those of the organization in which they continue to work. When this happens, they may question whether they still belong, and if they believe not, they may resign.

A few years ago, Ryder Truck Company successfully avoided losing employees on this basis by publicly reaffirming its corporate values. Ryder was facing a situation in which the company was not only expanding beyond its core truck leasing business but also facing changes due to deregulation (e.g., routes, tariffs, taxes). To help guide employees through the tumultuous time, chief executive Tony Burns went out of his way to reinforce the company's core values—support, trust, respect, and striving. He spread the message far and wide throughout the company, using videotaped interviews, articles in the company magazine, plaques, posters, and even laminated wallet-size cards carrying the message of the company's core values. Along with other Ryder officials, Mr. Burns is convinced that reiterating the company's values was responsible for the high level of affective commitment that the company enjoyed during this turbulent period.

Normative commitment.   A third type of organizational commitment is **normative commitment.** This refers to employees' feelings of obligation to stay with the organization because of pressures from others. People who have high degrees of normative commitment are greatly concerned about what others would think of them for leaving. They would be reluctant to disappoint their employers and concerned that their fellow employees may think poorly of them for resigning. Normative commitment, like the other two forms of commitment, is typically assessed using a paper-and-pencil questionnaire. (To see what questions measuring organizational commitment look like, and to assess your own degree of organizational commitment, see the **Self-Assessment Exercise** on p. 138.)

WHY STRIVE FOR A COMMITTED WORKFORCE?

As you might imagine, people who feel deeply committed to their organizations behave differently than those who do not. Specifically, several key aspects of work behavior have been linked to organizational commitment.[28]

Committed employees are unlikely to withdraw.   The more highly committed employees are to their organizations, the less likely they are to resign and be absent (what I referred to as *withdrawal behavior* in the context of job satisfaction). Being committed leads people to stay on their jobs and to show up when they are supposed to.[29]

This phenomenon has been demonstrated in a large-scale survey study in which dropout rates among U.S. Air Force cadets was traced over the four years required to get a degree. The more strongly committed to the service the cadets were upon entering the program, the less likely they were to drop out.[30] The finding that commitment levels could predict behavior so far into the future is a good indication of the importance of organizational commitment as a work-related attitude.

Committed employees are willing to make sacrifices for the organization. Beyond remaining in their organizations, those who are highly committed to them demonstrate a great willingness to share and make sacrifices required for the organization to thrive. For example, in the 1970s, when Chrysler Corporation was in serious financial trouble, CEO Lee Iacocca demonstrated his commitment to help the company through its difficult period by reducing his annual pay to only $1. Although this move was clearly symbolic of the sacrifices the company wanted all employees to make, there is no doubt that Iacocca's actions cost him a great deal of real money. Had he been less committed to saving Chrysler, now, Daimler Chrysler, there would have been little incentive for him to be so generous. In fact, a less strongly committed CEO may have been expected to bail out altogether.

This example should not be taken as an indication that only highly magnanimous gestures result from commitment. In fact, small acts of good organizational citizenship are also likely to occur among people who are highly committed to their organizations.[31] This makes sense if you consider that it would take people who are highly committed to their organizations to be willing to make the investment needed to give of themselves for the good of the company.

In view of these benefits of organizational commitment, it makes sense for organizations to take the steps necessary to enhance commitment among its employees. I will now describe various ways of doing this.

WAYS TO DEVELOP ORGANIZATIONAL COMMITMENT

Some determinants of organizational commitment fall outside of managers' spheres of control, giving them few opportunities to enhance these feelings. For example, commitment tends to be lower when the economy is such that employment opportunities are plentiful. An abundance of job options surely will lower continuance commitment, and there's not too much a company can do about it. However, although managers cannot control the external economy, they can do several things to make employees want to stay working for the company—that is, to enhance affective commitment.

1. *Enrich jobs.* People tend to be highly committed to their organizations to the extent that they have a good chance to take control over the way they do their jobs and are recognized for making important contributions. (You may recall reading about *job enrichment* as an approach to motivating employees discussed in Chapter 4.) This technique worked well for the Ford Motor Company. In the early 1980s, Ford confronted a crisis of organizational commitment in the face of budget cuts, layoffs, plant closings, lowered product quality, and other threats. In the words of Ernest J. Savoie, the director of Ford's Employee Development Office:

> The only solution for Ford, we determined was a total transformation of our company . . . to accomplish it, we had to earn the commitment of all Ford people. And to acquire that commitment, we had to change the way we managed people.[32]

With this in mind, Ford instituted its *Employee Involvement* program, a systematic way of involving employees in many aspects of corporate decision making. They not only got to perform a wide variety of tasks but also enjoyed considerable autonomy in doing them (e.g., freedom to schedule work and to stop the assembly line if needed). A few years after the program was in place, Ford employees became more committed to their jobs—so much so, in fact, that the acrimony that usually resulted at contract renewal time had all but vanished. Although employee involvement may not be the cure for all commitment ills, it was clearly highly effective in this case.

2. *Align the interests of the company with those of the employees.* Whenever making something good for the company also makes something good for its employees, those employees are likely to be highly committed to those companies. Many companies do this quite directly, by introducing **profit sharing plans**—that is, incentive plans in which employees receive bonuses in proportion to the company's profitability. Such plans are often quite effective in enhancing organizational commitment, especially when they are perceived to be administered fairly.

> *Prince Corporation gives its employees yearly bonuses based on several indices: the company's overall profitability, the employee's unit's profitability, and each individual's performance.*

For example, the Holland, Michigan, auto parts manufacturer, Prince Corporation gives its employees yearly bonuses based on several indices: the company's overall profitability, the employee's unit's profitability, and each individual's performance. Similarly, workers at Allied Plywood Corporation (a wholesaler of building materials in Alexandria, Virginia) receive cash bonuses based on company profits, but these are distributed monthly as well as yearly. The monthly bonuses are the same size for all, whereas the annual bonuses are given in proportion to each employee's individual contributions to total profit, days worked, and performance. These plans are good examples of some of the things companies are doing to enhance commitment. Although the plans differ, their underlying rationale is the same: By letting employees share in the company's profitability, they are more likely to see their own interests as consistent with those of their company. And when these interests are aligned, commitment is high.

3. *Recruit and select new employees whose values closely match those of the organization.* Recruiting new employees is important not only insofar as it provides opportunities to find people whose values match those of the organization but also because of the dynamics of the recruitment process itself. Specifically, the more an organization invests in someone by working hard to lure him or her to the company, the more that individual is likely to return the same investment of energy by expressing commitment toward the organization. In other words, companies that show their employees they care enough to work hard to attract them are likely to find those individuals strongly committed to the company.

In conclusion, it is useful to think of organizational commitment as an attitude that may be influenced by managerial actions. Not only might people be selected who are predisposed to be committed to the organization, but also various measures can be taken to enhance commitment in the face of indications that it is suffering.

SUMMARY: HAVE I MET THE LEARNING OBJECTIVES?

You can be certain that you have met the learning objectives for this chapter found on p. 111 if you understand the following:

1. **DISTINGUISH between prejudice, stereotypes, and discrimination**. *Prejudice* is an attitude, specifically, a negative feeling about people belonging to certain groups. These feelings are based on unfounded negative beliefs about members of these groups, referred to as *stereotypes*. Negative behavior following from prejudicial beliefs is known as *discrimination.*

2. **DISTINGUISH between affirmative action plans and diversity management programs**. *Affirmative action* plans encourage the hiring of qualified women and members of racial and ethnic minority groups to enhance their representation in the workforce. However, *diversity management* programs go beyond efforts to include different groups of people in the workplace. They involve creating supportive work environments for women and minorities by celebrating the differences between people, recognizing the unique contributions that people can make because of their differences.

3. **DESCRIBE four theories of job satisfaction.** The *two-factor theory* of job satisfaction distinguishes between two separate types of variables: those associated with the job itself (e.g., chances for growth and development), known as motivators, and those associated with conditions surrounding the job (e.g., pay, relations with others), known as hygiene factors. Motivators promote job satisfaction, and hygiene factors help avoid job dissatisfaction. Another approach to job satisfaction, *value theory,* claims that satisfaction results when there exist only small gaps between the things people want from their jobs and what they already have. The *social information processing model* specifies that people's job satisfaction is based on attitudes they develop by coming into contact with their coworkers. Finally, the *dispositional model* of job satisfaction acknowledges that some people are predisposed to be either satisfied or dissatisfied with their jobs, and tend to hold these attitudes over the course of their working lives.

4. **IDENTIFY the consequences of having dissatisfied employees and DESCRIBE ways of boosting job satisfaction.** When employees are dissatisfied with their jobs, they tend to be absent and to voluntarily resign from their positions. They also tend to refrain from doing things that go beyond what they are formally required to do, acts known as *organizational citizenship behaviors.* Job satisfaction may be enhanced by paying people fairly, by improving the quality of supervision, by decentralizing organizational power, and by matching people to jobs that fit their interests.

5. **DISTINGUISH between three forms of organizational commitment.** Organizational commitment refers to people's attitudes toward their organizations. Three types include continuance commitment (the desire to remain because of the high costs of quitting, such as a lack of alternative jobs), affective commitment (the desire to remain due to agreement with the company's values), and normative commitment (the desire to remain due to social pressures against leaving).

6. **IDENTIFY the benefits of having a committed workforce and DESCRIBE ways of developing organizational commitment.** Absenteeism and turnover are lower when people are highly committed to their organizations. Moreover, committed employees are likely to make the sacrifices needed for their companies to prosper. Organizational commitment can be enhanced by enriching jobs, by

aligning the interests of the company with those of the employees, and by recruiting and selecting prospective employees whose values closely match those of the organization.

You Be the Consultant

The president of a small manufacturing firm comes to you with a problem: The company is spending a lot of money training new employees, but 75 percent of them quit after working less than a year. Worse, they take jobs at the company's biggest competitor. Answer the following questions relevant to this situation based on the material in this chapter.

1. Drawing on research and theory on job satisfaction, what would you suspect is the cause of the turnover? What advice can you offer about how to eliminate the problem?
2. Drawing on research and theory on organizational commitment, what would you suspect is the cause of the turnover? What advice can you offer about how to eliminate the problem?
3. Suppose you find out that the greatest levels of dissatisfaction exist among employees belonging to minority groups. What would you recommend doing to eliminate the prejudice that may be responsible for the turnover?

SELF-ASSESSMENT EXERCISE

How Strongly Are You Committed to Your Job?

Questionnaires similar to the one presented here (which is based on established instruments) are used to assess three types of organizational commitment—continuance, affective, and normative.[33] Completing this scale will give you a good feel for your own level of job commitment, and how this important construct is measured.

Directions
In the space to the left of each of the 12 statements below, write the one number that reflects the extent to which you agree with it personally. Express your answers using the following scale: 1 = not at all, 2 = slightly, 3 = moderately, 4 = a great deal, 5 = extremely.

_____ 1. I stay on my job more because I have to than because I want to.
_____ 2. I feel I strongly belong to my organization.
_____ 3. I am reluctant to leave a company once I have been working there.
_____ 4. Leaving my job would entail a great deal of personal sacrifice.
_____ 5. I fee l emotionally connected to the company for which I work.
_____ 6. My employer would be very disappointed if I left my job.
_____ 7. I don't have any other choice but to stay on my present job.
_____ 8. I feel like I am part of the family at the company in which I work.
_____ 9. I feel a strong obligation to stay on my job.

_____ 10. My life would be greatly disrupted if I left my present job.
_____ 11. I would be pleased to work the rest of my life for this organization.
_____ 12. I stay on my job because people would think poorly of me for leaving.

Scoring
1. Add the scores for items 1, 4, 7, and 10. This reflects your degree of *continuance commitment*.
2. Add the scores for items 2, 5, 8, and 11. This reflects your degree of *affective commitment*.
3. Add the scores for items 3, 6, 9, and 12. This reflects your degree of *normative commitment*.

Questions to Ask Yourself
1. Which form of commitment does the scale reveal you have most? Which do you have least? Are these differences great, or are they highly similar?
2. Did the scale tell you something you didn't already know about yourself, or did it merely reinforce your intuitive beliefs about your own organizational commitment?
3. To what extent is your organizational commitment, as reflected by this scale, related to your interest in quitting your job and taking a new position?
4. How do your answers to these questions compare to those of your classmates? Are your responses similar to theirs or different from them? Why do you think this is?

_____ (**GROUP EXERCISE**)

Auditing Organizational Biases

Is your organization biased against certain groups of people? Even if you answer "no," chances are good that you may have missed some subtle and unintentional forms of prejudice lurking about. This exercise is designed to help you uncover some of these.

Directions
1. Reproduce the checklist below, making one copy for each member of the class.
2. Guided by this checklist, gather the information indicated for the organization in which you work (or, if you don't work, for any organization to which you have access) and check off all items that apply.
3. In answering, either use your existing knowledge of the company, or ask those who might know. (If you do ask others, be sure to tell them that it's for a class project!)
4. Report back to the class after one week.

Does Your Organization . . .
_____ 1. Have signs and manuals in English only although several employees speak other languages?
_____ 2. Ignore important holidays celebrated by people of certain cultures, such as Martin Luther King Day, Yom Kippur, Cinco de Mayo, or Chinese New Year?

_____ 3. Limit social events to married people?

_____ 4. Restrict training opportunities available to women and people from minority groups?

_____ 5. Emphasize male-oriented sporting events, such as football?

_____ 6. Limit its recruitment efforts to colleges and universities that have predominately white students?

_____ 7. Hire predominantly females for secretarial positions?

_____ 8. Discourage styles of dress that allow for the expression of varied cultural and ethnic backgrounds?

Questions for Discussion

1. How many of the eight items did you check off? How about other members of the class? What was the class average?

2. What items represented the biggest sources of bias? What are the potential consequences of these actions?

3. What steps could be taken to change these practices? Do you think the company would be willing to do so?

4. Going beyond this checklist, what other subtle (or not-so-subtle) signs of institutional prejudice can you identify in your company?

5. To what extent do you believe that your own awareness of prejudicial practices has been enhanced by this exercise?

NOTES

Case Notes

[1]Labich, K. (1999, September 6). No more crude at Texaco. *Fortune,* pp. 205–206, 208, 210, 212.
Roberts, B., & White, J. E. (1999). *Roberts vs. Texaco: A true story of race and corporate America.* New York: Avon.

Chapter Notes

[1] U.S. Bureau of Labor Statistics (2000). *Labor participation rates.* Washington, DC: Author.

[2] Gill, D. (1999, December 6). Diversity 101. *Business Week,* p. F12.

[3] Conlin, M., & Zellner, W. (1999, November 22). The CEO still wears wingtips. *Business Week,* pp. 85-86, 88, 90.

[4] Tsui, A. S., Egan, T. D., & O'Reilly, C. A., III. (1992). Being different: Relational demography and organizational attachment. *Administrative Science Quarterly, 37,* 549-579.

[5] Gregory, R. F. (2001). *Age discrimination in the American workplace: Old at a young age.* New Brunswick, NJ: Rutgers University Press.

[6] Raines, C. (1997). *Beyond generation X: A practical guide for managers.* Menlo Park, CA: Crisp.

[7] Magill, B. G. (1999). *Workplace accommodations under the ADA.* Washington, DC: Thompson Publishing Group.

[8] Morris, K. (1998, November 23). You've come a short way, baby. *Business Week,* pp. 82-83, 86, 88.

[9] Steinberg, R., & Shapiro, S. (1982), Sex differences in personality traits of female and male master of business administration students. *Journal of Applied Psychology, 67,* 306-310.

[10] Catalyst (2000). *The glass ceiling in 2000.* New York: Author (from the World Wide Web: www.catalystwomen.org/press/factslabor00.html. Bureau of Labor Statistics, 1999; Catalyst, 1999 Census of Women Corporate Officers and Top Earners; 1999 Census of Women Board Directors of the *Fortune* 1000.

[11] Hereck, G. M. (1998). *Stigma and sexual orientation: Understanding prejudice against lesbians, gay men, and bisexuals*. Newbury Park, CA: Sage.

[12]Martinez, M. N. (1993, June). Recognizing sexual orientation is fair and not costly. *HRMagazine,* pp. 66-68, 70-72 (quote, p. 68).

[13]Yang, C. (1993, June 21). In any language, it's unfair: More immigrants are bringing bias charges against employers. *Business Week,* pp. 110-112 (quote, p. 111).

[14] Kravitz, D. A., & Klineberg, S. L. (2000). Reactions to two versions of affirmative action among whites, blacks, and Hispanics. *Journal of Applied Psychology, 85,* 597-611.

[15] Polus, S. (1996). Ten myths about affirmative action. *Journal of Social Issues, 52,* 25-31.

[16]Thomas, R. R., Jr. (1992). Managing diversity: A conceptual framework. In S. E. Jackson (Ed.), *Diversity in the workplace* (pp. 306-317). New York: Guilford Press.

[17] Richard, O. C. (2000). Racial diversity, business strategy, and firm performance: A resource-based view. *Academy of Management Journal, 43,* 164-177.

[18] See p. 5-34)

[19] Gingold, D. (2000, July 26). Diversity today. *Fortune,* special section. Rosen, R. H. (1991). *The healthy company*.

[20] Wah, L. (1999, July-August). Diversity at Allstate: A competitive weapon. *Management Review,* pp. 24-30 (quote, p. 24).

[21] See Note 20.

[22] Herzberg, F. (1966). *Work and the nature of man*. Cleveland, OH: World.

[23] Salancik, G. R., & Pfeffer, J. R. (1978). A social information processing approach to job attitudes. *Administrative Science Quarterly, 23,* 224-252. Zalesny, M. D., & Ford, J. K. (1990). Extending the social information processing perspective: New links to attitudes, behaviors, and perceptions. *Organizational Behavior and Human Decision Processes, 47,* 205-246.

[24] Judge, T. A. (1992). Dispositional perspective in human resources research. In G. R. Ferris & K. M. Rowland (Eds.), *Research in personality and human resources management* (Vol. 10, pp. 31-72). Greenwich, CT: JAI Press.

[25] Reingold, J. (1999, March 1). Why your workers might jump ship. *Business Week,* p. 8. To attract talent, you've gotta give 'em all. (1999, July-August). *Management Review,* p. 10. Employee loyalty surprisingly strong. (1999, July-August). *Management Review,* p. 9. The List: Hot Seat in the Corner Office (2000, February 14). *Business Week,* p. 8.

[26] Meyer, J. P,. Allen, N. J., & Smith, C. A. (1993). Commitment to organizations and occupations: Extension and test of a three-component conceptualization. *Journal of Applied Psychology, 78,* 538-551.

[27] O'Reilly, B. (1994, June 13). The new deal: What companies and employees owe each other. *Fortune,* pp. 45, 47, 50, 52 (quote, p. 45).

[28] Lee, K., Carswell, J. J., & Allen, N. J. (2000). A meta-analytic review of occupational commitment: Relations with person- and work-related variables. *Journal of Applied Psychology, 85,* 799-811.

[29] Clugston, M. (2000). The mediating effects of multidimensional commitment on job satisfaction and intent to leave. *Journal of Organizational Behavior, 21,* 477-486.

[30] Lee, T. W., Ashford, S. J., Walsh, J. P., & Mowday, R. T. (1992). Commitment propensity, organizational commitment, and voluntary turnover: A longitudinal study of organizational entry processes. *Journal of Management, 18,* 15-32.

[31] Hui, C., Lam, S. S. K., & Law, K. K. S. (2000). Instrumental values of organizational citizenship behavior for promotion: A field quasi-experiment. *Journal of Applied Psychology, 85,* 822-828.

[32] See Note 18 (quote, pp. 71-72).

[33] Meyer, J. P., & Allen, N. J. (1991). A three-component conceptualization of organizational commitment. *Human Resource Management Review, 1,* 61-89.

6

Interpersonal behavior in the workplace

LEARNING OBJECTIVES

After reading this chapter, you will be able to:

1. DESCRIBE two types of psychological contracts in work relationships and the types of trust associated with each.

2. DESCRIBE organizational citizenship behavior and ways it may be promoted.

3. IDENTIFY ways cooperation can be promoted in the workplace.

4. DESCRIBE competition and what makes it inevitable in organizations.

5. DESCRIBE the causes and effects of conflict in organizations.

6. IDENTIFY two forms of deviant organizational behavior and how to minimize their occurrence.

THREE GOOD REASONS WHY YOU SHOULD CARE ABOUT. . .

Interpersonal Behavior in the Workplace

You should care about interpersonal behavior in the workplace because:

1. Cooperation between people can make life on the job not only more pleasant, but more productive.

2. The effects of conflict can be beneficial in organizations if managed properly, but harmful if mismanaged.

3. Managers can take several effective steps to reduce the likelihood of deviant organizational behavior, thereby avoiding its high costs.

141

Making the Case for... Interpersonal Relationships at Work

Starbucks Brews a Tall Cup of Trust

Think of sipping coffee at a café, and the name Starbucks is likely to come to mind. With over 2,600 shops in North America and 15 international locations, and at least one new store opening each day, it's difficult to think otherwise. As chairman and CEO of Starbucks Coffee, that suits Howard Schultz just fine. There can be no doubt that with revenues approaching $2 billion and a considerable lead over the competition in the coffeehouse business, Schultz sits atop a successful coffee empire. But Schultz will be the first to tell you that Starbucks is less about numbers than it is about people. In fact, Schultz claims that the company's success stems in a large part from the way it treats its employees.

When Schultz was a young boy growing up in the housing projects of Brooklyn, New York, he saw his father move through a succession of poor-paying blue-collar jobs that offered virtually no benefits, dashing any hopes his father ever had of achieving financial stability for his family. These bitter memories inspired Schultz to treat his own employees far better. Indeed, people who work at Starbucks acknowledge that it is like no other place they've ever worked before. At Starbucks, employees refer to each other as "partners," which they are: Each receives up to 14 percent of his or her base pay in stock options each year—even those who work part time. They also receive comprehensive medical, dental, and vision insurance, as well as a generous retirement plan. It's no wonder that Starbucks's turnover rate, under 60 percent, is four to five times lower than the national average for similar businesses—a whopping 250 percent. Although shareholders were at first skeptical about Schultz's apparent generosity, they soon realized that the low turnover rates helped the company save far more than it spent. Investing in people paid off on the bottom line.

With figures like these to support his case, Schultz claims that being benevolent is not so much an added cost as it is a way of building people's emotional ties to the company, enriching their lives as well as the company's profitability. At the core of Schultz's approach lies his belief in the importance of trust. To help promote trust, Schultz regularly meets with his partners, allowing them to understand each other better and giving them a sense of his vision for the company. In too many companies, Schultz observes, nothing of this nature goes on: "One of the outgrowths of the last 10 to 15 years in business is that there has been a fracturing of trust between senior management and rank-and-file employees....You have to change that," he adds, "but it can't be in words; it has to be in everyday actions....Once you break that trust, the ability to inspire people is over."

In sharing the company's success with those who have helped create it, most of the 40,000 people who work at Starbucks likely would agree that Schultz practices what he preaches. They also would have to acknowledge that Schultz epitomizes the first guiding principle in his company's mission statement: "To provide a great work environment and to treat each other with respect and dignity." Few would argue with him when he says, "I take these kinds of issues very, very seriously," adding, "the ability to get people to think passionately and do things as if it were their own business can only be achieved when they are truly part of the business." And, at Starbucks, that sentiment amounts to more than just a hill of beans.

The lesson we can learn from the way Howard Schultz treats his "partners" at Starbucks is important: Respecting the welfare of others, being trustworthy, and promoting harmony are key ingredients to a successful workplace. As you know, however, not all executives follow this lead. Although there are times when people do help each other, they sometimes work at cross-purposes or even go out of their way to harm one another purposely. It is these processes of working with others and against them that is the focus of this chapter on **interpersonal behavior** at work. Specifically, I will summarize a wide array of interpersonal behaviors that occur in the workplace and describe how they influence the way people work and how they feel about their jobs and organizations.

Figure 6.1 identifies the major forms of interpersonal behavior in the workplace reviewed in this chapter. This diagram organizes interpersonal behaviors along a continuum ranging from those that involve working *with* others, shown on the left, to those involving working *against* others, shown on the right. This forms a useful road map of how we will proceed in this chapter. Beginning on the left, we first will examine *prosocial behavior*—the tendency for people to help others on the job, sometimes even when there doesn't appear to be anything in it for them. Following this, we will discuss situations in which people help each other and receive help from them—that is, the tendency to *cooperate*. In the world of business, as you know, people and entire companies don't always work with each other; they also *compete* against each other—that is, as one tries to win, it forces the other to lose. Under such circumstances, it is not unusual

FIGURE 6.1 Varieties of Interpersonal Behavior

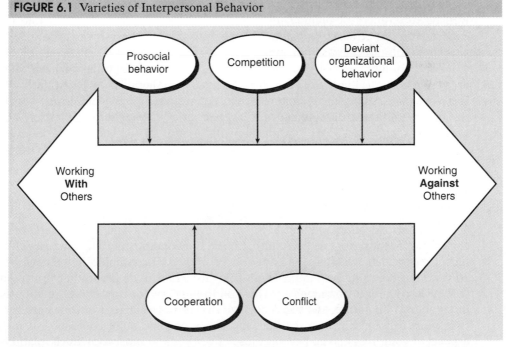

The five types of interpersonal behavior observed in organizations, and presented in this chapter, can be summarized as falling along a continuum ranging from those involving working with other people to those involving working against them.

for *conflict* to emerge, breeding ill will. And, when taken to the extreme, this results in *deviant* behavior—extreme acts such as stealing from the company or even harming other people. Before examining these various forms of behavior, I will begin by describing some of the basic dynamics that guide all forms of interpersonal behavior in the workplace.

The Dynamics of Interpersonal Relationships

To understand interpersonal behavior in organizations we must have a basic understanding of the basic building blocks of social relationships in general. What factors influence the kinds of relationships people develop between them? Although the answer to this question is more complicated than we can address here, we can identify two important factors—*psychological contracts* and *trust*.

PSYCHOLOGICAL CONTRACTS: OUR EXPECTATIONS OF OTHERS

Whenever people have relationships with each other, they are bound to have certain expectations about what things will be like in that relationship. Leave a phone message for a friend, for example, and you expect him or her to return your call. Put in a fair day's work for your boss, and you expect to get paid in return. These examples illustrate what is known as the **psychological contract**—a person's beliefs about what is expected of another in a relationship.[1]

Although these are not legal contracts, they guide what we expect of others in much the same way. However, unlike legal contracts, in which the terms are made explicit, psychological contracts are perceptual in nature. Not surprisingly, there may well be differences of opinion regarding psychological contracts: What one person expects may not be exactly what the other expects. As you know from experience, such perceptual disagreements often make interpersonal relationships challenging.

As you might imagine, the nature of the psychological contracts we have with others depends on the kind of relationships we have with them. This is particularly clear in the workplace. Suppose, for example, that you are a temporary employee working in the order-fulfillment department of a large retail e-business during the busy holiday period. You know that your relationship with your employer will have a definite ending and that it is based on a clearly defined set of economic terms. You go to work each day as scheduled, you do your job as directed, you get your paycheck, and at the end of the season, it's over. In this case, you would be said to have a **transactional contract** with your employer.[2] This relationship is characterized by an exclusively economic focus, a brief time span, an unchanging nature, and is narrow and well defined in scope.

By contrast, other relationships between employers and employees are much closer and far more complex in nature. In fact, they operate more like marriages—long term in scope, ever changing, and not clearly defined. For example, if you have worked 20 years for the same boss in the same company, chances are good that your relationship is based not only on money but also on friendship. You expect that relationship to last well into the future, and you recognize that it may change over the years. In addition, your relationship with the boss has likely become quite complex and involves aspects of your lives that go beyond those of worker and supervisor. Such relationships are based on **relational contracts**. Compared to the transactional contracts that short-term employees are likely to have with their supervisors, long-term employees are

FIGURE 6.2 Two Kinds of Psychological Contracts: A Comparison

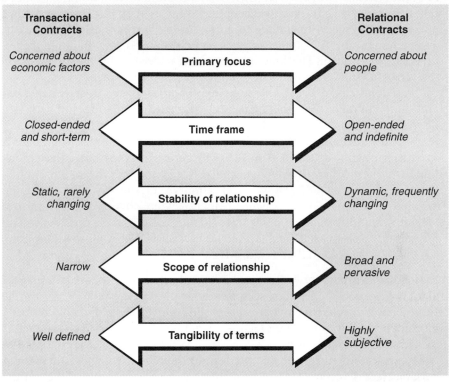

Transactional Contracts		Relational Contracts
Concerned about economic factors	Primary focus	Concerned about people
Closed-ended and short-term	Time frame	Open-ended and indefinite
Static, rarely changing	Stability of relationship	Dynamic, frequently changing
Narrow	Scope of relationship	Broad and pervasive
Well defined	Tangibility of terms	Highly subjective

Psychological contracts may be considered either transactional or relational. The characteristics of each type are summarized here. (*Source*: Based on suggestions by Rousseau & Parks, 1993; see Note 4.)

likely to have relational contracts. For a summary of the defining characteristics of transactional and relational contracts, see Figure 6.2.

THE IMPORTANCE OF TRUST IN RELATIONSHIPS

One thing that makes relationships based on transactional contracts so different from those based on relational contracts is the degree to which the parties trust each other. By **trust**, I am referring to a person's degree of confidence in the words and actions of another.[3] Suppose, for example, that your supervisor, the local sales manager, will be talking to his own boss, the district sales manager, about getting you transferred to a desirable new territory. You are counting on your boss to come through for you because he says he will. To the extent you believe that he will make a strong case on your behalf, you trust him. However, if you believe that his recommendation will not be too enthusiastic, or that he will not recommend you at all, you will trust him less.

Two major types of trust.   These examples illustrate two different types of trust, each of which is linked to different kinds of relationships we have with others. The first is known as **calculus-based trust**, a kind of trust based on deterrence.[4] Calculus-based trust exists whenever people believe that another person will behave as promised out of fear of getting punished. We trust our employers to withhold the proper amount of taxes from our paychecks, for example, insofar as they risk fines and penalties from government agencies for failing to do so. People develop calculus-based trust slowly and incrementally: Each time they behave as promised, they build up the level of trust others have for them. This kind of trust is characteristic of professional relationships—the very kind in which people develop transactional contracts.

A second kind of trust, known as **identification-based trust**, is based on accepting and understanding the other person's wants and desires. Identification-based trust occurs when people know and understand each other so well that they are willing to allow that individual to act on his or her behalf. For example, you might allow your spouse or a very good friend to select furniture for your house based on the belief that his or her judgment will be much like yours and that this person would not make any decisions of which you would disapprove. In short, you trust this person. The example described earlier in which you allow your boss to discuss your transfer with a higher-ranking official also illustrates identification-based trust. As you might imagine, identification-based trust is likely to be found in very close relationships, be they personal or professional in nature—those based on relational contracts.

How does trust develop?   Even when people first meet, chances are good that they already have some level of trust or distrust in each other. What is responsible for this? In other words, what factors are responsible for the development of trust? Scientists have identified two important factors.

First, as you may already know from experience, some people tend to be more trusting than others. Indeed, the predisposition to be trusting of others is a personality variable (see Chapter 3). You probably know some people at the extremes in this regard: Whereas some individuals are cynical and hardly ever trust anyone, there are still others who are overly trusting of people even when not warranted, to the point of being gullible.

Second, people develop reputations for being trustworthy or not trustworthy. That is, you may have learned by dealing with others directly that they will let you down and are not to be trusted. Importantly, based on their reputations, we also may judge someone to be trustworthy or untrustworthy even if we never met that person. Because violating one's trust is such an affront, we are all very sensitive to this, making such information likely to be passed along to others—either by way of offering praise about never having been let down, or by way of warning about the likelihood of getting let down (e.g., "don't trust him!").

How to promote trust in working relationships.   Obviously, it is important to be thought of as being a trustworthy individual. The success of your relationships with others depends on it. That said, the question arises as to what we can do to get others to trust us. Clearly, the key is to not let others down. But, this is easier said than done. Fortunately, there are specific things we all can do to build others' trust in us. These are as follows:

1. *Always meet deadlines.* If you promise to get something done on time, it is essential to meet that deadline. Although one or two incidents of lateness may be

overlooked, people who are chronically late in meeting deadlines rapidly gain a reputation for being untrustworthy. And when others believe that you will not meet important deadlines, they are likely to overlook you when it comes to getting any important, career-building assignments.

2. *Follow through as promised.* It is not only important to do things on time, but to perform those tasks in the manner in which others expect them to be done. Suppose, for example, that more often than not, the manager of your department gives you incomplete figures needed for you to complete important sales reports for which you are responsible. His inconsistency, not behaving as promised, will lead you to be distrusting of him. And as this individual develops a reputation within the company for not being trustworthy, he or she may come across some serious barriers to promotion.

3. *Spend time sharing personal values and goals.* Remember, identification-based trust requires a keen understanding and appreciation of another. And getting this understanding requires spending time together discussing common interests, common objectives, and the like. If you think about it, this is the key to Howard Schultz's success (described on p. 142). By taking time to get to know his employees and by sharing ideas with each other, they get to know what he is like. And this is key to developing trust.

Prosocial Behavior: Helping Others

At Starbucks, Howard Schultz goes out of his way to help his employees. Not only is he polite and attentive, as you might imagine, but he also does things to help them get ahead in life. Indeed helping others is essential to making work not only a pleasant experience but also a productive one for both individuals and their organizations. Scientists refer to such acts that benefit others in organizations as **prosocial behavior**. I will now discuss two important forms of prosocial behavior.

ORGANIZATIONAL CITIZENSHIP BEHAVIOR:
ABOVE AND BEYOND JOB REQUIREMENTS

Imagine the following scene. It's coming up on 5:00 P.M. and you're wrapping up your work for the day. You're anxiously looking forward to getting home and relaxing. While this is going on, the scene is quite different at the next cubicle. One of your colleagues has been working feverishly to complete an important report, but appears to have hit a snag. She now has little hope of getting the report on the boss's desk before he leaves for the day—that is, without your help. Pitching in to help your colleague is something you don't have to do. After all, there's nothing in your formal job description that makes it necessary for you to do so. What's more, you're quite weary after your own long day's work. However, when you see the bind your colleague is in, you put aside your own feelings and offer to stay and help her out.

In this case, although you're probably not going to win any medals for your generosity, you are being helpful, and you have gone "above and beyond the call of duty." Actions such as these, that exceed the formal requirements of one's job, are known as **organizational citizenship behavior** (or **OCB**, for short).[5] It is easy to imagine how such behaviors, although informal and sometimes minor in nature, play a very important

TABLE 6.1 Organizational Citizenship Behavior: Specific Forms and Examples

Organizational citizenship behavior (OCB) can take many different forms, most of which fall into the five major categories shown here.

Form of OCB	Examples
Altruism	Helping a coworker with a project
	Switching vacation dates with another person
	Volunteering
Conscientiousness	Never missing a day of work
	Coming to work early if needed
	Not spending time on personal calls
Civic virtue	Attending voluntary meetings and functions
	Reading memos; keeping up with new information
Sportsmanship	Making do without complaint ("Grin and bear it!")
	Not finding fault with the organization
Courtesy	"Turning the other cheek" to avoid problems
	Not "blowing up" when provoked

role when it comes to the smooth functioning of organizations. The example I just gave of volunteering to help one of your coworkers is just one of five different forms that OCB can take. For a summary of all five, including examples of each, see Table 6.1.

Why does OCB occur?   As you know, people sometimes are selfish and do not engage in OCB. What, then, lies behind the tendency to be a good organizational citizen? Although there are several factors involved, evidence strongly suggests that people's beliefs that they are being treated fairly by their organization (especially their immediate supervisors) is a critical factor. The more people believe they are treated fairly by the organization, the more they trust its management, and the more willing they are to go the extra mile to help out when needed. By contrast, those who feel that their organizations are taking advantage of them are untrusting and not at all likely to engage in OCB.

Does OCB really matter?   As you might imagine, the effects of OCB are difficult to assess because OCB is generally not included as part of any standard performance measures that a company gathers about its employees. However, OCB does have important effects on organizational functioning. Specifically, people's willingness to engage in various types of OCB is related to such work-related measures as job satisfaction and organizational commitment, which, as described in Chapter 5, are related to organizational functioning in a number of complex ways.[6] In addition, being a good organizational citizen can have important effects on recruiting efforts. The more positive statements current employees make about the companies where they are employed, the more effectively those companies will be able to recruit the best new employees.[7] In conclusion, although the effects of OCB may be indirect and difficult to measure, they can be very profound.

Tips for promoting OCB.   Given the importance of OCB, it makes sense to highlight some specific ways of bringing it about. Several potentially useful suggestions may be made.

1. *Go out of your way to help others*. The more you help your colleagues, the more likely they will be to help you. Soon, before you know it, with everyone helping everyone else, prosocial behavior will become the norm—that is, a widely accepted practice in the company.
2. *Be an example of conscientiousness*. Employees are inclined to model the citizenship behavior of their supervisors. If, as a manager, you set a good example by coming to work on time and not making personal phone calls, your subordinates may be expected to follow your lead. Although it might not be this easy, at least you have some credibility when you do insist that your subordinates refrain from these forms of poor citizenship.
3. *Make voluntary functions fun*. It only makes sense that employees will not be motivated to attend voluntary meetings or corporate functions of one kind or another (e.g., picnics, award banquets) unless these are enjoyable. People are more likely to show the good citizenship associated with attending corporate functions when the company makes it worthwhile for them to do so. After all, the more desirable it is for someone to be prosocial, the more likely that individual will be a good organizational citizen.
4. *Demonstrate courtesy and good sportsmanship*. When something goes wrong, don't "make a stink," rather, just "grin and bear it." Someone who "blows up" at the slightest provocation not only is a poor organizational citizen, but also may discourage good citizenship among others.

Although these suggestions all seem like common sense, they certainly are not common practice. Even if you have only limited work experience you probably can tell a few tales about one or more individuals who behaved just the opposite of the manner outlined here. Keeping in mind how unpleasant these people made life in your organization may be just the incentive you need to follow these guidelines. Doing so will keep you from becoming a bad organizational citizen yourself—and from encouraging others to follow suit.

WHISTLE-BLOWING: HELPING THROUGH DISSENT

Sometimes employees face situations in which they recognize that their organization is behaving in an improper fashion. To right the wrong they reveal the improper or illegal practice to someone who may be able to correct it—an action known as **whistle-blowing**.[8] Formally, whistle-blowing is the disclosure by employees of illegal, immoral, or illegitimate practices by employers to people or organizations able to affect action.

Is whistle-blowing a prosocial action? From the point of view of society, it usually is. In many instances, the actions of whistle-blowers can protect the health, safety, or security of the general public. For example, an employee of a large bank who reports risky or illegal practices to an appropriate regulatory agency may be protecting thousands of depositors from considerable delay in recovering their savings. Similarly, an individual who blows the whistle on illegal dumping of toxic chemicals by his or her company may save many people from serious illness. For a summary of some actual cases of whistle-blowing, see Table 6.2.[9]

As you might imagine, blowing the whistle on one's employer is likely to be a very costly act for employees, as they often find themselves facing a long, uphill battle attempting to prove the wrongdoing. They also frequently face ostracism and loss of

TABLE 6.2 Whistle-blowing: Some Examples

As the following examples illustrate, employees blow the whistle on many different types of organizations accused of committing a wide range of questionable activities. (*Sources:* See Note 9.)

Whistleblower	Action
Paul van Buitenen	Went public in 1999 with claims of fraud and corruption within the European Commission
An unnamed U.S. Customs inspector	Alerted Congress of security problems at the Miami airport in 1995 after management took no action
Tonya Atchinson	This former internal auditor at Columbia-HCA Healthcare Corp. charged the company with illegal Medicare billing
Daniel Shannon	An in-house attorney for Intelligent Electronics protested the company's alleged misuse of marketing funds from computer manufacturers
Robert Young	This agent for the Prudential Insurance Co. in New Jersey accused company agents of encouraging customers to needlessly sell some policies and buy more expensive ones, boosting their commissions
Bill Bush	This manager at the National Aeronautics and Space Administration (NASA) went public with the administration's policy of discouraging the promotion of employees older than 54 years of age

their jobs in response to disloyalty. For example, five agents from State Farm Insurance were fired recently after they accused the company of various consumer abuses.[10] Although various laws prevent employers from firing people directly because they blew the whistle, organizations frequently find alternative official grounds for dismissing "troublemakers."[11] It is not surprising, therefore, that six senior employees of the company that runs the 900–mile Trans–Alaskan pipeline chose to remain anonymous when voicing their complaints about safety violations to BP Amoco.[12] It is interesting to note that although whistle-blowing often involves considerable personal cost, the importance of the action motivates some people to go through with it.

Cooperation: Providing Mutual Assistance

Thus far, our discussion has focused on one person's giving help to another. However, it is probably even more common in organizations to find situations in which assistance is mutual, with two or more individuals, teams, or organizations working together toward some common goal. Such efforts are known as acts of **cooperation**. As you know from experience, people do not always cooperate with each other. As you might imagine, cooperation is essential to organizational success. Unless individuals, teams, and entire organizations cooperate with each other, all are likely to fall short of their objectives. With this in mind, it makes sense to consider the factors that bring about cooperation, both within organizations and between them as well.

COOPERATION WITHIN ORGANIZATIONS

Several factors affect the tendency for people to cooperate with each other within organizations. I will review some of the key ones here:

The reciprocity principle.   We all know that The Golden Rule admonishes us to do unto others as we would have them do unto us. However, this doesn't describe exactly the way people behave. Instead of treating others as we would like to be treated, most people treat others as they have been treated in the past by them. In short, we are more inclined to follow a different principle: "An eye for an eye and a tooth for a tooth." Social scientists refer to this as the principle of **reciprocity**—the tendency to treat others as they have treated us.

> *Instead of treating others as we would like to be treated, most people treat others as they have been treated in the past by them.*

To a great extent, the principle of reciprocity describes the way people behave when cooperating with others.[13] The key task in establishing cooperation in organizations is straightforward: getting it started. Once individuals or teams have begun to cooperate, the process may be largely self-sustaining. That is, one unit's cooperation encourages cooperation among the others. To encourage cooperation, therefore, managers should attempt to get the process under way.

Personal orientation.   As you know from experience, some people tend to be more cooperative, by nature, than others. In contrast, other people tend to be far more competitive—interested in doing better than others in one way or another. Not surprisingly, scientists have found that people can be reliably classified into four different categories in terms of their natural predispositions toward working with or against others.[14] These are as follows:

- **Competitors**—People whose primary motive is doing better than others, besting them in open competition
- **Individualists**—People who care almost exclusively about maximizing their own gain, and don't care whether others do better or worse than themselves
- **Cooperators**—People who are concerned with maximizing joint outcomes, getting as much as possible for their team
- **Equalizers**—People who are primarily interested in minimizing the differences between themselves and others

Although there are individual differences, men as a whole tend to favor a competitive orientation, attempting to exploit others around them. By contrast, women tend to favor a cooperative orientation, preferring to work with other people rather than against them, and they also tend to develop friendly ties with others.[15] Still, it would be a mistake for managers to assume that men and women automatically fall into certain categories. Instead, it is widely recommended that managers take the time to get to know their individual workers' personal orientations and then match these to the kinds of tasks to which they may be best suited. For example, competitors may be effective in negotiation situations whereas cooperators may be most effective in teamwork situations. (To get a sense of which category best describes you, complete the **Self-Assessment Exercise** on p. 164.)

Organizational reward systems.   It is not only differences between people that leads them to behave cooperatively, but differences in the nature of organizational reward systems as well. Despite good intentions, companies all too often create reward systems that lead their employees to compete against each other. This would be the case, for example, in a company in which various divisions sell products that compete with each other. Sales representatives who receive commissions for selling their division's products have little incentive to help the company by attempting to sell another division's products. In other words, the company's reward system discourages cooperative behavior.

With an eye toward eliminating such problems, and fostering cooperation, many of today's companies are adopting **team-based rewards**.[16] These are organizational reward systems in which at least a portion of an individual's compensation is based on the performance of his or her work group. The rationale behind these incentive systems is straightforward (and follows from the principle of reinforcement described in Chapter 2): People who are rewarded for contributing to their groups' performance will focus their energies on group performance. In other words, they will cooperate with each other. Although there are many difficult challenges associated with setting up team-based reward programs that are manageable (e.g., based on measurable rewards that really matter) and that people find acceptable (e.g., ones that are administered fairly), companies that have met these challenges have reaped benefits in terms of increased job satisfaction and productivity.

COMPETITION: THE OPPOSITE OF COOPERATION

Question: If competition is so beneficial, why does it not always occur? In other words, why do people or organizations with similar goals not always join forces? To a large extent, the answer is that some goals cannot be shared. There can be only one winner of the Super Bowl and one winner of the World Series; the teams cannot share these prizes. Similarly, when several large companies are courting the same small company as a takeover candidate, there can be only one winner as well. Such conditions breed **competition**—a pattern of behavior in which each person, group, or organization seeks to maximize its own gains, often at the expense of others. For a graphic summary of the differences between cooperation and competition, see Figure 6.3.

It is important to recognize that competition and competition might be occurring at the same time. That is, people may have **mixed motives**—the motive to cooperate and the motive to compete may be operating simultaneously. Take the game of baseball, for example. Players may cooperate with each other, such as when it comes to getting a double play (where the shortstop might flip a ground ball to the second baseman, who then throws it to the first baseman). At the same time, they also may be competing against each other for individual records. And, of course, they are working together to compete against the other team. Clearly, there are a lot of things going on in such situations: The motives to cooperate and to compete often coexist within the same situation.

In business, competition is the natural order of things. Employees in the same company compete for a promotion, companies compete for the same government contract, and of course, retail businesses compete for the same customers. In recent years, for example, several start-up companies, such as Victory and Excelsior-Henderson have made high-quality motorcycles that compete very favorably with "cruisers" from the legendary Harley-Davidson.[17] They are trying to attract customers by offering more bike for

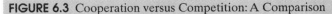

FIGURE 6.3 Cooperation versus Competition: A Comparison

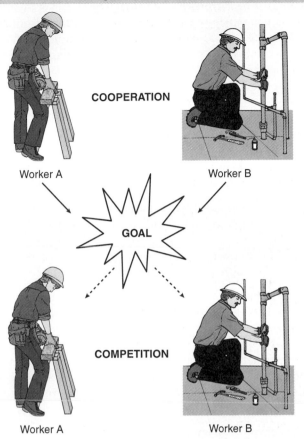

When *cooperating* with each other, people work together to attain the same goal, which they share. However, when *competing* against one another, each person works to attain the same goal at the exclusion of the other.

the money, while Harley fans continue to be attracted to something less tangible—that company's reputation. Although only time will tell the outcome of this competition, it is clear that no matter what happens, companies will always be competing against each other.

Conflict: The Inevitable Result of Incompatible Interests

If we conceive of prosocial behavior and cooperation as being at one end of a continuum (such as in Figure 6.1), then it makes sense to conceive of *conflict as* approaching the other end. In the context of organizations, **conflict** may defined as a process in which one party perceives that another party has taken or will take actions that are

> *About 20 percent of managers' time is spent dealing with conflict and its effects.*

incompatible with one's own interests. As you might imagine, conflict occurs quite commonly in organizations. In fact, about 20 percent of managers' time is spent dealing with conflict and its effects.[18] Considering this, it makes sense to examine the causes and consequences of conflict, and ways to effectively manage conflict that occurs in the workplace.

CAUSES OF CONFLICT

The conflicts we face in organizations may be viewed as stemming from a variety of causes, including both our interactions with other people and the organization itself. Here are just a few of the most important sources of organizational conflict.

Grudges.   All too often, conflict is caused when people who have lost face in dealing with someone attempt to "get even" with that person by planning some form of revenge. Employees involved in this kind of activity are not only going out of their way to harm one of their coworkers, but by holding a grudge, they are wasting energy that could be devoted to more productive organizational endeavors.

Malevolent attributions.   Why did someone do something that hurt us? To the extent that we believe that the harm we suffer is due to an individual's malevolent motives (e.g., the desire to hurt us), conflict is inevitable. However, whenever we believe that we suffered harm because of factors outside someone's control (e.g., an accident), conflict is less likely to occur. (This is an example of the attribution process addressed in Chapter 2.) This causes problems in cases where we falsely attribute the harm we suffer to another's negative intent when, in reality, the cause was externally based.

Destructive criticism.   Communicating negative feedback in organizations is inevitable. All too often, however, this process arouses unnecessary conflict. The problem is that some people make the mistake of using **destructive criticism**—that is, negative feedback that angers the recipient rather than helps this person do a better job. The most effective managers attempt to avoid conflict by using constructive criticism instead. For some important comparisons between these two forms of criticism, see Table 6.3.

Distrust.   The more strongly people suspect that some other individual or group is out to get them, the more likely they are to have a relationship with that person or group that is riddled with conflict. In general, companies that are considered great places in which to work are characterized by high levels of trust between people at all levels.

Competition over scarce resources.   Because organizations never have unlimited resources (such as space, money, equipment or personnel), it is inevitable that conflicts will arise over the distribution of those resources. This occurs in large part because of a self-serving tendency in people's perceptions (see Chapter 2)—that is, people tend to overestimate their own contributions to their organizations. Believing that we made greater contributions leads us to feel more deserving of resources than others. Inevitably, conflict results when others do not see it this way.

TABLE 6.3 Constructive versus Destructive Criticism: A Comparison	

The factors listed here distinguish constructive criticism (negative feedback that may be accepted by the recipient to improve his or her performance) from destructive criticism (negative feedback likely to be rejected by the recipient and unlikely to improve his or her performance).

Constructive Criticism	*Destructive Criticism*
Considerate—protects the recipient's self-esteem	Inconsiderate—harsh, sarcastic, biting
Does not contain threats	Contains threats
Timely—occurs as soon as possible after the substandard performance	Not timely—occurs after an inappropriate delay
Does not attribute poor performance to internal causes	Attributes poor performance to internal causes (e.g., lack of effort, motivation, ability)
Specific—focuses on aspects of performance that were inadequate	General—a sweeping condemnation of performance
Focuses on performance, not on the recipient	Focuses on the recipient—his or her personal characteristics
Motivated by desire to help the recipient improve	Motivated by anger, desire to assert dominance over the recipient, desire for revenge
Offers concrete suggestions for improvement	Offers no concrete suggestions for improvement

CONSEQUENCES OF CONFLICT: BOTH BAD AND GOOD

The word *conflict* doubtlessly brings to mind negative images—thoughts of anger and confrontation. Indeed, there is no denying the many negative effects of conflict. But, as you will see, conflict has a positive side as well. With this in mind, I will now identify the many consequences of conflict in organizations, both negative and positive.

Negative consequences of conflict. The major problem with conflict, as you know from experience, is that it yields strong negative emotions. However, these emotional reactions mark only the beginning of a chain of reactions that can have harmful effects in organizations.

The negative reactions, besides being quite stressful, are problematic in that they may divert people's attention from the task at hand. For example, people who are focused on getting even with a coworker and making him look bad in front of others are unlikely to be attending to the most important aspect of their jobs. In particular, communication between individuals or teams may be so adversely affected that any coordination of effort between them is compromised. Not surprisingly, such lowered coordination tends to lead to decrements in organizational functioning. In short, organizational conflict has costly effects on organizational performance. For some helpful suggestions on how to avoid many of these problems, see Table 6.4.[19]

Positive consequences of conflict. Have you ever worked on a team project and found that you disagreed with someone on a key matter? If so, how did you react? Chances are good that you fell short of sabotaging that person's work or acting aggressively. In fact,

TABLE 6.4 How to Manage Conflict Effectively

Although conflict is inevitable, there are concrete steps that managers can take to avoid the negative consequences that result from conflict between people in the workplace. (*Source*: Based on suggestions by Bragg, 1999; see Note 19.)

- Agree on a process for making decisions *before* a conflict arises. This way, when a conflict needs to be addressed, everyone knows how it is going to be handled.
- Make sure everyone knows his or her specific areas of responsibility, authority, and accountability. Clarifying these things avoids potential conflicts when people either avoid their responsibilities or overstep their authority.
- Recognize conflicts stemming from faulty organizational systems, such as a pay system that rewards one department at the expense of another. In such cases, work to change the system rather than training employees.
- Recognize the emotional reactions to conflict. Conflicts will not go away until people's hurt feelings are addressed.
- Consider how to avoid problems rather than assigning blame for them. Questions such as "Why did you do that?" only make things worse. It is better to ask, "How can we make things better?"
- Conflicts will not go away by making believe they don't exist; doing so will only make them worse. Avoid the temptation not to speak to the other party and discuss your misunderstandings thoroughly.

the conflict may have even brought the two of you to the table to have a productive discussion about the matter at hand. As a result of this discussion you may have even improved relations between the two of you and the quality of the decisions that resulted from your joint efforts. If you can relate to this scenario, then you already recognize an important fact about organizational conflict—that some of its effects are positive.

Specifically, organizational conflict can be the source of several benefits. Among these are the following.

- Conflict may improve the quality of organizational decisions (as in the above example).
- Conflict may bring out into the open problems that have been previously ignored.
- Conflict may motivate people to appreciate each others' positions more fully.
- Conflict may encourage people to consider new ideas, thereby facilitating change.

In view of these positive effects of conflict, the key is to make sure that more of these benefits occur as opposed to costs. It is with this goal in mind that managers work so diligently to manage organizational conflict effectively. We will now examine some of the ways they go about doing this.

REDUCING CONFLICT THROUGH NEGOTIATION

When conflicts arise between individuals, groups, or even entire organizations, the most common way to resolve them is to work together to find a solution that is acceptable to all the parties involved. This process is known as **bargaining** (or **negotiation**).

Formally, we may define bargaining as the process in which two or more parties in dispute with each other exchange offers, counteroffers, and concessions in an attempt to find a mutually acceptable agreement.

Obviously, bargaining does not work when the parties rigidly adhere to their positions without budging—that is, when they "stick to their guns." For bargaining to be effective, the parties involved must be willing to adjust their stances on the issues at hand. And, for the people involved to be willing to make such adjustments, they must believe that they have found an acceptable outcome—one that allows them to claim victory in the negotiation process. For bargaining to be most effective in reducing conflict, this must be the case for all sides. That is, outcomes must be found for all sides that allow them to believe that they have "won" the negotiation process—results known as **win–win solutions**. In win–win solutions, everybody wins, precisely as the name implies.

Tips for negotiating win-win solutions.   Several effective ways of finding such win–win solutions may be identified. (For practice in putting these techniques to use, see the **Group Exercise** on p. 165.)

1. *Avoid making unreasonable offers*. Imagine that a friend of yours is selling a used car with an asking price of $10,000—the car's established "book value." If you were to attempt to "low ball" the seller by offering only $1,000, your bad-faith offer might end the negotiations right there. A serious buyer would offer a more reasonable price, say $9,000—one that would allow both the buyer and the seller to come out ahead in the deal. In short, extreme offers tend to anger one's opponents, sometimes ending the negotiation process on a sour note, allowing none of the parties to get what they want.
2. *Seek the common ground*. Often people in conflict with others assume that their interests and those of the other party are completely incompatible. When this occurs, they tend to overlook the fact that they actually might have several areas of interest in common. When parties focus on the areas of agreement between them, it helps bring them together on the areas of disagreement. So, for example, in negotiating the deal for purchasing the used car, you might establish the fact that you agree to the selling price of $9,000. This verifies that the interests of the buyer and the seller are not completely incompatible, thereby encouraging them to find a solution to the area in which they disagree, such as a payment schedule. By contrast, if either party believed that they were completely far apart on all aspects of the deal, it would be less likely to negotiate a win–win solution.
3. *Broaden the scope of issues considered*. Sometimes, parties bargaining with each other have several issues on the table. When this occurs, it is often useful to consider the various issues together as a total package. Labor unions often do this in negotiating contracts with company management whenever they give in on one issue in exchange for compensation on another issue. So, for example, in return for not freezing wages, a company may agree to concede to the union's other interests, such as gaining representation on key corporate committees. In other words, compared to bargaining over single issues (e.g., the price of the used car), when the parties get to bargaining across a wide array of issues, it often is easier to find solutions that are acceptable to all sides.

4. *Uncover "the real" issues.* Frequently, people focus on the conflicts between them in only a single area although they may have multiple conflicts between them—some of which are hidden. Suppose, for example, that your friend is being extremely stubborn when it comes to negotiating the price of the used car. He's sticking firmly to his asking price, refusing to budge despite your reasonable offer, possibly adding to the conflict between you. However, it may be the case that there are other issues involved. For example, he may be trying to "get even" with you for harming him several years ago. In other words, what may appear to be a simple conflict between two people may actually have multiple sources. Finding long-lasting solutions requires identifying all the important issues—even the hidden ones—and bringing them to the table.

As you might imagine, it is almost always far easier to say these things than to do them. Indeed, when people cannot come to an agreement about something, they sometimes become irrational, not seeking common ground, and not taking the other's perspective needed to find a win–win solution, but only thinking of themselves. In such circumstances, third parties can be useful to break the deadlock. For a description of a popular approach for doing this, see the **Winning Practices** section on the next page.

Deviant Organizational Behavior

As you know from experience, some employees do things that intentionally violate the norms of organizations or the formal rules of society, resulting in negative consequences. We refer to such acts as **deviant organizational behavior**. For example, more people than you might imagine steal from their employers: Three-quarters of all employees have stolen company property at least once. Some individuals do things like taking excessively long breaks and evading orders, and in extreme cases, vandalizing the workplace, sabotaging others, even committing acts of physical violence. Deviant organizational behavior represents the extreme right side of the continuum in Figure 6.1, reflecting acts against others. Although there are many different forms of deviant organizational behavior, we will discuss the two best understood—*workplace aggression* and *employee theft*.

WORKPLACE AGGRESSION: WHEN THINGS GET OUT OF HAND

All too often, our newspapers are full of stories of ex-employees who went berserk and returned to the workplace to murder their former bosses and coworkers. Despite all the publicity that such acts get, they, quite fortunately, are very rare. Although over 800 people are murdered at work each year in the United States (and even more in some other countries), most of these crimes are committed by outsiders, such as customers.[22]

Although over 800 people are murdered at work each year in the United States (and even more in some other countries), most of these crimes are committed by outsiders, such as customers.

Such violent acts are merely one form of more general reaction to conflict known as **workplace aggression**. This term refers to acts of harming other people in one's organization or the organization itself. This can take many dramatic forms that fall short of all-out violence. For example, workplace

Settling Disputes Quickly and Inexpensively Out of Court: Alternative Dispute Resolution

When a customer canceled a $60,000 wedding reception, Anthy Capetola, a caterer from Long Island, New York, was able to fill that time slot with an event bringing in only half as much.[20] Although Capetola was harmed by the customer's actions, as you might imagine, that customer was unwilling to cough up the lost revenue. Many business owners in Capetola's shoes would seek restitution by taking the customer to court, resulting in a delay of many months, or even years, and a huge bill for litigation, not to mention lots of adverse publicity. Fortunately, in their contract, Capetola and the customer agreed to settle any future disagreements using what is known as **alternative dispute resolution (ADR)**. This refers to a set of procedures in which disputing parties work together with a neutral party who helps them settle their disagreements out of court.

There are two popular forms of ADR—*mediation* and *arbitration*. **Mediation** involves having a neutral party (the *mediator*) work together with both sides to reach a settlement. Typically, mediators meet together and separately with each side and try to find a common ground that will satisfy everyone's concerns. Mediators do not consider who's wrong and who's right, but set the stage for finding a resolution. And that they do! In fact, by one recent estimate mediators help disputing parties find solutions about 85 percent of the time. As you might imagine, however, for mediation to work the two sides must be willing to communicate with each other. When this doesn't happen, ADR may take the form of **arbitration**. This involves having a neutral third party listen to the facts presented by each side who then makes a final, binding decision.

ADR is very popular these days because it helps disputants reach agreements rapidly (often in a matter of a day or two, compared to months or years for court trials) and inexpensively (usually for just a few thousand dollars split between the parties, compared to astronomical sums for attorney fees). Moreover, it keeps people who otherwise might end up in court out of the public eye, which could be damaging to their reputations—even the party in whose favor the judgment goes. Because it is low-key and nonconfrontational, mediation is particularly valuable in cases in which the parties have an ongoing relationship (business or personal) that they do not want to go sour.[21] After all, the mediation process brings the parties together, helping them see each other's side—something that is usually lost for sure in the heat of a courtroom battle.

Not surprisingly, the popularity of ADR these days has led to the development of several companies specializing in rendering mediation and arbitration services. The largest of these, the American Arbitration Association, boasts offices in half the U.S. states, with a caseload pushing 80,000 per year. It maintains a file of some 18,000 arbitrators and mediators (typically lawyers, businesspeople, and former judges), enabling it to find a neutral party who is experienced in just about any kind of dispute that people are likely to have.

Questions for Discussion

1. For what kinds of disputes would ADR be most effective?
2. What challenges are mediators most likely to face in the course of resolving disputes?
3. What do you consider the major drawbacks of ADR?

aggression may include a wide range of behaviors, such as bringing a lawsuit against the company, sabotaging an associate's work, or even saying negative things about someone else or the company itself.[23] In short, although some of these behaviors are more destructive than others, these are all extremely negative ways in which people sometimes respond to conflicts that they are having.

Causes of workplace aggression.   As you might imagine, some people, by nature, are more inclined than others to behave aggressively. Indeed, we all probably know someone who has a "short fuse," and is prone to "explode" at the slightest provocation. Of course, managers must be sensitive to how they treat such individuals. However, this isn't always easy. With few exceptions, most people don't show any advance signs that they're going to behave aggressively. Indeed, when bystanders are interviewed about the employee who "went postal" by killing his coworkers, they typically say that he "seemed normal" and that they "couldn't see it coming." So, short of subjecting everyone to intense psychological testing, screening these individuals is not always practical.

Fortunately, however, most acts of aggression are not extreme, and they are committed by everyday people who just happen to be reacting strongly to adverse situations they have experienced. Typically, aggressive behavior in the workplace is the result of two different factors. The first is *unfair treatment*. Indeed, people who believe they have been unfairly passed up for raises or promotions sometimes believe that they have been treated unfairly. Perhaps they believe that their boss is biased against them, "has it in for them," or that the company's entire human resources system is corrupted in some fashion. It is not unusual for workers harboring such beliefs to express hostility openly (e.g., belittling their boss), to impede the work of others (e.g., not returning phone calls), or in some cases to behave violently by destroying company property.

Workplace aggression also results when changes make people feel insecure about their futures with their companies. For example, corporate downsizing and layoffs threaten people's livelihoods. It is not surprising, therefore, that individuals who are affected by such moves have been known to go on strike against their companies. In so doing, they are attempting to harm the company that threatens to harm them. Not surprisingly, some strikes become violent, as picketers lash out at "scabs" who break their picket lines, frustrating their efforts.

Tips for managing workplace aggression.   Although all workplace aggression cannot be eliminated, practicing managers can take several concrete steps to minimize its occurrence. Here are three such tips:

1. *Establish clear disciplinary procedures*. It is not unusual for people to curb aggressive reactions in organizations that have clearly understood disciplinary procedures in place. Such programs send strong messages that inappropriate behavior will not be tolerated and that it will be punished if it occurs. Such deterrents go a long way toward many forms of workplace aggression.[24]

2. *Treat people fairly*. To the extent that people behave aggressively in response to unfair treatment, it follows that managers may reduce reactions of this type by behaving fairly. In particular, people are highly sensitive to what is called **interactional justice**—people's perceptions of the fairness of the way they are treated by others. Managers who belittle their subordinates and who fail to

show them the dignity and respect they deserve unknowingly may be promoting aggressive behavior. In some cases, this takes the form of people suing their former employers on the grounds of wrongful termination. Individuals who file such lawsuits are clearly striking back at their former employers, attempting to get even with them for harming them. Recent research has shown that the more unfairly people believe they have been treated on the job (i.e., the less dignity and respect they have been shown), the more likely they are to file lawsuits against their former employers.[25] Obviously, this provides a strong lesson to managers about the importance of treating people fairly, something that is easily under their control.

3. *Train managers in ways to recognize and avoid aggression.* Although we all recognize aggressive behavior when it occurs, too few of us know how to recognize potentially dangerous situations before they become serious. Managers should be trained in techniques for recognizing threats and be familiar with ways to defuse those threats. Probably the most significant tip in this regard: Take all threats seriously. Never assume that someone is merely making a joke. Talking calmly and rationally to someone who appears to be troubled can go a long way toward avoiding a potentially explosive situation.

EMPLOYEE THEFT: TAKING WHAT'S NOT YOURS

Retail stores are very concerned with problems of shoplifting, as you know. What you might not know, however, is that companies lose more money and goods from their own employees than from customers. Although estimates of costs of employee theft are quite varied, it is clear that the figures are staggering. For some recent figures on the costs and scope of employee theft in several types of organizations, see Table 6.5.[26]

The problem with employee theft is that almost everyone takes home some office supplies now and again. Although these acts may seem innocent and innocuous enough,

---

TABLE 6.5   Employee Theft: Some Facts and Figures

The following statistics will give you a sense of the scope and serious nature of employee theft today. (*Sources:* See note 26.)

- In the restaurant business, theft by employees costs between $15 billion and $25 billion per year.
- Although fewer consumers are stealing wireless phone service than ever before, there has been a significant rise in theft of service by employees of wireless companies.
- Most employees dislike the use of video surveillance cameras at work. At a Virginia restaurant, seven cashiers resigned the day before they believed closed-circuit surveillance cameras were going to be installed.
- Fraud cost American businesses about $400 billion a year.
- The average convenience stores loses $20,000 per year due to employee theft.
- In Asian retail businesses, about 3 percent of the staff steals every day and 8 percent steals every week.
- Breaches of computer security are on the rise, but most of the people who break into corporate or government computers illegally are current employees rather than outsiders.

petty theft is so common that cumulatively, it costs companies far more than the few acts of grand theft that grab newspaper headlines.[27]

Why do employees steal?   It's hardly surprising that many employees steal because they are troubled in some way (e.g., they are in serious debt or have a narcotics or gambling habit). Although this is undoubtedly true in some cases, it doesn't account for everyone.

Lots of people steal for a very simple reason—because *they see their coworkers doing it*. To the extent that everyone around you is taking home tools, office supplies, and even petty cash, it quickly seems not so inappropriate. After all, we rationalize, "everyone is doing it" and "the company expects us to do it." Although this doesn't make it right, of course, and it clearly costs the company money, people are quick to convince themselves that petty theft is "no big deal," and not worth worrying about.

Similarly, many employees engage in theft because in some companies, *not* stealing goes against the *informal norms* of the workgroup.[28] Unspoken rules go a long way toward determining how people behave on the job (as we will discuss in Chapter 9), and in some companies, an employee has to steal to feel accepted and to belong.

Finally, employees frequently also engage in theft because *they want to "even the score"* with employers who they believe have mistreated them. In fact, people who believe they have been underpaid frequently steal from their employers because in so doing they are righting a wrong by taking what they should have had all along.

Tips for reducing employee theft.   Although you see security cameras just about everywhere, it's clear that they are not completely effective. After all, many people keep on stealing. As a practicing manager, there are several things you can do to help chip away at the problem. While you won't be able to stop theft completely, it's encouraging to know that you can make a difference by following these practical suggestions.

1. *Involve employees in the creation of a theft policy*. It is not always clear what constitutes theft. Does your company prohibit the use of personal phone calls or the copy machine for personal purposes? If so, violating these policies constitutes theft of company resources, although chances are good that few will think of them as such. The trick is to develop very clear policies about employee theft and to involve employees in the process of doing so. The more involved they are, the more they will "buy into" the policies and follow them. Once such policies are developed, of course, it is critical to articulate them carefully in a formal document (such as a policy manual or code of ethics) and to carefully train all employees in them.
2. *Communicate the costs of stealing*. Chances are good that someone in the accounting department of any company has a good idea of how much the company is losing each year due to employee theft. To the extent that this information is shared with other employees, along with a clear indication of how it costs them (e.g., through smaller raises and bonuses), many employees will think twice before they take company property for personal use.
3. *Be a good role model*. One of the most effective things managers can do to discourage theft is not to engage in theft themselves. After all, to the extent that employees see their managers making personal phone calls, padding their expense accounts, or taking home office supplies, they are left with the message

that doing these kind of things is perfectly acceptable. When it comes to discouraging employee theft, "walking the talk" is very important.

SUMMARY: HAVE I MET THE LEARNING OBJECTIVES?

You can be certain that you have met the learning objectives for this chapter found on p. 141 if you understand the following:

1. **DESCRIBE two types of psychological contracts in work relationships and the types of trust associated with each**. One type of psychological contract is the *transactional contract*. It is characteristic of relationships that have an exclusively economic focus, last for a brief period of time, are unchanging in nature, and have a narrow, well-defined scope. *Calculus-based trust*—trust based on deterrence—is associated with transactional contracts. A second type of contract is the *relational contract*. Such contracts are based on friendship and exist in relationships in which the parties take a long-term perspective. Such relationships are characterized by *identification-based trust*—that is, trust based on accepting and understanding another.

2. **DESCRIBE organizational citizenship behavior and ways it may be promoted**. Organizational citizenship behavior consists of acts that go above and beyond one's formal job requirements in helping one's organization or fellow employees. It can be promoted by going out of the way to help others, being an example of conscientiousness, making voluntary functions fun, and demonstrating good sportsmanship and courtesy.

3. **IDENTIFY ways cooperation can be promoted in the workplace**. Although by nature some people are more cooperative than others, interpersonal cooperation may be promoted by following the reciprocity principle and by adopting reward systems (e.g., *team-based pay*) that encourage cooperation with others.

4. **DESCRIBE competition and what makes it inevitable in organizations**. Competition occurs when two or more people, groups, or organizations seek to maximize their own gains at the expense of others. This is inevitable insofar as in many situations valued resources can go to only one party—that is, the winner. Competition is a defining aspect of business relationships, although in many situations people have *mixed motives*—that is, they both cooperate and compete.

5. **DESCRIBE the causes and effects of conflict in organizations**. Conflict is caused by a wide variety of factors, including grudges, malevolent attributions, destructive criticism, distrust, and competition over scarce resources. Conflict not only can be a source of negative emotions but also can lead to a lack of coordination, which can make performance suffer in organizations. However, conflict also can have beneficial effects. These include improving the quality of organizational decisions, bringing out into the open problems that have been previously ignored, motivating people to appreciate each others' positions more fully, and encouraging people to consider new ideas.

6. **IDENTIFY two forms of deviant organizational behavior and how to minimize their occurrence**. *Workplace aggression* is one form of deviant organizational behavior. It can be minimized by establishing clear disciplinary procedures, treating people fairly, and training managers in ways to recognize and avoid

aggression. *Employee theft* is another form of deviant organizational behavior. It can be reduced by involving employees in the creation of a theft policy, communicating the costs of stealing, and by having managers be a good role model by not stealing themselves.

You Be the Consultant

Life in your company has become tumultuous. Not only are people always at each others' throats, but sometimes they get downright hostile to each other, sabotaging others' work. Even those who have not been involved are suffering the consequences, and good employees are resigning. Answer the following questions using the material in this chapter.

1. What possible causes of the problem would you consider, and why?
2. Assuming that these causes are real, what advice would you offer about how to eliminate the problem?
3. What steps would you recommend so as to avoid deviant behavior?

SELF-ASSESSMENT EXERCISE

Assessing Your Personal Orientation Toward Others

On page 151 you read descriptions of four different personal orientations toward others—competitors, individualists, cooperators, and equalizers. As you read these, you probably developed some ideas as to which orientation best described you. This exercise is designed to help you find out.

Directions
Use the following scale to indicate how well each of the following statements describes you.

1 = Does not describe me at all/never
2 = Describes me somewhat/some of the time
3 = Describes me moderately/half of the time
4 = Describes me greatly/much of the time
5 = Describes me perfectly/all of the time

_____ 1. I don't care how much money one of my coworkers earns, so long as I make as much as I can.
_____ 2. When playing a game with a close friend, I always try to keep the score close.
_____ 3. As long as I do better than the next guy, I'm happy.
_____ 4. I will gladly give up something for myself if it can help my team get ahead.
_____ 5. It's important to me to be the best in the class, even if I'm not doing my personal best.
_____ 6. I feel badly if I do too much better than my friends on a class assignment.

_____ 7. I want to get an A in this class regardless of what grade you might get.

_____ 8. I enjoy it when the people in my work team all pitch in together to beat other teams.

Scoring

Insert the numbers corresponding to your answers to each of the questions in the spaces corresponding to those questions. Then, add the numbers in each column (these can range from 2 to 10). The higher your score, the more accurately the personal orientation heading that column describes you.

Competitor	*Individualist*	*Cooperator*	*Equalizer*
3. _____	1. _____	4. _____	2. _____
5. _____	7. _____	8. _____	6. _____
Total = _____	Total = _____	Total = _____	Total = _____

Questions for Discussion

1. What did this exercise reveal about yourself?
2. Were you surprised at what you learned, or was it something you already knew?
3. Do you tend to maintain the same orientation most of the time, or are there occasions in which you change from one orientation to another? What do you think this means?

(**GROUP EXERCISE**)

Negotiating the Price of a Used Car

This exercise is designed to help you put into practice some of the skills associated with being a good negotiator. In completing this exercise, follow the steps for negotiating a win–win solution found on pages 157-158.

Steps

1. Find a thorough description of a recent-model used car in the newspaper.
2. Divide the class into groups of six. Within each group, assign three students to the role of buyer and three to the role of seller.
3. Each group of buyers and sellers should meet in advance to plan their strategies. Buyers should plan on getting the lowest possible price; sellers should seek the highest possible price.
4. Buyers and sellers should meet to negotiate the price of the car within the period of time specified by the instructor. Feel free to meet within your groups at any time to evaluate your strategy.
5. Write down the final agreed-upon price and conditions that may be attached to it.

Discussion Questions

1. Did you reach an agreement? If so, how easy or difficult was this process?
2. Which side do you think "won" the negotiation? What might have changed the outcome?
3. How might the negotiation process or the outcome have been different had this been a real situation?

NOTES

Case Notes

Neff, T. J., & Citrin, J. M. (1999). *Lessons from the top.* New York: Currency Doubleday (quotes, pp. 262-264); Howard Schultz: Starbucks' CEO serves a blend of community, employee commitment. (1998, April 21) *Nation's Restaurant News,* pp. 162–163. Starbucks Website: www.starbucks.com/company.

Chapter Notes

[1] Robinson, S. L., & Morrison, E. W. (2000). The development of psychological contract breach violation: A longitudinal study. *Journal of Organizational Behavior, 21,* 525–546.

[2] Rousseau, D. M., & Parks, J. M. (1993). The contracts of individuals and organizations. In L. L. Cummings & B. M. Staw (Eds.), *Research in organizational behavior* (Vol. 15, pp. 1–43). Greenwich, CT: JAI Press. Turnley, W. H., and Feldman, D. C. (2000). Re-examining the effects of psychological contract violations: Unmet expectations and job dissatisfaction as mediators. *Journal of Organizational Behavior, 21,* 25–42.

[3] Lewicki, R. J., McAllister, D. J., & Bies, R. J. (1998). Trust and distrust: New relationships and realities. *Academy of Management Review, 23,* 438–458.

[4] Lewicki, R. J., & Wiethoff, C. (2000). Trust, trust development, and trust repair. In M. Deutsch and P. T. Coleman (Eds.), *The handbook of conflict resolution* (pp. 86–107). San Francisco: Jossey-Bass.

[5] Podsakoff, P. M., MacKenzie, S. B., Paine, J. B., & Bachrach, D. G. (2000). Organizational citizenship behaviors: A critical review of the theoretical and empirical literature and suggestions for future research. *Journal of Management, 26,* 513–563.

[6] See Note 1.

[7] Fomburn, C. J. (1996). *Reputation.* Boston: Harvard Business School Press.

[8] Miceli, M., & Near, J. (1992). *Blowing the whistle.* Lexington, MA: New Lexington Press.

[9] Paul van Buitenen: Paying the price of accountability. (2000, April). *Accountancy, 125*(1), 280. Taylor, M. (1999, September 13). Another Columbia suit unsealed. *Modern Healthcare, 29*(37), 10. Ettore, B. (1994, May). Whistleblowers: Who's the real bad guy? *Management Review,* pp. 18–23.

[10] Gjersten, L. A. (1999). Five State Farm Agents fired after accusing company of consumer abuse. *National Underwriter, 103*(51), 1, 23.

[11] Martucci, W. C., & Smith, E. W. (2000). Recent state legislative development concerning employment discrimination and whistle-blower protections. *Employment Relations Today, 27*(2), 89–99.

[12] Jones, M., & Rowell, A. (1999). Safety whistleblowers intimidated. *Safety and Health Practitioner, 17*(8), p. 3.

[13] Falk, A., Gachter, S., & Kovacs, J. (1999). Intrinsic motivation and extrinsic incentives in a repeated game with incomplete contracts. *Journal of Economic Psychology, 20,* 251–284.

[14] Knight, G. P., Dubro, A. F., & Chao, C. (1985). Information processing and the development of cooperative, competitive, and individualistic social values. *Developmental Psychology, 21,* 37–45.

[15] Knight, G. P., & Dubro, A. F. (1984). Cooperative, competitive, and individualistic social values: An individualized regression and clustering approach. *Journal of Personality and Social Psychology, 46,* 98–105.

[16] DeMatteo, J. S., Eby, L. T., & Sundstrom, E. (1998). Team-based rewards: Current empirical evidence and directions for future research. In B. M. Staw and L. L. Cummings (Eds.), *Research in organizational behavior* (Vol. 20, pp. 141–183). Greenwich, CT: JAI. Heneman, R.L, (2000). *Business-driven compensation policies.* New York: AMACOM.

[17] Teerlink, R., & Ozley, L. (2000). *More than a motorcycle: The leadership journey at Harley-Davidson.* Boston: Harvard Business School Press.

[18] Thomas, K. W., & Schmidt, W. H. (1976). A survey of managerial interests with respect to conflict. *Academy of Management Journal, 10,* 315–318.

[19] Bragg, T. (1999, October). Ten ways to deal with conflict. *IIE Solutions,* pp. 36–37.

[20] Lee, M. (1998, October 12). "See you in court—er, mediation." *Business Week Enterprise,* pp. ENT22, ENT24.

[21] Bordwin, M. (1999). Do-it-yourself justice. *Management Review*, pp. 56–58.

[22] National Institute for Occupational Safety and Health, Centers for Disease Control and Prevention. (1993). *Homicide in the workplace.* [Document # 705003]. Atlanta, GA: Author.

[23] Robinson, S. L., & Greenberg, J. (1998). Employees behaving badly: Dimensions, determinants, and dilemmas in the study of workplace deviance. In D. M. Rousseau and C. Cooper (Eds.), *Trends in organizational behavior* (Vol. 5). New York: John Wiley.

[24] Trevino, L. K., & Weaver, G. R. (1998). Punishment in organizations: Descriptive and normative perspectives. In M. Schminke (Ed.), *Managerial ethics: Moral management of people and processes* (pp. 99–114). Mahwah, NJ: Lawrence Erlbaum Associates.

[25] Lind, E. A., Greenberg, J., Scott, K. S., & Welchans, T. D. (2000). The winding road from employee to complainant: Situational and psychological determinants of wrongful-termination claims. *Administrative Science Quarterly,* 557–590.

[26] Kooker, N. R. (2000, May 22). Taking aim at crime—stealing the profits: Tighter controls, higher morale may safeguard bottom line. *Nation's Restaurant News, 34*(21), pp. 114–118. Young, D. (2000, May 1). Inside jobs. *Wireless Review, 17*(9), pp. 14–20. Rosner, B. (1999, October). How do you feel about video surveillance at work? *Workforce, 78*(10), pp. 26–27. As new CCTV system goes live, cashiers quit. (1999, May). *Security, 36*(5), p. 40. Wells, J. T. (1999, August). A fistful of dollars. *Security Management, 43*(8), pp. 70–75. Vara, B. (1999, June). The "steal trap." *National Petroleum News, 91*(6), pp. 28–31. Wimmer, N. (1999, June). Fingers in the till. *Asian Business, 35*(6). pp. 59–60. Golden, P. (1999, May). Dangers without, dangers within. *Electronic Business, 25*(5), 65–70.

[27] Jabbkerm A. (2000, March 29). Agrium seeks $30 million in damages in embezzlement case. *Chemical Week, 162*(13), 22.

[28] Greenberg, J. (1998). The cognitive geometry of employee theft: Negotiating "the line" between taking and stealing. In R. W. Griffin, A. O'Leary-Kelly, and J. M. Collins (Eds.), *Dysfunctional behavior in organizations: Non-violent dysfunctional behavior* (pp. 147–194). Stamford, CT: JAI Press.

Joining up and fitting in:
socialization and career development

LEARNING OBJECTIVES

After reading this chapter, you will be able to:

1. DEFINE organizational socialization.

2. DESCRIBE the three stages of organizational socialization.

3. EXPLAIN how the mentoring process works in organizations.

4. DEFINE career.

5. DESCRIBE the three stages of career development.

6. EXPLAIN the impact of the growth of entrepreneurship, the dominance of dual-career couples, and the use of career coaches on careers today.

THREE GOOD REASONS WHY YOU SHOULD CARE ABOUT . . .

Socialization and Career Development

You should care about socialization and career development because:

1. Your effectiveness as an employee is greatly determined by how effectively you are socialized into the organization's ways of doing things.

2. Mentoring plays an important role in both individual and organizational success.

3. Developing a career is a complex process, but one that can be managed effectively if you understand the challenges involved.

Making the Case for... Socialization and Career Development

For Today's MBAs, Job Choice Is Dot-Complicated

Only a few years ago, the formula used to be simple: Go to a top-tier business school, and get on the fast track for a top-tier job in a top-tier company. That's precisely the path Patrick Mullane had in mind when he entered the MBA program at the prestigious Harvard Business School. But, somewhere along the way, he changed his mind. A month before graduating, Andersen Consulting offered him a six-figure starting salary and a $30,000 signing bonus, and agreed to pay back his $50,000 student loan. He turned it down. Before concluding that Mullane is crazy to reject such a lucrative offer, you should know that decisions like these are being made all the time. In fact, so many of today's top business students are spurning blue-chip offers that companies such as General Motors, Coca-Cola, and Procter & Gamble are finding it difficult to fill important slots.

What's going on is that droves of top business school grads are opting for the lure of working for smaller Internet start-ups rather than traditional positions in the corporate world. As Mullane explains, "I didn't want to miss the next Industrial Revolution. I didn't want to have any regrets." Although the starting pay and bonuses aren't anywhere near as lucrative, Mullane and those like him are betting on the future of these much smaller firms, hoping to get in on the ground floor, where in just a few years they can be part of something big. Then, they stand to make more money than they could ever imagine. Meanwhile, for Mullane and many of his classmates, it's not all about money. There's also the matter of lifestyle. The corporate world typically requires lots of time on the road, and an even longer trip up the corporate ladder—even for fast-trackers.

Sharon Goldstein, a graduate of Northwestern University's Kellogg Graduate School of Management, is one of those fast-trackers. Like Mullane, she had offers from major consulting firms, but turned them down in favor of a much more modest-paying position in the media systems group of RealNetworks in Seattle. While in school, she spent a summer there as an intern and grew to love the laid-back lifestyle. Believing that the corporate world was too bureaucratic and too confining for her, she is convinced she made the right choice.

Mullane is also certain of his decision. At Harvard, he was wooed by many big companies, but like Goldstein, he couldn't imagine carving out a place for himself in the bureaucratic world of corporate America. So, where did he end up? A few of his classmates were writing a business plan for a Web-based business whose mission is to help manufacturers reduce their supply-chain costs. He liked what he saw, and he joined them, beginning his career as director of marketing for the start-up, SupplierMarket.com. In exchange for the big bucks he turned down up front, Mullane opted for enough money to sustain his family today and "as much equity as I could get," in the hope of a huge payoff tomorrow.

Mullane and Goldstein probably would be the first to tell you that they are fortunate to have had the opportunities they turned down. After all, not everyone has a chance at a good position in a prestigious company. Yet, these two young people chose nontraditional paths, opting to invest the early stages of their work lives in positions that could make them wealthy later on. Maybe you can relate to what these individuals have done, or maybe, like many of us, your options are more limited. In either case, like all of us, they will follow a sequence of jobs over their lives, known as *careers*. Although careers are changing these days, all have several characteristics in common that are worth knowing. The better we understand how these operate, the better equipped we are to take control over our own careers. It is with this in mind that I will review the topic of career development in this chapter.

No matter what career you choose, there is one aspect of life at work that all people have in common—the experience of being new to the job. Indeed, everyone has a first day, and everyone has to learn the ropes. The process of becoming a member of an organization and learning all about it is known as *organizational socialization*. This important process is the first major topic covered in this chapter.

Organizational Socialization: Becoming Part of the Company

It's your first day on the job. After years of training and experience, you have all the skills needed to succeed, but you still have a lot to learn. Some things may be minor, such as finding out where to find the coffee machine or the water fountain. Others may be more critical, such as policies regarding the treatment of customers or informal standards about how hard to work. The process through which people move from outsiders to effective, participating members of their organizations is referred to as **organizational socialization**. In this section of the chapter, I will describe this process and the ways organizations go about making the socialization process effective.

THE THREE STAGES OF SOCIALIZATION

As you might imagine, people do not become fully socialized members of their organizations instantly, or even after a few weeks. Rather, organizational socialization is a gradual process that occurs in three discrete stages over a matter of years (for a summary, see Figure 7.1).[1]

Anticipatory socialization.   The first stage, **anticipatory socialization**, is concerned with "getting in." This involves learning about an organization from the outside, before one may even consider becoming a part of it. If this sounds strange, just ask yourself if there is a specific organization in which you would be interested in working someday. What makes you attracted to it? If you can answer this question, even tentatively, it's clear that you know something about an organization even before you begin working there.

How do such expectations develop? First, as friends or relatives who work in an organization share their experiences with you, you may develop an image of the company. Second, there also are formal sources, such as professional journals, magazine and newspaper articles, and corporate annual reports. These also provide information that may help cultivate an impression of what it would be like to work in a certain organization. Unfortunately, both formal and informal sources of information may be biased. For example, you may hear your acquaintances talk about their jobs only when they have negative things to say. Likewise, press reports about organizations are often reserved for sensationalistic accounts of either extremely positive news (e.g., record-breaking earnings) or negative news (e.g., illegal activities). Thus, although we often

FIGURE 7.1 The Three Stages of Socialization

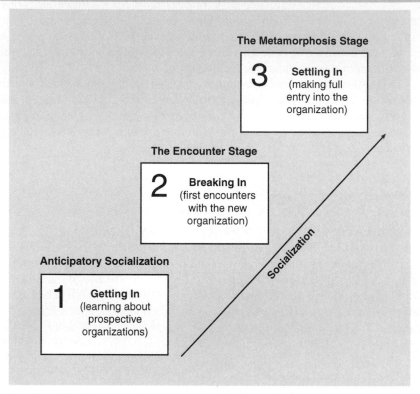

Organizational socialization generally follows the three stages summarized here: *anticipatory socialization*, which involves getting in; the *encounter stage*, which involves breaking in; and the *metamorphosis stage*, which involves settling in.

rely on secondhand information from personal contacts and the popular press as bases for our judgments about organizations, it is important to keep in mind that the information they provide may be questionable.

The most direct way to learn about an organization is to get the information "straight from the horse's mouth," so to speak—that is, by listening to corporate recruiters. Sometimes, however, these individuals paint overly rosy pictures of their organizations. In response to intense competition for the best job candidates, they may describe their companies in glowing terms, glossing over internal problems and emphasizing the positive aspects. As a result, potential employees often receive unrealistically positive impressions of what it would be like to work in those organizations. Then, when new employees actually arrive on the job and find their expectations are unmet, strong feelings of disappointment, confusion, and disillusionment may result—what is referred to as **entry shock**. In fact, the less employees' job expectations are met, the less satisfied and committed they are, and the more likely they are to think about quitting and to actually do so.

With this in mind, the trick for corporate recruiters is not to give job candidates unrealistically positive descriptions, but rather, highly accurate descriptions—both positive and negative—of the jobs they will perform and the organizations they will enter. Such descriptions are called **realistic job previews**.[2] Research has shown that people exposed to realistic job previews later report higher satisfaction and show lower turnover than those who receive glowing, but often unrealistic, information about the companies in question. By making their expectations more realistic, employees are less likely to resign when they confront negative conditions. For this reason, it makes sense for recruiters not only to inform prospective employees about the many benefits of working for their companies (as they are already prone to do), but also to supplement this information with realistic accounts of what life will be like in the organization.[3]

Several companies have been doing just this. For example, recruiters at AT&T have used realistic job previews to recruit operators and customer service representatives, and at NBD Bank they have been used to recruit tellers. Using realistic job previews also has been found to increase the amount of time cooperative extension service field agents stay on their jobs.[4] In probably the largest-scale example, realistic job previews are used in the process of recruiting men and women for all branches of the Canadian Armed Forces. Clearly, these organizations have a great deal of confidence in realistic job previews as a tool for avoiding entry shock and avoiding problems associated with turnover.

In probably the largest-scale example, realistic job previews are used in the process of recruiting men and women for all branches of the Canadian Armed Forces.

The encounter stage. The second stage of organizational socialization, the **encounter stage**, begins when individuals actually assume their new duties. During this stage, they face several key challenges. First, of course, they must master the skills required by their new jobs. Second, they must become oriented to the practices and procedures of the new organization—that is, the way things are done there. Third, new members of an organization must establish good social relations with others. They must get to know these people and gain their acceptance. Only when they do can they become effectively functioning members of the work team.

It is during the encounter stage that formal **corporate orientation programs** are conducted. These are sessions designed to teach new employees about their organizations.[5] This includes not only the ways they operate, but also information about their histories, missions, and traditions. Such programs are considered a vital part of employee training insofar as they help new employees fit in and understand what their organization is all about. Although much of what is covered in such sessions may be picked up informally over time, formal orientation programs are highly efficient ways of indoctrinating new employees and introducing them to company officials. Of course, such efforts are merely supplements to the informal socialization between coworkers that may be expected to go on continuously.

The metamorphosis stage. The third stage of organizational socialization, the **metamorphosis stage**, occurs as the individual enters an organization and attains full member status. Just as a caterpillar undergoes a metamorphosis when it becomes a butterfly, so too does a trainee develop fully when he or she eventually becomes a full-fledged member of the organization. Sometimes, this entry is marked by a formal event, such as a dinner, reception, or graduation ceremony. The ceremony in which cadets graduate from a police academy is a good example insofar as it marks their transition from students to police officers. At this time, we can expect one's title to change from a temporary one, such as trainee or apprentice, to a permanent one, such as associate or partner. In other cases, especially when training has been short or informal, full acceptance into the work group may not be marked by any specific ceremony at all. Instead, it may be acknowledged by informal actions, such as being invited to lunch by one's new coworkers.

Whatever form it takes, the metamorphosis phase of socialization marks important shifts both for individuals and for organizations. Employees now make permanent adjustments to their jobs (e.g., they resolve conflicting demands between their jobs and their personal lives). And organizations begin treating them as if they will be long-term members of their work teams.

MENTORING: SOCIALIZING PEOPLE INDIVIDUALLY

Some of the most effective forms of socialization involve the one-on-one contact between senior and junior people. For example, at Fu Associates Ltd. (a computer consulting firm in Arlington, Virginia) all new employees start out working directly with a midlevel manager who shows them the ropes. After a few months, Ed Fu, the owner and senior systems analyst, selects a few of the more promising new employees to work with him on important projects. This is an example of **mentoring**—the process by which a more experienced employee, known as a **mentor**, advises, counsels, and otherwise enhances the personal development of a new employee, known as a **protégé**. If you've ever had an older, more experienced employee take you under his or her wing and guide you, then you probably already know how valuable mentoring can be. Indeed, mentoring is strongly associated with career success: The more mentoring people receive, the more promotions and pay raises they subsequently receive during their careers.[6]

Development of the mentoring process. As you might expect, mentor–protégé relationships do not develop in a haphazard fashion. Rather, they follow certain regular patterns. Notably, mentors are usually older than their protégés (by about 8 to 15 years). They also tend to be individuals with considerable power and status in their companies. As a result, they can assist rising young stars without feeling threatened themselves. On some occasions, mentor–protégé relationships are initiated by the mentor, who recognizes something impressive about the junior person. However, it is also possible for junior employees to approach prospective mentors about the possibility of entering into a mentoring relationship. Regardless of who initiates the relationship, for it to succeed, both parties must enter into it willingly—and, of course, the organization must be supportive of this association.

Some organizations believe so strongly in the benefits of mentoring that they are unwilling to leave the process to chance, and formally encourage or even require men-

At the hosiery division of Sara Lee Corporation, a "women's information network" was formed in which groups of lower-ranking female employees meet regularly with higher-ranking female employees to discuss career-path opportunities.

toring in corporate-wide programs. For example, at Colgate-Palmolive, all new white-collar employees are assigned higher-ranking employees who serve as mentors. Other companies make mentoring more of a group process. For example, at the hosiery division of Sara Lee Corporation, a "women's information network" was formed in which groups of lower-ranking female employees meet regularly with higher-ranking female employees to discuss career-path opportunities. These are only two examples of a wide variety of different types of mentoring in use today.

Despite their different formats, most mentor–protégé relationships pass through several distinct phases. The first, known as *initiation*, lasts from six months to a year and represents a period during which the relationship gets started and takes on importance for both parties. The second phase, known as *cultivation*, may last from two to five years. During this time, the bond between mentor and protégé deepens, and the young individual may make rapid career strides because of the skilled assistance he or she is receiving.

The third phase, *separation*, begins when the protégé feels it is time to assert independence and strikes out on his or her own, or when there is some externally produced change in their roles (e.g., the protégé is promoted, or the mentor is transferred). Separation also can occur if the mentor feels unable to continue providing support and guidance to the protégé (e.g., if the mentor becomes ill). As you might imagine, this phase can be quite stressful if the mentor resents the protégé's growing independence, or if the protégé feels that the mentor has prematurely withdrawn support.

If this separation is successful, the relationship may enter its final phase, termed *redefinition*. Here, both parties perceive their bond primarily as one of friendship. They come to treat each other as equals, and the roles of mentor and protégé fade away completely. However, the mentor may continue to take pride in the accomplishments of his or her former protégé. Likewise, the protégé may continue to feel a debt of gratitude toward the former mentor. Although there is bound to be variation in the way mentor–protégé relationships actually develop, these four phases accurately depict the way in which these important relationships generally unfold (see summary in Figure 7.2).

Benefits of mentoring. Mentors do many important things for their protégés.[7] For example, they provide much-needed emotional support and confidence. For those who are just starting out and are likely to be insecure about their abilities, this can be a big help. Mentors also help pave the way for their protégés' job success, such as by nominating them for promotions and by providing opportunities for them to demonstrate their competence. They also suggest useful strategies for achieving work objectives—especially ones that protégés might not generate for themselves. In doing all these things, they help bring the protégé to the attention of top management—a necessary first step for advancement. Finally, mentors often protect their protégés from the repercussions of errors and help them avoid situations that may be risky for their careers.

FIGURE 7.2 Mentoring: A Four-Stage Process

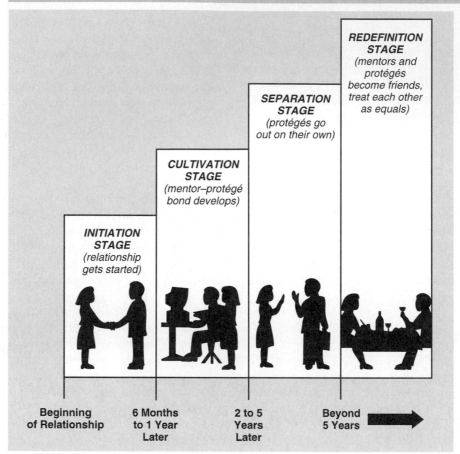

REDEFINITION STAGE
(mentors and protégés become friends, treat each other as equals)

SEPARATION STAGE
(protégés go out on their own)

CULTIVATION STAGE
(mentor–protégé bond develops)

INITIATION STAGE
(relationship gets started)

| Beginning of Relationship | 6 Months to 1 Year Later | 2 to 5 Years Later | Beyond 5 Years |

Relationships between mentors and their protégés tend to develop following the four stages summarized here.

As you might suspect from these benefits, organizations generally come out ahead when their employees engage in mentoring. At Scotiabank, for example, mentoring was used to reduce the time required for newly minted MBAs to become loan officers. This was necessary because these recent grads maintained traditional, not particularly service-oriented, beliefs about banking, which were holding them back. Through Scotiabank's Competency-Based Mentoring Program, however, branch managers reinforced what these new employees learned about service in their training programs. As a result, training time was reduced from a full year to nine months, allowing the bank to get these new employees fully functioning that much sooner.

"True mentoring is a process by which you buy into another's dream," according to Ben Borne, a human resources consultant. "It is a dynamic partnering that benefits all the participants."[8] The main benefits to protégés, of course, are the various types of career support just described. Still, Borne is correct in implying that mentor–protégé relationships may benefit the mentor as well. Indeed, it would be misleading to depict mentors as totally selfless benefactors who seek nothing in return for their guidance.

Often, people become mentors because they are so very appreciative of having received such help earlier in their careers. For example, Borne recalls how senior managers at Motorola and Kaiser Aluminum helped him get started some 35 years ago. Knowing what it's like to have people pay attention to you, he is pleased to be in the position to offer help to junior colleagues who now need his assistance. In other words, mentors may reap psychological benefits from feeling needed and a sense of accomplishment in helping the younger generation.

However, gratification is not the only source of benefit for mentors. In exchange for their guidance, mentors often expect certain things from their protégés. First, they expect their protégés to work hard at the tasks assigned to them, which makes for highly productive employees. Second, mentors often expect protégés to be loyal supporters within their organization. (After all, they are now members of the mentor's team!) Third, mentors may gain recognition from others in the company for their work in helping nurture young talent and can feel proud of their protégés' successes.

Costs of mentoring. This discussion of benefits is not meant to imply that mentor–protégé relationships are totally without costs. Indeed, there are several potential risks. For example, protégés may find that their own success hinges on the success of their mentor. If the mentor should happen to be a falling star in the company and suffers setbacks, the protégé's own career may be in jeopardy. Likewise, because the protégé's behavior reflects on the mentor, any failures on the part of the protégé may harm the mentor's reputation. In addition, there's always the risk that a mentor's advice might not be as good as it should be. This can be problematic regardless of whether the protégé follows the bad advice (and receives a negative outcome) or does not follow it (and risks insulting the mentor). To the extent that the mentor and protégé blame each other for the poor result, their relationship is likely to develop an uncomfortable level of conflict.

Finally, there's always a risk that protégés will become so highly dependent on their mentors that they will become slow to develop as self-reliant individuals. Similarly, it's possible for mentors to grow overly reliant on their protégés for help, delegating too many responsibilities that they should be discharging themselves. It is, of course, one thing to guide someone, and quite another to take advantage of them by having them do too much of your work. In conclusion, whereas mentoring offers many possible rewards to mentors, protégés, and their companies, it is wise to keep in mind the potential problems of such relationships as well. In view of the rewards and costs of mentoring, it makes sense to consider ways of making the mentoring experience successful for all involved. For some useful suggestions in this regard, see Table 7.1.[9] (To get a better sense of the benefits and costs of mentoring, perform the **Group Exercise** on p. 192.)

Mentoring members of diverse groups. When you think of a mentor, the image probably comes to mind of an older, white male executive helping a younger male manager work his way up the corporate ladder by introducing him to the most influential people in the organization. Typically, these are men who wield most of the power in the organization—what is known as the **old boy network**. By definition, any old *boy* network is sexist. Not surprisingly, because women frequently are left out, they generally have more limited access to suitable mentors than men.[10]

TABLE 7.1   Ten Tips for Successful Mentoring

The long-term success of mentoring can be enhanced by adhering to the suggestions identified here. Both mentors and protégés should familiarize themselves with these guidelines before entering into a relationship. (*Source*: Based on suggestions by Wickman & Sjodin, 1997; see Note 9.)

Mentors should . . .

1. Be responsible *to* protégés, not *for* them.
2. Make the mentoring relationship fun and enjoyable.
3. Recognize that their involvement with their protégé extends beyond the workday.
4. Listen carefully to their protégés.
5. Openly acknowledge their failures as well as their successes.
6. Protect their protégés and expect their protégés to protect them.
7. Give their protégés not only directions but also options.
8. Recognize and encourage their protégés' small successes and accomplishments.
9. Encourage independent thinking among their protégés.
10. Focus not only on job skills but also on ethical values.

Likewise, mentoring often fails to occur among members of minority groups who are not well represented in their companies. After all, insofar as people tend to be more comfortable with others who are similar to them, members of minority groups often tend to be denied informal mentoring opportunities simply because there are few others like them around. This is problematic given that people who don't have mentors face a barrier to success in the corporate world. And, insofar as affirmative action programs and diversity management programs (reviewed in Chapter 5) demand giving opportunities to women and minorities, providing mentors is essential. Fortunately, several companies have developed formal programs that bring together mentors and protégés from diverse groups. For some examples, see Table 7.2. Not only have such programs helped minority group members get the mentoring they need to succeed, they also have been quite effective in promoting diversity in the workplace (see Chapter 5).

Careers: Sequences of Work Experiences

Over the course of our lives we tend to find ourselves becoming socialized to many different jobs in several different organizations, a journey that exposes us to a variety of organizational cultures. In fact, during the course of his or her working life, the average American holds eight different jobs. In most cases, these positions are interconnected in some systematic way, weaving a path, however twisted and indirect, representing a career. Formally, a career can be defined as the evolving sequence of work experiences over time. In this section of the chapter, we will turn our attention to careers. Specifically, we will focus on the ways careers develop, and various personal strategies for managing your own career.

At the risk of oversimplifying the pleasures of living, it's clear that our lives tend to progress in systematic fashion, and with it, different foci: school, then marriage, children, and before you know it, grandchildren. The same can be said with respect to the paths taken by our careers. At the risk of oversimplifying these, organizational scien-

TABLE 7.2 Mentoring Diverse Groups: What Some Companies Are Doing		

Many of today's companies have taken successful steps to ensure that women and members of minority groups are receiving proper mentoring. Some of these practices, and the resulting benefits, are summarized here.

Company	*Mentoring Activity*	*Result*
Chubb & Son (insurance)	In its Sponsorship Program, women managers are assigned to higher-ranking female protégés.	Over half of the women were promoted within two years.
Dow Jones	"Quad Squads" of high-level mentors are grouped with three others, including a white male, a woman of any race, and a minority group member of either gender.	More members of minority groups are finding mentors than ever before, and racial tensions are minimal.
DuPont	Protégés are paired with mentors of different races so as to broaden each individual's exposure to new ideas and ways of looking at things.	The proportion of minorities in top management positions has risen from 10 percent to 30 percent, even as the overall number of management jobs has dropped.

tists have distinguished between various issues arising at three stages of careers, referred to as *early career*, *middle career*, and *late career* stages. As we describe these, you may find it useful to refer to the summary in Figure 7.3.

EARLY CAREER: GETTING STARTED

The question "what do you want to be when you grow up?" surely is among the most commonly considered ones throughout childhood (if not later, too). Before you know it, you have to answer seriously. Indeed, when we are beginning our careers, usually in our twenties, we are faced with the issue of **career planning**—the process of deciding what jobs and activities we wish to be doing in the future. When making these choices, we rely on our perceptions of our own talents, abilities, needs, motives, attitudes, and values.

Career anchors. By our mid-thirties, we are usually guided strongly by our own perceptions as we make our career choices. Scientists have referred to these self-perceptions as **career anchors** insofar as they firmly attach people's careers to their underlying abilities, needs, and values. Five major career anchors have been identified.[11] These are as follows:

- *Technical or functional*—Concentration on jobs focusing on specific content areas (e.g., auto mechanics, graphic arts)
- *Managerial competence*—Focus on jobs that allow for analyzing business problems and dealing with people
- *Security and stability*—Attraction to jobs that are likely to continue into the future (e.g., the military)

FIGURE 7.3 The Three Stages of Career Development

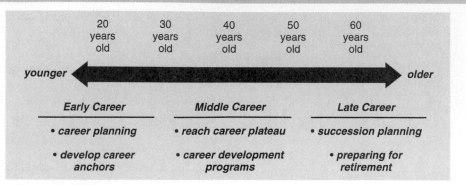

Careers generally develop in three stages, each of which occurs at different ages and is associated with different issues.

- *Creativity or entrepreneurship*—Primary interest in starting new companies from visions of unique products or services, but not necessarily running them
- *Autonomy and independence*—Attraction to jobs that allow for freedom from constraints, and to work at one's own pace (e.g., novelists and creative artists)

Beyond developing career anchors, people in the early stages of their careers typically confront frequent job changes. In fact, most new graduates with MBA degrees expect to stay at their first jobs for no more than four years.[12] It is easy to understand that as we begin our careers, we may find that a particular job may not be as desirable as expected. Similarly, we may find that it is difficult or impossible to gain entry into some professions. (If you have ever tried to become a professional actor, you probably know only too well what I mean!) The result, in either case, is the same: You pursue a different job. As a general rule, people are far more likely to change jobs during this early period in their lives, when career expectations are just forming, and life responsibilities make it easier to be mobile.

MIDDLE CAREER: CONFRONTING THE CAREER PLATEAU

If early-career issues pertain to people in their twenties and thirties, then middle-career issues apply to the 40-something crowd. This is sometimes a difficult period in which people look down the road and realize that they may never fulfill their career aspirations. The point at which one's career has peaked and is unlikely to develop further is known as a **career plateau**. Today, as companies are reducing the sizes of their staffs and competition for jobs becomes intense, more and more people are reaching their plateaus earlier than expected. Faced with poor chances for promotion and few alternatives for employment, they may feel unmotivated and simply stick with their jobs until they retire from them.

If you think this picture is depressing, imagine how serious the problem becomes when companies are faced with large cohorts of midcareer employees who are unmotivated because their careers have plateaued. Surely, a workforce composed of people who are merely "going through the motions" will be neither very productive nor satisfied. So, to avoid these problems, organizations have been relying on **career develop-**

ment interventions—systematic efforts to help manage people's careers while simultaneously helping the organizations in which they work.

Several of these are quite interesting. For example, at Chevron, employees are counseled to seek outside hobbies during periods in which their jobs offer little gratification. Some are encouraged to make lateral moves within the company in order to keep their work lives stimulating. Not only have Chevron employees done this, but so too have thousands of employees at General Motors, where the white-collar workforce has been reduced dramatically over the last few years. In fact, it has been reported that GM

> *GM has spent some $10 million per year helping employees whose careers have reached plateaus find appropriate new positions within the company.*

has spent some $10 million per year helping employees whose careers have reached plateaus find appropriate new positions within the company.

Much of what goes on in career development interventions involves helping employees assess the skills and interests they have so that they may be placed into positions for which they are well suited. Some companies, such as Hewlett-Packard and Lawrence Livermore Laboratories, provide *self-assessment exercises* for this purpose. Others, such as Coca-Cola and Disneyland, rely on *individualized counseling sessions* in which employees meet with trained professionals. Still others, including AT&T, IBM, Ford, Shell Oil, and Kodak, take it a step further, offering *organizational assessment programs* through which employees are systematically tested to discover their profiles of skills and interests. (For an overview of what such tests look like, and a chance to examine your own career aspirations, see the **Self-Assessment Exercise** on p. 191.)

At the very least, companies such as CBS, Merck, Aetna, and General Electric all provide services, such as job posting systems and career resource centers, through which employees can learn about new career options within their companies. And when companies find that they must reduce the size of their workforces, terminated employees at Exxon, Mutual of New York, General Electric, and other companies receive the services of **outplacement programs**. These generally include assistance in developing the skills needed to find new jobs (such as networking, interviewing skills, résumé writing, and the like).

A recent trend observed among plateaued midcareer employees is that they completely abandon their traditional jobs and start their own small businesses. In recent years, such "dropouts" have been referred to as **corporate refugees**. Although it is quite difficult to begin new business ventures, corporate refugees are generally not looking for an easy way out. Instead, they seek to regain the challenges left behind in their corporate jobs and to find a more fulfilling existence.

LATE CAREER: FOCUSING ON SUCCESSION AND RETIREMENT

When we speak of late-career issues, the image probably comes to mind of the faithful employee retiring after some 40 years of employment with the same company, proudly showing off the gold watch he or she just received to an audience of adoring soon-to-be-former coworkers. Indeed, preparation for retirement is an important issue faced during one's sixties. Psychologically, there is a reorientation from being directed in one's life by work activities to an increased focus on leisure time activities.

Preparing for retirement also involves careful planning to meet the special challenges faced by retired workers, including adjustment to reduced earnings. Fortunately, it has been shown that through careful planning, people can greatly enjoy the new era of their lives that begins when their working lives end. To help ensure that this occurs, many companies are offering intensive counseling services to their employees to prepare them for retirement. For example, employees of the Walt Disney Company and their spouses are invited to seminars in which their incomes and financial needs are carefully investigated before it's time to retire. As a result, when the day that the gold watch comes, employees will not have to hock it to pay their bills.

> *Employees of the Walt Disney Company and their spouses are invited to seminars in which their incomes and financial needs are carefully investigated before it's time to retire.*

Today, rather than retiring from work altogether, many people in their sixties are opting for brand-new careers. In fact, only about 37 percent of recent retirees never expect to return to work. The rest plan on staying active by working at least part time.[13] Apparently, the image of retirees spending their golden years leisurely golfing and playing with their grandkids is fading fast. Speaking of golf, many professional golfers who find that aging makes it hard for them to compete against the likes of Tiger Woods no longer have to retire from the game. Instead, they are discovering second careers by competing in the Senior PGA tour, where at age 50, they once again can rise to the top of their game.[14] Although precious few of us have the luxury of making a living by playing golf, many companies are finding it beneficial to hire semiretired executives as consultants. Instead of putting these talented, experienced people out to pasture, so to speak, they are taking full advantage of the expertise they can bring to the job—especially as mentors to young employees.[15]

Before people retire—whether to a world of leisure or an entirely new career—high-level executives typically assist their companies to prepare for the void created by their departure. Typically, this involves **succession planning**—the process of identifying who will take over key organizational positions after job incumbents retire. After one spends years building a successful business, it's unlikely that he or she would feel comfortable retiring without taking steps to preserve what has been done and to ensure that the company is left in good hands. People generally also want to pass the baton to another whose goals and values match their own. And, of course, careful planning of this nature is in the best interests of the company as well. One way of identifying successors, particularly for top executives, is by having the retiring individual identify and develop a successor (over a course of years, if possible). Mentoring at this level not only assures the retiring executive that he or she will have a successor qualified to fill the post, but also helps prepare the successor for the job and eases his or her transition within the organization.

To summarize, careers progress through the three distinct stages noted in Figure 7.3. Each stage is associated with a series of unique issues that must be faced. Increasingly, organizations are growing sensitive to the special needs of employees at each career stage and offer various forms of assistance to help meet the challenges they confront.

MAKING CAREER CHOICES: A LIFELONG CHALLENGE

How do people go about making vocational choices? Although this issue certainly is very complicated, three major factors appear to be involved. The first one is **person–organization fit**. That is, people tend to choose jobs that match their skills, interests, and values. Second, people also select jobs that match their self-concepts—that is, their images of who they are. In other words, we tend to match ourselves to prototypes of job incumbents, our beliefs about what the typical holder of a job is like. So, for example, if you see yourself as being more like a musician than a banker, you are probably more likely to pursue a job in the world of music. Of course, *which* particular job you take will depend on your career anchor. This may lead you to play guitar in a rock band, be an artist's agent or manager, a record producer, or the head of a record company.

Today, almost any option is considered acceptable, and people are considering a wide choice of options. Thirty-seven percent of business school graduates choose to work for a top global company—particularly in the fields of management consulting (where the firm McKinsey is the top choice), the Internet (Amazon.com is the second-most popular place to work), and investment banking (Goldman Sachs is the third-most popular choice).[16] Still, about 18 percent—like Patrick Mullane and Sharon Goldstein profiled in the opening case—opt to work for smaller start-up companies. Importantly, it is not only newly minted MBAs who are opting to work for Internet start-ups, but experienced executives as well. In fact, seven out of ten executives leaving large companies are putting their faith in the *new economy* by taking jobs of this type.[17]

Finally, a note of realism: People's vocational choices are guided largely by options and opportunities. No matter how much you are attracted to the romantic image of the old village blacksmith, it's unlikely that you will be able to pursue this line of work today. By contrast, however, there are many different careers in which opportunities abound and options are plentiful. And, as people learn about these types of jobs early in their careers, they stand good chances of preparing for them, and subsequently succeeding in them. As you might imagine, some of today's fastest-growing and most lucrative jobs are in the field of high technology.[18] Given how rapidly this field moves, it probably comes as no surprise that jobs in high-tech fields appear and disappear rapidly as well. The key to getting the hot job is to stay ahead of the curve. With this in mind, I present in Table 7.3 some new jobs that are expected to grow in popularity with advances in the Internet-based economy. Getting these jobs, of course, also relies on high technology. For a close-up look at how one prominent company is using its own technical prowess to help recruit employees, see the **Winning Practices** section on page 185.

Personal Strategies for Career Management

Almost all of us care greatly about becoming successful in our careers, and most of us expect to attain some measure of success. In fact, a recent survey by the firm Ernst & Young found that over 70 percent of MBAs and undergraduates expect to become millionaires—and over half expect to retire in their fifties.[19] With this in mind, we had better get right down to several important considerations for having a successful career.

ENTREPRENEURSHIP: SHOULD YOU START YOUR OWN BUSINESS?

You all know the legendary story of Bill Gates, who, with partner Paul Allen, dropped out of Harvard to found Microsoft and made it one of the world's most successful

TABLE 7.3 High-Tech Jobs for the Internet Economy

The popularity of the Internet has led to the development of many new jobs. Some particularly interesting new positions—and ones that we can expect to see more of in the future—are noted here. (*Source*: Based on information in Donahue, 1999; see Note 19.)

Title	Description	Essential Skills
New Metrics Analyst	They carefully and thoroughly analyze patterns in the way people use various Websites (e.g., how long people visit, when do they shop, etc.), allowing companies to set advertising rates and identify selling opportunities.	Database experience and ability to perform quantitative analysis. A strong knowledge of business is required to suggest how the numbers translate into a useful course of action.
Content Engineer	Working with marketing and information technology specialists, they are responsible for the overall organization and presentation of the content of a Website.	Technical background is necessary, as is a solid background of the content as well as the audience the site is serving.
Chief Community Strategist	Relying on feedback from e-mail, message boards, and face-to-face meetings, these individuals serve as a link between a Web site's online community of visitors and a company's top executives.	General management and operations skills are necessary, along with a good sense of what the online community wants.
Ethical Hacker	Companies pay these individuals to attempt to break into their networks by simulating attacks from the Net or internally. They then work with clients to find ways of reducing these threats.	Must have expertise in several different operating systems, security systems, and networking protocols—along with a reputation for being trustworthy.
E-Mail Channel Specialist	These experts design customized e-mail subscription services for clients, sending them messages of greatest interest about the company's products and services.	In addition to knowing how to develop software, these specialists also must understand the needs of the company's customers.
Chief Knowledge Officer (CKO)	These individuals are responsible for developing and managing a company's *knowledge management* efforts, building databases of the available skills and knowledge of people throughout the company (see Chapter 2).	Technical skills in database development and management are essential, along with a sense of how the company's employees work together.
Chief Internet Officer (CIO)	A person in this position oversees all online operations and strategies.	Good general management and leadership skills are required, along with a willingness to act quickly and take risks.

Pounding the Virtual Pavement:
The Art and Science of "E-Cruiting" at Cisco Systems

Traditionally, people looking for jobs scoured the "help wanted" section of their local newspapers, checking out the offerings of various companies classified by the type of work involved. Although this practice is still widely used, today it is eclipsed by job searches conducted online. In fact, to make up for lost revenue from such ads, many newspapers have gotten into the business of posting job offerings online (if you can't beat 'em, join 'em).[20] Almost 30,000 Web sites offer job-posting services—the most popular of which are Monster.com and CareerPath.com, with over 2 million and 1 million unique visitors per month, respectively.[21]

Today, almost all companies do at least some of their recruiting online, and spend about $1.7 billion on this process. As you might imagine, technically oriented companies are most actively engaged in this process. The most aggressive of these is Cisco Systems. This $10-billion-a-year networking company receives 81 percent of its résumés via the Web and selects two-thirds of its new hires from the Web. It doesn't do this by sitting by passively and hoping visitors to its Website check out employment opportunities. Instead, visitors are lured into what has been characterized as "a Venus flytrap of attractions."[22] Among these are opportunities to place jobs of interest in a shopping cart, allowing visitors to learn about each one after gathering those that seem most interesting. Anyone who's curious about what Cisco's San Jose campus looks like is free to take a virtual tour of the facility. This is not to say that there isn't also a personal touch. The MakeFriends@Cisco program puts visitors in touch with a real live person from the department in which the visitor expressed interest.

No résumé handy? No problem. Cisco's friendly Profiler helps prospects build one online, using a friendly, humorous interface. Because 90 percent of visitors log on while at work, the Cisco Web site even has an "Oh No! My Boss Is Coming" button, which removes any telltale signs of looking for a job and replaces them with "Seven Habits of a Successful Employee." Once you've left the Cisco site, you're not really out of touch. The company uses technology that tracks where visitors to its Website go after leaving and places employment banner ads on those sites. But it doesn't do this for just anyone—only those who might be interested in working for Cisco, such as those visiting from the Web sites of competing high-tech firms, such as Lucent Technologies and 3Com.

Apparently, these tactics work quite well. Compared to an industry average of $10,800 to recruit employees, Cisco's cost per hire is only $6,556. Even more importantly, using this technology has helped reduce the amount of time taken to fill an open position down to an average of 45 days from 113 days previously. Given that Cisco's job openings fill a 463-page book, these time savings are precious.

Questions for Discussion

1. Have you ever been involved in searching for a job online? If so, how is the experience different from the traditional, low-tech method?
2. What limitations, if any, do you suspect may result from recruiting the way Cisco does?
3. To what extent do you think that this high-tech method of recruiting appeals only to those looking for jobs in high-tech firms? Do you think this technique can be used by other kinds of companies as well?

companies. However, you probably never heard of Robert F. Young, who in only four years made his company, Red Hat, one of today's fastest-growing software companies (on the strength of its Linux operating system)—increasing his net worth some $2 billion in the process. You also probably never heard of Alain Rossmann, although if you have ever used an Internet browser in a wireless phone, chances are good that you used a product developed by the wildly successful company he founded, Phone.com.[23] Like Gates, Young and Rossmann are people who started their own companies—individuals known as **entrepreneurs**.

Today, growing numbers of people are turning away from the corporate world, opting instead to start their own businesses. In fact, in the United States, 8.30 percent of the population is involved in a start-up company, and 5.51 percent have invested in one—making it the leading nation in terms of the number of entrepreneurs.[24] So commonplace is the entrepreneurship movement, in fact, that two-thirds of teenagers report being interested in starting a business of their own someday.[25]

Given its popularity, it probably comes as no surprise that people today consider entrepreneurship as a viable career option. This is especially the case among young people. The general reasons for this boil down to the fact that young entrepreneurs are prepared to ride the wave of technology, have cheap capital available to them, and have boundless optimism.[26] For a more detailed look at some of the forces that keep young entrepreneurs going today, see Table 7.4.

Despite these considerations, it is important to note that success as an entrepreneur cannot be assured. In fact, many of today's once-thriving Internet start-up companies have disappeared. Clearly, to start a company is one thing, but to make it successful is quite another. In fact, the statistics are sobering: About 60 percent of all businesses fail within the first two years.[27] A survey of entrepreneurs indicated that 32 percent say they failed because they were undercapitalized (i.e., they didn't begin with enough money to develop the business properly). The other major reasons for failure

---

TABLE 7.4 Why Are Young Entrepreneurs So Prevalent Today?

Several recent trends in business and technology have made entrepreneurship a very popular and viable option among today's young people. (*Source*: Based on suggestions by Rosenberg, 1999; see Note 26.)

1. Young people are more *tech-savvy* than the generation ahead of them. In fact, many of today's entrepreneurs grew up in an era in which they never knew life without computers.
2. *The Internet* makes it easy for entrepreneurs to gain access to new markets and permits sophisticated research to be conducted inexpensively.
3. Because many companies are *downsizing*, security in the corporate world cannot be assured, reducing people's interest in scaling the corporate ladder.
4. Small businesses have opportunities because many larger companies are *outsourcing* specialized services.
5. *Entrepreneurship programs* have become commonplace in both undergraduate and graduate-level business programs, thereby giving today's students the basic skills needed to become an entrepreneur.
6. The fact that many start-ups become successful has attracted *venture capitalists* to finance start-up companies, making them viable.

noted are a slow economy (30 percent), creditor problems (8 percent), slow receivables (8 percent), and tax problems (6 percent).[28]

Even if your company can make a go of it, it's important to note that an entrepreneur's life is not always as glamorous as one hears. In fact, it can be rather difficult. Typically, founders of companies work longer and harder than they ever worked before—often giving up much of their personal time in the process.[29] Making things worse, they usually find that they do not make any money for the first few years, making it difficult for them to stay afloat personally. Thus, although stories abound of people who made it big on a shoestring—even from their college dormitory rooms (as was Michael Dell's case, the founder of Dell Computers)—adding to the allure of entrepreneurship, it is important to note that entrepreneurs face a long, difficult challenge ahead of them.[30]

> *Typically, founders of companies work longer and harder than they ever worked before—often giving up much of their personal time in the process.*

MANAGING DUAL CAREERS

It's no secret that today's families are quite different from those of just one generation ago.[31] Thirty years ago, the typical nuclear family consisted of a husband who worked outside the home, a wife working as a homemaker, and two children. Today, however, this configuration exists in less than 4 percent of all American households. In fact, in well over half of all American families both spouses work outside the home. These are known as **dual-career couples**. In addition, about twice as many children are currently being raised in single-parent families (mostly mothers) compared to 1970, and two-thirds of these single parents work outside the home.

As you might imagine, these changing demographics have had a considerable impact on the nature of people's careers, and organizational scientists have been highly involved in studying them. When both members of married couples work outside the home, it becomes particularly challenging to be able to balance the demands of one's job (e.g., to work late to meet special projects) with the demands of one's family life (e.g., playing with the children)—what has been referred to as a **work–family conflict** (see Chapter 3). Research has shown that work–family conflicts are major sources of stress that can have a profound negative impact on people's satisfaction with both their work lives and their family lives, increasing depression and lowering overall life satisfaction.[32] In addition, because the demands of one's family life can interfere with one's work, job performance can suffer, and lowered income may result.

In view of the changing nature of the workplace and the adjustments that people must make, many companies are making special efforts to resolve some of the problems of work–family conflict and the logistical problems faced by dual-career couples. For a summary of some of the key approaches that are being taken today, see Table 7.5.

By adopting *family-responsive programs* such as these, companies derive several important benefits. First, they help retain highly valued employees—not only keeping them from competitors but also saving the costs of having to replace them. In fact, officials at AT&T found that the average cost of letting new parents take up to a year of unpaid parental leave was only 32 percent of an employee's annual salary, compared with a 150 percent cost to replace that person permanently. Second, by alleviating the

TABLE 7.5 Family-Responsive Practices for Helping Dual-Career Couples

With an eye toward alleviating some of the work–family conflicts that dual-career couples have, many companies have adopted programs like those summarized here.

Program	Description	Example
Flextime programs	These are policies that give employees some discretion over when they can arrive and leave work, thereby making it easier to adapt their work schedules to the demands of their personal lives. Typically, employees must work a common core of hours, such as 9:00 A.M. to 12 noon and 1:00 P.M. to 3:00 P.M. Scheduling of the remaining hours, within certain spans (such as 6:00 to 9:00 A.M. and 3:00 to 6:00 P.M.) is then left up to the employees themselves.	Companies such as Pacific Bell and Duke Power company have found that flexible work scheduling has helped their employees meet the demands of juggling their work and family lives.
Family leave programs	These are policies that give employees time off their jobs (often some portion of which is paid) to devote to starting a new family.	Aetna Life & Casualty found dramatic increases in the number of female employees who returned to their jobs, saving the company considerable time and money it would have cost to replace them.
Child-care facilities	These are sites at or near company locations where parents can leave their children while they are working.	America West believes so strongly in providing child care that it offers these services 24 hours a day. (The company even maintained this benefit while it was going through bankruptcy proceedings in 1991.)
Personal support policies	These are a wide variety of practices that help employees meet the demands of their family lives, freeing them to concentrate on their work.	The SAS Institute (Cary, North Carolina) offers its employees nutritious take-home dinners. Wilton Connor Packaging (Charlotte, North Carolina) provides on-site laundry, high school equivalency classes, door-to-door transportation, and a children's clothing swap center.
Job sharing	This is the practice of allowing pairs of employees to assume the responsibilities of a single job, giving them the flexibility of being able to work while having time off for family obligations.	At Xerox, several sets of employees share jobs, including two female employees who were sales rivals, but who joined forces to share one job when they each faced the need to reduce their working hours so they could devote time to their new families.

distractions of having to worry about nonwork issues, employees are freed to concentrate on their jobs and to be their most creative. Commenting on this idea, Ellen Galinsky, copresident of the Families & Work Institute, said, "There's a cost to *not* providing work and family assistance."[33] A third benefit is that such policies help attract the most qualified human resources, giving companies that use them a competitive edge over those that do not. In conclusion, family-responsive policies represent a key element in the arsenal of tools used by today's human resources professionals.

HIRING A CAREER COACH

Not everyone is fortunate enough to have a mentor—especially top executives who have few others available to guide them. However, such individuals are not necessarily without the help they need to improve their lives at work and at home. They can—and in increasing numbers, often do—hire *career coaches*. According to the Internal Coach Federation, which boasts 10,000 coaches working worldwide, a **career coach** is an expert hired for purposes of helping someone accomplish his or her career objectives.[34]

Coaches are personal consultants, sounding boards, and therapists all rolled into one. People who don't know how to handle a delicate situation at work, or who are experiencing very stressful situations (see Chapter 3), simply can pick up their phones and find their coaches at the other end ready, willing, and able to lend a hand. Many employees find this highly personal service preferable to, say, confiding in a mentor who may not know what to do, or a superior to whom people would prefer to keep their vulnerabilities confidential. Most coaching services today are provided via either telephone or online connections; few coaches actually meet face-to-face with their clients.[35]

This form of coaching was pioneered in the 1980s by Thomas J. Leonard, a Seattle-based financial planner who discovered that his clients wanted to talk more about life issues than tax and investment advice.[36] Soon, Leonard gave up his financial planning practice and began what he calls a "life planning" service, which his clients referred to as coaching. There was so much demand for his services that, in 1992, Leonard began a formal program for training other coaches, known as Coach University. Although coaching services are not inexpensive (they range in price from $600 to $2,000 per month for three or four 30- to 60-minute phone calls), many executives have benefited so much from these services that they more than pay for themselves. Because of this, several large companies, such as IBM, Kodak, and Goldman Sachs, have brought coaches aboard to help their employees become more productive. For example, at AT&T, executive coach Cheryl Weir inspired managers to shoot for and attain such high goals that the company's investment in coaching services was recovered in only one week.

SUMMARY: HAVE I MET THE LEARNING OBJECTIVES?

You can be certain that you have met the learning objectives for this chapter found on p. 169 if you understand the following:

1. **DEFINE organizational socialization**. Organizational socialization is the process through which people become participating members of their organizations.
2. **DESCRIBE the three stages of organizational socialization**. During the earliest stage, anticipatory socialization, people consider what it would be like to be-

come a member of an organization. To help avoid disappointments, and subsequent turnover, it helps for corporate recruiters to provide *realistic job previews*—accurate descriptions of both the negative and positive aspects of a job likely to be encountered. Once people enter the organization, the encounter stage, they are likely to be exposed to corporate orientation programs designed to socialize them systematically with respect to the operations of the organization as well as its history and traditions. Finally, in the metamorphosis stage, new employees become full-fledged members of the organization, a passage sometimes marked by formal ceremonies.

3. **EXPLAIN how the mentoring process works in organizations**. Mentoring is a special one-on-one form of socialization. It involves a *mentor,* a generally older, more experienced person who counsels and advises a younger, less experienced person, a *protégé*. Relationships between mentors and their protégés offer benefits to both parties, although they have potential costs as well. Such relationships pass through regular stages during which mentors and protégés work closely together and then begin to separate, as the protégé goes off on his or her own. Several of today's companies have been helping women and members of minority groups gain from mentoring experiences.

4. **DEFINE career**. A career is an evolving sequence of work experiences that people have over the course of their lives.

5. **DESCRIBE the three stages of career development**. In the *early-career stage,* during their twenties and thirties, people make career choices that are guided by perceptions of their own talents, referred to as career anchors. After working at a career for a while, in the *middle-career stage,* many people reach the point where their careers have peaked and are unlikely to develop further, known as career plateaus. To help such employees feel better about their work, or to find suitable new work, companies offer career development interventions. These generally include some form of vocational counseling. During one's fifties and sixties, the *late-career stage,* two major issues arise—planning for retirement and preparing for a replacement, or succession planning.

6. **EXPLAIN the impact of the growth of entrepreneurship, the dominance of dual-career couples, and the use of career coaches on careers today**. More people than ever before are turning away from the corporate world and starting their own businesses, becoming *entrepreneurs*. Fueled by their knowledge of technology, the availability of cheap capital, and boundless optimism, many young people are drawn in this direction. However, the vast majority of entrepreneurial businesses fail because they are undercapitalized. Today's *dual-career couples*—those in which both adult members of the household work outside the home—can find it difficult to balance their personal demands with their work demands. To help, growing numbers of companies have *family-responsive programs* (e.g., flextime, job sharing) that help alleviate some of these problems, making it possible for them to maintain their jobs. In recent years, employees who have questions about their careers and their lives have turned to *career coaches* for help. These professionals, hired either individually or by companies for their employees, are providing useful guidance to people in today's complex world.

You Be the Consultant

You are the VP of human resources for "Rubbish World," a private trash removal service located in a large metropolitan area. For some time, customers have been complaining that their trash hasn't always been picked up on time. After investigating the matter, the dispatcher discovered that quite a few drivers have been taking time off their routes to run personal errands. You are concerned because you don't want the problem to continue with the new employees you hire. At a high-level meeting, you are asked to provide advice on this matter. Answer the following questions based on the material in this chapter.

1. How might you use realistic job previews to help select new employees who would not be predisposed to goofing off?
2. What would you do to socialize prospective employees about the company's values? Do you think a corporate orientation program would help? If so, what should it emphasize? How about mentors? Would they be effective in this case? Why or why not?
3. After interviewing some employees, you lean that work–family conflicts might lay at the root of the problem. What steps can the company take to help alleviate such conflicts?

SELF-ASSESSMENT EXERCISE

Finding the Right Career for You

An important part of selecting an appropriate career begins with understanding who you are, and what special personality characteristics you bring with you to your job. This exercise is a highly simplified version of one kind of test that is sometimes used in career counseling.[37] Complete it to get a feel for what such tests are like, and to learn something about your own career interests. Such a simple exercise cannot be completely accurate, of course, but considering your answers carefully may give you some interesting self-insights.

Directions
For each of the seven following sets of adjectives, select the letter corresponding to the one adjective that best describes yourself.

1. (a) forceful	(b) enthusiastic	(c) systematic	(d) patient
2. (a) adventurous	(b) outgoing	(c) diplomatic	(d) loyal
3. (a) demanding	(b) emotional	(c) conscientious	(d) stable
4. (a) daring	(b) sociable	(c) conventional	(d) team oriented
5. (a) decisive	(b) generous	(c) analytical	(d) calm
6. (a) self-assured	(b) convincing	(c) sensitive	(d) deliberate
7. (a) competitive	(b) trusting	(c) accurate	(d) passive

Scoring
1. Add the number of times you selected the adjectives corresponding to each letter.
2. If the majority of your choices were in the "a" category, you are likely to excel at jobs requiring the generation of new ideas, making decisions, solving problems, and taking charge. Careers in management might be right for you.
3. If the majority of your choices were in the "b" category, you are likely to excel at jobs requiring motivating others and generating enthusiasm in them, interacting with people, and lending them assistance. Careers in teaching might be right for you.
4. If the majority of your choices were in the "c" category, you are likely to excel at jobs requiring the careful following of orders and performing jobs with great care and precision. Careers in scientific laboratory work might be right for you.
5. If the majority of your choices were in the "d" category, you are likely to excel at jobs requiring patience and understanding of others, loyalty, and being a good listener. Careers in the clergy might be right for you.

Questions for Discussion
1. What would you say are the underlying assumptions of this test, and are these reasonable?
2. Did you find it easy or difficult to describe yourself by using only these adjectives? Was it hard for you to select only one adjective? Why or why not?
3. Do you agree with the conclusions about the career best suited to your characteristics based on the scoring? Why or why not?
4. Did this exercise tell you something about yourself that you didn't know? Or, did it merely confirm things you already believed? If so, does this limit the value of the test, or might it still be useful? Explain.
5. What would you consider the limitations of tests such as this when it comes to career counseling?

(**GROUP EXERCISE**)

Assessing Mentorship Experiences

This exercise is designed to help you understand the nature of people's experiences to mentoring in the workplace—both positive and negative.

Directions
1. As a class, generate a master list of people you know (e.g., friends or relatives) who work in various companies.
2. Select from your class a partner with whom you would like to work on this project.
3. Each student should call one individual whom he or she knows, and ask if that person has had experience as either a mentor or a protégé. For those who say yes to either, politely ask permission to interview them about these experiences. Set up a time for this interview that is acceptable to you, the employee, and your partner on this project.
4. During the interview, one of you should ask questions, and the other partner should take careful notes on how the person answers each of the following questions:

      a. Were you ever someone's mentor on the job? (If yes, go to b, c, d, and e. If not, go to f.)

      b. What exactly did you do to help this individual?

      c. Did this relationship develop informally, or was it part of a formal program?

      d. What were the major benefits you got out of the experience?

      e. What were the major problems, if any, you experienced in this relationship?

      f. Were you ever someone's protégé on the job? (If yes, go to g, h, i, and j.)

      g. If so, how exactly did this individual help you?

      h. Did this relationship develop informally, or was it part of a formal program?

      i. What were the major benefits you got out of the experience?

      j. What were the major problems, if any, you experienced in this relationship?

5. As a team, repeat this process with another interviewee. This time, reverse roles as questioner and note taker.

6. Compare each team's results with the entire class.

Questions for Discussion

1. What were the major benefits people reported about being a mentor?

2. What were the major problems people reported about being a mentor? In your opinion, how might these be overcome?

3. What were the major benefits people reported about being a protégé?

4. What were the major problems people reported about being a protégé? In your opinion, how might these be overcome?

NOTES

Case Note

Morris, B. (1999, August 2). MBAs get .com fever. *Fortune*, pp. 60–66.

Chapter Notes

[1] Feldman, J. C. (1976). A socialization process that helps new recruits succeed. *Personnel, 57*, 11–23.

[2] Wanous, J. P., & Coella, A. (1989). Organizational entry research: Current status and future directions. In G. Ferris & K. Rowland (Eds.), *Research in personnel and human resources management* (Vol. 7, pp. 59–120). Greenwich, CT: JAI Press.

[3] Wanous, J. P., Poland, T. D., Premack, S. L., & Davis, K. S. (1992). The effects of met expectations on newcomer attitudes and behaviors: A review and meta-analysis. *Journal of Applied Psychology, 77*, 288–297.

[4] Harvey, M. E. (1991). The effects of a realistic job preview on the tenure and satisfaction of cooperative extension service field agents. *Dissertation Abstracts International, 51*(10A), 3303.

[5] Wanous, J. P. (1993). Newcomer orientation programs that facilitate organizational entry. In H. Schuler & J. L. Farr (Eds.), *Personnel selection and assessment: Individual and organizational perspectives* (pp. 125–139). Hillsdale, NJ: Lawrence Erlbaum Associates.

[6] Darwin, A. (2000). Critical reflections on mentoring in work settings. *Adult Education Quarterly, 50*, 197–211.

[7] Ragubsm, B. R., & Scandura, T. A. (1999). Burden or blessing? Expected costs and benefits of being a mentor. *Journal of Organizational Behavior, 20*, 493–509.

[8] Rothman, H. (1993, April). The boss as mentor. *Nation's Business*, pp. 66–67 (quote, p. 66).

[9] Wickman, F., & Sdodin, T. (1997). *Mentoring*. Chicago: Richard D. Irwin.

[10] Ragins, B. R. (1999). Gender and mentoring relationships: A review and research agenda for the next decade. In G. N. Powell (Ed.), *Handbook of gender and work* (pp. 347–370). Thousand Oaks, CA: Sage.

[11] Schein, E. H. (1978). *Career dynamics: Matching individual and organizational needs*. Reading, MA: Addison-Wesley.

[12] Branch, S. (1998, March 16). MBAs: What they really want. *Fortune*, p. 167.

[13] Forum for Investor Advice. (1999, July 26). Work 'til you drop. *Business Week*, p. 8.

[14] Decker, J. P. (1999, November 22). Why pro golfers can't wait to hit the big five-oh. *Fortune*, p. 76.

[15] Thornton, E. (1999, August 9). No room at the top. *Business Week*, p. 50.

[16] Daniels, C. (2000, April 17). So where do you want to work? *Fortune*, p. 217.

[17] Poe, R., & Courter, C. L. (2000, January). Small is beautiful again. *Across the Board*, p. 9.

[18] Donahue, S. (1999, July). New jobs for the new economy. *Business 2.0*, pp. 102–104, 106–109.

[19] Poe, R., & Courter, C. L. (1999, November–December). Great expectations. *Across the Board*, p. 7.

[20] Vesely, R. (1999, June). Pounding the virtual pavement. *Business 2.0*, pp. 24, 26.

[21] Useem, J. (1999, July 5). For sale online: You. *Fortune*, pp. 67–70, 74, 76.

[22] See Note 21. (quote p. 70)

[23] The top entrepreneurs. (2000, January 10). *Business Week*, pp. 80–82.

[24] Global Entrepreneurship Monitor. (1999, July 19). Startup nation. *Business Week*, p. F4.

[25] Berman, D. (1999, December 6). One iota. *Business Week*, p. F8.

[26] Rosenberg, H. (1999, March 1). This generation is all business. *Business Week*, pp. ENT4, ENT6, ENT8.

[27] Meadors, A. L. (2000). Common reasons for business failure. From the World Wide Web: http://members.tripod.com/mysec/flag/failure.html.

[28] Barker, R. (1999, March 29). Lessons from a survivor. *Business Week*, pp. ENT18–ENT20.

[29] Lundstrom, M. (1999, December 20). Mommy, do you love your company more than me? *Business Week*, p. 175.

[30] MacLean, R. (1999, October 19). Big manager on campus. *Inc.*, pp. 62–64, 66.

[31] Jiping, Z., & Tang, S. (2000). Breadwinner status and gender ideologies of men and women regarding family roles. *Sociological Perspectives, 43*, 29–43.

[32] Jackson, A. P., Brown, R. P., & Patterson-Stewart, K. E. (2000). African-Americans in dual-career commuter marriages: An investigation of their experiences. *Family Journal–Counseling and Therapy for Couples and Families, 8*, 22–36.

[33] Galen, M., Palmer, A. T., Cuneo, A., & Maremont, M. (1993, June 28). Work and family. *Business Week*, pp. 80–84, 86, 88 (quote, p. 83).

[34] Schatz, R. D. (1999, October 11). Put me in, coach. *Business Week*, p. F48.

[35] Harrington, A. (1998, September 28). A sounding board in cyberspace. *Fortune*, pp. 301–302.

[36] Morris, B. (2000, February 21). So you're a player. Do you need a coach? *Fortune*, pp. 144–146, 148, 150, 152, 154,

[37] Adapted from Morrison, E. K. (1994). *Leadership skills*. Tucson, AZ: Fisher Books.

8

Organizational communication

LEARNING OBJECTIVES

After reading this chapter, you will be able to:

1. DEFINE communication and DESCRIBE the various steps in the communication process.

2. RECOGNIZE the differences between formal and informal communication in organizations.

3. DISTINGUISH between verbal and nonverbal communication, and the factors that make each effective.

4. IDENTIFY various inspirational techniques that can be used to enhance one's effectiveness as a communicator.

5. DESCRIBE what it takes to be a supportive communicator.

6. EXPLAIN how to meet the challenges associated with communicating with people from different cultures.

THREE GOOD REASONS WHY YOU SHOULD CARE ABOUT . . .

Organizational Communication

You should care about organizational communication because:

1. Although managers spend a great deal of time communicating with others, they tend not to do so as effectively as possible.

2. Properly managing organizational communication is key to individual and organizational effectiveness.

3. Being a good communicator can help you advance to higher organizational positions.

Making the Case for... Organizational Communication

US West: Information Sharing in Real Time

If we are living in the information age, then surely US West's network-reliability operations center in Littleton, Colorado, is ground zero. Admittedly, the huge, beige corrugated-metal building doesn't look like much from the outside, but inside it's a different story. With massive display panels positioned at one end of the cavernous facility facing banks of computer terminals, it looks a lot like *Star Trek*'s legendary USS *Enterprise*. And, with crowds of people checking out the rows of names and numbers on the screens, you'd think you were in the operations room of a Las Vegas sports-betting parlor.

In reality, however, the scene is neither science fiction nor gambling fancy. Rather, the high-tech displays report the real-time status of telecommunications in a 14-state region. Data on performance of customers' telephone lines are updated every five minutes and reported on eight large display screens. The idea is to provide all employees with critical information needed to help resolve service problems or to avoid them in the first place. This information alerts workers to the nature and location of any outages they spot, allowing them to take appropriate action. Technical managers, seated at the front of the room, diagnose the problem, seeking help from hundreds of technicians seated behind them. These experts range from those who monitor equipment in the field to those who set up lines for new service. When they succeed at what they're doing, problems are resolved so quickly that most customers don't know they ever existed.

One day, for example, the board showed an exceptionally busy pattern of traffic that was threatening to tie up telephone service in a small area. As it worked out, the problem was caused by thousands of people trying to call a merchant who just received a shipment of Beanie Babies. Activity on the trunk line was so great that merchants in neighboring stores couldn't make any outgoing calls—that is, until technicians at the center made appropriate adjustments to the equipment.

Aware that phone service may be affected by more than just a shipment of Beanie Babies, US West also receives continuous feeds from the Weather Channel and CNN. This enables it to take advance precautions when serious weather or major news events threaten to increase phone traffic into or out of its service area. A good example is the tragic 1999 shooting at Columbine High School, just a few miles away. By getting a lead on the breaking story, technicians were able to anticipate the increased phone traffic, making appropriate adjustments so that nobody's service was disrupted.

Sixty-five percent of the outages stem not from bad weather or breaking news, but from human error. To avoid these problems, weekly meetings are held in which the previous week's most significant service problems are reviewed to assess how they began and to consider how they may be avoided in the future. Nobody is singled out by name, and no blame is assigned. The emphasis is on recognizing problems so that people can be better trained to anticipate them. And, given US West's outstanding service, it seems to be working quite well.

Beyond the technological marvel that is US West's network-reliability operations center lies a good demonstration of the importance of sharing information in organizations. Instead of having one person gather information on his or her computer terminal and shares it with others, as is typical in many companies, US West's approach allows all technicians to access the same information at once. This is a good example of efficient *communication*—the processes through which people send information to others and receive information from them. As you might imagine, successful communication is required for organizations to succeed. With this in mind, in this chapter I will explain how the communication process works and ways of fostering communication in organizations.

The Communication Process

For organizations to function, individuals and groups must carefully coordinate their efforts and activities. Waiters must take their customers' orders and pass them along to the chef. Store managers must describe special promotions to their sales staffs. And the football coach must tell his team what play to run. Clearly, communication is the key to these attempts at coordination. Without it, people would not know what to do, and groups and organizations would not be able to operate effectively—if at all!

With this in mind, it should not be surprising that communication has been referred to as "the social glue . . . that continues to keep organizations tied together,"[1] and "the essence of organizations."[2] Given the importance of communication in organizations, you may not be surprised to learn that managers spend as much as 80 percent of their time communicating in one form or another (e.g., writing a report, speaking to others, etc.). I will begin reviewing organizational communication by formally describing the communication process and then identifying some of the forms it takes. Then, building on this foundation, I will discuss several ways of improving organizational communication.

STEPS IN THE COMMUNICATION PROCESS

Formally, **communication** is defined as the process by which a person, group, or organization (the *sender*) transmits some type of information (the *message*) to another person, group, or organization (the *receiver*). Figure 8.1 clarifies this definition and further elaborates on the process.

Encoding.   The communication process begins when one party has a message it wishes to send another (either party may be an individual, a group, or an entire organization). It is the sender's mission to transform the idea into a form that can be sent to, and understood by, the receiver. This is what happens in the process of **encoding**—translating an idea into a form, such as written or spoken language, that can be recognized by a receiver. We encode information when we select the words we use in an e-mail message or when we speak to someone in person.

Transmission via communication channels.   After a message is encoded it is ready to be transmitted over one or more **channels of communication** to reach the desired receiver. There are many different pathways over which information travels, including telephone lines, radio and television signals, fiber-optic cables, mail routes, and even the airwaves that carry the vibrations of our voices. Thanks to modern technology, people sending messages have a wide variety of communication channels available to them for sending both visual and oral information. Whatever channel is used, the communicator's goal is the same: to send the encoded message accurately to the desired receiver.

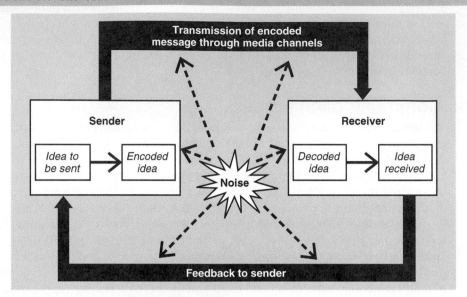

FIGURE 8.1 The Communication Process

Communication generally follows the steps outlined here. Senders *encode* messages and *transmit* them via one or more communication channels to receivers, who then *decode* these messages. The process continues as the original receiver then sends *feedback* to the original sender. Factors distorting or limiting the flow of information—known collectively as *noise*—may enter into the process at any point.

Decoding.   Once a message is received, the recipient must begin the process of **decoding**—that is, converting that message back into the sender's original ideas. This can involve many different processes, such as comprehending spoken and written words, interpreting facial expressions, and the like. To the extent that a sender's message is accurately decoded by the receiver, the ideas understood will be the ones intended.

As you might imagine, our ability to comprehend and interpret information received from others is far from perfect. This would be the case, for example, if we were conducting business in a foreign country and lacked the language skills needed to understand the speaker. However, even when it comes to understanding one's own native language it's only too easy to imagine how we sometimes misunderstand what others intend to say.

Feedback.   Once a message has been decoded, the process of communication continues, but in reverse. In other words, the person receiving the message now becomes the sender of a new message. This new message is then encoded and transmitted along a communication channel to the intended recipient, who then decodes it. This part of the communication process is known as **feedback**—providing information about the impact of messages on receivers. Receiving feedback allows senders to determine whether their messages have been understood properly. Of course, once received, feedback can trigger another idea from the sender, initiating yet another cycle of communication and triggering another round of feedback. It was with this cyclical nature of the communication process in mind that we characterize the communication process in Figure 8.1 as being continuous.

Noise.   Despite its apparent simplicity, it probably comes as no surprise that the communication process rarely operates as flawlessly as I have described it here. As you will see, there are many potential barriers to effective communication. **Noise** is the name given to factors that distort the clarity of messages that are encoded, transmitted, or decoded in the communication process. Whether noise results from unclear writing (i.e., poorly encoded messages), a listener's inattentiveness (i.e., poorly decoded messages), or static along a telephone line (i.e., faulty communication media), ineffective communication is inevitably the result.

FORMAL COMMUNICATION IN ORGANIZATIONS

Imagine a CEO of a large conglomerate announcing plans for new products to a group of stockholders. Now imagine a supervisor telling his or her subordinates what to do that day on the job. Both examples describe situations in which someone is sharing official information with others who need to know this information. This is referred to as **formal communication**. The formally prescribed pattern of interrelationships existing between the various units of an organization is commonly described by using a diagram known as an **organization chart**. Such diagrams provide a graphic representation of an organization's structure, and an outline of the planned, formal connections between its various units—that is, who is supposed to communicate with whom.

An organization chart revealing the structure of a small part of a fictitious organization, and an overview of the types of communication expected to occur within it, is shown in Figure 8.2. Each box represents a particular job, as indicated by the job titles noted. The lines connecting the boxes show the formal lines of communication between the individuals performing those jobs—that is, who is supposed to communicate with whom. This particular organization chart is typical of most in that it shows that people communicate formally with those immediately above them and below them, as well as those at their own levels.

Downward communication.   Formal communication differs according to people's positions in an organization chart. Suppose, for example, that you are a supervisor. How would you characterize the formal communication that occurs between you and your subordinates—that is, communication down the organization chart? Typically, *downward communication* consists of instructions, directions, and orders—that is, messages telling subordinates what they should be doing. We also would expect to find feedback on past performance flowing in a downward direction. A sales manager, for example, may tell the members of his or her sales force what products they should be promoting.

As formal information slowly trickles down from one level of an organization to the next lowest level (as occurs when information is said to "go through channels"), it becomes less accurate. This is especially true when that information is spoken. In such cases, it is not unusual for at least part of the message to be distorted and/or omitted as it works its way down from one person to the next lowest-ranking person. (Anyone who has ever played the game of "telephone" has experienced this firsthand.) To avoid these problems, many companies have introduced programs in which they communicate formal information to large numbers of people at different levels all at one time.

FIGURE 8.2 The Organization Chart: A Summary of Formal Communication Paths

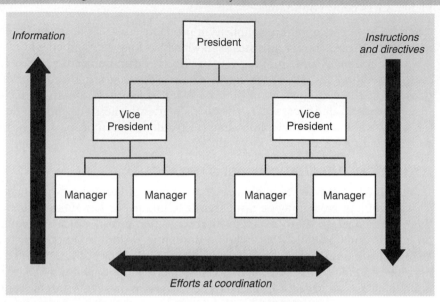

Diagrams known as *organization charts* indicate the formal pattern of communication within an organization. They reveal which particular people, based on the jobs they hold, are required to communicate with each other. The types of messages generally communicated across different levels are identified here.

Upward communication.   When information flows from lower levels to higher levels within an organization, such as messages from subordinates to their supervisors, it is known as *upward communication*. Typically, these messages involve information that managers need to do their jobs, such as data required to complete projects. This may include suggestions for improvement, status reports, reactions to work-related issues, and new ideas.

Although logically, upward communication is the opposite of downward communication, there are some important differences between them resulting from the difference in status between the communicating parties. For example, it has been established that upward communication occurs far less frequently than downward communication. In fact, one classic study found that 70 percent of assembly-line workers initiated communication with their supervisors less than once a month. And when people do communicate upward, their conversations tend to be far shorter than the ones they have with others at their own level.

> *One classic study found that 70 percent of assembly-line workers initiated communication with their supervisors less than once a month.*

Even more importantly, when upward communication does occur, the information transmitted is frequently inaccurate. Given that employees are interested in "putting their best foot forward" when communicating with their bosses, they have a tendency to highlight their accomplishments and to downplay their mistakes. As a result, negative information tends to be ignored or disguised. This tendency for people to purposely avoid communicating bad news to their supervisors is known as the **MUM effect**. We are concerned about this phenomenon because supervisors can make good decisions only when they have good information available to them. And when subordinates are either withholding or distorting information so as to avoid looking bad, the accuracy of the information communicated is bound to suffer. As one executive put it, "All of us have our share of bonehead ideas. Having someone tell you it's a bonehead idea before you do something about it is really a great blessing."[3] Unfortunately, this does not occur as often as many executives would like. In fact, a recent survey has found that although 95 percent of CEOs say that they have an open door policy and will not harm those who communicate bad news, still half of all employees believe that they will be jeopardizing their positions by sharing bad news, and frequently refrain from doing so.[4]

Horizontal communication.   Within organizations, messages don't flow only up and down the organization chart, but sideways as well. **Horizontal communication** is the term used to identify messages that flow laterally, at the same organizational level. Messages of this type are characterized by efforts at coordination, or attempts to work together. Consider, for example, how a vice president of marketing would have to coordinate his or her efforts with people in other departments when launching an advertising campaign for a new product. This would require the coordination of information with experts from manufacturing and production (to see when the products will be available) as well as those from research and development (to see what features people really want).

Unlike vertical communication, in which the parties are at different organizational levels, horizontal communication involves people at the same level. Therefore, it tends to be easier and friendlier. It also is more casual in tone and occurs more readily, given that there are fewer social barriers between the parties. This is not to say that horizontal communication is without its potential pitfalls. Indeed, people in different departments sometimes feel that they are competing against each other for valued organizational resources, leading them to show resentment toward one another. And when an antagonistic, competitive orientation replaces a friendly, cooperative one, work is bound to suffer.

INFORMAL COMMUNICATION: BEYOND THE ORGANIZATION CHART

Imagine a bunch of workers standing around the coffee machine chatting about how tough the big boss is, or who was dancing with whom at the company party. These, too, are examples of organizational communication, but because they involve the sharing of unofficial information, they would be considered examples of **informal communication**. It's probably obvious to you that a great deal of information communicated in organizations goes far beyond formal messages sent up, down, or across organization charts—in other words, such information is shared without any formally imposed obligations or restrictions.

Hearing it "through the grapevine."   When people communicate informally, they are not bound by their organizational positions. Anyone can tell anything to anyone else. Although it clearly would be inappropriate for a mail room clerk to share his or her thoughts with a vice president about matters of corporate policy, both parties may be perfectly at ease exchanging funny stories. The difference lies in the fact that the funny stories are unofficial in nature and are communicated informally—that is, without following the formal constraints imposed by the organization chart.

When anyone can tell something informally to anyone else, it results in a very rapid flow of information along what is commonly called **the grapevine**. This term refers to the pathways along which unofficial information travels. In contrast to formal organizational messages, which might take several days to reach their destinations, information traveling along the organizational grapevine tends to flow very rapidly. In fact, it is not unusual for some messages to reach everyone in a large organization in a matter of a few hours. This happens not only because informal communication crosses organizational boundaries and is open to everyone, but also because it generally is transmitted orally, and oral messages not only reach more people, but do so more quickly than written messages.

As I noted earlier, however, oral messages run the risk of becoming inaccurate as they flow between people. Because of the possible confusion grapevines can cause, some people have sought to eliminate them. However, grapevines are not necessarily bad. In fact, informally socializing with our coworkers can help make work groups more cohesive, and they also may provide excellent opportunities for the pleasant social contacts that make life at work enjoyable. Moreover, the grapevine remains one of the most efficient channels of communication. Indeed, about 70 percent of what people learn about their companies they pick up by chatting with coworkers in the cafeteria, at the coffee machine, or in the corridors.[5]

> *About 70 percent of what people learn about their companies they pick up by chatting with coworkers in the cafeteria, at the coffee machine, or in the corridors.*

Rumors: The downside of informal communication.   Although the information communicated along the grapevine may be accurate in some respects, it may be inaccurate in others. In extreme cases, information may be transmitted that is almost totally without any basis in fact and is unverifiable. Such messages are known as **rumors**. Typically, rumors are based on speculation, someone's overactive imagination, and wishful thinking, rather than on facts.

Rumors race like wildfire through organizations because the information they contain is usually so interesting and vague. This ambiguity leaves messages open to embellishment as they pass orally from one person to the next. Before you know it, almost everyone in the organization has heard the rumor, and its inaccurate message comes to be taken as fact ("Everyone knows it, so it must be true"). Hence, even if there may have been, at one point, some truth to a rumor, the message quickly grows untrue.

If you personally have ever been the victim of a rumor, you know just how troublesome it can be. Now, imagine how many times more serious the consequences may be when an organization falls victim to a rumor. Two cases come to mind. In the late 1970s, a rumor circulated in Chicago that McDonald's hamburgers contained worms.

Also, in June 1993, stories appeared in the press stating that people had found syringes in cans of Pepsi-Cola. Although both rumors were proven to be completely untrue, they cost both McDonald's and Pepsi considerable sums of money due to lost sales, not to mention the costs of investigation and advertising.

With this in mind, the question arises: What can be done to counter the effects of rumors? You may be tempted to consider directly refuting a rumor. This approach works best whenever a rumor is highly implausible and is challenged immediately by an independent source. This was precisely what occurred when the Food and Drug Administration (FDA) carefully investigated Pepsi-Cola and announced that there were not, nor could there have been, syringes in cans of Pepsi. In the case of McDonald's, direct refutations (in the form of signs from the FDA stating that McDonald's used only wholesome ground beef in its burgers) had little effect because the rumor had spread so rapidly. In fact, directly challenging the rumor only led some customers to raise questions about why such official government statements were necessary in the first place, thereby fueling the rumor. What worked best at countering the rumor, research showed, was reminding people about other things they already believed about McDonald's (e.g., that it is a clean, family-oriented place).[6] Not surprisingly, advertising campaigns (including public relations efforts by politicians rumored to be involved in various scandals) frequently devote more time to redirecting the public's attention away from negative thoughts and toward positive ones that they already have.

Communicating With and Without Words: Verbal and Nonverbal Communication

By virtue of the fact that you are reading this book, I know that you are familiar with **verbal communication**—transmitting and receiving ideas using words. Verbal communication can be either oral—that is, using spoken language, such as face-to-face talks or telephone conversations—or written, such as faxes, letters, or e-mail messages. Despite their differences, these forms of communication share a key feature: They all involve the use of words. As you know, however, people also communicate a great deal without words, or nonverbally—that is, by way of their facial gestures, body language, the clothes they wear, and even where at a table they choose to sit. This is referred to as **nonverbal communication**. I will describe both verbal and nonverbal communication in this section of the chapter.

VERBAL MEDIA: THEIR FORMS AND EFFECTIVENESS

As you already know, organizations rely on a wide variety of verbal media. Some forms are considered rich because they are highly interactive and rely on a great deal of information. A face-to-face discussion is a good example. A telephone conversation may be considered a little less rich because it doesn't allow the parties to see each other. At the other end of the continuum are communications media that are considered lean because they are static (one-way) and involve much less information. Flyers and bulletins are good examples insofar as they are broadly aimed and focus on a specific issue. Letters are also a relatively lean form of communication. However, because letters are aimed at a specific individual, they may be considered not as lean as bulletins. For a summary of this continuum, please refer to Figure 8.3.

FIGURE 8.3 A Continuum of Verbal Communication Media

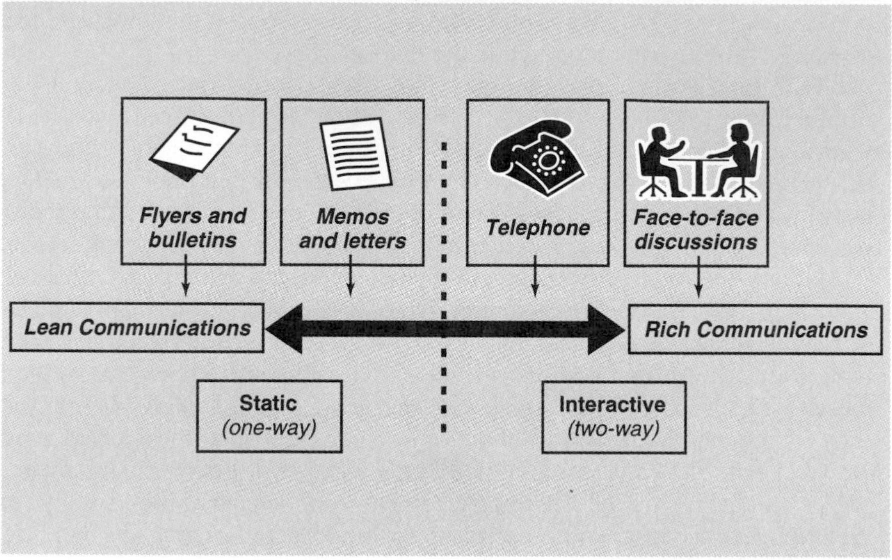

Verbal communication media may be characterized along a continuum ranging from highly rich, interactive media (e.g., face-to-face discussions) to lean, static media (e.g., flyers and bulletins).

Forms of written communication. Although organizations rely on a wide variety of written media, two particular forms—*newsletters* and *employee handbooks*—deserve special mention because of the important roles they play. **Newsletters** are regularly published internal documents describing information of interest to employees regarding an array of business and nonbusiness issues. Traditionally, these are printed on paper, but today, a great many company newsletters are published online, using the company's **intranet**—a Web site that can be accessed only by a company's employees. Many companies have found newsletters to be useful devices for explaining official policies and reminding everyone of important decisions made at group meetings. For example, at the Widemeyer-Baker Group, a 75-person media-relations firm, employees use the company's intranet site to access an online newsletter that provides key information about what's going on in the company.[7] Particularly popular is a column called "the Buzz," which serves as a sort of electronic water cooler around which people gather to share information about others in the company.

    Employee handbooks are also important vehicles of internal organizational communication. These are formal documents describing basic information about the organization—its formal policies, mission, and underlying philosophy. Handbooks are widely used today. Not only do they do an effective job socializing new employees into the company (see Chapter 7), but the explicit statements they provide may also help avoid serious misunderstandings and conflict between employees and their company's top management (see Chapter 6).

The effectiveness of verbal media: Matching the medium and the message. Given that people in organizations spend so much of their time using both oral and written communication, it makes sense to ask: Which is more effective? As you might imagine, the answer is rather complex. For example, we know that communication is most effective in organizations when it uses multiple channels—that is, *both* oral and written messages.[8] Oral messages help get people's immediate attention. Then, written follow-ups are helpful because they provide permanent documents to which people can later refer. Oral messages also have the benefit of allowing for immediate two-way communication between parties, whereas written messages frequently are either one-way or take too long for a response. Not surprisingly, in organizations two-way communications (such as face-to-face discussions and telephone calls) occur more frequently than one-way communications (e.g., memos).

The matter of how effectively a particular communications medium works depends on the kind of message being sent. In general, managers prefer using oral media when communicating ambiguous messages (e.g., directions on how to solve a complex technical problem), but written media for communicating clear messages (e.g., sharing a price list). Moreover, managers who follow this particular pattern of matching media with messages tend to be more effective on the job than those who do not do so. This suggests that demonstrating sensitivity to communicating in the most appropriate fashion is an important determinant of managerial success.

> *In general, managers prefer using oral media when communicating ambiguous messages (e.g., directions on how to solve a complex technical problem), but written media for communicating clear messages (e.g., sharing a price list).*

NONVERBAL COMMUNICATION

It has been estimated that people communicate at least as much *nonverbally* (i.e., without words) as they do verbally.[9] Indeed, there can be no doubt that many of the messages we send others are transmitted without words. Here are just a few examples of how we communicate nonverbally in organizations:

- *Mode of dress*—Much of what we say about ourselves to others comes from the way we dress. For example, despite the general trend toward casual clothing in the workplace, higher status people still tend to dress more formally than lower-ranking employees.[10]
- *Waiting time*—Higher-status people, such as managers and executives at all ranks, tend to communicate their organizational positions nonverbally by keeping lower-ranking people waiting to see them—a gesture that sends the message that their time is more important.[11]
- *Seating position*—Higher-ranking people also assert their higher status by sitting at the heads of rectangular tables, a position that not only has become associated with importance over the years, but that also enables important people to maintain eye contact with those over whom they are responsible.[12]

As you read this, you may be asking yourself, "What can I do to present myself more favorably to those around me on the job?" Specifically, what can you do nonverbally to cultivate the impression that you have the qualities of a good leader and that you are worthy of promotion? Just as you can say certain things to enhance your image

---

TABLE 8.1 How to Communicate Your Leadership Potential Nonverbally

People who are self-confident not only speak and write with assurance, but they also project their capacity to lead others in the various nonverbal ways summarized here. (*Source*: Based on suggestions by DuBrin, 2001; see Note 13.)

- Stand and sit using an erect posture. Avoid slouching.
- When confronted, stand up straight. Do not cower.
- Nod your head to show that you are listening to someone talk.
- Maintain eye contact and smile at those with whom you are talking.
- Use hand gestures in a relaxed, nonmechanical way.
- Always be neat, well-groomed, and wear clean, well-pressed clothes.

---

as a strong, effective employee, there are also several things you can do nonverbally that will enhance your image. For a summary of these, see Table 8.1.

Improving Your Communication Skills

There can be no doubt that successful employees at all levels, from the lowest-ranking person to the CEO, stand to benefit by improving their verbal communication skills. Although there are far too many ways of improving your verbal communication than I can possibly review here, two general approaches are worthy of mentioning. These include using inspirational tactics and being a supportive communicator.

USE INSPIRATIONAL COMMUNICATION TACTICS

Effective leaders know how to inspire others when they communicate with them. To become an effective leader, or even a more effective employee, it helps to consider several key ways of inspiring others when communicating with them.[13] These are as follows:

- *Project confidence and power with emotion-provoking words.* The most persuasive communicators attempt to inspire others by sprinkling their speech with words that provoke emotion. For example, it helps to use phrases such as "bonding with customers" instead of the more benign "being friendly." Effective communicators also use words in ways that highlight their power in an organization. For some linguistic tips in this regard, see Table 8.2.[14]
- *Be credible.* Communicators are most effective when they are perceived to be credible. Such perceptions are enhanced when one is considered trustworthy, intelligent, and knowledgeable. Bill Joy of Sun Microsystems (considered "the Thomas Edison of the Internet"), for example, has considerable credibility in the computer business because he is regarded to be so highly intelligent. At the very least, credibility is enhanced by backing up your claims with clear data. People might not believe you unless you support your ideas with objective information.
- *Pitch your message to the listener.* The most effective communicators go out of their way to send messages that are of interest to listeners. Assume that people will pay the greatest attention when they are interested in answering the question, "How is what you are saying important to me?" People will attend most carefully to messages that have value to them. Jürgen Schempp, the CEO of

TABLE 8.2	How to Project Confidence with Your Words

The most powerful and confident people tend to follow certain linguistic conventions. By emulating the way they speak, you, too, can enhance the confidence you project. (*Source*: Based on suggestions by DuBrin, 2001; see Note 13.)

Rule	*Explanation or Example*
Always know exactly what you want.	The more committed you are to achieving a certain end, the more clearly and powerfully you will be able to sell your idea.
Use the pronoun "I", unless you are a part of a team.	This allows you to take individual credit for your ideas.
Downplay uncertainty.	If you are unsure of your opinion, make a broad but positive statement, such as "I am confident this new accounting procedure will make things more efficient."
Ask very few questions.	You may come across as being weak or unknowledgeable if you have to ask what something means or what's going on.
Don't display disappointment when your ideas are challenged.	It is better to act as though opposition is expected and to explain your viewpoint.
Make bold statements.	Be bold about ideas, but avoid attacking anyone personally.

Daimler-Chrysler, appeared to have this rule in mind when he explained how his plan for organizing the company into three divisions would result in higher salaries and bonuses for employees, as well as greater autonomy.

* *Avoid "junk words" that dilute your message.* Nobody likes to listen to people who constantly use phrases such as "like," "know what I mean?" and "you know." Such phrases send the message that the speaker is ill-prepared to express himself or herself clearly and precisely. Because many of us use such phrases in our everyday language, it helps to practice by tape-recording what you are going to say so you can keep track of the number of times you say these things. Make a conscious effort to stop using these words, and use your tape recordings to monitor your progress.
* *Use front-loaded messages.* The most effective communicators come right out and say what they mean. They don't beat around the bush, and they don't embed their most important message in a long speech or letter. Instead, they begin by making the point they are attempting to communicate and then use the remainder of the message to illustrate it and flush out the details.
* *Cut through the clutter.* People are so busy these days that they easily become distracted by the many messages that come across their desks (see Figure 8.4).[15] The most effective communicators attempt to cut through the clutter, such as by making their messages interesting, important, and special. Dull and uninspired messages are likely to get lost in the shuffle.

FIGURE 8.4 We All Are Bombarded by Messages

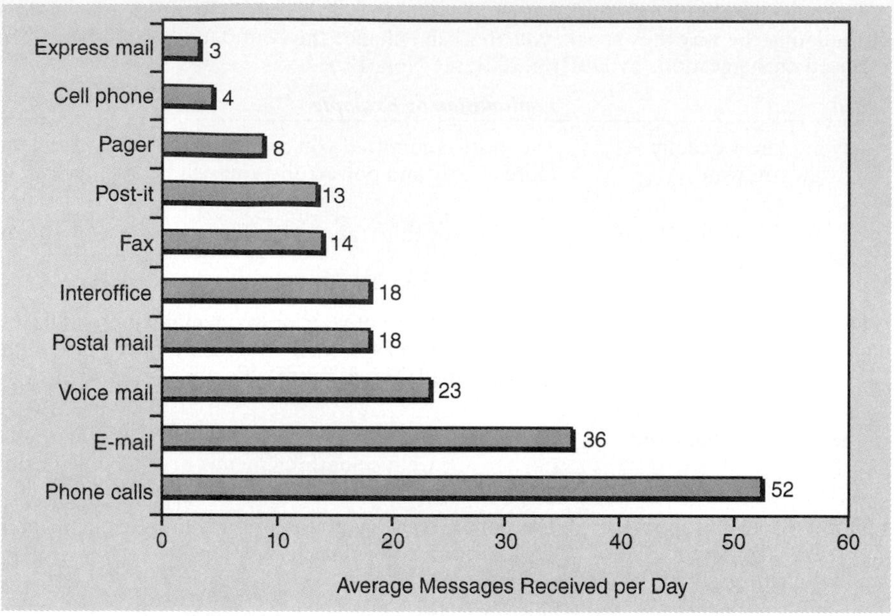

The average U.S. office worker receives 189 messages per day—that's over 23 per hour. As summarized here, they come in many different forms. (*Source*: Wurman, 2000; see Note 15.)

BE A SUPPORTIVE COMMUNICATOR

Thus far, I have been describing a way of being an effective communicator by being forceful and inspiring people. Good communicators, as you know, are also highly people-oriented, requiring a low-key approach. To communicate effectively with others, we need to show that we are interested in what the other person has to say and respond in ways that strengthen the relationship between ourselves and the target of our messages. In short, we need to demonstrate what is called **supportive communication**. Doing this requires adhering to the following rules:[16]

- *Focus on the problem instead of the person.* Although people are generally receptive to ways of making things better, we all naturally resist suggestions that we somehow need to change ourselves. Saying, for example, "You need to be more creative," would lead most of us to become defensive and to turn off the speaker. However, saying something more supportive, like "See if you can find a way of finding more solutions to this problem," is bound to meet with a far better reaction.
- *Match your words and your body language.* You can be a far more effective communicator when the things you say with your body match the words you use. For example, sending the message that you are excited about someone's idea is amplified by verbally explaining your satisfaction and nonverbally showing your excitement, such as by sitting up, looking alert, and opening your eyes widely. By contrast, crossing your arms, closing your eyes, and slumping while

saying the same words would only detract from your message—if it even comes across at all.

- *Acknowledge the other person's ideas.* Even if you disagree with what someone is saying, you don't want to make that individual feel badly about expressing his or her ideas. Not only is this rude, but it is a good way of getting people to keep their ideas to themselves, which interferes with effective management. So, for example, if you have to reject someone's suggestion, don't make that person feel badly by suggesting that the idea is silly and devoid of merit. Instead, it would be far more supportive to highlight the good aspects of that person's ideas and to explain precisely why it would be inappropriate to implement it right now.
- *Keep the conversation going.* One sure way to block the exchange of ideas is to say or do things that stop conversations in their tracks. Long pauses may do this, as will saying things that change the topic. Effective communication requires keeping the conversation going, and this can be accomplished by listening carefully to what someone says and building upon it when responding.

ENCOURAGE OPEN FEEDBACK

In theory, it's simple: If accurate information is the key to effective communication, then organizations should encourage feedback since, after all, feedback is a prime source of information. However, I say "in theory" because it is natural for workers to be afraid of the repercussions they may face when being extremely open with their superiors. Likewise, high-ranking officials may be somewhat apprehensive about hearing what's really on their workers' minds. In other words, people in organizations may be reluctant to give and to receive feedback—a situation that can wreak havoc on organizational communication.

People in organizations may be reluctant to give and to receive feedback—a situation that can wreak havoc on organizational communication.

These problems would be unlikely to occur in an organizational climate in which top officials openly and honestly seek feedback and in which lower-level workers believe they can speak their minds with impunity. But how can this be accomplished? Although this is not easy, several successful techniques for opening feedback channels have been used by organizations. Some of the more popular approaches are listed below. For a close-up look at one company's novel approach to addressing this problem, see the **Winning Practices** section on page 210.

- **360-degree feedback**—Formal systems in which people at all levels give feedback to others at different levels and receive feedback from them, as well as outsiders—including customers and suppliers. This technique is used in such companies as Alcoa, BellSouth, General Mills, Hewlett-Packard, Merck, Motorola, and 3M.
- **Suggestion systems**—Programs that invite employees to submit ideas about how something may be improved. Employees are generally rewarded when their ideas are implemented. For example, the idea of mounting film boxes onto cards that hang from display stands, which is so common today, originally came from a Kodak employee.

WINNING PRACTICES

Mistake of the Month

If your company has an important message to communicate to customers, the press, employees, financial analysts, or any such group, Delahaye Medialink can do research to help you find the most effective way of communicating with them. Given that this Portsmouth, New Hampshire–based company is in the communication research business, it probably comes as no surprise that it uses a particularly effective, yet counterintuitive, way of communicating within its ranks.[17]

It all started in 1989 when the founder and CEO, Katie Paine, made a serious mistake: She overslept, causing her to miss a flight to an important meeting with a client. Despite her obvious embarrassment from her big mistake, Paine learned a vital lesson about the importance of getting up on time. But why, she thought, should this lesson be kept solely with her? After all, sharing it with others stood to benefit them as well. With this in mind, the next day Paine went to a staff meeting, where she put a $50 bill on the table and challenged her colleagues to tell a worse story about their own mistakes. That they did. One salesman described how he went on a sales call without his business cards, and another admitted to having scheduled a presentation at Coca-Cola but left the presentation materials behind.

So many people learned so many things about ways to mess things up—and how to avoid doing so—that the "Mistake of the Month" soon became a feature of staff meetings at Delahaye. It works like this: At each monthly staff meeting, a half hour is devoted to identifying and discussing everyone's mistakes. Each is written on a board, and everyone gets to vote on two categories of mistakes—the one from which they learned the most and the one from which they learned the least. The person whose mistake is identified as helping the most is awarded a highly coveted downtown parking space for the next month. The person from whose mistake people learned the least is required to speak at the next meeting about what he or she is doing to ensure that it will never happen again. The time spent on this exercise is considered a wise investment insofar as it allows all employees to learn from everyone else's mistakes.

During the program's first 10 years, more than 2,000 mistakes have been identified—but few ever have been repeated, creating a positive effect on the company's work. Paine also notes that the program helps her identify steps she needs to take to improve things at Delahaye. She also says that sharing mistakes has been "a bonding ritual," adding "once you go through it, you're a member of the club."

Questions for Discussion

1. What problems, if any, do you envision as resulting from Delahaye's "Mistake of the Month" program?
2. How do you think a similar "Mistake of the Month" program would work at the company at which you are employed?
3. What mistake did you ever make on the job from which you think others might benefit from knowing?

- **Corporate hot lines**—Telephone lines staffed by corporate officials ready to answer questions and listen to comments. These are particularly useful during times when employees are likely to be full of questions because their organizations are undergoing change. For example, AT&T used hot lines in the early 1980s during the period of its antitrust divestiture.

USE SIMPLE LANGUAGE

No matter what field you're in, chances are good that it has its own special language—its **jargon**. Although jargon may greatly help communication within specialized groups, it can severely interfere with communication among the uninitiated.

The trick to using jargon wisely is to know your audience. If the individuals with whom you are communicating understand the jargon, using it can help facilitate communication. However, when addressing audiences whose members are unfamiliar with specialized language, simple, straightforward language is bound to be most effective. In either case, the rationale is the same: Communicators should speak the language of their audiences. Although you may be tempted to try to impress your audience by using big words, you may have little impact on them if they don't understand you. My advice is clear: Follow the **K.I.S.S. principle**—that is, **k**eep **i**t **s**hort and **s**weet.

AVOID OVERLOAD

Imagine this scene: You're up late one night at the end of the term as you're writing a paper and studying for finals (or at least trying to) all at the same time. Your desk is piled high with books when your roommate comes in to explain what you should do to prepare for the end-of-semester party. If this sounds at all familiar to you, then you probably know only too well that it's unlikely that you'd be able to give everything you're doing your most careful attention. After all, when people are confronted with more information than they can process at any given time, their performance tends to suffer. This condition is known as **overload**.

Staying competitive in today's hectic world often requires doing many things at once—but without threatening the performance that often results when communication channels are overloaded. Fortunately, several things can be done to avoid, or at least minimize, the problem of overload. Among these are the following:

- *Rely on gatekeepers.* People whose jobs require them to control the flow of information to potentially overloaded individuals, groups, or organizations are known as **gatekeepers**. In making appointments for top executives, administrative assistants are providing a gatekeeping service.
- *Practice queuing.* A "queue" is a line. So, **queuing** involves lining up incoming information so that it can be attended to in an orderly fashion. Air traffic controllers do this when they "stack" incoming planes in a holding pattern so as to prevent them from tragically "overloading" the runway.

WALK THE TALK

When it comes to effective communication, action definitely speaks louder than words. Too often, communication is hampered by the practice of saying one thing but doing another. And whenever implicit messages (e.g., "we may be cutting jobs") contradict official messages (e.g., "don't worry, the company is stable"), confusion is bound to result.

This is especially problematic when the inconsistency comes from the top. In fact, one of the most effective ways of fostering effective organizational communication is for CEOs to "walk the talk," that is, to match their deeds to their words. After all, a boss would lose credibility if she told her employees, "My door is always open to you," but then was never available for consultation. Good communication demands consistency. And, for the words to be heard as loud as the actions, they must match up.

BE A GOOD LISTENER

Effective communication involves more than just presenting messages clearly. It also involves doing a good job of comprehending others. Although most of us take listening for granted, effective listening is an important skill. In fact, given that managers spend about 40 percent of their time listening to others, but are only 25 percent effective, listening is a skill that could stand to be developed in most of us. When we speak of *effective listening* we are not referring to the passive act of just taking in information, which so often occurs. Rather, effective listening involves three important elements.:

- Being nonjudgmental while taking in information from others
- Acknowledging speakers in ways that encourage them to continue speaking
- Attempting to advance the speaker's ideas to the next step

It is worthwhile to consider what we can do to improve our own effectiveness as listeners. Fortunately, experts have offered several good suggestions, some of which are summarized in Table 8.3.[18] Although it may require some effort, incorporating these suggestions into your own listening habits cannot help but make you a more effective listener.

TABLE 8.3   Tips for Improving Your Listening Skills

Being a good listener is an important skill that can enhance the effectiveness of communication in organizations. Although it may be difficult to follow the suggestions outlined here, the resulting benefits make it worthwhile to try to do so. (*Source*: Based on suggestions by Morrison, 1994; see Note 18.)

Suggestion	*Description*
Do not talk while being spoken to.	It is difficult, if not impossible, to listen to another while you are speaking to that person.
Make the speaker feel at ease.	Help the speaker feel that he or she is free to talk as desired.
Eliminate distractions.	Don't focus on other things: Pay attention only to the speaker.
Show empathy with the speaker.	Try to put yourself in the speaker's position, and make an effort to see his or her point of view.
Be as patient as possible.	Take the time needed to hear everything the speaker has to say.
Hold your arguments.	If you're busy forming your own arguments, you cannot focus on the speaker's points.
Ask questions.	By asking questions, you demonstrate that you are listening and make it possible to clarify areas of uncertainty.

Given its importance, it should not be surprising that many organizations are working hard to improve their employees' listening skills. For example, Unisys has long used seminars and self-training audiocassettes to train thousands of its employees in effective listening skills. Such systematic efforts at improving listening skills represent a wise investment insofar as good listening definitely pays off. Indeed, research has shown that the more effective one is as a listener, the more likely he or she is to get promoted to a top management position—and to perform effectively in that role. (To practice your own listening skills, and to help others do the same, see the **Group Exercise** on p. 220.)

MEETING THE CHALLENGES
OF CROSS-CULTURAL COMMUNICATION

By this point in the chapter, you are likely to have reached the conclusion that effective communication in organizations cannot be taken for granted. Making things even more challenging are two fundamental facts of contemporary organizational life: (1) the global nature of business relationships and (2) the multilingual nature of the workforce. As you might imagine, these characteristics pose critical challenges that must be met for organizations to be as effective as they must be to thrive—or even to survive.

Communication in a global economy. It's no secret that businesses operate in a global economy. Approximately two-thirds of the large companies in Europe, Australia, and New Zealand have employees in six or more countries (compared to 56 percent of Asian companies, 43 percent of North American companies, and 33 percent of Latin American companies).[19] Keeping the economy going requires a keen understanding of the complexities of communicating with people from different countries. This is far easier said than done—and mistakes can readily offend your hosts, even unintentionally.

Imagine, for example, that you are at home in a large U.S. city, where you are entertaining a group of potential business partners from abroad. As you enter a restaurant, you find it odd that your guests are reluctant to check their coats, taking them to the table instead, although the inside temperature is quite comfortable. Upon prompting, your guests admit that they have heard all about the crime problem in the United States and were advised against ever letting something of value out of their sight. If you are not immediately offended, you would feel at the very least uncomfortable about the message your visitors are sending about their trust of Americans— a likely problem given that you are considering partnering with them. Clearly, when visiting abroad, it pays not only to learn the language spoken there (even if only somewhat, as a gesture of politeness) but also to familiarize yourself carefully with the local customs.[20] For a summary of some of the most easily recognized pitfalls of international communication, see Figure 8.5. (To see how familiar you are with the unique ways people from different cultures communicate, see the **Self-Assessment Exercise** on p. 219.)

Beyond these, and other, specific rules about communicating within other countries, there are several general rules that everyone should follow when doing business with people from other countries.[21] These are as follows:

- *Learn local cultural rules*. By acknowledging that there are likely to be cultural differences between yourself and people from another country, learn what you

FIGURE 8.5 "When in Rome": Understanding National Customs

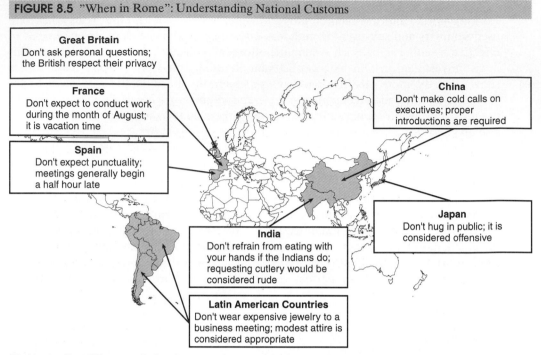

Great Britain
Don't ask personal questions; the British respect their privacy

France
Don't expect to conduct work during the month of August; it is vacation time

Spain
Don't expect punctuality; meetings generally begin a half hour late

China
Don't make cold calls on executives; proper introductions are required

Japan
Don't hug in public; it is considered offensive

India
Don't refrain from eating with your hands if the Indians do; requesting cutlery would be considered rude

Latin American Countries
Don't wear expensive jewelry to a business meeting; modest attire is considered appropriate

Understanding differences in local customs is essential when conducting business in today's global economy. A few important customs that might come as a surprise to American businesspeople are summarized here. (*Source*: Based on information in Lewis, 1999; see Note 20.)

can do to avoid embarrassing these people. Many Americans make this mistake, for example, when they publicly praise Asian visitors. Although this would be considered a very kind thing to do in American culture, Asians are likely to find it a source of discomfort inasmuch as their cultures value group performance more highly than individual performance. Pay special attention to rules of etiquette regarding how to address people (by first name, last name, or title). To avoid embarrassment, it's a good idea to check with local experts to ensure that you are doing this correctly.

- *Don't take anything for granted*. It is important when communicating with people from other nations to challenge your cultural assumptions. Don't assume, for example, that everyone values the same things that you do. Although it may come as a shock to many Americans, concepts such as equal achievement, autonomy, and individual accomplishment are not recognized as appropriate throughout the world.

- *Show respect for everyone*. We often find it funny when someone says or does something that runs counter to what we expect. However, giggling or telling someone that they have a funny accent is not only disrespectful, but it imposes a tall barrier to effective communication. In this connection, it helps to focus on *what* people are saying, rather than how they are saying it or how they look.

- *Speak slowly, clearly, and in straightforward language.* Even after you have studied a foreign language for a few years in high school or college, you may be surprised to find just how little you understand when you visit a country where that is the native language. "If they only spoke more slowly and clearly," you think to yourself, "I'd probably understand them." Indeed, you might. With this in mind, it's important for you to speak slowly and clearly (but not louder) when talking to people in languages that are not their native tongue. Moreover, it's important to avoid colloquial words or phrases that you take for granted, but which they might not know.

- *Try to speak the local language—at least a little.* People always appreciate the effort you make to speak their language, so give it a try. It's a good way to show goodwill and to break the barriers between you. Whatever you do, however, check with a native speaker to make sure that your pronunciation is accurate and that you are not offending anyone by using the wrong words or gestures.

- *Be aware of nonverbal differences.* The same gestures that mean one thing in one country may mean quite another in another country. For example, an American may not think twice about hugging a colleague who has done well or touching another's arm to acknowledge him or her. However, these same acts would be considered not only inappropriate but also offensive to people from Korea. Bottom line: You have not completely learned a foreign language until you have learned its nonverbal language as well.[22] For some examples of cross-cultural differences in nonverbal behavior, see Figure 8.6 on the next page.

The multilingual workforce: "You say tomato, I say domates, or pomidor, or tomate." In the Book of Genesis, the Bible tells us of the Tower of Babel that the descendants of Noah built to reach up to heaven and make them like God. However, the story tells us that God prevented them from completing the tower by confusing their language so that they could no longer understand one another. From that time forward, according to the Bible, the peoples of the earth would speak different languages. Just as language differences kept the tower from completion in Biblical times, so too do language differences between people threaten to interfere with people's work today.

Just because you go to work at an American company in the United States, there's no assurance that everyone around you will be a native speaker of English. Especially in states like California and New York, where as many as one person in four is foreign-born, there's good reason to expect that many of your coworkers will speak English with a foreign accent—if they speak it at all. The communication challenges this situation creates are not difficult to imagine. After all, business operations are sure to falter when people cannot understand each other because they are speaking different languages.

To combat this problem, several companies have implemented *English-only rules*, requiring all employees to speak only English while on the job. The underlying idea is that workplaces in which people speak only one language will be ones in which communications are clear and efficient and in which safety is enhanced. In recent years, however, the courts have not looked favorably on such policies, claiming they interfere with an employee's rights to use whatever language he or she wishes. For example, a Washing-

FIGURE 8.6 Beware of Nonverbal Miscommunication in Different Countries

When a person from the United States does this	it means ...	BUT	When the same thing is done by a person from	it means ...
 stands close to another while talking	the speaker is considered pushy		 Italy	the speaker is behaving normally
 looks away from another	the speaker is shy		 Japan	the speaker is showing deference to authority
 extends the palm of his or her hand	the person is extending a greeting, such as a handshake		 Greece	the person is being insulted
 joins the index finger and thumb to form an "O"	"okay"		 Tunisia	"I'll kill you"

Although people preparing to conduct business abroad may study their host country's spoken language, they frequently fail to learn the nonverbal language. As summarized here, this can lead to some serious miscommunication. (*Source*: Based on information in Barnum & Wolanainsky, 1989; see Note 22.)

Legally, for companies to insist that their employees speak fluent English, they must establish clearly that an employee who cannot do so will perform poorly on the job.

ton court awarded a Cambodian-born immigrant $389,000 by the bank that employed him, ruling that he was unfairly denied a promotion because of his lack of fluency in English.[23] Legally, for companies to insist that their employees speak fluent English, they must establish clearly that an employee who cannot do so will perform poorly on the job.

Instead of insisting that everyone speak only English, companies with diverse customer bases generally are delighted to have employees who speak several different languages. For example, fluency in English is important for sales associates at Longo Toyota in El Monte, California, and three-quarters of the sales staff speak at least one additional language (in fact, 20 different languages are spoken at Longo). This has helped the dealership sell cars to people from the community who were not as well served by the competition, helping it become one of the top-grossing car dealerships in the United States.

Although it is often useful to be able to speak a second language, most U.S. companies find it necessary to ensure that their employees speak English so that they can understand instructions, notices, and memos. With this in mind, many businesses have arranged for their employees to take classes in English as a second language. This is done at Kayem Foods, a meat processing and packaging company in Chelsea, Massachusetts, where English is a second language for 60 to 70 percent of the employees, most of whom have Spanish or Polish as their native tongue. This is so important that it's not relegated to something the company hopes workers will do on their own time off the job. Rather, teachers are brought into the facility to train workers during their shifts.

Learning to communicate in English is particularly important in the hospitality industry, where doing so is required to cater to American tourists. For example, before the Four Seasons Hotel and Resort opened on the southern tip of the island of Bali in Indonesia, none of the 10,000 applicants could speak English. In fact, nobody could pass a simple test of English required to perform any of the 580 jobs the resort was attempting to fill. The solution was intensive training in English-language terms used in the hospitality industry—nine hours per day for almost a month. Although staff members might not be able to understand the entire language, they now know enough English to serve their customers' needs.

In some locations, a company's customer base is so ethnically diverse that it must go out of its way to hire employees who speak foreign languages. What happens, however, if the one or two employees who speak an unusual language are not available? Detroit Edison, the electric utility company serving ethnically diverse southeast Michigan, has faced this challenge by using AT&T's Language Line service. This service provides around-the-clock translation services in any of 140 different languages by accessing a toll-free phone number. Customers who speak a language that is unknown to any of Detroit Edison's service representatives are put on a conference call with someone from the company and the Language Line service. In conclusion, it's easy to see how very important it is for people to respond to the challenge of using language—be it one or many—to communicate effectively with their coworkers and their customers.

SUMMARY: HAVE I MET THE LEARNING OBJECTIVES?

You can be certain that you have met the learning objectives for this chapter found on p. 195 if you understand the following:

1. **DEFINE communication and DESCRIBE the various steps in the communication process**. *Communication* is the process through which people send information to others and receive information from them. The process of communication involves *encoding* ideas into messages, *transmitting* messages over channels of communication, and *decoding* the original message back into the original ideas. This process continues in reverse as *feedback* is given on the original ideas. Imperfections in the communication process are referred to as *noise*.

2. **RECOGNIZE the differences between formal and informal communication in organizations**. Compared to *formal communication*, which deals with official information and is guided by an organization's structure, *informal communication* is not so restricted. It deals with unofficial information, and flows freely and quickly between any interested parties. In contrast, formal communication carefully follows the *organization chart. Downward communication* is characterized by the sending of instructions, directions, and orders. *Upward communication* involves sending messages that managers need to do their jobs. *Horizontal communication* involves efforts at coordination and getting people to work together.

3. **DISTINGUISH between verbal and nonverbal communication, and the factors that make each effective**. *Verbal communication* media vary along a continuum from those that are considered "rich" because they are highly interactive and rely on a great deal of information (e.g., face-to-face conversation) at one end to those that are considered "lean" because they are static and involve less information (e.g., flyers). Communication is effective when oral messages are used to communicate ambiguous information and written messages are used to communicate clear information. *Nonverbal communication* occurs without words. Effectively communicating nonverbally requires understanding and adhering to the norms of organizations and cultures with respect to dress, the use of time, and space.

4. **IDENTIFY various inspirational techniques that can be used to enhance one's effectiveness as a communicator**. Inspirational communication tactics include: (a) projecting confidence and power by using emotion-producing words, (b) being credible, (c) pitching your message to the listener, (d) avoiding "junk words" that dilute your message, (e) using front-loaded messages, and (f) cutting through the clutter of other messages.

5. **DESCRIBE what it takes to be a supportive communicator**. Supportive communicators behave in ways that demonstrate their interest in what the other person has to say. Being a supportive communicator requires the following: (a) focusing on the problem instead of the person, (b) matching your words and your body language, (c) acknowledging the other person's ideas, and (d) saying things that keep the conversation going.

6. **EXPLAIN how to meet the challenges associated with communicating with people from different cultures**. To communicate effectively with people from other cultures, it helps to do the following: (a) Learn local cultural rules; (b) don't take anything for granted; (c) show respect for everyone; (d) speak slowly, clearly, and in straightforward language; (e) try to speak the local language—at least a little; and (f) be aware of nonverbal differences.

You Be the Consultant

"Everyone is moving in different directions. No one seems to have any sense of what the company is and where it is going. Making things worse, people around here aren't paying any attention to each other, and everyone is doing his or her own thing." These are the words of an operations director of a large credit card processing center, who asks you to look into these problems in your capacity as manager of human resources. Answer the following questions relevant to this situation based on the material in this chapter.

1. Casting the problem as one of poor communication between company officials and lower-level employees, what steps could be taken to fill everyone in on the company's plans, goals, and activities?
2. What specific tactics would you advise the company's managers use so as to improve communication within its ranks?
3. In what ways might differences in nationality be responsible for this state of affairs, and what can be done to help improve communication despite these differences?

(SELF-ASSESSMENT EXERCISE)

How Familiar Are You with Foreign Communication Practices?

Expert communicators in today's global business world must have considerable familiarity with cultural differences in communication style around the world. This questionnaire is designed to assess your familiarity with many such communication practices. It is important to note that although people in any given country are not all alike, their cultural backgrounds lead them to share certain communication styles and practices. (*Source* Based on information in Rosen et al., 2000, see Note 19; and Lewis, 1999, see Note 20.)

Directions

Match each country in the left column to the communication characteristic that best describes its people in the column on the right.

1. _____ Russia		a. Chivalry and gallantry are important; first names are reserved for use only with close friends.
2. _____ Brazil		b. Show respect for speakers by being silent; tend to be shy and to refrain from open disagreement.
3. _____ Germany		c. Women are deferent to men; good bargainers, who expect you to negotiate with them.
4. _____ Australia		d. Raise voice and use gestures when excited; formal dress and style is typical at meetings.
5. _____ Japan		e. Punctuality is important; perfectionists, who demand lots of information from others.
6. _____ Philippines		f. Use humor a great deal, such as to break up tension; take time to make decisions.
7. _____ Poland		g. Talk tough when they believe they have an advantage; tend to drink between meetings.

8. _____ France   h. Being an hour or two late is not unusual; leadership is based on family name, age, and connections.
9. _____ Great Britain   i. Very talkative and long-winded; tend to interrupt conversations with their own ideas.
10. _____ India   j. Tend to be cynical and distrust people who praise them too enthusiastically.

Scoring

Using the following key, count how many correct matches you made: 1 = g, 2 = i, 3 = e, 4 = j, 5 = b, 6 = h, 7 = a, 8 = d, 9 = f, 10 = c.

Questions for Discussion

1. How many correct matches did you make? How does this compare to how you expected to score before you began this exercise?
2. Based on your own experiences, to what extent do you believe these descriptions are generally accurate as opposed to merely stereotypic?
3. How would you characterize your own nation's culture relative to those described in this exercise?

(**GROUP EXERCISE**)

Sharpening Your Listening Skills

Are you a good listener, a *really* good listener? Do you understand exactly what others are saying and get them to open up even more? Most of us tend to think that we are much better than we really are when it comes to this important skill. After all, we've been listening to people our whole lives—and, with that much practice, we must be at least reasonably acceptable. However, being a truly effective listener is an active skill, and it takes some practice to master. The following exercise will help you gain some insight into your own listening skills.

Directions

1. Divide the class into pairs of people who do not already know each other. Arrange the chairs so that the people within each pair are facing one another but are separated from the other pairs.
2. Within each pair, select one person as the speaker and the other as the listener. The speaker should tell the listener about a specific incident on the job in which he or she was somehow harmed (e.g., disappointed by not getting a raise, being embarrassed by another, getting fired, and so on), and how he or she felt about it. This discussion should last about 10 to 15 minutes.
3. Listeners should carefully attempt to follow the suggestions for good listening summarized in Table 8.3 (on p. 212). To help, the instructor should discuss these with the class.
4. After the conversations are over, review the suggestions with your partner. Discuss which ones the listener followed and which ones were ignored. Try to be as open and honest as possible about assessing your own and the other's strengths

and weaknesses. Speakers should consider the extent to which they felt the listeners were really paying careful attention to them.

5. Now, repeat steps 2 through 4, but change roles. Speakers now become listeners, and listeners now become speakers.
6. As a class, share your experiences as speakers and listeners.

Questions for Discussion
1. What did this exercise teach you about your own skills as a listener? Are you as good as you thought? Do you think you can improve?
2. Was there general agreement or disagreement in the class about each listener's strengths and weaknesses? Explain.
3. Which particular listening skills were easiest and which were most difficult for you to put into practice? Do you think there may be certain conditions under which good listening skills may be especially difficult to implement?

NOTES

Case Note
Lieber, R. (1999, November). Information is everything. *Fast Company*, pp. 246–249, 253–254.

Chapter Notes
[1] Roberts, K. H. (1984). *Communicating in organizations*. Chicago: Science Research Associates (quote, p. 4).
[2] Weick, K. E. (1987). Theorizing about organizational communication. In F. M. Jablin, L. L. Putnam, K. H. Roberts, & L. W. Porter (Eds.), *Handbook of organizational communication* (pp. 97–122). Newbury Park, CA: Sage.
[3] Daft, R. L., Lengel, R. H., & Trevino, L. K. (1987). Message equivocality, media selection, and manager performance: Implications for information systems. *MIS Quarterly, 11*, 355–366.
[4] Stromberg, R. M. (1998, September). No, it couldn't happen here. *American Management Association International*, p. 70.
[5] Poe, R., & Courter, C. L. (1998, September). The great coffee grapevine. *Across the Board*, p. 7.
[6] Walton, E. (1961). How efficient is the grapevine? *Personnel, 28*, 45–49.
[7] Esterson, E. (1998). Inner beauties. *Inc. Tech*, pp. 78–80, 84, 86, 88, 90.
[8] Level, D. A. (1972). Communication effectiveness: Methods and situation. *Journal of Business Communication, 28*, 19–25.
[9] Mehrabian, A., & Weiner, B. (1967). Decoding of inconsistent communications. *Journal of Personality and Social Psychology, 6*, 109–114.
[10] Rafaeli, A., Dutton, J. Harquail, C., & Mackie-Lewis, S. (1997). Navigating by attire: The use of dress by female administrative employees. *Academy of Management Journal, 40*, 9–45.
[11] Greenberg, J. (1989). The organizational waiting game: Time as a status-asserting or status-neutralizing tactic. *Basic and Applied Social Psychology, 10*, 13–26.
[12] Zweigenhaft, R. L. (1976). Personal space in the faculty office: Desk placement and student–faculty interaction. *Journal of Applied Psychology, 61*, 628–632.
[13] Dubrin, A. J. (2001). *Leadership (3rd ed.)*. Boston: Houghton-Mifflin.
[14] Tannen, D. (1998, February 2). How you speak shows where you rank. *Fortune*, p. 156.
[15] Wurman, R. S. (2000). *Understanding*. Newport, RI: TED Conferences.
[16] Whetten, D. E., & Cameron, K. S. (1998). *Developing management skills (4th ed.)*. Upper Saddle River, NJ: Prentice Hall.

[17] Labarre, P. (1998, November). Screw up, and get smart. *Fast Company*, p. 58.

[18] Morrison, K. E. (1994). *Leadership skills*. Tucson, AZ: Fisher Books.

[19] Rosen, R., Digh, P., Singer, M., & Phillips, C. (2000). *Global literacies*. New York: Simon & Schuster.

[20] Lewis, R. D. (1999). *When cultures collide*. London: Nicholas Brealey Publishing.

[21] See Note 9.

[22] Barnum, C., & Wolaninsky, N. (1989, April). Taking cues from body language. *Management Review*, pp. 3–8.

[23] Dutton, G. (1998, December). One workforce, many languages. *Management Review*, pp. 42–47.

9

Group dynamics and teamwork

LEARNING OBJECTIVES

After reading this chapter, you will be able to:

1. DEFINE group and DISTINGUISH between various types of groups.

2. DESCRIBE the role of norms in organizations.

3. DESCRIBE the social facilitation effect and the social loafing effect.

4. DEFINE team and EXPLAIN what makes a team different from an ordinary work group.

5. DESCRIBE the general effectiveness of work teams.

6. IDENTIFY ways of making work teams effective.

THREE GOOD REASONS WHY YOU SHOULD CARE ABOUT . . .

Group Dynamics and Teamwork

You should care about group dynamics and teamwork because:

1. The dynamics between people in groups is largely responsible for both the successes and failures of many work groups, as well as the satisfaction of the individuals working in them.

2. Groups and teams can be very effective if you know how to manage them properly.

3. Teams are a fact of organizational life—the most popular way of coordinating the activity of people on the job. Knowing how they work will give you an edge.

Making the Case for... Group Dynamics and Teamwork

People Power at Consolidated Diesel

Whitakers, North Carolina, is a small town with a very large building—the 1.2-million-square-foot factory operated by Consolidated Diesel Company. As out of scale as the facility is with its surrounding rural community, what's going on inside is equally out of scale with the world of manufacturing. A brand-new diesel engine for a tractor, truck, combine, or bus rolls off the assembly line amazingly fast—every 72 seconds. Unlike other factories, where layoffs are common and turnover is high, Consolidated Diesel has never had a major layoff, and the annual turnover rate is under 2 percent. Also unique is the fact that managers are responsible for four times as many employees as those in the average factory—100, as opposed to 25, saving Consolidated Diesel an estimated $1 million per year. And as if all this is not special enough, the injury rate at the plant is only about one-fifth the national average.

Obviously, something special is going on at this factory, but what? Anyone at the plant will tell you that the answer lies in the fact that employees work together in teams. What's more, they've been working this way since 1980 when the factory opened its doors. Exactly how they do this is based on several key practices. Possibly the most important thing the company does is give teams total responsibility over everything they do. Team members not only routinely solve their own problems, but they also are responsible for hiring—and, when necessary, firing—their own members. The decisions they make are the ones they live by.

The company's second key to success involves extensively cross-training everyone. Consolidated Diesel's employees know how to do many different jobs. One day someone may be operating a machine, and the next day he may be making quality inspections. The idea is that people who know how to do someone else's job have respect for what that person is doing, and this breeds a sense of cooperation.

Third, Consolidated Diesel executives listen to their employees and enlist their help in finding ways to improve plant operations. Recently, for example, a third-shift skeleton crew was added to help meet the growing demand for engines. Overtime costs grew, but performance remained flat. After teams got involved, a better solution was found: New, flexible schedules were developed. Soon, shifts returned to eight-hour days and Saturday work was eliminated. As general manager Jim Lyons explains, "Sometimes the fact that it's the teams' plan and not a plan dictated by management means everything. The teams will make it work."

All of these practices are effective because none of the employees believe that the company is out to hurt them. Instead, they feel that the company treats them fairly. The good and the bad are distributed equally. For example, either everyone gets a bonus or nobody gets one. And the burden of working the night shift is shared equally as well. Entire teams move from working days to working nights every two weeks. Labor and management trust each other and get along extremely well. The typical barriers found between executives and laborers are not to be found at Consolidated Diesel. Most of the employees call the plant supervisor by his first name, and state-of-the-plant meetings are regularly held in which information about operations is openly shared. Quarterly, the plant supervisor meets with each of the 1,400 employees in small groups in which information and ideas are freely exchanged. Still more information is made available over the in-house newsletter and even a closed-circuit TV network.

The interesting thing about Consolidated Diesel's operations is that everyone has grown to expect superior results. Mediocrity is not tolerated. The expectations are considerable, but for the most part, they have been self-imposed. Everybody expects a great deal from everyone else, and delivering it is the general rule.

Obviously, many things about working life at Consolidated Diesel are very special and amazingly effective. Although this company may be extreme in many ways, elements of what it does may be seen in factories and offices everywhere. Indeed, *teams* are growing in popularity in all kinds of organizations—and, in view of Consolidated Diesel's experiences, there's little wonder why. Because so many companies are using work arrangements they refer to as teams, it is not always clear exactly what teams are. With this in mind, I will clarify the nature of teams and then review cases in which teams have been used in organizations. Of course, sometimes teams are as highly effective as they are at Consolidated Diesel, but as you might imagine, they do not always work so well. Clearly, several things must be done to make teams effective. I will review these considerations in the final part of this chapter.

Before turning attention to the special kinds of groups known as teams, however, I will describe the basic nature of *groups* in general. As you know, a great deal of the work performed in organizations is done by people working together in groups. In view of this, it makes sense to understand the types of groups that exist and the variables governing the interrelationships between them and individuals—commonly referred to as *group dynamics*. This will be our focus in the first half of this chapter. Then, after understanding the basic nature of groups, you will be in a good position to understand the operation of teams.

The Nature of Groups

To understand the operation of groups in organizations, it is necessary to define exactly what a group is and the types of groups that exist.

WHAT IS A GROUP?

Imagine waiting in a line at the bank one day along with five other people. Now compare this collection of individuals to your company's board of directors. Although in our everyday language we may refer to the people waiting in line as a group, they certainly are not a group in the same sense as the members of the board are. Obviously, a group is more than simply a collection of people. But, what exactly is it that makes a group a group?

Social scientists have defined the **group** as a collection of two or more interacting individuals with a stable pattern of relationships between them who share common goals and who perceive themselves as being a group. Let's consider the various elements of this definition separately.

- *Groups are composed of two or more people in social interaction.* In other words, the members of a group must have some influence on each other. Whether the interaction between the parties is immediate and occurs face-to-face, such as in committee meetings, or is delayed, such as might occur when a written draft of a document is circulated for comments, to be considered a group, the parties must have some impact on each other.
- *Groups possess a stable structure.* Although membership can change, there must be some stable relationships that keep group members functioning together as a unit. A collection of individuals that constantly changes (e.g., those waiting on the bank line with you) cannot be thought of as a group.

- *Group members share common interests or goals.* For example, members of a company's safety committee all share the common goal of keeping the workplace free of danger.
- *Groups are composed of individuals who perceive themselves as members.* Groups are composed of people who recognize each other as a member of their group and can distinguish these individuals from nonmembers. Whether it's the members of a corporate board of directors or a company softball team, people know who is in their group and who is not.

As these four characteristics suggest, groups are very special collections of individuals. Despite these specific requirements, there are a wide variety of different types of groups that may be identified within organizations.

TYPES OF GROUPS

Although a military combat unit, the president's cabinet, and the three-person cockpit crew of a commercial airliner are certainly all very different from each other, they are all groups. So, to clarify our understanding of the nature of groups, it is helpful to describe the different types of groups that exist (for a summary, see Figure 9.1).[1]

Formal groups. Groups created by the organization that are designed to direct members toward some important organizational goal are known as **formal groups.** One type of formal group is a **command group**—a group determined by the connections between individuals who are a formal part of the organization. For example, a command group may be formed by the vice president of marketing who gathers together her regional marketing directors from around the country to hear their ideas about a

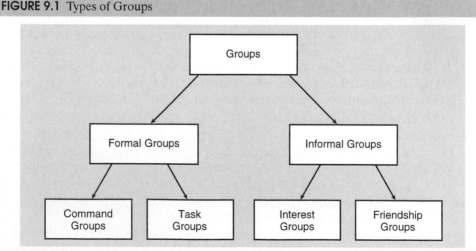

FIGURE 9.1 Types of Groups

Groups may be categorized as *formal groups,* such as command groups and task groups, as well as *informal groups,* such as interest groups and friendship groups.

new national advertising campaign. Command groups are determined by the organization's rules regarding who reports to whom, and usually consist of a supervisor and his or her subordinates.

A formal organizational group also may be formed around some specific task. Such a group is referred to as a **task group.** Unlike command groups, task groups may be composed of individuals with some special interest or expertise in a specific area regardless of their positions in the organizational hierarchy. For example, a company may have a committee on equal employment opportunities whose members monitor the fair hiring practices of the organization. It may be composed of personnel specialists, corporate vice presidents, and workers from the shop floor. Whether they are permanent committees, known as *standing committees,* or temporary ones formed for special purposes (such as a committee formed to recommend solutions to a parking problem) known as *ad hoc committees* or *task forces,* task groups are commonly found in organizations.

Informal groups. Not all groups are as formal as those I have identified; many are informal in nature. **Informal groups** develop naturally among an organization's personnel without any direction from the management of the organization within which they operate. A key factor in the formation of informal groups is a common interest shared by its members. For example, a group of employees who band together to seek union representation, or who march together to protest their company's pollution of the environment, may be called an **interest group.** The common goal sought by members of an interest group may unite workers at many different organizational levels. The key factor is that membership in an interest group is voluntary—it is not dictated by the organization, but encouraged by an expression of common interests.

Of course, sometimes the interests that bind individuals together are far more diffuse. Groups may develop out of a common interest in participating in sports or going to the movies or just getting together to talk. These kinds of informal groups are known as **friendship groups.** Friendship groups extend beyond the workplace because they provide opportunities for satisfying the social needs of workers that are so important to their well-being (as you may recall from our discussion of Maslow's need hierarchy theory in Chapter 4).

Informal work groups are an important part of life in organizations. Although they develop without direct encouragement from management, friendships often originate out of formal organizational contact. For example, three employees working alongside each other on an assembly line may get to talking and discover their mutual interest in basketball, and decide to get together after work to shoot hoops. Such friendships on the job bind people together, helping them cooperate with each other, having beneficial effects on organizational functioning.

> *Friendships on the job bind people together, helping them cooperate with each other, having beneficial effects on organizational functioning.*

organizational functioning. (Our discussion thus far has suggested that people have many different reasons for joining groups. For a look at some of the key reasons—and to see which ones apply to you—see the **Self-Assessment Exercise** on p. 246.)

Group Dynamics:
People Working with Others

To understand groups it is essential to consider the way groups influence individuals and the way individuals influence groups, which is known as **group dynamics**. We will examine several ways in which this occurs in this section of the chapter.[2]

GROUP NORMS: UNSPOKEN RULES OF GROUP BEHAVIOR

From your own experiences in groups you probably already know one important way in which groups influence people—that is, by imposing ways of thinking and acting that are considered acceptable. If anyone has ever told you, "that's not the way we do things around here," then you probably already know how potent these effects can be. What you might not know, however, is that such informal forces constitute a key aspect of group dynamics known as **norms.** Specifically, a norm is a generally agreed-upon set of rules that guides the behavior of group members.[3]

Norms differ from organizational policies in that they are informal and unwritten. In fact, norms may be so subtle that group members may not even be aware that they are operating. Yet, their effects can be quite profound. For example, group norms may regulate such key behaviors as honesty (e.g., whether or not to steal from the company), manners of dress (e.g., a coat and tie are required), and the punctuality of meetings and appointments (e.g., whether or not they generally begin on time). In so doing, norms help regulate groups and keep them functioning in an orderly fashion.

It is important to note that norms can be either *prescriptive*—dictating what should be done—or *proscriptive*—dictating the behaviors that should be avoided. For example, groups may develop prescriptive norms to follow their leader or to help a group member who needs assistance. They also may develop proscriptive norms to avoid absences, or to refrain from blowing the whistle on each other. Sometimes the pressure to conform to norms is subtle, as in the dirty looks given a manager by his peers for going to lunch with one of the assembly-line workers. Other times, normative pressures may be quite severe, such as when one production worker sabotages another's work because he is performing at too high a level, making his coworkers look bad.

Norms develop over time because of four key factors. These are as follows:

- *Precedents set over time.* Whatever behaviors emerge at a first group meeting will usually set the standard for how that group is to operate. Initial group patterns of behavior frequently become normative, such as where people sit, and how formal or informal the meeting will be. Such routines help establish a predictable, orderly interaction pattern.
- *Carryovers from other situations.* Group members usually draw from their previous experiences to guide their behaviors in new situations. The norms governing professional behavior apply here. For example, the norm for a physician to behave ethically and to exercise a pleasant bedside manner is generalizable from one hospital to another.
- *Response to an explicit statement by a superior or coworker.* As described in Chapter 5, newcomers to groups quickly "learn the ropes" when people describe what is expected of them. Such an explanation is an explicit statement of the group's or organization's norms insofar as it describes what one should do or avoid doing to be accepted by the group.

- *Critical events in the group's history*. If an employee releases an important organizational secret to a competitor, causing a loss to the company, a norm to maintain secrecy may develop out of this incident. To the extent that norms guide people away from similar mistakes, they may be a helpful way of ensuring that the group or organization learns from its past experiences.

SOCIAL FACILITATION: PERFORMING IN THE PRESENCE OF OTHERS

Imagine that you have been taking piano lessons for 10 years, and you are now about to go on stage for your first major solo concert performance. You have been practicing diligently for several months, getting ready for the big night. Now, you are no longer alone in your own living room, but on stage in front of hundreds of people. Your name is announced, and silence breaks the applause as you sit in front of the concert grand. How will you perform now that you are in front of an audience? Will you freeze, forgetting the pieces you practiced so intensely on your own? Or will the audience spur you on to your best performance yet? In other words, what impact will the presence of the audience have on your behavior?

After studying this question for a century, using a wide variety of tasks and situations, social scientists found that the answer to this question is not straightforward.[4] Sometimes people perform better in the presence of others than alone, and sometimes they perform better alone than in the presence of others. The key question is this: Under what conditions will performance be helped by the presence of others, and under what conditions will it be hindered? Research has shown that the answer depends on how well people know the task they are performing. When people are performing tasks they know quite well (e.g., a musical piece they have played for years), they generally perform better in front of an audience than alone. However, when people are performing tasks with which they are unfamiliar (e.g., a piece of music that is new to their repertoires), they generally perform better alone than in front of an audience. This

> *When people are performing tasks they know quite well (e.g., a musical piece they have played for years), they generally perform better in front of an audience than alone. However, when people are performing tasks with which they are unfamiliar (e.g., a piece of music that is new to their repertoires), they generally perform better alone than in front of an audience.*

tendency for the presence of others to enhance an individual's performance at times and to impair it at other times is known as **social facilitation.** (Although the word *facilitation* implies improvements in task performance, scientists use the term *social facilitation* to refer to both performance improvements *and* decrements stemming from the presence of others.) For a summary of the social facilitation effect, see Figure 9.2.

It's easy to imagine how the social facilitation effect may have a profound influence on organizational behavior. For example, consider the effects it may have on people whose work is monitored, either by others who are physically present or by connections made via computer networks. The rationale behind **performance monitoring**—the practice of supervisors observing subordinates while working—is that it will encourage

FIGURE 9.2 The Social Facilitation Effect

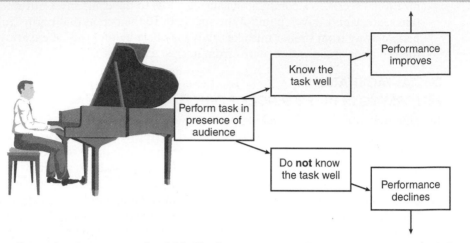

According to the phenomenon of social facilitation, a person's performance on a task will be influenced by the presence of others. Compared to performance when doing the task alone, performance in front of an audience will be enhanced if that task is well learned, but impaired if it is not well learned.

people to perform at their best. But does it really work this way? The concept of social facilitation suggests that monitoring should improve task performance only if the people monitored know their tasks extremely well. However, if they are relatively new at the task, their performance would suffer when monitored. In fact, research suggests that this is precisely what happens.[5] For employees who are not well-practiced at their jobs, performance monitoring does not have the intended effects. Accordingly, supervisors seeking to raise employees' performance levels by introducing performance monitoring should carefully consider the effects of social facilitation before doing so.

SOCIAL LOAFING: "FREE RIDING" WHEN WORKING WITH OTHERS

Have you ever worked with several others helping a friend move into a new apartment, each carrying and transporting part of the load from the old place to the new one? Or, how about sitting around a table with others stuffing political campaign letters into envelopes and addressing them to potential donors? Although these tasks may seem quite different, they actually share an important common characteristic: Performing each requires the efforts of only a single individual, but several people's work can be pooled to yield greater outcomes. Because each person's contributions can be added together with another's, such tasks have been referred to as **additive tasks.**

If you've ever performed additive tasks, such as the ones described here, there's a good chance that you found yourself contributing not quite as much as you would if you did them alone. For example, when working in a group on a class project, do you always contribute your fair share, or do you tend to go along for a "free ride," hoping the others will pick up the slack? How about the tips you leave a server at a restaurant when dining as part of a group? Many people leave less than they would if they were

FIGURE 9.3 The Social Loafing Effect

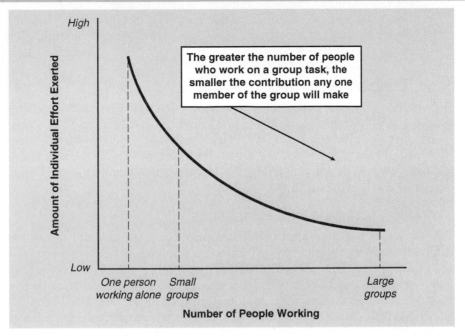

When individuals work together on additive tasks, the greater size of the group, the less effort each individual tends to exert. This phenomenon is known as *social loafing.*

dining alone, hoping that others will leave more and believing that no one will be able to identify them as the person not contributing his or her fair share to the tab. (By the way, it is because of this that many restaurants automatically add tips to the bills of larger parties.) Chances are good that you can relate to these examples because there is a general tendency for everyone performing additive tasks to contribute less to the joint product than an individual does when performing the same tasks alone.[6] This is known as the **social loafing effect,** the general form of which is shown in Figure 9.3. (To experience the social loafing effect firsthand, perform the **Group Exercise** on p. 247.)

Obviously, the tendency for people to reduce their effort when working with others could be a serious problem in organizations. Fortunately, there are several ways in which social loafing can be overcome. Some key recommendations in this regard are as follows:

- *Identify individual performance.* People are unlikely to loaf when they believe their individual performance can be identified. Companies that follow the practice of publicly posting individual performance on a wall chart find that employees are unlikely to loaf for fear of being embarrassed by being caught free riding.
- *Explain the importance of work.* People are unlikely to go along for free rides when they believe the tasks they are performing are vital to the organization. Loafing on unimportant jobs, however, is unlikely to cause problems and, therefore, is likely to occur.

- *Use punishment threats*. People are reluctant to engage in social loafing when they fear having to pay consequences for getting caught.
- *Form smaller work groups*. The tendency to loaf increases as the size of the group increases (as shown in Figure 9.3 on p. 231). As such, loafing will be less prevalent in smaller groups.

Teams: Empowered Work Groups

In recent years, as organizations have been striving to hone their competitive advantages, many have been organizing work around specific types of groups known as *teams*. Because the team movement frequently takes different forms, some confusion has arisen regarding exactly what teams are. In this section we will clarify the basic nature of teams by describing their key characteristics and then identifying the various types of teams that exist.

WHAT IS A TEAM? KEY CHARACTERISTICS

At the Miller Brewing Company in Trenton, Ohio, groups ranging from six to nineteen employees work together to perform all operations, including brewing (Miller Genuine Draft beer is made at this facility), packaging, and distribution. They schedule their own work assignments and vacations, conduct assessments of their peers' performance, maintain the equipment, and perform other key functions. Each group is responsible for meeting prespecified targets for production, quality, and safety—and to help, data regarding costs and performance are made available. Clearly, these groups are different in key respects from the ones we have been describing thus far, such as a budget committee or company ski club. The Miller employees are all members of special kinds of groups known as *teams*. Formally, we define a **team** as a group whose members have complementary skills and are committed to a common purpose or set of performance goals for which they hold themselves mutually accountable. Applying this definition to our description of the way work is done at Miller's Trenton plant, it's clear that teams are in use at this facility.

Given the complicated nature of teams, I will highlight some of their key characteristics and distinguish them from the traditional ways in which work is structured.[7] As you read these descriptions below, including the summary in Table 9.1, you will find general descriptions of many of the specific things done at Consolidated Diesel, as described in the opening case on p. 224:

1. *Teams are organized around work processes rather than functions*. Instead of having traditional departments (such as engineering, planning, quality control, and so on), focusing on a specialized function, it is likely that team members have many different skills and come together to perform key processes, such as designing and launching new products, manufacturing, and distribution. As an example, Sterling Winthrop (an Australian manufacturer of liquid analgesics) used to have 21 different departments looking into various aspects of the manufacturing process. Today, all facets of production (e.g., scheduling, blending, etc.) are carried out by members of teams who work together on the entire production process.
2. *Teams "own" the product, service, or processes on which they work*. By this I mean that people feel part of something meaningful and understand how their

TABLE 9.1 Teams versus Traditional Work Structures: Some Key Distinctions	

Teams differ from traditional work structures with respect to the six key distinctions identified here. (*Source:* Adapted from Wellins, Byham, and Dixon, 1994; see Note 7).

Traditional Structure	*Teams*
Design around functions	Design around work processes
No sense of ownership over the work products	Ownership of products, services, or processes
Workers have single skills	Team members have many skills
Outside leaders govern workers	Team members govern themselves
Support staff and skills are found outside the group	Support staff and skills are built into teams
Organizational decisions are made by managers	Teams are involved in making organizational decisions for themselves

work fits into the big picture (recall our discussion of the motivating properties of this belief in Chapter 4). For example, employees at Florida's Cape Coral Hospital work in teams within four minihospitals (surgical, general, specialty medical, and outpatient)—not only to boost efficiency, but to help them feel more responsible for their patients. By working in small units, team members have greater contact with patients and are more aware of the effects of their work on patient care. This is in contrast to the traditionally more distant way of organizing hospital work, in which employees tend to feel less connected to the results of their actions.

3. *Members of teams are trained in several different areas and have a variety of different skills.* For example, at Milwaukee Insurance, policies are now processed by team members who rate policies, underwrite them, and then enter them into the system. Before the switch to teams, these three tasks were performed by specialists in three separate departments. In fact, this is typical. Traditionally, people learned only single jobs and performed them over and over again, unless there was some need for retraining.

4. *Teams govern themselves.* And, as a result, team leaders may be thought of as *coaches* who help members of the team, rather than bosses who use more authoritarian means of leadership (see Chapter 11). For example, at Texas Instruments' defense electronics plant, teams appoint their own leaders, called "coordinators," who do exactly what the name implies—they work to ensure the smooth interaction between the efforts of team members. At some companies, such as Mine Safety Appliances, "team captains" are self-selected and handle all the paperwork for a few weeks, until the job is rotated to someone else.

5. *In teams, support staff and responsibilities are built in.* Traditionally, such functions as maintenance, engineering, and human resources operate as separate departments that provide support to other groups requiring their services. Insofar as this often causes delays, teams may contain members who have expertise in needed support areas. For example, at K Shoes, a British footwear manufacturing firm, there are no longer any quality inspectors. Instead, all team members are all trained in matters of inspection and quality control. Or sometimes, organizations

hire people with highly advanced or specialized skills who are assigned to work as members of several different teams at once. For example, teams at Texas Instruments have access to specialized engineering services in this way. Regardless of how it's done, the point is that teams do not rely on outside support services to help get their jobs done; they are relatively self-sufficient.

6. *Teams are involved in company-wide decisions.* This is in contrast to the traditional practice of using managers to make all organizational decisions. For example, team members at Tennessee Eastman, a manufacturer of chemicals, fibers, and plastics, participate actively on company-level committees that develop policies and procedures affecting everyone. The underlying idea is that the people who are closest to the work performed should be the ones most involved in making the decisions.

TYPES OF TEAMS

According to one expert, major U.S. companies are now either using some form of teams or are seriously considering using them. Although there has been a great amount of recent interest in teams, they have been around the workplace in one form or another for some time. In fact, many corporations (e.g., Cummins Engine, General Motors, Digital Equipment, and Ford Motor Company) have been using them for quite a few years—with some, such as Procter & Gamble, for well over three decades. In view of their widespread popularity, it should not be surprising to learn that there are many different kinds of teams. I will summarize some of the major kinds of teams here in terms of some of the key ways they may be distinguished from one another:

Work teams and improvement teams.   One way of distinguishing between teams has to do with their major *purpose or mission*. In this regard, some teams—known as **work teams**—are primarily concerned with the work done by the organization, such as developing and manufacturing new products, providing services for customers, and so on. Their principle focus is on using the organization's resources to effectively create its results (either goods or services). The several examples of groups noted thus far are of this type. Other teams—known as **improvement teams**—are primarily oriented toward the mission of increasing the effectiveness of the processes that are used by the organization. For example, Texas Instruments has relied on teams to help improve the quality of operations at its plant in Malaysia.

Temporary and permanent teams.   A second way of distinguishing between types of teams has to do with *time*. Specifically, some teams are only **temporary** and are established for a specific project with a finite life. For example, a team set up to develop a new product would be considered temporary. As soon as its job is done, it disbands. However, other kinds of teams are **permanent** and stay intact as long as the organization is operating. For example, teams focusing on providing effective customer service tend to be permanent parts of many organizations.

Work groups and self-managed work teams.   Teams also differ with respect to the degree of autonomy they have. At one extreme are **work groups,** in which leaders make decisions on behalf of group members, whose job it is to follow the leader's orders. This traditional form is becoming less popular, as more organizations are allowing employees to make their own key decisions. Groups of the latter type are known as

self-managed work teams or **self-directed teams.** In such teams, small numbers of employees (typically about 10) take on duties once performed by their supervisors, such as making work assignments, deciding on the pace of work, and so on.[8] About 20 percent of U.S. companies use self-managed work teams, and this figure is growing rapidly. Some companies, such as Procter & Gamble, Cummins Engine, and General Motors, have used self-managed work teams for over three decades.

Intact and cross-functional teams. Another way to distinguish teams is with respect to the team's connection to the organization's overall *authority structure*—that is, the connection between various formal job responsibilities. In some organizations, **intact teams** work together all the time and do not apply their special knowledge to a wide range of products. Teams in such organizations, such as Ralston-Purina, do not have to stray from their areas of expertise.

With growing frequency, however, teams are crossing over various functional units (e.g., marketing, finance, human resources, and so on). Such teams, referred to as **cross-functional teams,** are composed of employees at identical organizational levels but from different specialty areas. Cross-functional teams are an effective way of bringing people together from throughout the organization to cooperate on large projects. To function effectively, the boundaries between cross-functional teams must be permeable—that is, employees must be members of more than one team. For example, members of an organization's manufacturing team must carefully coordinate their activities with members of its marketing team. To the extent that people are involved in several different kinds of teams, they may gain broader perspectives and make more contributions that are important to their various teams. Chrysler used cross-functional teams to develop the Neon, and Boeing used them to develop its latest 777 aircraft.

> *Cross-functional teams are an effective way of bringing people together from throughout the organization to cooperate on large projects.*

Real and virtual teams. The teams I have been describing thus far may be considered **real teams** insofar as they involve people who physically meet to work together. Although teams have operated this way for many years, and will continue to do so, technology has made it possible for teams to exist without ever having their members physically meet. Teams of this sort—which operate across space, time, and organizational boundaries, communicating with each other only through electronic technology—are known as **virtual teams.**[9]

Sometimes, virtual teams form quite unintentionally, such as when valued team members begin *telecommuting* (working from home, but communicating via e-mail). They also may be formed very deliberately, such as when it is important to bring together on a project the most talented people in the world.[10] Sun Microsystems did this, for example, when it developed a new electronic customer order system. The virtual team was composed of 15 engineers from three different companies in three different countries.[11] They worked together over a seven-month period without ever being together in the same room. Instead, intranets, teleconferencing, conference calls, and e-mails were used to bring the members together.

Today, virtual teams are possible because technology allows them to exist. To the extent that computer-based technology makes possible communication over long distances, the fact that team members are far away from each other becomes irrelevant. This is known as the **law of telecosm**—the idea that as computer networks expand, distances become irrelevant.[12] In today's global economy, it is safe to say that virtual teams are not only possible, but that they are a clear necessity.

How Effective Are Work Teams? Sorting Through the Evidence

Now that you understand the basic nature of teams, you are prepared to explore the issue of how successful teams have been in organizations. The most direct way to learn about companies' experiences with work teams is to survey the officials of organizations that use them. One large-scale study did just this.[13] The sample consisted of several hundred of the 1,000 largest companies in the United States. About 47 percent used some work teams, although these were typically in place in only a few selected sites, not throughout the entire organizations. Where they were used, however, they were generally highly regarded. Moreover, teams were viewed as becoming increasingly popular over time.

Case studies.   These optimistic results are further supported by in-depth case studies of numerous teams in many different organizations.[14] Research of this type, although difficult to quantify and to compare across organizations, provides some interesting insight into what makes teams successful and why. Consider, for example, the work teams used in General Motors' battery plant in Fitzgerald, Georgia. The 320 employees at this facility operate in various teams, including managers working together in *support teams,* middle-level teams of *coordinators* (similar to foreman and technicians), and *employee teams,* natural work units of three to nineteen members performing specific tasks.   Although the teams work closely together, coordinating their activities, they function almost as separate businesses. Because plant employees must perform many different tasks in their teams, they are not paid based on their positions, but for their knowledge and competence. In fact, the highest-paid employees are individuals who have demonstrated their competence (usually by highly demanding tests) on all the jobs performed in at least two different teams.   This is GM's way of rewarding people for broadening their perspectives, appreciating "the other guy's problems." By many measures, the Fitzgerald plant has been very effective. Its production costs are lower than comparable units in traditionally run plants. Furthermore, employee turnover is also much lower than average. Employee satisfaction surveys also reveal that job satisfaction at this plant is among the highest found at any General Motors facility.

Teams also have been successful in service businesses. For example, consider IDS, the financial services subsidiary of American Express. In response to rapid growth in the mid-1980s, IDS officials realized that their operations were becoming highly inefficient and created several teams to work on reorganizing the company's operations. Like many companies, the move to teams wasn't readily accepted by all employees. Particularly resistant were individuals who, before teams, had high-status jobs, with high pay to match. Naturally, they resented becoming co-equals with others when teams were formed. Still, these employees—and all others, for that matter—soon

> *With the help of employee teams, IDS's operations became so efficient that response time improved by 96 percent: from several minutes to only a few seconds.*

benefited from the company's improved operations. Accuracy in the processing of paperwork (e.g., orders to buy or sell stock) rose from 70 percent before teams were created to over 99 percent afterward. With the help of employee teams, IDS's operations became so efficient that response time improved by 96 percent: from several minutes to only a few seconds. During the stock market crash of October 1987, this quick response capability is credited for saving the day (not to mention lots of money) for IDS's customers.

These cases are two examples of very different companies that used teams in different ways, but with something in common—high levels of success (albeit not without some difficulties). And there are many more.[15] Although there are far too many cases to review here, I think you'll find it fascinating to review the summary of company experiences with teams in Table 9.2.[16]

Empirical studies. Although case studies report successful experiences with teams, they are not entirely objective. After all, companies may be unwilling to broadcast their failures to the world. This is not to say that case studies cannot be trusted. Indeed, when the information is gathered by outside researchers (such as those reported here), the stories they tell about how teams are used, and the results of using them, can be quite revealing.[17] Still, there is a need for completely objective, empirical studies of team effectiveness.

Research objectively assessing the effectiveness of work teams has recently been done. In one such investigation comparisons were made between various aspects of work performance and attitudes of two groups of employees at a railroad car repair facility in Australia: those who were assembled into teams that could freely decide how to do their jobs, and those whose work was structured in the more traditional, nonautonomous fash-

TABLE 9.2 The Effectiveness of Teams: Some Impressive Results

Teams have helped many organizations enjoy dramatic gains in productivity. Here is a sampling of these impressive results. (*Sources*: Based on information in Redding, 2000; see Note 23; and Blanchard & Bowles, 2001; see Note 17.)

Company	*Result*
Wilson Sporting Goods	Average annual cost savings of $5 million
Kodak Customer Assistance Center	Accuracy of responses increased 100 percent
Corning	Defects dropped from 1,800 ppm to 3 ppm
Sealed Air	Waste reduced by 50 percent
Exxon	$10 million saved in six months
Carrier	Unit turnaround reduced from two weeks to two days
Xerox	Productivity increased by 30 percent
Westinghouse	Product costs down 60 percent
Texas Instruments	Costs reduced by more than 50 percent

ion.[18] After the work teams had been in place for several months, it was found that they had significantly fewer accidents, as well as lower rates of absenteeism and turnover.

Not all empirical studies, however, paint such an optimistic picture of the benefits of work teams. For example, in one study examining work teams in an English manufacturing plant it was found that employees were more satisfied with their jobs in teams compared to those in conventional work arrangements (in which individuals take orders from a supervisor)—but, they were individually no more productive.[19] However, because the use of teams made it possible for the organization to eliminate several supervisory positions, the company became more profitable.

What's the conclusion? Are teams effective?   Taken together, research suggests that teams are well received. Most people enjoy working in teams, at least after they have adjusted to them. Certainly, teams help create commitment among employees, and as I described in Chapter 5, there are benefits to be derived from this (e.g., reduced absenteeism and turnover). From an organizational perspective, teams appear to be an effective way of eliminating layers of management, thereby getting more work done by fewer people, which also is a valuable contribution. All of these benefits are tangible. However, it is important to keep in mind that teams are not always responsible for making individuals and organizations any more productive. Cases of companies becoming wildly successful after adopting teams, although valid, cannot always be generalized to all teams in all situations.

Having said this, the key question becomes—what can be done to make your work team as effective as those extremely productive ones about which you may have read (including Consolidated Diesel, as I reported in this chapter's opening case on p.224)? I offer several important suggestions in the next section of this chapter.

Guidelines for Developing Effective Teams

Making teams work effectively is no easy task. Success is not automatic. Rather, teams need to be carefully nurtured and maintained for them to accomplish their missions.[20] As one expert expressed it, "Teams are the Ferrari of work design. They're high performance but high maintenance and expensive."[21] What, then, could be done to help make teams as effective as possible? Based on analyses of successful teams, several keys to success may be identified.[22]

PROVIDE PROPER TRAINING

To be effective, team members must have the right blend of skills needed for the team to contribute to the group's mission. Workers having high degrees of freedom and anonymity require a depth of skills and knowledge that surpasses that of people performing narrower, traditional jobs. For this reason, successful teams are those in which large investments are made in developing the skills of team members and leaders. In the words of one expert, "Good team members are trained, not born."[23]

Successful teams are those in which large investments are made in developing the skills of team members and leaders. In the words of one expert, "Good team members are trained, not born."

Illustrating this maxim is Development Dimensions International, a printing and distribution facility for a human resource company, located in Pittsburgh, Pennsylvania. This small company has each of its 70 employees spend some 200 hours in training (in such areas as interaction skills, customer service skills, and various technical areas) during their first year—even more for new leaders. Then, after this initial period, all employees receive a variety of training on an ongoing basis.

One key area in which all team members require training is in how to be a team member. Linda Godwin, a mission specialist at NASA's Johnson Space Center in Houston, likens team success to the kind of interpersonal harmony that must exist within space shuttle crews. "We have to be willing to compromise and to make decisions that benefit everyone as a whole," says Ms. Godwin, who is a veteran of two successful shuttle missions.[24] In this regard, there are several key interpersonal skills in which training is most useful, and these are summarized in Table 9.3.

COMPENSATE TEAM PERFORMANCE

Because the United States and Canada are highly individualistic cultures, most North American workers are used to highly individualistic compensation systems—ones that recognize individual performance. However, when it comes to teams, it is also very important to recognize group performance. Teams are no places for hot shots who want to make their individual marks—rather, teams require "team players." And the more organizations reward employees for their teams' successes, the more strongly team spirit will be reinforced. Several companies in which teams are widely used—including the Hannaford Brothers retail food distribution company in New York; Board na Mona, a peat-extraction company in Ireland; and Westinghouse's defense and commercial electronics plant in Texas—rely on **gain-sharing plans** to reward teams. These

TABLE 9.3 Interpersonal Skills Required by Team Members

Experts have advocated that team members be trained in the various interpersonal skills summarized here (many of which are described elsewhere in this book). (*Source*: Based on information in Caudron, 1993; see Note 23.)

Skill	*Description*
Advocating	Ways of persuading others to accept one's point of view (see Chapter 8)
Inquiring	Listening effectively to others and drawing information out of them (see Chapter 8)
Tension management	Managing the tension that stems from conflict with others (see Chapter 6)
Sharing responsibility	Learning to align personal and team objectives (see Chapter 5)
Leadership	Understanding one's role in guiding the team to success (see Chapter 11)
Valuing diversity	Acceptance—and taking advantage of—differences between members (see Chapter 5)
Self-awareness	Willingness to criticize others constructively and to accept constructive criticism from others (see Chapters 6 and 8)

plans reward all team members for reaching company-wide performance goals, allowing them to share in the company's profits.

In view of the importance of team members having a variety of different skills, many companies, including Milwaukee Insurance, Colgate-Palmolive, and Sterling Winthrop, have taken to paying employees for their demonstrated skills, as opposed to their job performance. Such a system is known as **skill-based pay.** A highly innovative skill-based pay system has been in use at Tennessee Eastman. This company's "pay-for-applied-skills-and knowledge" plan—or *PASK*, as it is known—requires employees to demonstrate their skills in several key areas, including technical skills and interpersonal skills. The pay scale is carefully linked to the number of skills acquired and the level of proficiency attained. By encouraging the development of vital skills in this manner, the company is ensuring that it has the resources for its teams to function effectively.

PROVIDE MANAGERIAL SUPPORT

> *For teams to survive, let alone thrive, it is essential for them to receive unqualified support from top management. In the absence of such support, the system may falter.*

For teams to survive, let alone thrive, it is essential for them to receive unqualified support from top management. In the absence of such support, the system may falter. Consider, for example, the experience at the Lenexa, Kansas, plant of the Puritan-Bennett Corporation, a manufacturer of respiratory equipment. After seven years of working to develop improved software for its respirators, product development teams failed to get the job done (despite an industry average for such tasks of only three years). According to Roger J. Dolida, the company's director of research and development, the problem is that management never made the project a priority, and refused to free up another key person needed to do the job. As he put it, "If top management doesn't buy into the idea . . . teams can go nowhere."[25]

Part of the problem is that some managers are unwilling to relinquish control. In general, good supervisors work their way up from the plant floor by giving orders and having them followed. However, team leaders have to build consensus and must allow team members to make decisions together. As you might expect, letting go of control isn't always easy for some to do. This problem emerged at Bausch & Lomb's sunglasses plant in Rochester, New York. In 1989 some 1,400 employees were organized into 38 teams. By 1992 about half the supervisors had not adjusted to the change, despite receiving thorough training in how to work as part of a team. They argued bitterly with team members whenever their ideas were not accepted by the team, and eventually they were reassigned.

An even tougher approach was taken at the Shelby Die Casting Company, a metal-casting firm in Shelby, Mississippi. When its former supervisors refused to cooperate as co-equals in their teams, the company eliminated their jobs and let the workers run their own teams. The result: The company saved $250,000 in annual wages, productivity jumped 50 percent, and company profits almost doubled. The message sent by both companies is clear: Those who cannot adjust to teamwork are unwelcome.

PROMOTE EMPLOYEE SUPPORT

In addition to support from managers, it is essential that the basis for the movement to teams be fully understood and accepted by the individuals who are involved. Unless employees can fully understand the importance of cooperating with each other, problems are likely to result. This happened a few years ago at Dow Chemical Company's plastics group in Midland, Michigan, where a team was put into place to create a new plastic resin. Some members (those in the research field) wanted to spend several months developing and testing new options, while others (those on the manufacturing end) wanted to slightly alter existing products and start up production right away. Neither side budged, and the project eventually stalled.

By contrast, when team members share a common vision and are committed to attaining it, they are generally very cooperative with each other, leading to success. For example, members of Hallmark's new-product development team (consisting of artists, designers, printers, and financial experts) work carefully together, contributing to the company's dominance in the greeting cards market. Similarly, by forming teams with highly cooperative members from different fields, Thermos was able to launch its highly successful electric grill.

COMMUNICATE THE URGENCY OF THE TEAM'S MISSION

The rationale is that team members are prone to rally around challenges that compel them to meet high performance standards. For example, a few years ago, employees at Ampex Corporation (a manufacturer of videotape equipment for the broadcasting industry) worked hard to make their teams successful when they recognized the changes necessitated by the shift from analog to digital technology. Unless the company met these challenges, the plug surely would be pulled. Realizing that the company's future was at stake, work teams fast-forwarded Ampex into a position of prominence in its industry.

PROMOTE COOPERATION WITHIN AND BETWEEN TEAMS

Team success requires not only cooperation within teams, but between them as well. As one expert put it:

> Time and time again teams fall short of their promise because companies don't know how to make them work together with other teams. If you don't get your teams into right constellations, the whole organization can stall.[26]

This problem occurred in General Electric's medical systems division when it assigned two teams of engineers, one in Waukesha, Wisconsin, and another in Hino, Japan, the task of creating software for two new ultrasound devices. Shortly, teams pushed features that had made their products popular only in their own countries and duplicated each other's efforts. When teams met, language and cultural barriers separated them, further distancing the teams from each other.

Boeing successfully avoided such problems in the development of its new 777 passenger jet—a project involving some 200 teams. As you might imagine, on such a large project coordination of effort between teams is essential. To help, regular meetings were held between various team leaders who disseminated information to members. And team members could go wherever needed within the organization to get the information required to succeed. As one Boeing employee, a team leader, put it, "I can go to the chief engineer. Before, it was unusual just to see the chief engineer."[27] Just as importantly, if after getting the information they need, team members find problems, they are empowered to take action without getting management approval. According to Boeing engineer, Henry Shomber: "We have the no-messenger rule. Team members must make decisions on the spot. They can't run back to their functions [department heads] for permission."[28]

WORK AT BUILDING TEAMS

Rather than simply putting teams together and hoping they work, many companies are taking proactive steps to ensure that team members will get along and perform as they should. Any formal effort directed toward making teams effective is known as **team building.** Team building is usually used when established teams are showing signs of trouble, such as when members lose sight of their objectives and when turnover is high.

Typically, team building involves having team members participate in several different exercises, such as the following:[29]

Role definition exercises.   Are team members doing what others expect them to be doing? Teams whose members answer "no" are destined for trouble. To avoid such problems, some team-building exercises ask members to describe their own roles and the roles of others on their team. Members then systematically discuss these perceptions and highlight areas of disagreement so these can be worked on.

Goal setting exercises.   As I described in Chapter 4, successful performance is enhanced by the setting of goals. As a team-building strategy, team members meet to clarify the various goals toward which they are working and to identify ways they can help achieve them.

Problem solving exercises.   Building successful teams requires ensuring that members are able to work together at solving important problems. To help in this regard, some team-building sessions require members to get together to systematically identify and discuss ways of solving problems more effectively.

Interpersonal process exercises.   Some of the most popular team-building activities involve activities that attempt to build trust and to open communication among members. After all, those members who harbor hostility toward each other or who have hidden agendas are unlikely to work together well. There is usually a fun aspect to interpersonal process training. Black & Decker, for example, had members of its design team participate in a Spider Web activity requiring members to crawl through a large web of woven rope suspended between two trees without touching the rope. The underlying idea is that by helping each other through these exercises, team members can develop more positive relationships with each other, and come to learn how they can influence each other's potential back on the job. In doing this, companies have used such diverse activities as trekking in the wilderness, going through obstacle courses, and having paintball wars. For a close-up example of one extreme form of building teams through interpersonal processes, see the **Winning Practices** section on the following page.

Is team building effective?   Although these various meetings and physical exercises may be fun, we must ask if they have any value. Are they worth the time and money

WINNING PRACTICES

Extreme Team Building: A Metaphor for the Internet Economy

In the fast-paced, eat-or-be-eaten world of e-business, start-up companies have few options but to grow big overnight. Mike Morford, CEO of Altrec.com, which sells outdoor and travel gear online, was well aware of this as he planned a way to develop a senior team that could pull off the near impossible task of finding large investors, launching a major advertising campaign, and overhauling its Web site—all while keeping at bay two equally hungry competitors.[30] Although his team of 10 star soloists looked good on paper, he realized that six were new to the company, and for things to gel, they had to learn how to work well together as a team.

Instead of bringing everyone together in the company's comfortable conference room in Bellevue, Washington, Morford opted for a more rugged venue—a 75-mile stretch of Idaho's lower Salmon River, one of the country's wildest waterways. There, in temperatures that reached 100 degrees, rode the fate of the company on an 18-foot rubber raft. They had four days to come up with a six-month plan for the company. If they didn't become a cohesive team by the end of the run, they faced a threat more ominous than business failure—"the Slide," at high water, the largest rapids in North America. The rationale was simple enough: The lessons learned about teamwork in the course of navigating the mine field of unknown hazards on the trip could be taken back to the office, where the more conventional hazards of e-business confronted them.

Although the technical specialists looked forward to the adventure (some, more than others), they all were somewhat skeptical about whether the "touchy-feely" trip would be anything more than a fun adventure. The first three days were just plain scary, but on the fourth, the team faced a "sink-or-swim" challenge. Amidst what the guide called particularly "flippy" rapids, the raft rose straight up into the air and plummeted from a height of a story and a half, dumping everyone into the water. Fortunately, everyone came out okay—or, even better than okay as they learned how to help each other confront a force bigger than themselves.

The real challenge began immediately after the adventure, as Altrec.com's senior management team put its words into practice. Two particular strategies emerged. First, team members realized there was tension due to the fact that nobody knew exactly what a particular employee was supposed to be doing. Because this individual happened to be close friends with Morford, everyone just sidestepped the issue and resentment built. During the trip, everyone agreed on a way to tackle the problem, and a plan was put in place to address it. Second, the team developed a strategy for development in four key areas: communication, feedback, decision making, and respect. After seeing his team in action, Morford, who welcomed a return to the dry, safe harbor of his office back in Bellevue, learned an important lesson himself: He has assembled a group of aggressive decision makers, and his job is to leverage, but not cripple, that strength.

Although everyone claims to have enjoyed the adventure, back at the office, team members are no more than cautiously optimistic about what the future holds for the company and the extent to which their river trip helped at all. If, after six months, the individuals begin working together as a team, none of the skeptical engineers is likely to bad-mouth the "touchy-feely" experience they had on—and in—the Salmon River.

Questions for Discussion

1. What do you think will be the outcome of Altrec.com's adventure on the Salmon River? Will it help the company become successful?
2. What else must be done for this exercise to have the intended effects?
3. Have you ever participated in a similar team-building exercise? If so, how was it similar to or different from this one?

invested in them? The answer is *only sometimes*. For team-building exercises to be effective they must be applied correctly. Too often, exercises are used without first thoroughly analyzing precisely what the team needs. When it comes to team building, one size does not fit all! Another problem is that team-building exercises often are used as a one-time panacea. To be most effective, team-building exercises should be repeated regularly to keep the team in tip-top shape or, at least, at the very first sign of problems. And then, when on the job, everyone should be reminded of the lessons learned off-site.

SELECT TEAM MEMBERS BASED ON THEIR SKILLS OR POTENTIAL SKILLS

Insofar as the success of teams demands that they work together closely on a wide variety of tasks, it is essential for them to have a complementary set of skills. This includes not only job skills but also interpersonal skills (especially since getting along with one's teammates is so very important).

Insofar as the success of teams demands that they work together closely on a wide variety of tasks, it is essential for them to have a complementary set of skills. This includes not only job skills but also interpersonal skills (especially since getting along with one's teammates is so very important). With this in mind, at Ampex (noted on p. 241) three-person subsets of teams are used to select their own new members insofar as they have the best ideas about what skills are needed and who would best fit into the teams. It is also frequently important for teams to project future skills that may be needed and to train team members in these skills. With this in mind, work teams at Colgate-Palmolive Company's liquid detergents plant in Cambridge, Ohio, initially receive 120 hours of training in such skills as quality management, problem solving, and team interaction, and subsequently receive advanced training in all these areas.

As part of keeping team members' skills fresh, it is important to *regularly confront members with new facts*. Fresh approaches are likely to be prompted by fresh information, and introducing new facts may present the kind of challenges that teams need to stay innovative. For example, when information about pending cutbacks in defense spending was introduced to teams at Florida's Harris Corporation (an electronics manufacturer), new technologies were developed that positioned the company to land large contracts in nonmilitary government organizations—including a $1.7 billion contract to upgrade the FAA's air traffic control system.

A CAUTIONARY NOTE: DEVELOPING SUCCESSFUL TEAMS REQUIRES PATIENCE

It is important to caution that although these suggestions are important, they alone do not ensure the success of work teams. Many other factors, such as the economy, the existence of competitors, and the company's financial picture are also important determinants of organizational success. Still, the fact that these practices are followed in many highly successful teams certainly makes them worthy of consideration. However, developing effective teams is difficult, and the path to success is riddled with obstacles. It is also time-consuming. According to management expert Peter Drucker, "You can't rush teams. It takes five years just to learn to build a team and decide what kind you want."[31] And it may take most organizations over a decade to make a complete transition to teams. Clearly, they are not an overnight phenomenon. But, with patience and careful attention to the suggestions I shared here, teams have ushered many companies to extraordinary gains in productivity.

SUMMARY: HAVE I MET THE LEARNING OBJECTIVES?

You can be certain that you have met the learning objectives for this chapter found on p. 223 if you understand the following:

1. **DEFINE group and DISTINGUISH between various types of groups.** A *group* is a collection of two or more interacting individuals with a stable pattern of relationships between them who share common goals and who perceive themselves as being a group. Within organizations there are both *formal groups* (e.g., command groups and task groups) and *informal groups* (e.g., interest groups and friendship groups). Formal groups are created by the organization for some specific purpose, whereas informal groups form in the absence of any official organizational reasons.

2. **DESCRIBE the role of norms in organizations.** *Norms* are generally agreed-upon rules that guide behavior. They can be either prescriptive, dictating what should be done, or proscriptive, indicating what should not be done. Norms develop due to precedents set over time, carryovers from other situations, responses to explicit statements by others, and critical events in a group's history.

3. **DESCRIBE the social facilitation effect and the social loafing effect.** *Social facilitation* refers to the tendency for people to perform better in the presence of others than alone when performing a well-learned task, but to perform worse in the presence of others than when alone when performing a poorly learned task. When people pool their efforts on additive group tasks (ones in which separate individual contributions are combined), each individual's contribution tends to be less than when the same task is done alone. The greater the size of the group, the less the size of the individual contributions to the joint product—a phenomenon known as *social loafing*.

4. **DEFINE team and EXPLAIN what makes a team different from an ordinary work group.** A *team* is a group whose members have complementary skills and are committed to a common purpose or set of performance goals for which they

hold themselves mutually responsible. Teams are distinguished from ordinary work groups in several ways: (1) Teams are organized around work processes rather than functions. (2) Teams "own" the product, service, or processes on which they work. (3) Members of teams are trained in several different areas and have a variety of different skills. (4) Teams govern themselves. (5) Teams have their own support staff and responsibilities built in. (6) Teams are involved in making company-wide decisions.

5. **DESCRIBE the general effectiveness of work teams.** Research has shown that teams can bring dramatic improvements in organizational performance. Although this might not stem from improvements in individual productivity, it may be the result of the fact that fewer people are needed to get the jobs done, thereby helping organizations become more efficient.

6. **IDENTIFY ways of making work teams effective.** To ensure the effectiveness of their work teams, companies may take several steps. Specifically, they should (1) provide proper training, (2) compensate employees for their contributions to the team, (3) provide managerial support, (4) promote employee support, (5) communicate the urgency of the team's mission, (6) promote cooperation within and between teams, (7) work at building teams, and (8) select team members based on their skills or potential skills.

You Be the Consultant

A large manufacturing company has been doing quite well over the years, but is now facing dramatic competition from overseas competitors that are undercutting its prices and improving on the quality of its goods. The company president has read a lot about teams in the popular press and has called upon you as a consultant to help implement a transition to teams for the organization. Answer the following questions relevant to this situation based on the material in this chapter.

1. What would you tell the company president about the overall record of teams in being able to improve organizational performance?
2. The company president notes that the current employees tend to have relatively poor skills and are generally disinterested in acquiring new ones. Will this be a problem when it comes to using teams? Why or why not?
3. The company president tells you that several people in the company—including some top executives—are a bit concerned about relinquishing some of their power to teams. Is this likely to be a problem, and if so, what can be done to help alleviate it?

SELF-ASSESSMENT EXERCISE

Why Do You Join Groups?

Groups are important in people's lives, and we join them for several different reasons. However, chances are good that you haven't given too much thought to the matter of why you may have joined certain groups in the first place. So, to identify these reasons, you may find it enlightening to complete the following questionnaire.

Directions

Think of a group you recently joined (e.g., a sports league, a campus club, a fraternity or sorority, a committee in your company). Then, indicate the importance of each of the following reasons for joining by using the following scale: 1 = not at all important, 2 = slightly important, 3 = moderately important, 4 = greatly important, 5 = extremely important.

I joined this group because . . .

_____ 1. I had something important in common with the other members.
_____ 2. By joining the group, I had greater clout.
_____ 3. People in the group shared my interests.
_____ 4. The group helped me feel safe and secure.
_____ 5. I enjoy being with other people.
_____ 6. I thought the people in the group would make me feel good about myself.
_____ 7. I wanted to feel less lonely.
_____ 8. I expected the group members to recognize my accomplishments.

Scoring

1. Add your responses to numbers 1 and 3. This score reflects your interest in joining the group *to seek the satisfaction of mutual interests and goals.*
2. Add your responses to numbers 2 and 4. This score reflects your interest in joining the group *to achieve security.*
3. Add your responses to numbers 5 and 7. This score reflects your interest in joining the group *to fill social needs.*
4. Add your responses to numbers 6 and 8. This score reflects your interest in joining the group *to seek the fulfillment of self-esteem (feeling good about yourself) that others can provide.*

Questions for Discussion

1. What were your strongest (highest score) and weakest (lowest score) reasons for joining this group?
2. Besides the eight reasons identified here, what other reasons did you have for joining this group?
3. Would your scores be different if you thought about another group you may have joined? Repeat the questionnaire to find out.

─── (**GROUP EXERCISE**)

Demonstrating the Social Loafing Effect

The social loafing effect is quite strong and is likely to occur in many different situations in which people make individual contributions to an additive group task. This exercise is designed to demonstrate the effect firsthand in your own class.

Directions

1. Divide the class into groups of different sizes. Between five and ten people should work alone. In addition, there should be a group of two, a group of three, a group of four, and so on, until all members of the class have been assigned to a group. If the class is small, assign students to groups of vastly different sizes, such as two, seven, and fifteen. Form the groups by putting people from the same group together at tables.
2. Each person should be given a page or two from a telephone directory and a stack of index cards. Then, have the individuals and the members of each group perform the same additive task—copying entries from the telephone directory onto index cards. Allow exactly 10 minutes for the task to be performed, and encourage everyone to work as hard as they can.
3. After the time is up, count the number of entries copied.
4. For each group, and for all the individuals, compute the average per-person performance by dividing the total number of entries copied by the number of people in the group.
5. At the board, the instructor should graph the results. Along the vertical axis show the average number of entries copied per person. Along the horizontal axis show the size of the work groups—one, two, three, four, and so on. The graph should look like the one in Figure 9.3.

Questions for Discussion

1. Was the social loafing effect demonstrated? On what basis do you draw this conclusion?
2. If the social loafing effect was not found, why do you think this occurred? Do you think it might have been due to the possibility that your familiarity with the effect led you to avoid it? Test this possibility by replicating the exercise using people who do not know about the phenomenon (e.g., another class), then compare the results.
3. What could have been done to counteract any "free riding" that may have occurred in this demonstration?

NOTES

Case Note

Sittenfeld, C. (1999, July–August). Power by the people. *Fast Company*, pp. 178–181, 185–189.

Chapter Notes

[1] Turner, M. E. (2000). *Groups at work: Theory and research*. Mahwah, NJ: Lawrence Erlbaum Associates.
[2] Toothman, J. (2000). *Conducting the experiential group: An introduction to group dynamics*. New York: John Wiley.
[3] Forsyth, D. L. (1983). *An introduction to group dynamics*. Monterey, CA: Brooks/Cole.
[4] Geen, R. (1989). Alternative conceptualizations of social facilitation. In P. B. Paulus (Ed.), *Psychology of group influence (2nd ed.)* (pp. 15–51). Hillsdale, NJ: Lawrence Erlbaum Associates.
[5] Aiello, J. R., & Svec, C. M. (1993). Computer monitoring of work performance: Extending the social facilitation framework to electronic presence. *Journal of Applied Social Psychology, 23,* 537–548.

[6] Shepperd, J. A. (1993). Productivity loss in performance groups: A motivation analysis. *Psychological Bulletin, 113,* 67–81.

[7] Wellins, R. S., Byham, W. C., & Dixon, G. R. (1994). *Inside teams.* San Francisco: Jossey-Bass.

[8] Robbins, H., & Finley, M. (2000). *The new why teams don't work.* New York: Berrett-Koehler.

[9] Duarte, D. L., & Snyder, N. T. (2000). *Mastering virtual teams: Strategies, tools, and techniques that succeed.* San Francisco: Jossey-Bass. Lipnak, J., & Stamps, J. (2000). *Virtual teams: People working across boundaries with technology (2nd ed.).* New York: John Wiley.

[10] Coovert, M. D., & Foster, L. L. (2001). *Computer supported cooperative work.* New York: John Wiley.

[11] Lipnak, J., & Stamps, J. (1997). *Virtual teams: Reaching across space, time, and organizations with technology.* New York: John Wiley.

[12] Gilder, G. (2000). *Telecosm: How infinite bandwidth will revolutionize our world.* New York: Free Press.

[13] Lawler, E. E., III, Mohrman, S. A., & Ledford, G. E., Jr. (1992). *Employee involvement and total quality management.* San Francisco: Jossey-Bass.

[14] Hackman, J. R. (Ed.) (1990). *Groups that work (and those that don't).* San Francisco: Jossey-Bass.

[15] Wellins, R. S., Byham, W. C., & Wilson, J. M. (1991). *Empowered teams.* San Francisco: Jossey-Bass.

[16] Osburn, J. D., Moran, L., Musselwhite, E., & Zenger, J. H. (1990). *Self-directed work teams.* Burr Ridge, IL: Richard D. Irwin.

[17] Blanchard, K. H., & Bowles, S. M. (2001). *High five: The magic of working together.* New York: William Morrow.

[18] Pearson, C. A. L. (1992). Autonomous workgroups: An evaluation at an industrial site. *Human Relations, 45,* 905–936.

[19] Wall, T. D., Kemp, N. J., Jackson, P. R., & Clegg, C. W. (1986). Outcomes of autonomous workgroups: A long-term field experiment. *Academy of Management Journal, 29,* 280–304.

[20] Salas, E., Edens, E., & Bowers, C. A. (2000). *Improving teamwork in organizations.* Mahwah, NJ: Lawrence Erlbaum Associates.

[21] Dumaine, B. (1994, September 5). The trouble with teams. *Fortune,* pp. 86–88, 90, 92 (quote, p. 86).

[22] Barner, R. W. (2001). *Team troubleshooter.* Palo Alto, CA: Davies-Black. Katzenbach, J. R., & Smith, D. K. (1993). *The wisdom of teams.* Boston: Harvard Business School Press.

[23] Redding, J. C. (2000). *The radical team handbook: Harnessing the power of team learning for breakthrough results.* New York: John Wiley. Caudron, S. (1994, February). Teamwork takes work. *Personnel Journal,* pp. 41–46, 49 (quote, p. 43).

[24] See Caudron, 1994; Note 23 (quote, p. 41).

[25] Stern, A. (1993, July 18). Managing by team is not always as easy as it looks. *New York Times,* p. B14 (quote, p. B14).

[26] See Note 21 (quote, p. 88).

[27] See Note 21 (quote, p. 90).

[28] See Note 21 (quote, p. 88).

[29] Sundstrom, E., DeMeuse, K. P., & Futrell, D. (1990). Work teams: Applications and effectiveness. *American Psychologist, 45,* 128–137.

[30] Balf, T. (1999, November). Extreme off-site. *Fast Company,* pp. 384–388, 390, 396, 398.

[31] Anonymous. (1994, December). The facts of life for teambuilding. *Human Resources Forum,* p. 3.

10

Making decisions in organizations

LEARNING OBJECTIVES

After reading this chapter, you will be able to:

1. IDENTIFY the steps in the decision-making process.

2. DESCRIBE the effects of culture on decision making, and the major reasons why people sometimes make unethical decisions.

3. DESCRIBE the varieties of decisions people make in organizations.

4. IDENTIFY factors that lead to imperfect decisions in organizations.

5. DESCRIBE the conditions under which individuals make better decisions than groups and groups make better decisions than individuals.

6. EXPLAIN how the Delphi technique and the nominal group technique are used to improve the quality of decisions made by groups.

THREE GOOD REASONS WHY YOU SHOULD CARE ABOUT. . .

Decision Making in Organizations

You should care about decision making in organizations because:

1. Human decision making is inherently imperfect, although these imperfections can be overcome if you know what they are and how they operate.

2. Functioning effectively in today's business environment requires awareness of cultural differences in the way people make decisions.

3. Groups are widely used to make organizational decisions despite the fact they often are ineffective at dealing with the kinds of tasks they are likely to face.

Making the Case for... Decision Making in Organizations

Keeping the New Orleans Saints Marching Down the Field

Bruce Lemmerman spends 363 days per year preparing for important decisions that have to be made in just a few minutes during the other two days. As director of college scouting for the New Orleans Saints, he visits colleges and universities throughout the United States in search of football players who are good enough to be selected for the "Big Show" (slang for the National Football League) during the NFL's two-day college draft each April.

The key to Lemmerman's mission is gathering all pertinent information so that it can be called up when Saints officials need to make decisions about which prospects to select as their draft choices. With this in mind, Lemmerman is almost always on the road, going to as many as 70 schools in four months. While there, he closely watches players during games or in practice sessions—live from the sidelines when he can, but at least on videotape. He also talks to coaches and trainers, getting their slant on each athlete's strengths and weaknesses.

He routinely gathers detailed information on a player's physical qualities, such as his height, weight, speed, percentage of body fat, and height of vertical leap, but that's not all. Lemmerman also pays close attention to personal qualities and intangible characteristics, such as a player's "football intelligence," his work ethic, competitiveness, and workout habits during the off-season.

Traditionally, the records were written by hand and kept in folders, resulting in disarray. Player profiles were kept in blue folders in the team's conference room, medical evaluations were in the trainer's office, and scouting reports were someplace else. Getting all the critical information on a player was a hopelessly difficult task—and it was only made worse by the fact that until Lemmerman joined the Saints in 1994, much of the recruiting was outsourced. His first mission was to assist in developing a database so that anyone in the front office could access whatever information was needed at any time.

Acknowledging that such a system is only as good as the data entered into it, Lemmerman spends a great deal of time entering information about players into his notebook computer. But he can't run up and down the sidelines while typing notes. Neither is a handheld computer practical because the screen is too small. So, Lemmerman prefers doing things the old-fashioned way—he takes notes on paper forms attached to a clipboard while speaking his impressions into a microcassette recorder. Then, either while on the plane or back at the hotel, he enters all of this information into the notebook computer and transmits it back to the main computer on his desktop in New Orleans.

As tedious as this process may be, Lemmerman realizes that it's necessary to enable the team to make the best possible recruiting decisions. As he puts it, "Imagine it's the fourth quarter and you're tired. You want to quit, but you suck it up and play anyway. At times like that it's easy to be less sharp and to take shortcuts." However, knowing that there are multimillion-dollar decisions at stake, Lemmerman does his part for the team by keeping the recruiting records in impeccable form.

––––––––––––

Management theorists agree that *decision making* is one of the most common, but vitally important, of all work activities.[1] As Bruce Lemmerman would freely admit, it's the reason why he gathers information, both objective and subjective, and why he works so hard to keep that information in a usable form. After all, without good scouting information, the New Orleans Saints would not know which college players to draft each April, jeopardizing the team's record. Although Lemmerman is probably too modest to admit it, the team's success all begins with him.

Although you might not be a big-time football scout, you undoubtedly make decisions in whatever work you do. Some of these may be mundane, but others may be very important. Whatever these may be, understanding how decisions are made and how they can be improved is a major goal of the field of OB. With this in mind, I will review in this chapter the various concepts and practices associated with managerial decision making. Specifically, I will review the basic characteristics of individual decisions and group decisions. For each, I will identify factors that adversely affect the quality of decisions and techniques for improving the quality of decisions. Before getting to this, however, I will examine the general process of decision making and the varieties of decisions made in organizations.

The Fundamental Nature of Decision Making

I begin this chapter by describing the fundamental nature of decision making. Specifically, I will focus on two things. First, I will describe a general model of the decision-making process. Second, I will address a fundamental question about decision making: Are we all alike in the way we make decisions?

A GENERAL MODEL OF DECISION MAKING

Traditionally, scientists have found it useful to conceptualize the process of decision making as a series of steps that groups or individuals take to solve problems.[2] A general model of the decision-making process can help us understand the complex nature of organizational decision making (see Figure 10.1). This model highlights two important aspects of the decision-making process: *formulation*, the process of understanding a problem and making a decision about it, and *implementation*, the process of carrying out the decision made. As I outline this model, keep in mind that all decisions might not fully conform to the neat, eight-step pattern described (e.g., steps may be skipped and/or combined). However, for purposes of pointing out the general way the decision-making process operates, the model is quite useful.

1. *Identify the problem.* To decide how to solve a problem, one must first recognize and identify it. For example, an executive may identify as a problem the fact that the company cannot meet its payroll obligations. This step isn't always as easy as it sounds. People frequently distort, omit, ignore, and/or discount information around them that provides important cues regarding the existence of problems. This, of course is problematic. After all, a problem cannot be solved if it is never recognized.

2. *Define objectives.* After a problem is identified, the next step is to define the objectives to be met in solving it. It is important to conceive of problems in such a way that possible solutions can be identified. The problem identified in our example may be defined as "inadequate cash flow." By looking at the problem in this way, the objective is clear: increase available cash reserves. Any possible solution to the problem should be evaluated relative to this objective.

3. *Make a predecision.* A **predecision** is a decision about how to make a decision. By assessing the type of problem in question and other aspects of the situation,

FIGURE 10.1 The Decision-Making Process

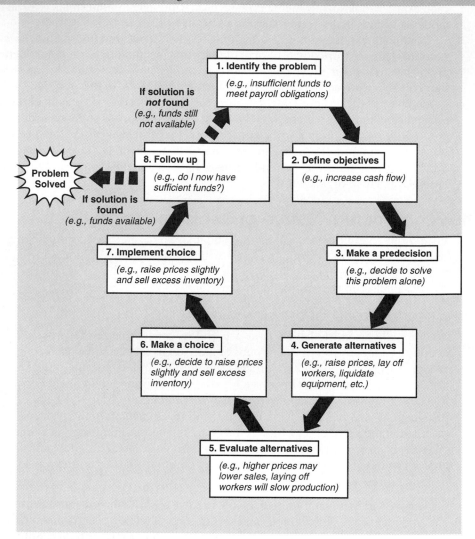

The process of *decision making* tends to follow the eight steps outlined here. The running example illustrates how a particular problem—insufficient funds to meet payroll obligations—can be applied to each step. (*Source*: Based on suggestions by Wedley & Field, 1984; see Note 2.)

managers may opt to make a decision themselves, delegate the decision to another, or have a group make the decision. Predecisions should be based on research that tells us about the effectiveness of decisions made under different circumstances, many of which we will review later in this chapter. Much of this information is summarized in computer programs known as **decision support systems** (**DSS**). These techniques are generally quite effective in helping people make decisions about complex problems.

4. *Generate alternatives.* Possible solutions to the problem are identified in this stage. Whenever possible in attempting to come up with solutions, people tend to rely on previously used approaches that may provide ready-made answers. In our example, some possible ways of solving the revenue shortage problem include reducing the workforce, liquidating unnecessary equipment, and increasing sales.

5. *Evaluate alternative solutions.* Because not all possible alternatives may be equally feasible, the fifth step calls for evaluating the various alternatives identified. Which solution is best? What would be the most effective way of raising the revenue needed to meet the payroll? The various alternatives need to be identified. Some may be more effective than others, and some may be more difficult to implement than others. For example, although increasing sales would certainly help, that is much easier said than done. It is a solution, but not an immediately practical one.

6. *Make a choice.* After several alternatives are evaluated, one that is considered acceptable is chosen. As I will describe shortly, different approaches to decision making offer different views of how thoroughly people consider alternatives and how optimal their chosen alternatives are. Choosing which course of action to take is the step that most often comes to mind when we think about the decision-making process.

7. *Implement the chosen alternative.* In following this step, whatever alternative was chosen is now carried out.

8. *Follow up.* Monitoring the effectiveness of the decisions they put into action is important to the success of organizations. Does the problem still exist? Have any new problems been caused by implementing the solution? In other words, it is important to seek feedback about the effectiveness of any attempted solution. For this reason, the decision-making process is presented as circular in Figure 10.1. If the solution works, the problem may be considered solved. If not, a new solution will have to be attempted.

CULTURAL DIFFERENCES IN DECISION MAKING

Having outlined the basic steps through which people go in making decisions, you may assume that everyone makes decisions the same way. This would be misleading. Although the basic steps involved in making decisions may be identical, there are widespread differences in the way people from various nations go about putting them into practice.[3] Because we take for granted our own ways of making decisions, differences between people from different cultures may seem strange to us. However, it is important to become aware of such differences when doing business with people from around the world. Accordingly, it makes sense to ask how people from different countries differ in the way they make decisions.

> *Although the basic steps involved in making decisions may be identical, there are widespread differences in the way people from various nations go about putting them into practice.*

Recognizing problems. As I noted earlier, decision making begins by observing a problem. As obvious as this may seem, people from different countries do not always agree on what constitutes a problem. Suppose, for example, you are managing a large construction project and discover that your most important supplier will deliver some important materials several months late. If you are from the United States, Canada, or Western Europe, you may decide to get another supplier. However, if you are from Thailand, Indonesia, or Malaysia, you would be likely to accept the situation as fate and allow the project to be delayed.

Preference for decision-making unit.   In the United States, where people tend to have a highly **individualistic orientation** (i.e., their primary focus is on themselves as individuals), people are apt to make decisions by themselves. However, in Asian countries, people have a more **collectivistic orientation** (i.e., their primary focus is on the groups to which they belong). As such, it would be inconceivable for a Japanese businessperson to make a decision without first checking with his or her colleagues. Individuals from such cultures are inclined to make group decisions, rather than individual ones.

Who makes the decisions?   In Sweden, employees at all levels expect to be involved in making whatever decisions involve them. In fact, employees of the auto manufacturers Saab and Volvo routinely make decisions about how to do their jobs (see Chapter 5). In India, by contrast, the hierarchy of an organization matters a great deal. People there expect decisions to be made by others of higher rank. Empowered decision making (which I will describe more fully later in this chapter) is not well accepted.

Time taken to make decisions.   In the United States, we generally respect people who make decisions quickly, referring to them as "decisive," a quality that is valued. In other cultures, however, time urgency is downplayed. For example, in the Middle East, quickly reaching a decision is seen as a sign of being overly hasty. In Egypt, the more important the matter, the more time one is expected to take when making a decision about it.

As these examples illustrate, there are some interesting and important differences in how people from various countries formulate and implement decisions. Understanding such differences is an important first step toward developing appropriate strategies for conducting business at a global level.[4]

WHY DO PEOPLE SOMETIMES MAKE UNETHICAL DECISIONS IN ORGANIZATIONS?

As you know, most people consider ethical factors at least to some degree when making decisions. Their tendency to do so, known as **bounded discretion,** reflects the fact that individual decisions are constrained by ethical considerations. For example, many individuals would refrain from padding their expense accounts even if they believed they could not get caught, simply because they believe that it is wrong to do so. As you know, however, unethical behavior in organizations is not uncommon. While psychologists have argued whether or not people are by nature ethical, and sociologists have debated the general degradation of moral standards in society, organizational behavior experts agree that unethical behavior occurs for two key reasons.

Organizations sometimes encourage behavior that violates ethical standards.   It is easy to understand that people may behave unethically on the job to the extent that they are encouraged to do so. Consider, for example, how some business executives are expected to say nothing about ethically dubious behavior they've witnessed in the company. In fact, in many companies it is considered not only acceptable but also desirable to be secretive and deceitful. For example, the practice of **stonewalling**—willingly hiding relevant information—is quite common. One reason for this is that organizations may actually punish those who are too open and honest. As a case in point, consider the disclosure that B. F. Goodrich allegedly rewarded employees who falsified and withheld data on the quality of aircraft brakes to win certification. This example illustrates how the **counternorms** of secrecy and deceitfulness were accepted and supported by the organization. By counternorms, I am referring to accepted organizational practices that run contrary to society's prevailing ethical standards. For a summary of some of the most common counternorms found in organizations, see Figure 10.2.[5]

FIGURE 10.2 Ethical Norms versus Organizational Counternorms

Ethical Norms		Organizational Counternorms
Be open and honest	vs.	Be secretive and deceitful
Follow the rules at all costs	vs.	Do whatever it takes to get the job done
Be cost-effective	vs.	Use it or lose it
Take responsibility	vs.	Pass the buck
Be a team player	vs.	Take credit for your own actions: grandstand

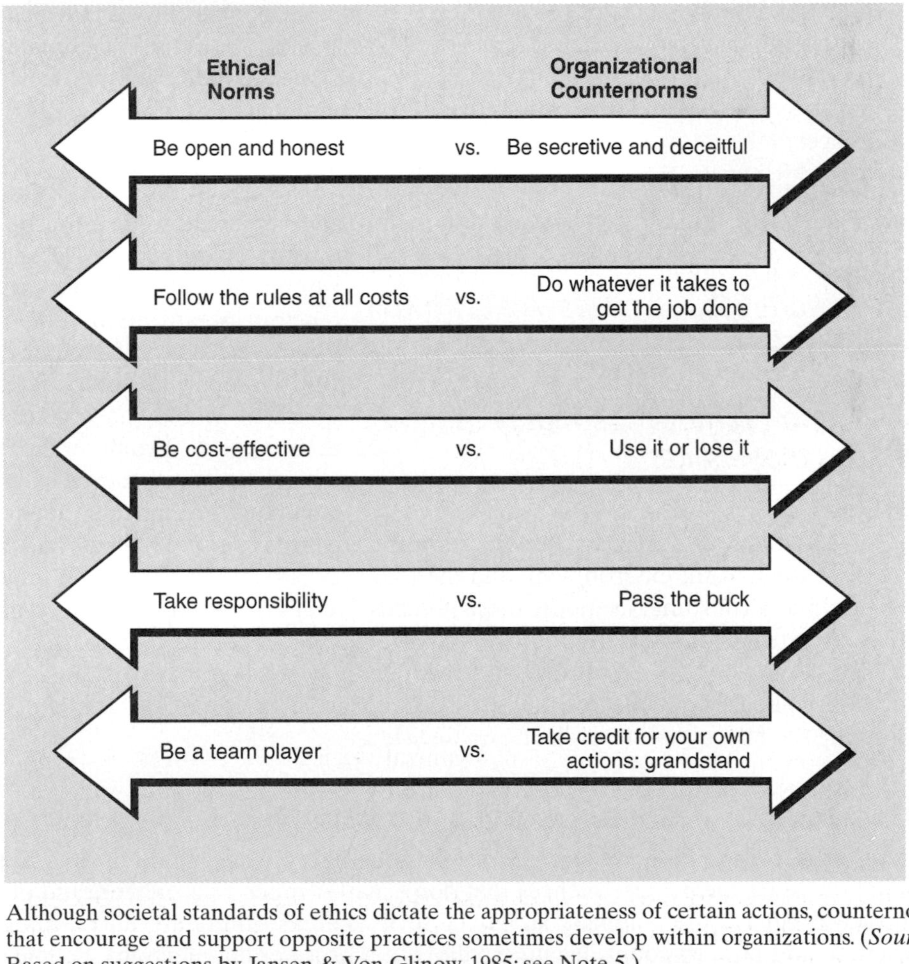

Although societal standards of ethics dictate the appropriateness of certain actions, counternorms that encourage and support opposite practices sometimes develop within organizations. (*Source*: Based on suggestions by Jansen & Von Glinow, 1985; see Note 5.)

Some managerial values undermine integrity. Most managers appear to believe that "good ethics is good business." However, some managers have developed ways of thinking that lead them to make unethical decisions. Given how very influential top leaders are when it comes to influencing others in their organizations, it should not be surprising that unethical managerial values promote unethical organizational decisions.[6] Several well-known forms of unethical thinking are as follows:[7]

- **Bottom-line mentality**—This line of thinking supports financial success as the only value to be considered. It promotes short-term decisions that are immediately financially sound, despite the fact that they may cause long-term problems for the organization.
- **Exploitative mentality**—This view encourages "using" people in a way that promotes stereotypes and undermines empathy and compassion. This highly selfish perspective sacrifices concern for others in favor of benefits to one's own immediate interests.
- **Madison Avenue mentality**—This perspective suggests that anything is right if the public can be made to see it as right. The idea is that executives may be more concerned that their decisions appear to be right than about their legitimate morality. This kind of thinking leads some companies to hide their unethical behavior (e.g., dumping toxic waste under cover of night) or to otherwise justify it as acceptable.

Recognizing the problems associated with these various orientations is not difficult. Their overemphasis on short-term monetary gain may lead to decisions that not only hurt individuals in the long run but also threaten the very existence of organizations. Some executives, such as Anita Roddick of the Body Shop[8] and Tom Chappell of Tom's of Maine,[9] have gone out of their way to promote the highly ethical decisions they make. These company founders have long engaged in highly ethical practices with respect to the treatment of animals and preservation of the natural environment, and their companies have prospered in great part because many consumers support these policies. However, because not all companies are run by such highly socially conscious individuals, many people tend to make unethical decisions every day. Because it isn't always easy to tell if you are making an ethical decision yourself, you will find the self-test appearing in Table 10.1 a useful way of assessing the ethical nature of your own decisions.

Varieties of Organizational Decisions

Consider for a moment the variety of decisions likely to be made in organizations. Some decisions have consequences that don't matter much (e.g., what brand of paper clips to order for the company supply closet), whereas others are far-reaching (e.g., whether, and how, to count disputed ballots in a presidential election). People sometimes make decisions in situations in which the likely outcomes are relatively well

TABLE 10.1 Guidelines for Making Ethical Decisions: A Self-Test	

Although making ethical decisions is far easier said than done, there are certain things anyone can do to increase the odds of making ethical decisions. Experts believe that ethical decisions can be enhanced by asking yourself the following questions.

Question	*Explanation*
Does it violate the obvious "shall-nots"?	We too often rationalize that it is acceptable to do something that we know is wrong, such as lie or cheat.
Will anyone get hurt?	To the extent that someone may get hurt by the decision you make, it probably is unethical.
How would you feel if your decision was reported on the front page of your newspaper?	If you would be displeased about having your decision made public, it's probably not the right thing to do.
What if you did it 100 times?	If something is wrong 100 times, it also is wrong once.
How would you feel if someone did it to you?	If you find yourself not liking what would happen to you if the tables were turned, your own actions probably are suspect.
What's your gut feeling?	If that "little voice inside your head" tells you something is wrong, you should listen.

known (e.g., the decision to underwrite life insurance on the basis of actuarial data), whereas at other times the outcomes are much more uncertain (e.g., the decision to invade a hostile nation for purposes of freeing hostages). Finally, some decisions are issued from the top (e.g., an order from the department head that work will begin sharply at 8:00 A.M.), whereas other decisions are made by the very individuals who will be affected by them (e.g., a team whose members decide whom to hire).

These examples illustrate the three major characteristics of organizational decisions I will now describe: (1) how structured or unstructured the situation is, (2) how much certainty or risk is involved in the decision, and (3) how much employees are involved in making the decisions affecting them.

PROGRAMMED VERSUS NONPROGRAMMED DECISIONS

Think of a decision that is made repeatedly, according to a preestablished set of guidelines. For example, a word processing operator may decide to make a backup diskette of the day's work, or a manager of a fast-food restaurant may decide to order hamburger buns as the supply starts to get low. Decisions such as these are known as **programmed decisions**—routine decisions, made by lower-level personnel, that rely on predetermined courses of action.

By contrast, people also make **nonprogrammed decisions**—ones for which there are no ready-made solutions. The decision maker confronts a unique situation in which the solutions are novel. The research scientist attempting to find a cure for a rare disease faces a problem that is poorly structured. Unlike the order clerk whose course of action is clear when the supply of paper clips runs low, the scientist in this example must rely on creativity rather than preexisting answers to solve the problem at hand.

Certain types of nonprogrammed decisions are known as **strategic decisions.** Typically, because these decisions have important long-term implications for the organization, they are made by coalitions of high-level executives.[10] Strategic decisions reflect a

TABLE 10.2   Strategic Decisions: Some Highly Successful Examples

Decisions that guide the future directions of organizations are known as *strategic decisions*. Some of the best-known and most successful strategic decisions are shown here. (*Source*: Based on material in Crainer, 1998; see Note 11.)

Company	*Decision Made*
Toyota	In the aftermath of World War II, the company decided to emphasize high-quality manufacturing techniques.
Coca-Cola	During World War II, the company developed brand loyalty by selling bottles of Coke to members of the armed services.
IBM	In 1924, founder Thomas Watson, Sr. changed the company's name from the Computing-Tabulating-Recording Company to International Business Machines although it had no international operations at the time, boldly declaring its ambitions.
Microsoft	In 1981, Bill Gates decided to license MS-DOS to IBM, which relinquished control of the operating system for all non-IBM personal computers.
Apple	Steve Jobs decided to build his company around sales of a simple computer that could be used by individuals.
Sears	In 1905, the company decided on a way to bring its products to a wider audience by introducing a mail-order catalog.
Johnson & Johnson	In 1982, the company pulled all bottles of Tylenol capsules off store shelves after a few capsules were found to be poisoned.
Sony	In 1980, the company introduced the Walkman after officials noticed that young people like to have music with them wherever they go.
Hewlett-Packard	In 1979 the company decided to exploit an engineer's observation that metal heated in a certain way tended to splatter, resulting in the development of the ink-jet printer.

way of directing an organization in some specified fashion—that is, according to an underlying organizational philosophy or mission. For example, an organization may make a strategic decision to grow at a specified yearly rate, or to be guided by a certain code of corporate ethics. Both of these decisions are likely to be considered "strategic" because they guide the future direction of the organization. Some excellent examples of highly successful strategic decisions may be found in Table 10.2.[11]

CERTAIN VERSUS UNCERTAIN DECISIONS

Think of how easy it would be to make decisions if we knew exactly what the future held in store. Making the best investments in the stock market would simply be a matter of looking up the changes in tomorrow's newspaper. Of course, we never know for sure what the future holds, but we can be more certain at some times than others. Certainty about the factors on which decisions are made is highly desired in organizational decision making.

Degrees of certainty and uncertainty are expressed as statements of risk. All organizational decisions involve some degree of risk—ranging from complete certainty (no risk) to complete uncertainty, "a stab in the dark" (high risk). To make the best possible decisions in organizations, people seek to "manage" the risks they take—that is, to minimize the riskiness of a decision by gaining access to information relevant to the decision.

What makes an outcome risky or not is the probability of obtaining the desired outcome. Decision makers attempt to obtain information about the probabilities, or odds, of certain events occurring given that other events have occurred. For example, a financial analyst may report that a certain stock has risen 80 percent of the time that the prime rate has dropped, or a meteorologist may report that the precipitation probability is 50 percent (i.e., in the past it rained or snowed half the time certain atmospheric conditions existed). These data may be considered reports of *objective probabilities* because they are based on concrete, verifiable data. Many decisions are also based on subjective probabilities—personal beliefs or hunches about what will happen. For example, a gambler who bets on a horse because it has a name similar to one of his children's, or a person who suspects it's going to rain because he just washed his car, is basing these judgments on *subjective probabilities*.

Obviously, uncertainty is an undesirable characteristic in decision-making situations. We may view much of what decision makers do in organizations as attempting to reduce uncertainty so they can make better decisions. In general, what reduces uncertainty in decision-making situations? The answer is *information*. Knowledge about the past and the present can be used to help make projections about the future. A modern executive's access to data needed to make important decisions may be as close as the nearest computer terminal. A variety of online information services are designed to provide organizational decision makers with the latest information relevant to the decisions they are making.

Of course, not all information needed to make decisions comes from computers. Many managerial decisions are also based on the decision maker's experiences and intuition. This is not to say that top managers rely on subjective information in making decisions (although they might), but that their history of past decisions—both successes and failures—is often given great weight in the decision-making process. In other words, when it comes to making decisions, people often rely on what has worked for them in the past. (To help reduce the riskiness of their decisions, many of today's top company officials are relying on high-tech devices. For a look at how this is done in a popular retail store, see the **Winning Practices** section on the following page.)

TOP-DOWN VERSUS EMPOWERED DECISIONS

Traditionally, the job of making all but the most menial decisions has belonged to managers.[13] Subordinates collect information and give it to their superiors, who then use it to make decisions. Known as **top-down decision making,** this approach puts the power to make decisions in the hands of managers, leaving lower-level workers with little or no opportunity to make decisions.

Today, however, a new approach has come into vogue. The idea of **empowered decision making** allows employees to make the decisions required to do their jobs without seeking supervisory approval. As the name implies, this approach gives employees the power to do their jobs effectively. The rationale is straightforward: Allow the people who actually do certain jobs to make decisions about them. This practice is generally very useful insofar as it is likely to lead to effective decisions. In addition, it also helps build commitment to decisions. After all, people are more committed to the results of decisions they made themselves than those their bosses have made for them.

WINNING PRACTICES

Adaptive Agents as Decision Aids

To make good decisions, it helps to know in advance how things will work out. With this in mind, scientists are developing sophisticated computer models that capture the rules of complex human behavior. The so-called **adaptive agents** created by engineers and consultants at PricewaterhouseCoopers are software-based "people" programmed to behave in the same ways as human beings.[12] Their goal is ambitious: to be able to mimic what people will do in certain situations, thereby allowing managers to see the impact of their decisions without ever making them in the real world.

This would be the ultimate way of reducing the uncertainty of decisions. Although even the most sophisticated computer programs cannot perfectly predict the future, they will be able to provide extremely useful information to decision makers about likely outcomes. I use the future tense here because this technology is in its infancy. Still, optimistic about how it will facilitate complex decision making, several companies have invested in its development, hoping to bring this technology to fruition. For example, Macy's is relying on using the technology to help it determine the number of salespeople to schedule in each store department and where to locate service desks and cash registers within stores. It also wants to know how a sales associate's age, gender, and length of service will influence sales by consumers. US West also has expressed interest in the technology, hoping to be able to predict how both competitors and customers will respond to different pricing and promotion plans.

As useful as this technology is, scientists freely admit that they have a long way to go before it's perfected. Still, it already has seen some successes. For example, the group at PricewaterhouseCoopers has developed 40,000 adaptive agents for a major entertainment company. Cloned from a survey of actual moviegoers, programming these agents has made it possible to forecast first-week box-office receipts 30 percent more accurately than traditional methods.

The real benefit from creating adaptive agents comes from the fact that you can simulate in just a few minutes what it otherwise would take entire days or weeks to find out. And, of course, mistakes have no cost because you're playing "what if" games with a simulated public. Those of you who have crashed airplanes while playing with flight simulation programs surely can appreciate the safety of using simulated decisions. At the same time, just as what you learn about real flying using a flight simulator can be invaluable, so too can what you learn about the behavior of real people when using simulated ones.

As promising as this technology may be, experts caution that it's only as good as the assumptions built into it (which, of course, requires considerable research in organizational behavior). And, while adaptive-agents could be useful as decision aids, they certainly won't be replacing actual human decision makers anytime soon.

Questions for Discussion

1. Beyond what's described here, how else might adaptive agents be used?
2. What types of information do you believe will be most difficult to program into adaptive agents?
3. Do you envision any potentially ethical concerns associated with the use of adaptive agents?

> *The Ritz-Carlton hotel chain offers a good example of empowered decision making. This upscale hotel chain, renown for its service, has empowered chambermaids to authorize expenditures (up to $2,000 per day) for maintenance of hotel facilities they find to be in need of repair.*

The Ritz-Carlton hotel chain offers a good example of empowered decision making. This upscale hotel chain, renown for its service, has empowered chambermaids to authorize expenditures (up to $2,000 per day) for maintenance of hotel facilities they find to be in need of repair. So, instead of filling out a form to repair, say, a broken lamp, which normally would get passed from one person to another for approval, chambermaids now can go straight to the appropriate person who can get the job done. What's more, they are empowered to follow up by making sure that the repair has been made, and overseeing its reinstallation in the hotel.

The Imperfect Nature of Human Decisions

We all like to think of ourselves as "rational" people who make **rational decisions**—that is, decisions that maximize the attainment of individual, team, or organizational goals. However, as you know from experience, people do not always act in completely rational ways. It's not that decision makers do not want to behave rationally, or that they are somehow irrational. Rather, innate limits in people's ability to make decisions as well as impediments in the work environment make it virtually impossible to make completely rational, perfect decisions.

To illustrate this point, consider how a personnel department might select a new receptionist. After several applicants are interviewed, the personnel manager might choose the best candidate seen so far and stop interviewing. Had the person been completely rational, he or she would have had to interview *all* possible candidates before deciding on the best one. But, he or she did not. Instead, the manager in this example used a far simpler approach, one that typifies the way people go about making decisions.

CHARACTERISTICS OF DECISIONS IN ORGANIZATIONS

Because people are not machines, we don't always make perfect decisions—in fact, we rarely, if ever, do so. And whatever limitations we have as human decision makers are aggravated by the realities of life in organizations. These limitations can be characterized in several key ways.

Decision makers have a limited view of the problems confronting them.   The number of solutions that can be recognized or implemented is limited by the capabilities of the decision maker and the available resources of the organization. Also, because decision makers do not have perfect information about the consequences of their decisions, they cannot tell which one is best. The idea is that people lack the cognitive skills required to formulate and solve highly complex business problems in a completely objective, rational way—what is known as **bounded rationality**.[14]

Decision makers consider solutions as they become available.   Although it might be best to consider all possible solutions, making an **optimal decision**, people don't do so.

Instead, they decide on the first alternative that meets their criteria for acceptability. Thus, the decision maker selects a solution that may be just good enough, although not optimal. Such decisions are referred to as **satisficing decisions**. In most situations satisficing decisions are acceptable and are more likely to be made than optimal ones. The following analogy has been used to compare the two types of decisions: Making an optimal decision is like searching a haystack for the sharpest needle, but making a satisficing decision is like searching a haystack for a needle just sharp enough with which to sew.

Decision makers face time constraints. Many important organizational decisions are made under severe time pressure. Under such circumstances, it is often impossible for exhaustive decision making to occur. This is particularly the case when organizations face crisis situations requiring immediate decisions. Under such conditions, when decision makers feel "rushed into" taking action, they frequently restrict their search for information and consideration of alternatives that may otherwise help them make effective decisions.

Decision makers are sensitive to political "face-saving" pressure. In other words, people may make decisions that help them look good to others, although the resulting decisions might not be in the best interest of their organizations. Decisions frequently are made with an eye toward cultivating a good impression, although they may not always be the best ones for their organizations.

SYSTEMATIC BIASES IN INDIVIDUAL DECISIONS

Beyond the fundamental limitations of people's capacity to process information, it also is important to be aware of the fact that people approach the decisions they make in ways that are systematically biased. I will describe several of these types of biases here.

Framing effects: "Half full or half empty?" One well-established decision-making bias has to do with the tendency for people to make different decisions based on how the problem is presented to them—that is, the **framing** of a problem. Scientists have found that problems framed in a manner that emphasizes the positive gains to be received tend to encourage conservative decisions (i.e., decision makers are said to be *risk averse*), whereas problems framed in a manner that emphasizes the potential losses to be suffered lead to *risk-seeking* decisions. Consider the following example:

> The government is preparing to combat a rare disease expected to take 600 lives. Two alternative programs to combat the disease have been proposed, each of which, scientists believe, will have certain consequences. *Program A* will save 200 people, if adopted. *Program B* has a one-third chance of saving all 600 people, but a two-thirds chance of saving no one. Which program do you prefer?

When such a problem was presented to a group of people, 72 percent expressed a preference for *Program A*, and 28 percent for *Program B*. In other words, they preferred the "sure thing" of saving 200 people over the one-third possibility of saving them all. However, a curious thing happened when the description of the programs was framed in negative terms. Specifically:

> *Program C* was described as allowing 400 people to die, if adopted. *Program D* was described as allowing a one-third probability that no one would die, and a two-thirds probability that all 600 would die. Now which program would you prefer?

Compare these four programs. *Program C* is just another way of stating the outcomes of *Program A*, and *Program D* is just another way of stating the outcomes of *Program B*. However, *Programs C* and *D* are framed in negative terms, which led to opposite preferences: Twenty-two percent favored *Program C* and 78 percent favored *Program D*. In other words, people avoided risk when the problem was framed in terms of "lives saved" (i.e., in positive terms), but sought risk when the problem was framed in terms of "lives lost" (i.e., in negative terms). To see if you are risk seeking or risk averse, see the **Self-Assessment Exercise** on p. 276.

Scientists believe that such effects are due to the tendency for people to perceive equivalent situations framed differently as not really equivalent. In other words, focusing on the glass as "half full" leads people to think about it differently than when it is presented as being "half empty," although they might recognize intellectually that the two are really the same. Such findings illustrate that people are not completely rational decision makers, but are systematically biased by the cognitive distortions created by simple differences in the way situations are framed.

Heuristics. Framing effects are not the only cognitive biases to which decision makers are subjected. It also has been established that people often attempt to simplify the complex decisions they face by using **heuristics**—simple rules of thumb that guide them through a complex array of decision alternatives. Although heuristics are potentially useful to decision makers, they represent potential impediments to decision making. Two very common types of heuristics may be identified:

- **The availability heuristic**—This is the tendency for people to base their judgments on information that is readily available to them—although it may be inaccurate. Suppose, for example, that an executive needs to know the percentage of entering college freshmen who go on to graduate. There is not enough time to gather the appropriate statistics, so she bases her judgments on her own recollections of when she was a college student. If the percentage she recalls graduating, based on her own experiences, is higher or lower than the usual number, her estimate will be off accordingly.
- **The representativeness heuristic**—This is the tendency to perceive others in stereotypical ways if they appear to be good representatives of the category to which they belong. For example, suppose you believe that accountants are bright, mild-mannered individuals, whereas salespeople are less intelligent, but much more extroverted. Further, imagine that there are twice as many salespeople as accountants at a party. You meet someone at the party who is bright and mild-mannered. Although mathematically the odds are two-to-one that this person is a salesperson rather than an accountant, chances are you will guess that the individual is an accountant because he or she possesses the traits you associate with accountants.

It is important to note that heuristics do not always deteriorate the quality of decisions made. In fact, they can be quite helpful. People often use rules of thumb to help simplify the complex decisions they face. For example, management scientists employ many useful heuristics to aid decisions regarding such matters as where to locate warehouses or how to compose an investment portfolio. We also use heuristics in our everyday lives, such as when we play chess ("control the center of the board") or blackjack ("hit on 16, stick on 17"). However, the representativeness heuristic and the availability heuristic may be recognized as impediments to superior decisions insofar as they discourage people from collecting and processing as much information as they should. Making judgments based on only readily available information, or on stereotypical beliefs, although making things simple for the decision maker, does so at a potentially high cost—poor decisions.

Escalation of commitment: Throwing good money after bad.   It is inevitable that some organizational decisions will be unsuccessful. What would you say is the rational thing to do when a poor decision has been made? Intuitively, it makes sense for the ineffective action to be stopped or reversed, to "cut your losses and run." However, people don't always respond this way. In fact, it is not unusual to find that ineffective decisions are sometimes followed up with still further ineffective decisions.

Imagine, for example, that you have invested money in a company, but as time goes on, it appears to be failing. Rather than lose your initial investment, you may invest still more money in the hope of salvaging your first investment. The more you invest, the more you may be tempted to save those earlier investments by making later investments. That is to say, people sometimes may be found "throwing good money after bad" because they have "too much invested to quit." This phenomenon is known as **escalation of commitment**—the tendency for people to continue to support previously unsuccessful courses of action because they have sunk costs invested in them. For a summary of the escalation of commitment phenomenon, see Figure 10.3.

Although this might not seem like a rational thing to do, this strategy is frequently followed. Consider, for example, how large banks and governments may invest money in foreign governments in the hope of turning them around even though such a result

FIGURE 10.3 Escalation of Commitment

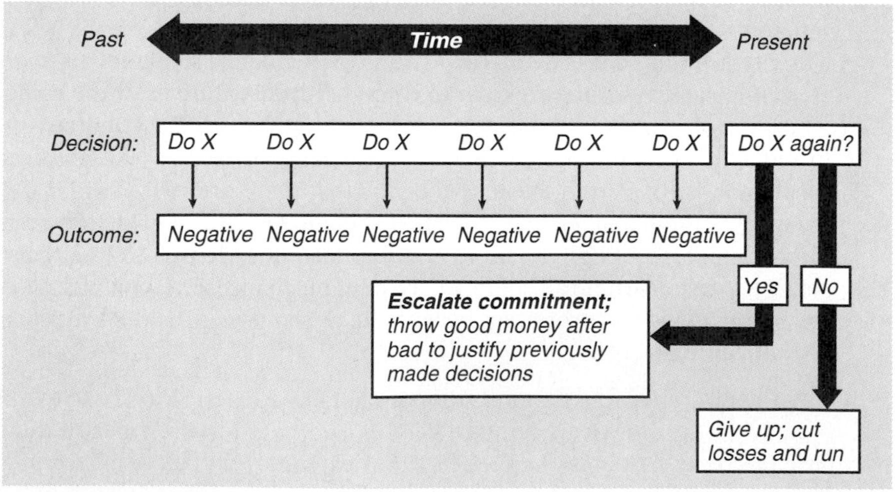

According to the *escalation of commitment* phenomenon, people who have repeatedly made poor decisions will continue to support those failing courses of action in the future so that they may justify their original decisions.

becomes increasingly unlikely. Similarly, the organizers of Expo '86 in British Columbia continued pouring money into the fair long after it became apparent that it would be a big money-losing proposition.[15]

Why do people do this? If you think about it, you may realize that the failure to back your own previous courses of action in an organization would be taken as an admission of failure—a politically difficult act to face in an organization. In other words, people may be very concerned about "saving face"—looking good in the eyes of others. Scientists believe that this tendency for self-justification is primarily responsible for people's inclination to protect their beliefs about themselves as rational, competent decision makers by convincing themselves and others that they made the right decision all along and are willing to back it up.

Group Decisions: Do Too Many Cooks Spoil the Broth?

Decision-making groups are a well-established fact of modern organizational life. Groups such as committees, study teams, task forces, or review panels are often charged with the responsibility for making important business decisions. They are so common, in fact, that it has been said that some administrators spend as much as 80 percent of their time in committee meetings. Given this, it is important to consider the strengths and weaknesses of using groups to make organizational decisions.

> *It has been said that some administrators spend as much as 80 percent of their time in committee meetings.*

GROUP DECISIONS: A DOUBLE-EDGED SWORD

There is little doubt that much can be gained by using decision-making groups. Several potential advantages of this approach may be identified. First, bringing people together may increase the amount of knowledge and information available for making good decisions. In other words, there may be a *pooling of resources*. A related benefit is that in decision-making groups there can be a *specialization of labor*. With enough people around to share the work load, individuals can perform only those tasks at which they are best, thereby potentially improving the quality of the group's efforts. Another benefit is that group decisions are likely to enjoy *greater acceptance* than are individual decisions. People involved in making decisions may be expected to understand those decisions better and be more committed to carrying them out than decisions made by someone else.

Of course, there are also some problems associated with using decision-making groups. One obvious drawback is that groups are likely to *waste time*. The time spent socializing before getting down to business may be a drain on the group and be very costly to organizations. Another possible problem is that potential disagreement over important matters may breed ill will and *group conflict*. Although constructive disagreement can actually lead to better group outcomes, highly disruptive conflict may interfere with group decisions. Finally, we may expect groups to be ineffective sometimes because of members' *intimidation by group leaders*. A group composed of several "yes" men or women trying to please a dominant leader tends to discourage open and honest discussion of solutions.

Given the several pros and cons of using groups to make decisions, we must conclude that *neither groups nor individuals are always superior*. Obviously, there are important trade-offs involved in using either one to make decisions.

COMPARING GROUP AND INDIVIDUAL DECISIONS: WHEN ARE TWO (OR MORE) HEADS BETTER THAN ONE?

Since there are advantages associated with both group and individual decision makers, a question arises as to when each should be used.[16] That is, under what conditions might individuals or groups be expected to make superior decisions?

When are groups superior to individuals?   Imagine a situation in which an important decision has to be made about a complex problem—such as whether one company should merge with another. This is not the kind of problem about which any one individual working alone would be expected to make a good decision. Its highly complex nature may overwhelm even an expert, thereby setting the stage for a group to do a better job.

Whether a group actually will do better than an individual depends on several important considerations. First, who is in the group? Successful groups are composed of heterogeneous group members with complementary skills.[17] So, for example, a group composed of lawyers, accountants, real estate agents, and other experts may make much better decisions on the merger problem than would a group composed of specialists in only one field. Indeed, the diversity of opinions offered by group members is one of the major advantages of using groups to make decisions.

Second, for a group to be successful, its members also must be able to freely communicate their ideas to each other in an open, nonhostile manner. Conditions under which one individual (or group) intimidates another from contributing his or her expertise can easily negate any potential gain associated with composing groups of heterogeneous experts. After all, having expertise and being able to make a contribution by using that expertise are two different things. Only when the contributions of the most qualified group members are given the greatest weight does the group derive any benefit from that member's presence. Thus, for groups to be superior to individuals, they must be composed of a heterogeneous collection of experts with complementary skills who can freely and openly contribute to their group's product.

In contrast to complex decision tasks, imagine a situation in which a judgment is required on a simple problem with a readily verifiable answer. For example, imagine that you are asked to translate a phrase from a relatively obscure language into English. Groups might do better than individuals on such a task only because the odds are increased that someone in the group knows the language and can perform the translation on behalf of the group. However, there is no reason to expect that even a large group will be able to perform such a task better than a single individual who has the required expertise. In fact, an expert working alone may do even better than a group because that expert may be distracted by others and may suffer from having to convince them of the correctness of his or her solution. For this reason, exceptional individuals tend to outperform entire committees on simple tasks. In such cases, for groups to benefit from a pooling of resources, there must be some resources to pool. The pool-

FIGURE 10.4 Comparing Group and Individual Decisions

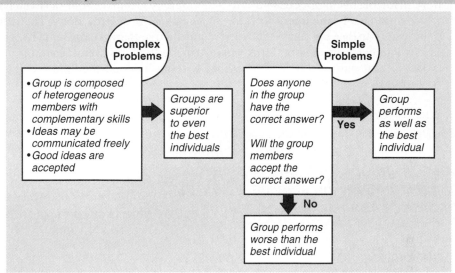

As summarized here, groups make better decisions than individuals do under some conditions, but individuals make better decisions than groups do under others.

ing of ignorance does not help. In other words, the question "Are two heads better than one?" can be answered this way: On simple tasks, two heads may be better than one *if* at least one of those heads has enough of what it takes to succeed.

In summary, whether groups perform better than individuals depends on the nature of the task performed and the expertise of the people involved. For an overview of these key considerations, refer to Figure 10.4.

When are individuals superior to groups?   Most of the problems faced by organizations require a great deal of creative thinking. For example, a company deciding how to use a newly developed adhesive in its consumer products is facing decisions on a poorly structured task. Although you would expect that the complexity of such creative problems would give groups a natural advantage, this is not the case. In fact, research has shown that on poorly structured, creative tasks, individuals perform better than groups.[18]

An approach to solving creative problems commonly used by groups is **brainstorming**. This technique was developed by an advertising executive as a tool for coming up with creative, new ideas.[19] The members of brainstorming groups are encouraged to present their ideas in an uncritical way and to discuss freely and openly all ideas on the floor. Specifically, members of brainstorming groups are required to follow four main rules: (1) Avoid criticizing others' ideas, (2) share even far-out suggestions, (3) offer as many comments as possible, and (4) build on others' ideas to create your own.

Does brainstorming improve the quality of creative decisions? To answer this question, researchers conducted a study comparing the effectiveness of individuals and brainstorming groups working on creative problems.[20] Specifically, participants were given 35 minutes to consider the consequences of situations such as "What if everybody went blind?" or "What if everybody grew an extra thumb on each hand?" Clearly, the novel nature of such problems requires a great deal of creativity. Comparisons were made of the number of solutions generated by groups of four or seven people and a like number of individuals working on the same problems alone. The results were clear: Individuals were significantly more productive than groups.

In summary, groups perform worse than individuals when working on creative tasks. A great part of the problem is that some individuals feel inhibited by the presence of others even though one rule of brainstorming is that even far-out ideas may be shared. To the extent that people wish to avoid feeling foolish as a result of saying silly things, their creativity may be inhibited when in groups. Similarly, groups may inhibit creativity by slowing down the process of bringing ideas to fruition.

> *To the extent that people wish to avoid feeling foolish as a result of saying silly things, their creativity may be inhibited when in groups. Similarly, groups may inhibit creativity by slowing down the process of bringing ideas to fruition.*

GROUPTHINK: TOO MUCH COHESIVENESS CAN BE A DANGEROUS THING

One reason groups may fare so poorly on complex tasks lies in the dynamics of group interaction (see Chapter 8). When members of a group develop a very strong group spirit—high levels of *cohesiveness*—they sometimes become so concerned about not disrupting the like-mindedness of the group that they may be reluctant to challenge the group's decisions. When this happens, group members tend to isolate themselves from outside information, and the process of critical thinking deteriorates. This phenomenon is referred to as **groupthink**.

The concept of groupthink was initially proposed as an attempt to explain ineffective decisions made by U.S. government officials that led to fiascoes such as the Bay of Pigs invasion in Cuba and the Vietnam War.[21] Analyses of each of these cases have revealed that the president's advisers actually discouraged more effective decision making. An examination of the conditions under which the decision was made to launch the ill-fated space shuttle *Challenger* in January 1986 revealed that it too resulted from groupthink.[22] Post-hoc analyses of conversations between key personnel suggested that the team that made the decision to launch the shuttle under freezing conditions did so while insulating itself from the engineers who knew how the equipment should function. Given that NASA had such a successful history, the decision makers operated with a sense of invulnerability. They also worked so closely together and were under such intense pressure to launch the shuttle without further delay that they all collectively went along with the launch decision, creating the illusion of unanimous agreement.

Groupthink doesn't occur only in governmental decision making, of course, but also in the private sector (although the failures may be less well publicized). For example, analyses of the business policies of large corporations such as Lockheed and Chrysler have suggested that it was the failure of top management teams to respond to changing market conditions that at one time led them to the brink of disaster. The problem is that members of very cohesive groups may have considerable confidence in their group's decisions, making them unlikely to raise doubts about these actions (i.e., "the group seems to know what it's doing"). As a result, they may suspend their own critical thinking in favor of conforming to the group. When group members become fiercely loyal to each other, they may ignore potentially useful information from other sources that challenges the group's decisions. The result of this process is that the group's decisions may be completely uninformed, irrational, or even immoral.

Fortunately, several strategies can effectively combat groupthink. A few proven techniques are summarized in Table 10.3. Given the extremely adverse effects group-think can have on organizations, practicing managers would be wise to press these simple suggestions into action.

TABLE 10.3 Guidelines for Avoiding Groupthink

The suggestions outlined here have been shown to be effective when it comes to avoiding the critical problem of groupthink.

Suggestion	*Explanation*
Use subgroups	Because the decision made by any one group may be the result of groupthink, basing decisions on the recommendations of two or more subgroups is a useful check. If the different groups disagree, a discussion of their differences is likely to raise important issues. However, if the two groups agree, you can be relatively confident that their conclusions are not the result of groupthink.
Admit shortcomings	When groupthink occurs, group members feel very confident that they are doing the right thing. Such feelings discourage people from considering opposing information. However, if group members acknowledge some of the flaws and limitations of their decisions, they may be more open to corrective influences. This may help avoid the illusion of perfection that contributes to groupthink.
Hold second-chance meetings	As people get tired of working on problems, they may hastily reach agreement on a solution. Before implementing a decision, hold sessions in which group members are asked to express any doubts and to propose any new ideas they may have (known as *second-chance meetings*). Second-chance meetings can be useful devices for seeing if a solution still seems good even after "sleeping on it."
Promote open inquiry	Remember, groupthink arises in response to group members' reluctance to "rock the boat." Group leaders should encourage members to be skeptical of all solutions and to avoid reaching premature agreements. It sometimes helps to play the role of *devil's advocate*, that is, to intentionally find fault with a proposed solution. Many executives have found that raising a nonthreatening question to force both sides of an issue can be a very helpful way to improve the quality of decisions.

Techniques for Improving Group Decisions

As explained in this chapter, certain advantages can be gained from sometimes using individuals and sometimes using groups to make decisions. A decision-making technique that combines the best features of groups and individuals, while minimizing the disadvantages, would be ideal. Two particular techniques designed to realize the "best of both worlds" have been used widely in organizations.

THE DELPHI TECHNIQUE

According to Greek mythology, people interested in seeing what fate the future held for them could seek the counsel of the Delphic oracle. Today's organizational decision makers sometimes consult experts to help them make the best decisions as well. A technique developed by the Rand Corporation, known as the **Delphi technique**, represents a systematic way of collecting and organizing the opinions of several experts into a single decision.[23] The steps in the process are summarized in Figure 10.5.

The Delphi process starts by enlisting the cooperation of experts and presenting the problem to them, usually in a letter. Each expert then proposes what he or she believes is the most appropriate solution. The group leader compiles all of these individual responses and reproduces them so they can be shared with all the other experts in a second mailing. At this point, each expert comments on the others' ideas and proposes another solution. These individual solutions are returned to the coordinater, who compiles them and looks for a consensus of opinions. If a consensus is reached, the

FIGURE 10.5 Steps in the Delphi Technique

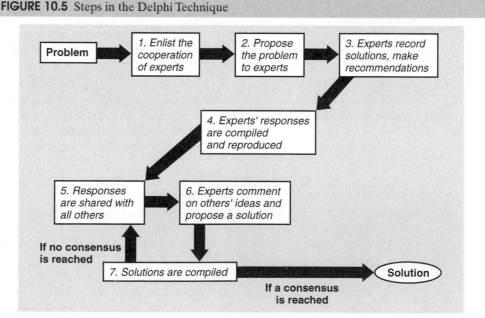

The *Delphi technique*, outlined here, allows decisions to be made by several experts without encountering many of the disadvantages of face-to-face groups.

decision is made. If not, the process of sharing reactions with others is repeated until a consensus is eventually obtained.

The obvious advantage of using the Delphi technique to make decisions is that it allows the collection of expert judgments without the great costs and logistical difficulties of bringing many experts together for a face-to-face meeting. However, the Delphi process can be very time-consuming. Sending out letters, waiting for everyone to respond, transcribing and disseminating the responses, and repeating the process until a consensus is reached can take quite a long time—often, several months. Given this limitation, the Delphi approach would not be appropriate for making decisions in crisis situations, or whenever else time is of the essence. However, the approach has been successfully employed to make decisions such as what items to put on a conference agenda and what the potential impact of implementing various new policies would be.

THE NOMINAL GROUP TECHNIQUE

When there are only a few hours available to make a decision, group discussion sessions can be held in which members interact with each other in an orderly, focused fashion aimed at solving problems. The **nominal group technique** (**NGT**) brings together a small number of individuals (usually about seven to ten) who systematically offer their individual solutions to a problem and share their personal reactions to others' solutions. The technique is referred to as nominal because the individuals involved form a group in name only. Participants do not attempt to agree as a group on any solution, but rather, vote on all the solutions proposed. For an outline of the steps in the process, see Figure 10.6.

The nominal group process begins by gathering group members together around a table and identifying the problem at hand. Members then write down their solutions. Next, one at a time, each member presents his or her solutions to the group as the facilitator records these on a chart. This process continues until all ideas have been expressed. Following this, each solution is discussed, clarified, and evaluated by the group members. Each member is given a chance to voice his or her reactions to each idea. After all the ideas have been evaluated, the group members privately rank-order their preferred solutions. The idea given the highest rank is taken as the group's decision. For practice running your own nominal group, see the **Group Exercise** on p. 277.

Although nominal groups traditionally meet in face-to-face settings, advances in modern technology enable nominal groups to meet even when its members are far away from each other. Specifically, a technique known as **automated decision conferencing** has been used, in which individuals in different locations participate in nominal group conferences by means of telephone lines or direct satellite transmissions. The messages may be sent either via characters on a computer monitor or images viewed during a teleconference. Despite their high-tech look, automated decision conferences are really just nominal groups meeting in a manner that approximates face-to-face contact.

The NGT has several advantages and disadvantages. I have already noted that it can be used to arrive at group decisions in only a few hours. Another benefit is that it discourages any pressure to conform to the wishes of a high-status group member because all ideas are evaluated and the preferences are expressed in private balloting.

FIGURE 10.6 Steps in the Nominal Group Technique

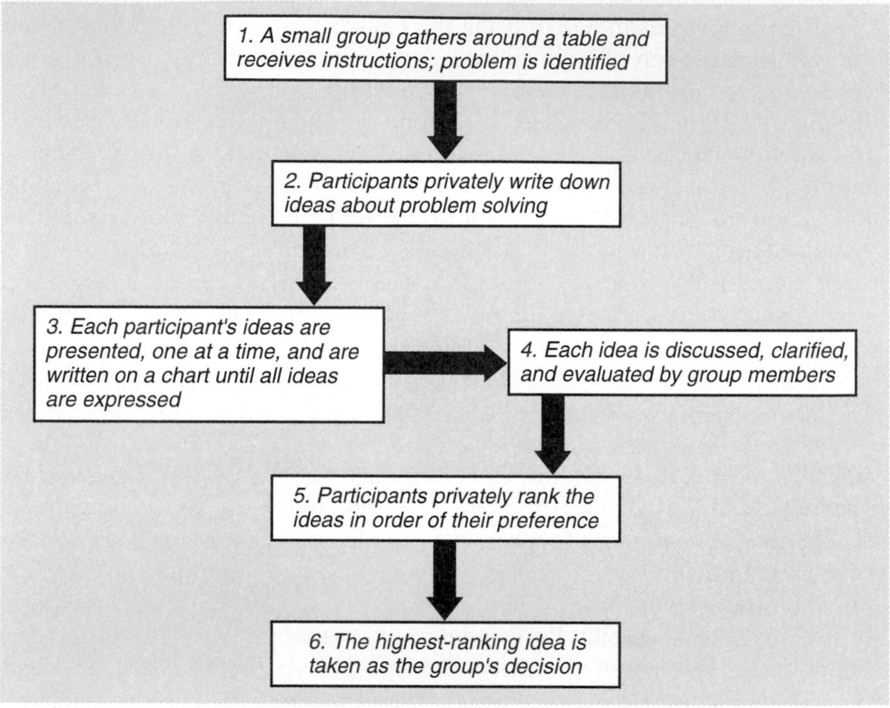

1. A small group gathers around a table and receives instructions; problem is identified

2. Participants privately write down ideas about problem solving

3. Each participant's ideas are presented, one at a time, and are written on a chart until all ideas are expressed

4. Each idea is discussed, clarified, and evaluated by group members

5. Participants privately rank the ideas in order of their preference

6. The highest-ranking idea is taken as the group's decision

The *nominal group technique*, whose steps are summarized here, structures face-to-face meetings in a way that allows for the open expression and evaluation of ideas.

The technique must be considered limited, however, in that it requires the use of a trained group facilitator. In addition, using NGT successfully requires that only one narrowly defined problem be considered at a time. So, for very complex problems, many NGT sessions would have to be run—and then only if the problem under consideration can be broken down into smaller parts.

SUMMARY: HAVE I MET THE LEARNING OBJECTIVES?

You can be certain that you have met the learning objectives for this chapter found on p. 251 if you understand the following:

1. **IDENTIFY the steps in the decision-making process.** Decision making is a multistep process. It involves (1) identifying a problem, (2) defining solution objectives, (3) making a predecision (a decision about how to make a decision), (4) generating alternatives, (5) evaluating alternatives, (6) choosing an alternative, (7) implementing the chosen alternative, and then (8) following up.
2. **DESCRIBE the effects of culture on decision making, and the major reasons why people sometimes make unethical decisions.** People from different national cultures make decisions differently in terms of: (1) the way they recognize problems, (2) their preference for making decisions individually or jointly, (3) who

makes the decisions (superiors or workers themselves), and (4) the amount of time taken to make decisions. Sometimes, people make unethical decisions because organizations may encourage behaviors that violate ethical standards and because some managerial values undermine integrity (e.g., the *bottom-line mentality*, the *exploitative mentality*, and the *Madison Avenue mentality*).

3. **DESCRIBE the different varieties of decisions people make in organizations.** The decisions made in organizations can be characterized as being either *programmed* (i.e., routine decisions made according to preexisting guidelines) or *nonprogrammed* (decisions requiring novel and creative solutions). Decisions also differ with respect to the amount of risk involved, ranging from those in which the decision outcomes are relatively *certain* to those in which the outcomes are highly *uncertain*. Uncertain situations are expressed as statements of probability based on either objective or subjective information. Finally, decisions differ in terms of whether they are *top-down* (i.e., made by higher-level executives and carried out by lower-level employees) or *empowered* (i.e., made by the individuals who will be affected).

4. **IDENTIFY various factors that contribute to imperfect decision making in organizations.** Decisions are imperfect insofar as decision makers (1) have a limited view of the problems facing them, (2) consider solutions as they become available—making *satisficing decisions* (ones that are not optimal, but good enough), (3) face time constraints, and (4) are sensitive to political "face-saving" pressure. Decisions also are made imperfect by several different systematic biases. These include *framing effects*, the use of *heuristics*, and the *escalation of commitment*.

5. **DESCRIBE the conditions under which individuals make better decisions than groups and groups make better decisions than individuals.** Groups have proven superior to individual members when they are composed of a heterogeneous mix of experts who possess complementary skills. However, groups may not be any better than the best individual when performing a task that has a simple, verifiable answer. Compared with individuals, face-to-face *brainstorming* groups tend to make inferior decisions on creative problems.

6. **EXPLAIN how the Delphi technique and the nominal group technique are used to improve the quality of decisions made by groups.** The quality of group decisions can be enhanced in several different ways. Using the *Delphi technique*, the judgments of experts are systematically gathered and used to form a single joint decision. The *nominal group technique* is a method of structuring group meetings to elicit and evaluate the opinions of all members.

You Be The Consultant

A business associate refers you to the president of a growing environmental management firm. The fact that the company is new and operates in a changing business environment makes all of its decisions especially crucial. As such, you are hired to assist in guiding the president in helping the company make decisions in the most effective possible way. Answer the following question relevant to this situation based on the material in this chapter.

1. The president has been making decisions about how to deal with governmental regulations all by himself. Should he consider delegating this task to a group instead? Why or why not?
2. What individual biases would be expected to interfere with the quality of the decisions made by individuals in this company?
3. In what ways might the group interaction limit the quality of decisions made? What steps can be taken to overcome these problems?

(SELF-ASSESSMENT EXERCISE)

Are You Risk Seeking or Risk Averse?

It's one thing to read about the effects of framing on riskiness, but quite another to experience it firsthand. This exercise will help you demonstrate the effects of framing for yourself.

Directions

Read each of the following descriptions of hypothetical situations. Then, for each, answer the following question: *Which project will you select: Alpha or Beta?*

Situation 1:   You are an executive whose policies have resulted in a $1 million loss for your company. Now you are considering two new projects. One of them, Alpha, will provide a definite return of $500,000. The other, Beta, will provide a fifty-fifty chance of obtaining either a $1 million return or a $0 return.

Situation 2:   You are considering one of two new projects to conduct in your company. One of them, Alpha, will provide a definite return of $500,000. The other, Beta, will provide a fifty-fifty chance of obtaining either a $1 million return or a $0 return.

Questions for Discussion

1. What choice did you make in situation 1? Most people would select Beta in such a situation because it gives them a fifty-fifty chance of undoing the loss completely. Such a risk-seeking decision is likely in a situation in which people are focusing on undoing loss.
2. What choice did you make in situation 2? Most people would select Alpha in such a situation because it gives them a sure thing, a "bird in the hand." Such a risk-averse decision is likely in a situation in which people are focusing on gains received.
3. Given that both situations are mathematically identical, why should people prefer one or the other?
4. Can you think of some key failures in history that may be seen as the result of taking high levels of risk?

(GROUP EXERCISE)

Running a Nominal Group: Try It Yourself

A great deal can be learned about nominal groups by running one—or, at least, participating in one—yourself. Doing so will not only help illustrate the procedure, but demonstrate how effectively it works.

Directions
1. Select a topic suitable for discussion in a nominal group composed of students in your class. It should be a topic that is narrowly defined, and on which people have many different opinions (these work best in nominal groups). Some possible examples include:
   - What should your school's student leaders be doing for you?
   - What can be done to improve the quality of instruction in your institution?
   - What can be done to improve the quality of jobs your school's students receive when graduating?
2. Divide the class into groups of approximately 10. Arrange each group in a circle, or around a table, if possible. In each group, select one person to serve as the group facilitator.
3. Following the steps outlined in Figure 10.6, facilitators should guide their groups in discussions regarding the focal question identified in step 1, above. Allow approximately 45 minutes to 1 hour to complete this process.
4. If time allows, select a different focal question and a different group leader, and repeat the procedure.

Questions for Discussion
1. Collectively, how did the group answer the question? Do you believe that this answer accurately reflected the feelings of the group?
2. How did the various groups' answers compare? Were they similar or different? Why?
3. What were the major problems, if any, associated with the nominal group experience? For example, were there any group members who were reluctant to wait their turns before speaking up?
4. If you conducted more than one nominal group discussion, with different leaders, was the process smoother the second time around, as everyone learned how it works?
5. How do you think your group experiences would have differed had you used a totally unstructured, traditional face-to-face group instead of a nominal group?

NOTES

Case Note
Esterson, E. (1998). Game plan. *Inc. Tech,* pp. 43–44.

Chapter Notes

[1] Hoch, S. L., Kunreuther, H., Hoch, S., & Gunther, R. (2001). *Wharton on making decisions.* New York: Free Press.

[2] Wedley, W. C., & Field, R. H. (1984). A predecision support system. *Academy of Management Review, 9,* 696–703.

[3] Brett, J. (2001). *Negotiating globally. How to negotiate deals, resolve disputes, and make decisions across cultural boundaries.* San Francisco: Jossey-Bass. Adler, N. J. (1991). *International dimensions of organizational behavior.* Boston: PWS Kent.

[4] Roth, K. (1992). Implementing international strategy at the business unit level: The role of managerial decision-making characteristics. *Journal of Management, 18,* 769–789.

[5] Jansen, E., & Von Glinow, M. A. (1985). Ethical ambivalence and organizational reward systems. *Academy of Management Review, 10,* 814–822.

[6] Brass, D. J., Butterfield, K. D., & Skaggs, B. C. (1998). Relationships and unethical behavior: A social-network perspective. *Academy of Management Review, 23,* 14–31.

[7] Wolfe, D. M. (1988). Is there integrity in the bottom line: Managing obstacles to executive integrity. In S. Srivastava (Ed.), *Executive integrity: The search for high human values in organizational life* (pp. 140–171). San Francisco: Jossey-Bass.

[8] Roddick, A. (1991). *Body and soul.* New York: Crown.

[9] Chappel, T. (1993). *The soul of a business.* New York: Bantam.

[10] Greenhalgh, L. (2001). *Managing strategic relationships: The key to business success.* New York: Free Press.

[11] Crainer, S. (1998, November). The 75 greatest management decisions ever made. *Management Review,* pp. 16–23.

[12] Byrne, J. A. (1998, September 21). Virtual management. *Business Week,* pp. 80–82.

[13] Simon, H. (1977). *The new science of management decisions (2nd ed.).* Englewood Cliffs, NJ: Prentice Hall.

[14] Gigerenzer, G., & Selten, R. (2001). *Bounded rationality: The adaptive toolbox.* Cambridge, MA: MIT Press.

[15] Ross, J., & Staw, B. M. (1986). Expo '86: An escalation prototype. *Administrative Science Quarterly, 31,* 274–297.

[16] Forman, E., H. & Selly, M. A. (2001). *Decision by objectives: How to convince others that you are right.* London: World Scientific.

[17] Salas, E., & Klein, G. (2001). *Linking expertise and naturalistic decision making.* Mahwah, NJ: Lawrence Erlbaum Associates.

[18] Hill, G. W. (1982). Group versus individual performance: Are N + 1 heads better than one? *Psychological Bulletin, 91,* 517–539.

[19] Osborn, A. F. (1957). *Applied imagination.* New York: Scribner's.

[20] Bouchard, T. J., Jr., Barsaloux, J., & Drauden, G. (1974). Brainstorming procedure, group size, and sex as determinants of the problem-solving effectiveness of groups and individuals. *Journal of Applied Psychology, 59,* 135–138.

[21] Janis, I. L. (1982). *Groupthink: Psychological studies of policy decisions and fiascoes (2nd ed.).* Boston: Houghton Mifflin.

[22] Morehead, G., Ference, R., & Neck, C. P. (1991). Group decision fiascoes continue: Space shuttle Challenger and a revised groupthink framework. *Human Relations, 44,* 539–550.

[23] Dalkey, N. (1969). *The Delphi method: An experimental study of group decisions.* Santa Monica, CA: Rand Corporation.

11

The quest
for leadership

LEARNING OBJECTIVES

After reading this chapter, you will be able to:

1. DEFINE leadership and IDENTIFY the major sources of power leaders have at their disposal.

2. DESCRIBE the trait approach to leadership and IDENTIFY the major characteristics of effective leaders.

3. IDENTIFY the types of behavior that have been most strongly associated with effective leadership.

4. DESCRIBE the basic tenets of LPC contingency theory and how it may be applied.

5. EXPLAIN the path-goal theory of leadership.

6. DESCRIBE the emerging trends and challenges in leadership practice.

THREE GOOD REASONS WHY YOU SHOULD CARE ABOUT...

Leadership

You should care about leadership because:

1. An organization's success is greatly determined by the quality of its leadership.

2. There are steps that anyone can take to enhance his or her effectiveness as a leader.

3. Changing business practices, such as globalization and the use of the Internet, have important implications for the practice of leadership.

Making the Case for... Leadership

Urban Box Office Loses Its Leader, Then the Business

The sad truth is that sometimes you don't know how important a leader is to an organization until he or she isn't around anymore. That's precisely the lesson the 300 employees of Urban Box Office learned when its CEO, George Jackson, died at age 42, two weeks after suffering a stroke in February 2000.

Jackson was CEO of Motown Records until 1998, when he joined his longtime friends Adam Kidron and Frank Cooper in starting an Internet business to serve the interests of millions of lovers of hip-hop music. Because Urban Box Office was just getting off the ground when Jackson passed away, it was uncertain if the company could continue in his absence. After all, Jackson not only had a keen vision of what the company should be, but he also had important qualities that kept the enterprise going.

Jackson was able to get people to buy into his dream, and he could keep them focused on doing whatever was necessary to keep them on-task. However, Kidron and Cooper pressed on without their esteemed leader and vowed to keep the business going—something that they would not have done had Jackson died even six months earlier.

In fact, after Jackson's passing, Urban Box Office launched several new Websites, including IndiePlanet, a site designed to help independent designers of film, music, and fashion sell their works online. This is in keeping with one of Jackson's goals for his enterprise: Using the Internet to promote groups that traditionally have not benefited from the boom in Web technology. Still, there's no doubt that Jackson's absence has been felt every day. Without him at the helm, everyone has been working much harder to keep the business afloat. Poignantly, Kidron even says that he sometimes has found himself dialing Jackson's number, forgetting that he no longer can be reached.

Unfortunately, investors failed to share Kidron and Cooper's optimism about being able to keep Urban Box Office afloat. Financing dried up, and on November 2, 2000, Urban Box Office declared bankruptcy, logging off for good.

While the demise of Urban Box Office was not directly attributed to the passing of George Jackson, those in the know would tell you otherwise. His magnetism and vision kept everyone optimistic about Urban Box Office. Because the business was still in its infancy, it depended on Jackson's magic to keep the music rolling. So when he died, investors feared that the business would no longer be viable, leading them to back out of their commitments. If you're thinking to yourself, "But he's just one person in an entire business," you are underestimating the importance of having a strong leader at the helm—especially when the business is new. In fact, if you asked a group of top executives to identify the single most important determinant of organizational success, most would likely reply, "effective leadership." Indeed, it is widely believed in the world of business that *leadership* is the key ingredient in the recipe for corporate achievement. And this view is by no means restricted to organizations. As you know, leadership also is important when it comes to politics, sports, and many other activities.

Is this view justified? Do leaders really play crucial roles in shaping the fortunes of organizations? A century of research on this topic suggests that they do. Effective leadership, it appears, is indeed a key determinant of organizational success. In view of this, I will devote this chapter to describing various approaches to the study of leadership as well as their implications for managerial practice. Before launching into this discussion, however, I will begin by defining what is meant by leadership and distinguish it from some other terms with which it is frequently associated.

What Is Leadership?
Some Fundamental Issues

Although we all have a good intuitive idea about what leadership is, and what leaders are like, it is important to begin this chapter with a formal definition of leadership and an overview of the ways in which leaders influence their followers.

A DEFINITION

When you think of a leader, what image comes to mind? For many, a leader is an individual—often with a title reflecting a high rank in an organization (e.g., president, director, etc.)—who is influential in getting others to behave as required by the organization. Indeed, social scientists think of leaders as people who have a great deal of influence over others. Formally, **leadership** is defined as the process by which an individual influences others in ways that help attain group or organizational goals.[1]

From this definition, it may seem that *leaders* and *managers* are quite similar. Indeed, the two terms are often used interchangeably. However, this is misleading insofar as they are conceptually distinct.[2] The primary function of a *leader* is to create the essential purpose or mission of the organization and the strategy for attaining it. By contrast, the job of the *manager* is to implement that vision. He or she is responsible for achieving that end, taking the steps necessary to

> The primary function of a leader is to create the essential purpose or mission of the organization and the strategy for attaining it. By contrast, the job of the manager is to implement that vision.

make the leader's vision a reality. The reason for the confusion is that the distinction between establishing a mission and implementing it is often blurred in practice. After all, many leaders, such as top corporate executives, are frequently called upon not only to create a vision but also to help implement it. Similarly, managers are often required to lead those who are subordinate to them while also carrying out their leader's mission. With this in mind, it has been observed that too many so-called leaders get bogged down in the managerial aspects of their job, creating organizations that are "overmanaged and underlead."[3]

HOW DO LEADERS INFLUENCE OTHERS?
SOURCES OF LEADERSHIP POWER

As our definition suggests, leaders influence others. To fully understand how leaders operate, it is necessary to identify how exactly they come by the power to exert influence. The basis for a leader's power resides in his or her formal position as well as the way followers respond to his or her personal qualities.[4]

Position power.   A great deal of the power that people have in organizations comes from the posts they hold in those organizations. In other words, they are able to influence others because of the formal power associated with their jobs. This is known as **position power**. For example, there are certain powers that the president of the United States has simply due to the authority given to the officeholder (e.g., signing bills into law, making treaties, and so on). These formal powers remain vested in the person and are available to anyone who holds that position. When the president's term is up, these powers transfer to the new officeholder. The four bases of position power are as follows:

- **Legitimate power**—The power that someone has because others recognize and accept his or her authority. For example, students recognize that their instructors have the legitimate power (i.e., authority) to make class policies and to determine grades.
- **Reward power**—The power to control the rewards others receive. For example, a supervisor has the power to reward one of his or her subordinates by recommending a large pay raise.
- **Coercive power**—The capacity to control punishment. For example, a boss may tell you to do something "my way or else." Typically, dictators are inclined to use coercive power, whereas leaders avoid it whenever possible.
- **Information power**—The power a person has by virtue of his or her access to valuable data or knowledge. Traditionally, people in top positions have available to them unique sources of information that are not available to others (e.g., knowledge of company performance, market trends, and so on). As they say, "knowledge is power," and such information greatly contributes to the power of people in many jobs.

As you read these descriptions of the different sources of position power, you may have found yourself wondering what you could do to enhance your own position power where you are working. If so, don't feel self-conscious about being "power hungry." To the contrary, you may find it comforting to know that building a strong power base is an important first step toward being an effective leader. With this in mind, you may find it interesting to review the various suggestions for enhancing position power summarized in Table 11.1.

Personal power.   In addition to the power leaders derive from their formal positions in organizations, they also derive power from their own unique qualities or characteristics. This is known as **personal power**. There are four sources of personal power, as follows:

- **Rational persuasion**—The power leaders have by virtue of the logical arguments and factual evidence they provide to support their arguments. Rational persuasion is widely used by top executives, such as when they present detailed reports in making a case as to why certain organizational policies should be changed.
- **Expert power**—The power leaders have to the extent that others recognize their expert knowledge on a topic. For example, athletes do what their coaches tell them in large part because they recognize and respect their coaches' expertise.
- **Referent power**—The power that individuals have because they are liked and admired by others. For example, senior managers who possess desirable qualities

TABLE 11.1 Position Power: How to Get It	

The following suggestions identify various ways of enhancing one's position power in organizations.

Suggestion	*Rationale*
Expand your network of communication contacts.	The more contacts you have, the more information you will have, and the more others will count on you.
Make some of your job responsibilities unique.	People have power to the extent that they are the only ones who can perform certain tasks.
Perform more novel tasks and fewer routine ones.	People who perform routine tasks readily can be replaced by others, whereas those who perform novel tasks are more powerful because they are indispensable.
Increase the visibility of your job performance by joining task forces and making contact with senior people.	The more involved you are in organizational decisions, and the more important others consider your input to be, the more power you will have.
Become involved with activities that are central to the organization's top priorities.	People performing peripheral activities have far less power than those whose activities are in line with the organization's primary mission and its top priorities.

and good reputations may have referent power over younger managers who identify with them and wish to emulate them.

- **Charisma**—The power someone has over others because of his or her engaging and magnetic personality. As I will describe later in this chapter, people with this characteristic are highly influential and inspire others to do things.

As I have outlined here, leaders derive influence from a variety of sources, some of which are based on the nature of the positions they hold and some of which are based on their individual characteristics. To assess the sources of power available to your own immediate supervisor, you may find it interesting to complete the **Self-Assessment Exercise** on p. 300.

The Trait Approach: Are Some People "Born Leaders"?

Common sense tells us that some people have more of "the right stuff" than others and are just naturally better leaders. And, if you look at some of the great leaders throughout history, such as Martin Luther King, Jr., Alexander the Great, and Abraham Lincoln, it is clear that such individuals certainly appear to be different from ordinary folks. The question is, "How are they different?" That is, what is it that makes great leaders so great?

GREAT PERSON THEORY

For many years, scientists have devoted a great deal of attention to the matter of identifying the specific traits and characteristics that are associated with leadership success. In so doing, they have advanced what is known as the **great person theory**—the approach that recognizes that great leaders possess key traits that set them apart from most others. Further, the theory contends that these traits remain stable over time and across different groups. Most organizational scientists today accept the idea that traits *do* matter—namely, that certain traits, together with other factors, contribute to leaders' success in business settings.[5] Specifically, as one team of scientists put it, "Leaders do not have to be great men or women by being intellectual geniuses or omniscient prophets to succeed, but they do need to have the 'right stuff' and this stuff is not equally present in all people."[6] (With this in mind, you may find it interesting to consider who the great leaders throughout the ages have been—a task that you will complete in the **Group Exercise** on p. 302.)

What are these traits? Table 11.2 lists and describes some of the key ones. Although you will readily recognize and understand most of these characteristics (e.g., drive, honesty and integrity, self-confidence), some require further clarification. For example, **leadership motivation** refers to a leader's desire to influence others—essentially, his or her interest in assuming a leadership role. It also is important to understand the role of **flexibility**—the ability to recognize what actions are required in a given situation and then to act accordingly. The most effective leaders are not prone to behave in the same ways all the time, but rather, to be adaptive, matching their styles to the demands of the situations they face. Today's most effective business leaders do an exceptional job of adapting to changing conditions. This quality is not only desirable but also essential for leaders of companies competing in the rapidly growing online marketplace.[7]

TRANSFORMATIONAL LEADERS: SPECIAL PEOPLE WHO MAKE THINGS HAPPEN

If you think about the great leaders throughout history, the names of Reverend Dr. Martin Luther King Jr. and President John F. Kennedy are sure to come to mind. These individuals surely were effective at envisioning ways of changing society and then bringing these visions to reality. People who do things to revitalize and transform the society of organizations are known as **transformational leaders**.[8] Reverend King's famous "I Have a Dream" speech inspired people to embrace the civil rights movement, and President Kennedy's shared vision of landing a man on the moon and

TABLE 11.2   Characteristics of Successful Leaders

Research indicates that successful leaders demonstrate the traits listed here.

Trait or Characteristic	Description
Drive	Desire for achievement: ambition; high energy; tenacity; initiative
Honesty and integrity	Trustworthy; reliable; open
Leadership motivation	Desire to exercise influence over others to reach shared goals
Self-confidence	Trust in own abilities
Cognitive ability	Intelligence; ability to integrate and interpret large amounts of information
Knowledge of the business	Knowledge of industry, relevant technical matters
Creativity	Originality
Flexibility	Ability to adapt to needs of followers and requirements of situation

returning him safely to Earth before 1970 inspired the "space race" of the 1960s. For these reasons, they are considered transformational leaders. Although these examples are useful, we must ask: Exactly what makes a leader transformational? The key characteristics of transformational leaders are as follows:

- *Charisma.* Transformational leaders have a mission and inspire others to follow them, often in a highly emotional manner.
- *Self-confidence.* Transformational leaders are highly confident in their ability and judgment, and others readily become aware of this.
- *Vision.* Transformational leaders have ideas about how to improve the status quo and do what it takes to change things for the better, even if it means making personal sacrifices.
- *Environmental sensitivity.* Transformational leaders are highly realistic about the constraints imposed upon them and the resources needed to change things. They know what they can and cannot do.
- *Intellectually stimulating.* Transformational leaders help followers recognize problems and show them ways of solving them.
- *Interpersonally considerate.* Transformational leaders give followers the support, encouragement, and attention they need to perform their jobs well.
- *Inspirational.* Transformational leaders clearly communicate the importance of the company's mission and rely on symbols (e.g., pins and slogans) to help focus their efforts.

A good example of a transformational leader is Jack Welch, the illustrious recently retired chairman and CEO of General Electric (GE).[9] Under Welch's leadership, GE has undergone a series of changes with respect to the way it does business.[10] At the individual level, GE has abandoned its highly bureaucratic ways and now does a good job of listening to its employees. Not surprisingly, GE has consistently ranked among the most admired companies in its industry in *Fortune* magazine's annual survey of corporate reputations (including a number-one ranking in several recent years!).[11] In the 1980s, Welch bought and sold many businesses for GE, using as his guideline the rule that GE would keep a company only if it placed either number one or number two in market share. If this meant closing plants, selling assets, and laying off personnel, he did it and got others to follow suit, earning him the nickname "Neutron Jack." Did Welch transform and revitalize GE? Having added well over $100 billion of value to the company, making it the most valuable company in the United States, there can be no doubt about it.[12]

What we know about the effectiveness of transformational leadership goes beyond anecdotal examples and is based on sound scientific research.[13] For example, a study of secondary school teachers found that the more highly transactional their schools' principals were (as measured using a special questionnaire), the more they engaged in organizational citizenship behavior (see Chapter 6) and had high levels of job satisfaction and organizational commitment among the teachers (Chapter 5).[14] Further research has shown managers at FedEx who are rated

Managers at FedEx who are rated by their subordinates as being highly transformational tend to be higher performers and are recognized by their superiors as being highly promotable.

TABLE 11.3   Guidelines for Becoming a Transformational Leader

Being a transformational leader is not easy, but following the suggestions outlined here may help leaders transform and revitalize their organizations. (*Source:* Based on suggestions by Yukl, 1998; see Note 1; and Bass, 1998; see Note 8.)

Suggestion	*Explanation*
Develop a vision that is both clear and highly appealing to followers.	A clear vision will guide followers toward achieving organizational goals and make them feel good about doing so.
Articulate a strategy for bringing that vision to life.	Don't present an elaborate plan; rather, state the best path toward achieving the mission.
State your vision clearly and promote it to others.	Visions must not only be clear, but made compelling, such as by using anecdotes.
Show confidence and optimism about your vision.	If a leader lacks confidence about success, followers will not try very hard to achieve that vision.
Express confidence in followers' capacity to carry out the strategy.	Followers must believe that they are capable of implementing a leader's vision. Leaders should build followers' self-confidence.
Build confidence by recognizing small accomplishments toward the goal.	If a group experiences early success, it will be motivated to continue working hard.
Celebrate successes and accomplishments.	Formal or informal ceremonies are useful for celebrating success, thereby building optimism and commitment.
Take dramatic action to symbolize key organizational values.	Visions are reinforced by things leaders do to symbolize them. For example, one leader demonstrated concern for quality by destroying work that was not up to standards.
Set an example; actions speak louder than words.	Leaders serve as role models. If they want followers to make sacrifices, for example, they should do so themselves.

---

by their subordinates as being highly transformational tend to be higher performers and are recognized by their superiors as being highly promotable.[15] These studies and similar evidence suggests that the benefits of being a transformational leader are considerable.[16] With this in mind, you may find it worthwhile to consider the ways of transforming your own organization summarized in Table 11.3.

The Behavior Approach: What Do Leaders Do?

The great person theory paints a somewhat fatalistic picture, suggesting that some people are, by nature, more prone to being effective leaders than others. After all, some of us have more of "the right stuff" than do others. However, other approaches to leadership—particularly, those focusing on what leaders do, rather than who leaders are—paint a more encouraging picture for those of us who aspire to leadership positions. This orientation is known as the **behavior approach**. By emulating the behavior of successful leaders, the possibility exists that anyone may become an effective leader.

TWO CRITICAL LEADERSHIP BEHAVIORS

Precisely what behaviors hold the key to leadership success? Although the answer to this question is quite complex, I can safely point to two very important leadership behaviors. The first is showing a *concern for people,* also known as **consideration**. In describing your boss, would you say that he or she cares about you as a person, is friendly, and listens to you when you want to talk? If so, he or she may be said to demonstrate a high amount of consideration.

The second main type of leadership behavior is showing a *concern for getting the job done,* also known as **initiating structure**. In describing your boss, would you say that he or she gives you advice, answers your questions, and lets you know exactly what is expected of you? If so, he or she may be said to demonstrate a high amount of initiating structure.

A large body of research suggests that leaders do differ greatly along these two dimensions. In these classic investigations subordinates completed questionnaires in which they described their leaders' behavior. Those leaders scoring high on initiating structure were mainly concerned with production and focused primarily on getting the job done. They engaged in actions such as organizing work, inducing subordinates to follow rules, setting goals, and making expectations explicit. In contrast, leaders scoring lower on this dimension showed less tendency to engage in these actions.

Leaders at the high end of the consideration dimension were primarily concerned with establishing good relations with their subordinates and being liked by them. They engaged in actions such as doing favors for subordinates, explaining things to them, and assuring their welfare. People who scored low on this dimension didn't care much about how they got along with subordinates.

It has been well established that leaders are likely to be most successful when they demonstrate high concern for both people (showing consideration) and production (initiating structure).

It has been well established that leaders are likely to be most successful when they demonstrate high concern for both people (showing consideration) *and* production (initiating structure). Showing consideration is beneficial insofar as it leads to high levels of group morale and low levels of turnover and absenteeism. At the same time, high levels of initiating structure are useful in promoting high levels of efficiency and performance. Not surprisingly, highly skilled leaders combine both orientations into their overall styles to produce favorable results.

Recently, two top executive recruiters analyzed the specific behaviors that characterize the way America's 50 most successful business leaders behave.[17] They found that these individuals shared a commitment to behaving in certain ways. Specifically, they all did the following:

- Demonstrated the utmost integrity in whatever they did
- Developed strategies for building on what the company does best
- Built a skilled management team whose members shared their own values
- Communicated so well that they inspired others to achieve greatness
- Made it possible for their organizations to make changes rapidly
- Developed compensation systems that reinforced the company's mission

Interestingly, this list is completely consistent with the well-established findings about the importance of paying attention to both people and the work itself. However, it provides a highly specific, and very insightful, list of some specific forms these behaviors take.

DEVELOPING SUCCESSFUL LEADER BEHAVIORS: GRID TRAINING

How can one go about developing these two forms of leadership behavior—demonstrating concern for production and concern for people? A technique known as **grid training** proposes a multistep process designed to cultivate these two important skills.[18]

The initial step consists of a *grid seminar*—a session in which an organization's managers (who have been previously trained in the appropriate theory and skills) help organization members analyze their own management styles. This is done using a specially designed questionnaire that allows managers to determine how they stand with respect to their *concern for production* and their *concern for people*. Each participant's approach on each dimension is scored using a number ranging from 1 (low) to 9 (high).

Managers who score low on both concern for production and concern for people are scored 1,1—showing evidence of *impoverished management*. Managers who are highly concerned about production but show little interest in people score 9,1, demonstrating the *task management* style. In contrast, those who show the opposite pattern— high concern with people but little concern with production—are described as having a *country club* style of management; they are scored 1,9. Managers scoring moderately on both dimensions, the 5,5 pattern, are said to follow a *middle-of-the-road* management style. Finally, there are individuals who are highly concerned with both production and people, those scoring 9,9. This is the most desirable pattern, representing what is known as *team management*. These various patterns are represented in a diagram like that shown in Figure 11.1, known as the *managerial grid®*.

After a manager's position along the grid is determined, training begins to improve concern over production (planning skills) and concern over people (communication skills) to reach the ideal, *9,9* state. This consists of organization-wide training aimed at helping people interact more effectively with each other. Then training is expanded to reducing conflict between groups that work with each other. Additional training includes efforts to identify the extent to which the organization is meeting its strategic goals and then comparing this performance to an ideal. Next, plans are made to meet these goals, and these plans are implemented in the organization. Finally, progress toward the goals is continuously assessed, and problem areas are identified.

Grid training is widely considered an effective way of improving the leadership behaviors of people in organizations. Indeed, the grid approach has been used to train hundreds of thousands of people in developing the two key types of leadership behavior.

Contingency Theories of Leader Effectiveness

It should be clear by now that leadership is a complex process. It involves intricate social relationships and is affected by a wide range of variables. In general, it may be said that leadership is influenced by two main factors—the characteristics of the individuals involved and the nature of the situations they face. This basic point lies at the heart of several approaches to leadership known as **contingency theories** of leader

FIGURE 11.1 The Managerial Grid®

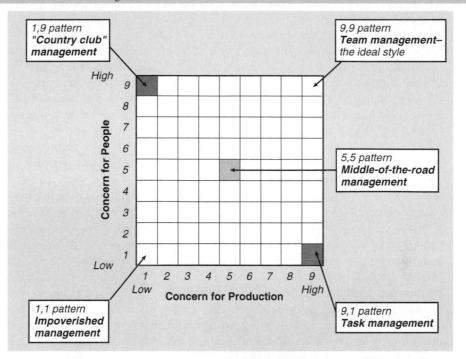

A manager's standing along two basic dimensions—*concern for production* and *concern for people*—can be illustrated by means of a diagram such as this, known as the managerial grid®. To promote effective leadership, people are trained to demonstrate high amounts of both dimensions. (*Source:* Based on suggestions by Blake and Mouton, 1969; see Note 18.)

> *Contingency theories seek to identify the conditions and factors that determine whether, and to what degree, leaders will enhance the performance and satisfaction of their subordinates.*

effectiveness. According to this approach, there is no one best style of leadership. Instead, they suggest that certain leadership styles may prove most effective under certain conditions. Contingency theories seek to identify the conditions and factors that determine whether, and to what degree, leaders will enhance the performance and satisfaction of their subordinates. I will describe two such approaches.

LPC CONTINGENCY THEORY: MATCHING LEADERS AND TASKS

Earlier, I explained that the behaviors associated with effective leadership fall into two major categories—concern for production and concern for people. Both types of behavior contribute to a leader's success. However, a more refined look at this issue leads us to ask exactly when each type of behavior works best. That is, under what conditions are leaders more successful when they demonstrate a concern for people compared to a concern for production?

The basics of the theory. This question is addressed by a widely studied approach to leadership known as **LPC contingency theory**. The contingency aspect of the theory reflected by the assumption that a leader's contribution to successful performance by his or her group is determined by the leader's own traits in conjunction with various features of the situation. Different levels of leader effectiveness occur under different combinations of conditions. To fully understand leader effectiveness, both types of factors must be considered.

The theory identifies *esteem (liking) for least preferred coworker* (**LPC** for short) as the most important personal characteristic. This refers to a leader's tendency to evaluate in a favorable or unfavorable manner the person with whom she or he has found it most difficult to work. Leaders who perceive this person in negative terms (low LPC leaders) are primarily concerned with attaining successful task performance. In contrast, those who perceive their least preferred coworker in a positive light (high LPC leaders) are mainly concerned with establishing good relations with subordinates. LPC is considered a leadership style that is relatively fixed and cannot be changed.

Which type of leader—one low in LPC or one high in LPC—is more effective? As suggested by the word *contingency* in the name, the answer is: "It depends." And what it depends on is the degree to which the situation is favorable to the leader—that is, how much it allows the leaders to have control over their subordinates. This, in turn, is determined largely by three factors: (1) the nature of the *leader's relations with group members* (the extent to which he or she enjoys their support and loyalty), (2) the *degree of structure* in the task being performed (the extent to which task goals and subordinates' roles are clearly defined), and (3) the leader's *position power* (as described earlier in this chapter). Combining these three factors, the leader's *situational control* can range from very high (positive relations with group members, a highly structured task, and high position power) to very low (negative relations, an unstructured task, and low position power).

What types of leaders are most effective under these various conditions? According to the theory, low LPC leaders (ones who are task-oriented) are superior to high LPC leaders (ones who are relations- or people-oriented) when situational control is either very low or very high. In contrast, high LPC leaders have an edge when situational control falls within the moderate range (refer to Figure 11.2).

The rationale for these predictions is quite reasonable. Under conditions of low situational control, groups need considerable guidance to accomplish their tasks. Without such direction, nothing would get done. For example, imagine a military combat group led by an unpopular platoon leader. Any chance of effectiveness this person has would result from paying careful attention to the task at hand, rather than hoping to establish better relations with the group. (In fact, in the military, it is often said that a leader in an emergency is better off giving wrong orders than no orders whatsoever.) Since low LPC leaders are more likely to provide structure than high LPC leaders, they usually will be superior in such cases.

Similarly, low LPC leaders are also superior under conditions that offer the leader a high degree of situational control. Indeed, when leaders are liked, their power is not challenged, and the demands of the task make it clear what a leader should be doing, it is perfectly acceptable for them to focus on the task at hand. Subordinates expect their leaders to exercise control under such conditions and accept it when they do so. And this leads to task success. For example, an airline pilot leading a cockpit crew is

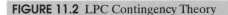

FIGURE 11.2 LPC Contingency Theory

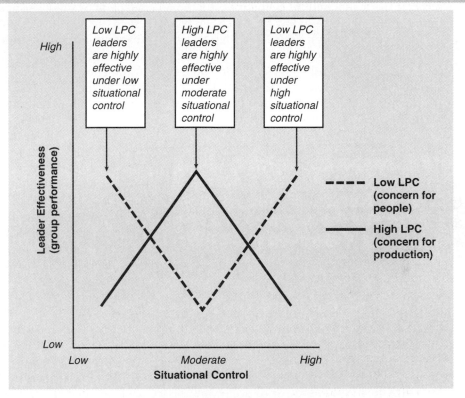

According to LPC contingency theory low LPC leaders (ones who are primarily task-oriented) will be more effective than high LPC leaders (ones who are primarily people-oriented) when situational control is either very low or very high. However, when situational control is moderate, high LPC leaders will be more effective than low LPC leaders.

expected to take charge, and not to seek the consensus of others as she guides the plane onto the runway for a landing. Surely, she would be less effective if she didn't take charge, but rather asked the copilot what he thought she should do.

Things are different, however, when situations offer leaders moderate situational control. Consider, for example, a situation in which a leader's relations with subordinates are good, but the task is unstructured, and the leader's power is somewhat restricted. This may be the case within a research and development team attempting to find creative new uses for a company's products. Here, it would be clearly inappropriate for a low LPC leader to impose directives. Rather, a highly nurturing leader who is considerate of the feelings of others would likely be most effective—that is, a high LPC leader.

Applying LPC contingency theory.   Practitioners have found LPC contingency theory to be quite useful when it comes to suggesting ways of enhancing leader effectiveness. Because the theory assumes that certain kinds of leaders are most effective under certain kinds of situations, and that leadership style is fixed, the best way to enhance effectiveness is to fit the right kind of leaders to the situations they face.

This involves completing questionnaires that can be used to assess both the LPC score of the leader and the amount of situational control he or she faces in the situation. Then, using these indexes, a match can be made such that leaders are put into the situations that best suit their leadership styles—a technique known as **leader match.** This approach also focuses on ways of changing the situational control variables— leader-member relations, task structure, and leader position power—when it is impractical to change leaders. For example, a high LPC leader should be moved to a job in which situational control is either extremely high or extremely low. Alternatively, the situation should be changed (such as by altering relations between leaders and group members, or raising or lowering his or her position power) to increase or decrease the amount of situational control encountered. Several companies, including Sears, have used the leader match approach with great success. In fact, research has found that this approach is a very effective way of improving group effectiveness.

> *Several companies, including Sears, have used the leader match approach with great success. In fact, research has found that this approach is a very effective way of improving group effectiveness.*

PATH-GOAL THEORY: LEADERS AS GUIDES TO VALUED GOALS

In defining leadership, I indicated that leaders help their groups or organizations reach their goals. This basic idea plays a central role in the **path-goal theory** of leadership.[19] In general terms, the theory contends that subordinates will react favorably to leaders who are perceived as helping them make progress toward various goals by clarifying the paths to such rewards. Specifically, the theory contends that the things a leader does to help clarify the nature of tasks and reduce or eliminate obstacles will increase subordinates' perceptions that working hard will lead to good performance and that good performance, in turn, will be recognized and rewarded. And, under such conditions (as you may recall from our discussion of expectancy theory in Chapter 4), motivation will be enhanced (which may help enhance performance).

How, precisely, can leaders best accomplish these tasks? Again, as in the case of LPC contingency theory, the answer is "It depends." (In fact, this answer is your best clue to identifying any contingency theory.) And what it depends on is a complex interaction between key aspects of *leader behavior* and certain *contingency* factors. Specifically, with respect to leader behavior, path-goal theory suggests that leaders can adopt four basic styles:

- **Instrumental** (directive)—An approach focused on providing specific guidance, establishing work schedules and rules
- **Supportive**—A style focused on establishing good relations with subordinates and satisfying their needs
- **Participative**—A pattern in which the leader consults with subordinates, permitting them to participate in decisions
- **Achievement-oriented**—An approach in which the leader sets challenging goals and seeks improvements in performance

FIGURE 11.3 Path-Goal Theory

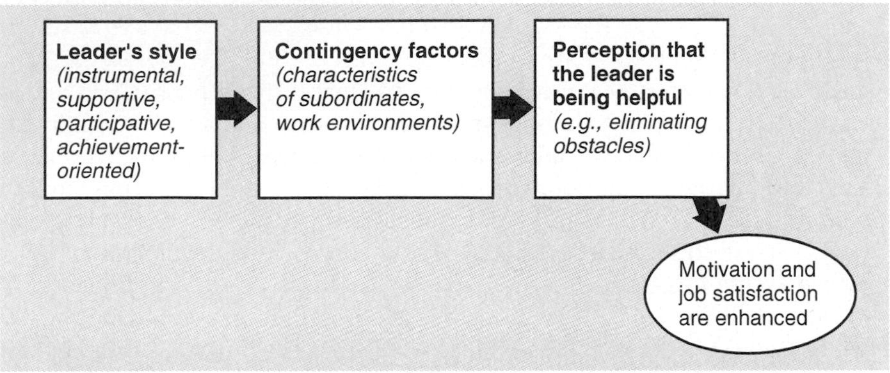

According to path-goal theory, perceptions among employees that leaders are helping them attain valued goals enhance their motivation and job satisfaction. Such perceptions are encouraged when a leader's style is consistent with the needs and characteristics of subordinates and various aspects of the work environment. (*Source:* Based on suggestions by House & Baetz, 1979; see Note 19.)

According to the theory, these styles are not mutually exclusive; in fact, the same leader can adopt them at different times and in different situations. Indeed, as I noted earlier in this chapter, showing such flexibility is key to being an effective leader.

Which of these styles is best for maximizing subordinates' satisfaction and motivation? The answer depends on several characteristics of subordinates. For example, if followers are high in ability, an instrumental style of leadership may be unnecessary; instead, a less structured, supportive approach may be preferable. On the other hand, if subordinates are low in ability, they may need considerable guidance to help them attain their goals. Similarly, people high in need for affiliation (i.e., those desiring close, friendly ties with others) may strongly prefer a supportive or participative style of leadership. Those high in the need for achievement may strongly prefer an achievement-oriented leader, one who can guide them to unprecedented levels of success.

The theory suggests that the most effective leadership style also depends on several aspects of the work environment. Specifically, path-goal theory predicts that when tasks are unstructured and nonroutine, an instrumental approach by the leader may be best; much clarification and guidance are needed. However, when tasks are structured and routine, such leadership may get in the way of good performance and may be resented by subordinates who think the leader is engaging in unnecessary meddling. (See Figure 11.3 for an overview of all these aspects of path-goal theory.)

Emerging Trends and Challenges in Leadership Practice

Now that your understanding of the nature of leadership has a solid foundation, you are prepared to appreciate several emerging trends and challenges that leaders face in today's rapidly changing business environment. I will describe four such issues: the practice of co-leadership, as well as the implications for leadership associated with today's global business world, the use of teams, and the digital economy.

CO-CEOS: THE BUCK SPLITS HERE

Traditionally, companies have only one chief executive officer (CEO), a top leader in charge of the company. These days, however, many companies are finding that there's good reason to have two talented leaders in charge—**co-CEOs**, who share power.[20] This trend has grown in popularity as the business world has become more global and complex, dictating the need for more than one top leader. Also, the wave of megamergers has led to the growth of co-CEOs as the newly created companies scramble to find places for the CEOs of the formerly individual firms. Moreover, the sheer size and geographic challenges of running these megacorporations makes having two CEOs somewhat of a necessity. For example, since Chrysler and Daimler-Benz merged in 1998, the new DaimlerChrysler has had as co-CEOs the former CEOs of the individual companies. But the DaimlerChrysler case is far from unique. In one recent year alone, three of the top ten largest mergers have led to the sharing of power by co-CEOs.[21]

> *Co-CEO arrangements frequently are well-received following mergers and acquisitions because they are friendly in tone (in contrast to the hostile takeovers that occurred in the 1980s). When the leaders of the two formerly separate companies work well together, they send a strong message to the rank-and-file employees that they are expected to do the same.*

Co-CEO arrangements frequently are well-received following mergers and acquisitions because they are friendly in tone (in contrast to the hostile takeovers that occurred in the 1980s). When the leaders of the two formerly separate companies work well together, they send a strong message to the rank-and-file employees that they are expected to do the same. However, co-CEOs don't exist only in newly merged firms. Unilever, for example, the world's second-largest consumer products company, has had co-CEOs since 1930. Instead of having two CEOs at once, Royal Dutch Shell has two executives who alternate turns as CEO (one from Royal Dutch Petroleum and the other from Shell Transport and Trading).

Another company that has benefited from co-CEOs is Sapient Corporation, an Internet services consulting firm.[22] For the past decade, co-CEOs Jerry Greenberg (not the author!) and Stuart Moore have run their company successfully despite—actually, because of—the fact that they have so little in common. They even live on opposite coasts. Greenberg focuses on sales and on financial matters, while Moore focuses on the personnel and technical issues. However, neither makes an important decision without consulting the other. It works because each recognizes the other's expertise and is willing to defer.

Unfortunately, not all such "professional marriages" are as successful. In fact, some experts say that companies with co-CEOs are unstable.[23] In the case of the proposed merger of the pharmaceutical giants Galaxo-Welcome and Smithkline Beecham, arguments about who would lead were so intense that the deal was canceled before it ever occurred. Attempts at installing co-CEOs failed in the merger between Time-Life and Warner Brothers (forming Time-Warner) and that between INA Corporation and Connecticut General (forming Cigna Corp.). In both cases, after the two CEOs tore their companies apart with their acrimony, the power-sharing arrangements were disbanded. Both companies now have single CEOs.

At this time, the future of co-leadership is not clear. Although it works sometimes, it's just as likely to be a failure. The keys to its success seem to be (1) the willingness of each party to yield power to the other, and (2) the recognition by each party that the other makes a vital contribution to the company. When these criteria are met, co-CEOs have a chance at sharing leadership successfully. Otherwise, it's unlikely to succeed.

MOLDING LEADERS FOR THE GLOBAL ECONOMY

Throughout this chapter, I have referred to several skills in which people have been trained to enhance their effectiveness as leaders. In today's global economy, the challenge of becoming an effective leader is more important than ever. In the words of C. R. "Dick" Shoemate, chairman and CEO of Bestfoods, "It takes a special kind of leadership to deal with the differences of a multicountry, multicultural organization such as ours." [24] Not surprisingly, most of the countries on *Fortune* magazine's list of the "Global Most Admired Companies" (such as General Electric, BASF, Berkshire Hathaway, and SBC Communications) pay considerable attention to training leaders to deal with the realities of today's global business world.[25]

Companies use a variety of approaches when it comes to training global leaders. In-house leadership seminars (focusing on many of the concepts in this chapter and the entire book) that have traditionally been used continue to be popular. However, these are being supplemented by carefully customized programs that prepare leaders for global assignments. Companies are intensely coaching individuals who take on overseas assignments and are carefully planning a succession of career assignments that prepare leaders for global business. For example, the pharmaceuticals giant Pfizer systematically assigns key managers and potential leaders to project teams that will give them overseas experience. Just as the company takes a long-term perspective on developing its products, Pfizer also "takes a long-term view of developing people," says Chick Dombeck, vice president of human resources.[26]

> *The pharmaceuticals giant Pfizer systematically assigns key managers and potential leaders to project teams that will give them overseas experience.*

Similarly, Shoemate refers to "cross-border assignments" in describing how Bestfoods prepares executives for learning about different cultures. American Express relies on a similar approach. Like other companies, it relies extensively on individual coaching, but also incorporates international assignments in its strategy for developing leaders. According to Linda Miindek, vice president of worldwide operations, American Express' goal is "to ensure our people have the required capabilities to lead the company to future success."[27] There can be no doubt that when it comes to developing leaders, today's companies are paying careful attention to the global world in which they do business.

THE CHALLENGE OF LEADING TEAMS

Traditionally, leaders make strategic decisions on behalf of followers, who are responsible for carrying them out. In many of today's organizations, however, where *teams* predominate (see Chapter 9), leaders are called upon to provide special resources to team members, who are empowered to implement their own missions in their own ways. Instead of "calling the shots," team leaders help subordinates take responsibility for their own work. As such, they are very different from the traditional "command-and-control" leadership role we have been discussing.[28] Because many people are new to working in teams, and because traditional leaders are generally unfamiliar with what is expected of them as leaders of teams, it is worth considering the guidelines for achieving success as a team leader outlined in Table 11.4.

As Table 11.4 suggests, leading teams is clearly very different from leading individuals in the traditional manner. The special nature of teams makes the leader's job very different. Although appreciating these differences is easy, making the appropriate adjustments may be extremely challenging—especially for individuals who are well-practiced in the ways of traditional leadership. However, given the prevalence of teams in today's work environment, the importance of making the adjustments cannot be overstated. Leading new teams using old methods is a surefire formula for failure. (In fact, as described in the **Winning Practices** section on the next page, the team approach to leadership has even found its way into the U.S. Navy.)

LEADING IN THE DIGITAL AGE

Most of what we know about leading people is derived from the era in which (1) there were clear hierarchies in organizations and everyone knew who was in charge, (2) changes

---

TABLE 11.4   Leading Groups Versus Leading Teams

The popularity of teams in today's organizations has important implications for how leaders go about fulfilling their roles. Some of the key differences between leading traditional work groups and leading teams are summarized here.

In traditional work groups, leaders . . .	*But, in teams, leaders . . .*
Tell people what to do.	Ask people what they think, and share responsibility for organizing and doing the work.
Take all the credit.	Share the limelight with all their teammates.
Focus on training employees.	Concentrate on expanding their team's capabilities by functioning primarily as coaches who build confidence in team members, cultivating their untapped potential.
Relate to others individually.	Create a team identity by helping the team set goals, helping members meet them, and celebrating when they have been met.
Work at reducing conflict between individuals.	Make the most of team differences by building respect for diverse points of view and ensuring that all team members' views are expressed.
React to change.	Recognize that change is inevitable and foresee it, better preparing the organization to make appropriate adaptations.

WINNING PRACTICES

Grassroots Leadership Aboard Ship

Until he was promoted to a top post in the U.S. Navy, for 20 months D. Michael Abrashoff was commander of the USS *Benfold,* one of the U.S. Navy's most modern, most technologically advanced, most lethal warships. Although you'd surely think that Commander Abrashoff ran this $1 billion floating computerized arsenal in the strict, top-down manner of most military companies, you couldn't be farther off.[29] In fact, he actually relied on a **grassroots leadership** approach in which the traditional management hierarchy is turned upside down. Aboard the *Benfold* it's the 300 sailors who are really in charge. The commander expressed it as follows:

> In most organizations today, ideas still come from the top. Soon after arriving at this command, I realized that the young folks on this ship are smart and talented. And I realized that my job was to listen aggressively—to pick up all of the ideas that they had for improving how we operate. The most important thing that a captain can do is to see the ship from the eyes of the crew.[30]

Abrashoff's approach to commanding the ship was highly personalized. Like all good team leaders do, he met face-to-face with each of the crew members in an attempt to understand their personal and professional goals. Moreover, he made decisions that paved the way for the sailors under his command to spend more time on mission-critical tasks and less time on unpleasant chores. No longer did they have to sand off rust and repaint the ship. Abrashoff arranged for an outside firm to replace rusting bolts with stainless steel hardware and to apply a special rust-inhibiting finish to the ship's surfaces. This not only relieved the sailors from having to perform tedious, demoralizing chores but also freed them to spend more time on their true purpose—preparing for combat.

Grassroots leadership has been an unqualified success aboard the *Benfold.* During Abrashoff's command, the ship became recognized as the best in the Pacific Fleet and as the most combat-ready ship in the entire U.S. Navy. In addition, the crew became so efficient that it was able to return a third of the budget allocated for maintenance. Finally, and perhaps most impressively, literally all of the career sailors aboard the *Benfold* reenlisted for a second tour of duty, enabling the Navy to get the most from its highly trained personnel.

It is not only aboard the USS *Benfold* where one can see grassroots leadership at work. The same basic approach also has been used very successfully at Royal Dutch Shell—which, like the U.S. Navy, is an organization with a strong tradition of top-down leadership.[31] The success of grassroots leadership in such rigid and traditional organizations is a good indication that this approach may have considerable value in a wide variety of organizations.

Questions for Discussion

1. As a leader, what concerns would you have about instituting a grassroots leadership program?
2. Why don't you think the sailors aboard the *Benfold* failed to take advantage of the freedom they were given?
3. How do you think you would enjoy working for a company whose management uses grassroots leadership?

were made slowly, and (3) people expected to follow their leaders' orders. Many of these characteristics do not apply to today's organizations, and none describes the high-tech world of Internet businesses. In today's digital economy, organizations are highly **decentralized**—that is, power to make decisions is spread out among many different people. What's more, the pace of change is so blindingly fast that leaders rarely have the luxury of making decisions with careful deliberation. Finally, unlike the traditional worker, many of today's employees demand independence and autonomy. In short, they are reluctant to be led in the traditional sense of having someone tell them precisely what to do.

As you might imagine, these considerations have important implications for the way today's dot-com leaders are required to operate. Some of the most important implications of the Internet economy for leadership are as follows:[32]

- *Growth occurs so quickly that strategies have to be changed constantly.* For example, Meg Whitman, the president and CEO of Ebay, Inc., says that the company grows so rapidly (often 40 to 50 percent each quarter!) that it becomes an entirely different company every few months. Leaders cannot take anything for granted, except the fact that whatever they decided to do yesterday may need to be changed tomorrow.

- *Leaders of Internet companies are not expected to have all the answers.* The highly technical nature of the business and the rapid pace of change make it impossible for just one or two people to make all the right decisions. According to Jonathan Buckeley, the CEO of Barnesandnoble.com, today's leaders "must be evangelists for changing the system, not preserving it."[33]

- *Showing restraint is critical.* There are so many opportunities available to Internet companies today that executives can too easily enter into a bad deal. For example, Andrew Jarecki, the cofounder and CEO of Moviefone, Inc., ignored the many suggestions he received to go into business with a big portal before agreeing to what proved to be the right deal—acquisition by AOL for $386 million in stock.

- *Hiring and retaining the right people is more important than ever.* In the world of the Internet, the average tenure of a senior executive is only 18 months. Constant change means that the people who are hired for today's jobs must meet the demands of tomorrow's jobs as well. As Jay Walker, founder and vice chairman of Priceline.com, puts it, "You've got to hire ahead of the curve," adding that "if you wait until you're actually doing [as much business as you expect] to hire the necessary talent, then you'll be too late."[34]

- *Today's leaders must not take anything for granted.* When Mark Cuban and his partner founded Broadcast.com (before selling it to Yahoo! four years later for $5.7 billion), they made lots of incorrect decisions. Instead of sticking by them, they quickly adjusted their game plan to fit the realities they faced.

- *Internet leaders must focus on real-time decision making.* Traditional leaders were trained to gather lots of data before making carefully researched decisions. According to Ruthann Quindlen, partner in Institutional Venture Partners, leaders can no longer afford to do so: "If your instinct is to wait, ponder, and perfect, then you're dead," adding that "leaders to have to hit the undo key without flinching."[35]

As I have outlined here, many of the traditional ways of leading need to be adjusted to accommodate to today's Internet economy. Before you think of ignoring everything you learned about leadership in this chapter, please note that the Internet world does not require us to rewrite all the rules about good leadership. For example, showing concern for people and concern for production have not gone out of style! In fact, to successfully accommodate to the fast-paced modern era, they may be considered more important than ever.

SUMMARY: HAVE I MET THE LEARNING OBJECTIVES?

You can be certain that you have met the learning objectives for this chapter found on p. 279 if you understand the following:

1. **DEFINE leadership and IDENTIFY the major sources of power leaders have at their disposal.** Leadership is the process whereby one individual influences other group members toward the attainment of defined group or organizational goals. Leaders derive power based on their formal positions, including their accepted authority in the organization, their capacity to administer rewards and punishments, and their access to important information. They also have power attributable to their personal characteristics, such as their ability to use rational persuasion, their recognized expertise, the fact that they are admired, and their charisma (i.e., their engaging and magnetic personalities).

2. **DESCRIBE the trait approach to leadership and IDENTIFY the major characteristics of effective leaders.** The trait approach to leadership claims that leaders differ from followers in certain key respects. They are higher in drive, honesty, leadership motivation, self-confidence, and several other traits. In addition, successful leaders appear to be high in flexibility—the ability to adapt their style to the followers' needs and to the requirements of specific situations. Some of the most effective leaders are considered transformational insofar as they do things that change and revitalize their organizations. They are highly charismatic, and they provide intellectual stimulation, individualized consideration, and inspirational motivation. Transformational leaders tend to be very effective.

3. **IDENTIFY the types of behavior that have been most strongly associated with effective leadership.** Leaders vary along two key dimensions: concern with maintaining favorable personal relations with subordinates—referred to as consideration—and concern with, and efforts to attain, successful task performance—referred to as initiating structure.

4. **DESCRIBE the basic tenets of LPC contingency theory and how it may be applied.** *LPC contingency theory* suggests that both a leader's characteristics and situational factors are crucial. Task-oriented leaders (termed low LPC leaders) are more effective than people-oriented leaders (termed high LPC leaders) under conditions in which the leader has either high or low control over the group in question. In contrast, people-oriented leaders are more effective under conditions in which the leader has moderate control. The theory claims that although someone's LPC score cannot be changed, successful leadership results when people, based on their LPC scores, are matched to those situations in which they may be expected to be most effective.

5. **EXPLAIN the path-goal theory of leadership.** *Path-goal theory* of leadership suggests that leaders' behavior will be accepted by subordinates and will enhance their motivation only to the extent that it helps them progress toward valued goals and provides guidance or clarification not already present in work settings.

6. **DESCRIBE the emerging trends and challenges in leadership practice.** Several of today's organizations are experimenting with the use of *co-CEOs,* two top leaders who share power. The effectiveness of this practice has been mixed. Another trend involves training leaders for the global economy. With this in mind, many companies that conduct business across national borders are systematically giving leaders experience in different countries' operations. The popularity of teams has changed the traditional ways in which leaders function. Instead of telling lower-level people what to do, team leaders provide the necessary resources for members to lead themselves (as is the case in *grassroots leadership*). Finally, because of the rapidly changing nature of the digital economy, leaders of Internet-based businesses find it especially important to make decisions without careful deliberation, and to hire and retain the most talented senior executive team.

You Be the Consultant

The president and founder of a large office furniture manufacturer, tells you, "Nobody around here has any respect for me. The only reason they listen to me is because this is my company." Company employees report that he is a highly controlling individual who does not let them do anything for themselves.

1. What behaviors should the president attempt to emulate to improve his leadership style? How may he go about doing so?
2. Under what conditions would you expect the president's leadership style to be most effective? Do you think that these conditions might exist in his company?
3. Would your advice be any different if he were in charge of a small Internet start-up instead of a large manufacturing company?

SELF-ASSESSMENT EXERCISE

What Forms of Power Does Your Supervisor Use?

One of the main ways of learning about power in organizations is to use questionnaires in which people are asked to describe the behaviors of their superiors. If a consistent pattern emerges with respect to the way subordinates describe their superiors, some very strong clues are provided about the nature of the supervisor's influence style. Questionnaires similar to this one are used for this purpose.[36] Complete this questionnaire to gain some indication of the types of social influence on which your supervisor relies.

Directions

Indicate how strongly you agree or disagree with each of the following statements as it describes your immediate supervisor. For each statement, select the number corresponding to the most appropriate response using the following scale: 1 = *strongly disagree,* 2 = *disagree,* 3 = *neither agree nor disagree,* 4 = *agree,* and 5 = *strongly agree.*

My supervisor can. . .

_____ 1. Recommend that I receive a raise.
_____ 2. Assign me to jobs that I dislike.
_____ 3. See that I get the promotion I desire.
_____ 4. Make my life at work completely unbearable.
_____ 5. Make decisions about how things get done.
_____ 6. Provide useful advice on how to do my job more effectively.
_____ 7. Comprehend the importance of doing things a certain way.
_____ 8. Make me want to look up to him or her.
_____ 9. Share with me the benefit of his or her vast job knowledge.
_____ 10. Get me to admire what he or she stands for.
_____ 11. Find out things that nobody else knows.
_____ 12. Explain things so logically that I want to do them.
_____ 13. Have access to vital data about the company.
_____ 14. Share a clear vision of what the future holds for the company.
_____ 15. Come up with the facts needed to make a convincing case about something.
_____ 16. Explain the company's mission clearly and convincingly.

Scoring

1. Add the numbers assigned to statements 1 and 3. This is the *reward power* score.
2. Add the numbers assigned to statements 2 and 4. This is the *coercive power* score.
3. Add the numbers assigned to statements 5 and 7. This is the *legitimate power* score.
4. Add the numbers assigned to statements 6 and 9. This is the *expert power* score.
5. Add the numbers assigned to statements 8 and 10. This is the *referent power* score.
6. Add the numbers assigned to statements 11 and 13. This is the *information power* score.
7. Add the numbers assigned to statements 12 and 15. This is the *rational persuasion* score.
8. Add the numbers assigned to statements 14 and 16. This is the *charisma* score.

Questions for Discussion

1. On which dimensions did your supervisor score highest and lowest? Are these consistent with what you would have predicted in advance?
2. How do you think your own subordinates would answer these same questions with respect to yourself?
3. What additional statements, beyond the two given here for each category, could be used to describe each form of influence?

Identifying Great Leaders in All Walks of Life

A useful way to understand the great person theory is to identify those individuals who may be considered great leaders and then to consider what it is that makes them so great. This exercise is designed to guide a class in this activity.

Directions
1. Divide the class into four equal-size groups, arranging each in a semicircle.
2. In the open part of the semicircle, one group member—the recorder—should stand at a flip chart, ready to write down the group's responses.
3. The members of each group should identify the 10 most effective leaders they can think of—living or dead, real or fictional—in one of the following fields: business, sports, politics-government, or humanitarian endeavors. One group should cover each of these domains. If more than 10 names come up, the group should vote on the 10 best answers. The recorder should write down the names as they are identified.
4. Examining the list, group members should identify the traits and characteristics that the people on the list have in common, but that distinguish them from others who are not on the list. In other words, what is it that makes these people so special? The recorder should write down the answers.
5. One person from each group should be selected to present his or her group's responses to members of the class. This should include both the names of the leaders identified and their special characteristics.

Questions for Discussion
1. How did the traits identified in this exercise compare to the ones described in Table 11.2 as important determinants of leadership? Were they similar or different? Why?
2. To what extent were the traits identified in the various groups different or similar? In other words, were different characteristics associated with leadership success in different walks of life? Or were the ingredients for leadership success more universal?
3. Were some of some traits identified surprising to you, or were they all what you would have expected?

NOTES

Case Notes
Leonard, D. (2000, March 20). Living without a leader. *Fortune,* p. 218. Hammer, B. (2000, November 2). Urban Box Office declares bankruptcy. *The Industry Standard,* p. 15.

Chapter Notes
[1] Yukl, G. (1998). *Leadership in organizations (4th ed.).* Upper Saddle River, NJ: Prentice Hall.
[2] Weathersby, G. B. (1999, March). Leadership vs. management. *Management Review,* p. 5.
[3] See Note 1.
[4] Yukl, G. (2000). Use power effectively. In E. A. Locke (Ed.), *The Blackwell handbook of principles of organizational behavior* (pp. 241-256). Oxford, England: Blackwell.

[5] Kirkpatrick, S. A. & Locke, E. A. (1991). Leadership: Do traits matter? *Academy of Management Executive, 5,* 41-60.

[6] See Note 5 (quote, p. 58).

[7] Editorial. (2000, January 10). The best managers: What it takes. *Business Week,* p. 158.

[8] Bass, B. M. (1998). *Transformational leadership: Industry, military, and educational impact.* Mahwah, NJ: Lawrence Erlbaum Associates.

[9] Colvin, G. (1999, November 22). The ultimate manager. *Fortune,* pp. 185-187. Slater, R. (1999). *Jack Welch and the GE way.* New York: McGraw-Hill.

[10] Tichy, N. M. (1993). *Control your destiny or someone else will.* New York: Doubleday Currency.

[11] Stewart, T. A. (1998, March 2). America's most admired companies. *Fortune,* pp. 70-82.

[12] Colvin, C. (2000, December 18). America's best and worst wealth creators. *Fortune,* pp. 207-208, 210, 212, 214, 216.

[13] Judge, T. A., & Bono, J. E. (2000). Five-factor model of personality and transformational leadership. *Journal of Applied Psychology, 85,* 751-765.

[14] Koh, W. L., Steers R., & Terborg, J. R. (1995). The effects of transformational leadership on teacher attitudes and student performance in Singapore. *Journal of Organizational Behavior, 16,* 319-333.

[15] Hater, J. J., & Bass, B. M. (1988). Superiors' evaluations and subordinates perceptions of transformational and transactional leadership. *Journal of Applied Psychology, 73,* 695-702.

[16] Hauser, M., & House, R. J. (2000). Lead through vision and values. In E. A. Locke (Ed.), *The Blackwell handbook of principles of organizational behavior* (pp. 257-273).

[17] Neff, T. J., & Citrin, J. W. (1999). *Lessons from the top.* New York: Doubleday.

[18] Blake, R. R., & Mouton, J. S. (1969). *Building a dynamic corporation through grid organizational development.* Reading, MA: Addison-Wesley.

[19] House, R. J., & Baetz, M. L. (1979). Leadership: Some empirical generalizations and new research directions. In B. M. Staw (Ed.), *Research in organizational behavior* (Vol. 1, pp. 341-424). Greenwich, CT: JAI Press.

[20] Bennis, W., & Heenan, D. A. (1999). *Co-leaders: The power of great partnerships.* New York: John Wiley.

[21] Troiano, P. (1999, February). Sharing the throne. *Management Review,* pp. 39-43.

[22] Whitford, D. (2000, January 24). The two-headed manager. *Fortune,* pp. 147-148.

[23] Sirower, M. (2000). *The synergy trap: How companies lose the acquisition game.* New York: Free Press.

[24] Molding global leaders. (1999, October 11). *Fortune,* p. 270.

[25] Stein, N. (2000, October 2). Global most admired companies: Measuring people power. *Fortune,* pp. 273-288.

[26] See Note 25 (quote, p. 283).

[27] See Note 25 (quote, p. 285).

[28] Zenger, J. H., Musselwhite, E., Hurson, K., & Perrin, C. (1994). *Leading teams: Mastering the new role.* Homewood, IL: Business One Irwin.

[29] LaBarre, P. (1999, April). The agenda—grassroots leadership. *Fast Company,* pp. 115-126.

[30] See Note 29 (quote pp. 116, 118).

[31] Pascale, R. (1998, April-May). Grassroots leadership: Royal Dutch Shell. *Fast Company,* pp. 110-120.

[32] Labarre, P. (1999, June). Unit of one: Leaders.com. *Fast Company,* pp. 95-98, 100, 102, 104, 108, 110, 112.

[33] See Note 32 (quote, p. 96).

[34] See Note 33 (quote, p. 100).

[35] See Note 32 (quote, p. 104).

[36] Hinkin, T. R., & Schreisheim, C. A. (1989). Development and application of new scales to measure the French and Raven (1959) bases of social power. *Journal of Applied Psychology, 74,* 561-567.

12

Culture, creativity, and innovation

LEARNING OBJECTIVES

After reading this chapter, you will be able to:

1. DEFINE organizational culture and IDENTIFY the various functions it serves in organizations.

2. IDENTIFY the ways in which organizational cultures differ and the mechanisms through which organizational culture is transmitted.

3. IDENTIFY the factors responsible for creating organizational culture and for getting it to change.

4. DEFINE creativity and DESCRIBE the basic components of individual and team creativity.

5. DESCRIBE various approaches to promoting creativity in organizations.

6. IDENTIFY the basic components of innovation and the various stages of the innovation process.

THREE GOOD REASONS WHY YOU SHOULD CARE ABOUT. . .

Culture, Creativity, and Innovation

You should care about culture, creativity, and innovation because:

1. Organizational culture exerts profound influences on employees, both positive and negative.

2. Managers play an important role in transmitting organizational culture.

3. Individual and team creativity is an important determinant of an organization's capacity to be innovative, which facilitates organizational survival.

Making the Case for... Culture, Creativity, and Innovation

IDEO: Where Silliness Is Taken Seriously

Although you probably never heard of IDEO, you most certainly are familiar with the products it has designed, including the optical computer mouse (for Apple Computer), the stand-up toothpaste tube (for Procter & Gamble's Crest), and 3Com's sleek Palm V personal digital assistant. IDEO's team of product design specialists even created the 25-foot robotic whale used in the movie *Free Willy*. Although we take such products for granted, coming up with them, as you might imagine, requires incredibly creative people. CEO and founder David Kelly knows that maintaining IDEO's status as the largest product design firm in the United States requires keeping ideas flowing from his 350-person staff, something he doesn't take for granted.

The key to nurturing creativity at IDEO is having fun—not just telling a few jokes, but playing games and acting goofy. Having fun for the sake of nurturing creativity permeates the atmosphere at IDEO. For example, when employees are not playing miniature golf or tossing Nerf balls in the corridors, they may be found racing desk chairs on the streets outside the company's Palo Alto, California, headquarters. According to Jim Hackett, the CEO of Steelcase (which bought an equity stake in IDEO after being impressed with its operations), this way of operating "appeals to the childlike aspirations of all of us to be continually creative," adding that at IDEO, "work doesn't look like work."

Although Kelly's approach is unconventional, there is a method to his madness. By creating an atmosphere in which people are encouraged to play and have fun, he believes that the barriers that keep people from sharing ideas with each other will be broken down. In other words, if you're willing to throw a Nerf ball at your boss, you also might be willing to toss a few crazy ideas across the table. In Kelly's own words, "You can be playful when everybody feels they're just as important as the next person." Given the company's phenomenal success at coming up with innovative new product designs, his approach seems to be working.

As its clients noticed IDEO's innovative—and highly effective—way of nurturing creativity, they soon became interested not only in *what* the firm designs, but *how* it goes about doing so. After several such inquiries, Kelly decided to diversify IDEO's services by teaching its customers its own special recipe for creativity. In fact, with clients such as NEC, Kodak, Canon McDonald's and Samsung, creativity training now accounts for a quarter of IDEO's revenues. Acknowledging the adage that genius is 99 percent perspiration and 1 percent inspiration, Dennis Boyle, one of IDEO's trainers, says, "Most companies have that 99 percent. It's that 1 percent that's really hard, and that's why our clients are asking us to work with their people and not just their products."

The question of how this elusive 1 percent is developed is one of the key issues I will describe in this chapter. In so doing, I will identify some of the approaches that IDEO takes, as well as several other successful approaches for enhancing *creativity*. As you probably know, people in some organizations, such as IDEO, regularly take novel, ingenious, and cutting-edge approaches to the problems they face. In addition, employees in companies such as 3M, General Electric, and Rubbermaid routinely do the nonroutine.

What accounts for such differences? Why are some organizations more *innovative* than others? It's tempting to speculate that because people have different personalities, the organizations in which they work are likely to be different from each other as well. However, when you consider that entire organizations are often so consistently different from each other, it's apparent that there's more involved than simply differences in the personalities of the employees. In fact, even in companies where employees are constantly changing, the organizations themselves do not reinvent themselves. In fact, it is often the new employees who themselves change rather than their organizations. In a sense, then, organizations have a stable existence of their own, apart from the unique combination of people of which they are composed at any given time. This is the idea behind *organizational culture*—the shared beliefs, expectations, and core values of people in an organization.[1]

Because organizational culture is a key determinant of individual creativity and an organization's tendency toward innovation, I will begin this chapter by examining the concept of organizational culture. Specifically, I will start by describing the basic nature of organizational culture, including the role it plays in organizations. Then, I will describe the processes through which organizational culture is formed and maintained. Finally, I will review the effects of organizational culture on individual and organizational functioning, and examine when and how culture is subject to change. Then, after having described the nature of organizational culture, I will turn the attention to questions of creativity and innovation, including not only basic descriptions, but specific tips and suggestions regarding how to bring out your own creativity and how to make your own company more innovative.

Organizational Culture: Its Basic Nature

So that you can fully appreciate organizational culture, I will begin by offering a formal definition, and then explain key features of its basic nature.

ORGANIZATIONAL CULTURE: A DEFINITION

Scientists define **organizational culture** as a cognitive framework consisting of assumptions and values shared by organization members.[2] For example, organizations tend to have different absence cultures—that is, the employees share different understandings about the appropriateness of taking off from work. At one organization, for example, healthy employees may feel that it's appropriate to call in sick if they have unused sick days available. However, at other companies, people wouldn't think of taking off unless they really are ill.

In both of these companies, employees take for granted these various *assumptions* about sick leave. They are said to be ingrained into the organizational culture and are taken for granted. As the definition indicates, organizational culture also reflects different *values* that are shared by members of the organization. By **values**, I am referring to stable, long-term beliefs about what is important. For example, at IDEO—and other companies, such as PeopleSoft—employees value the fun side of work. In contrast, a highly formal way of operating has long characterized the organizational culture at IBM. There, employees wouldn't think of throwing Nerf balls at their bosses (even if they would like to do so!).

In these, and all, companies, organizational culture serves three key functions. Specifically, it may be said that organizational culture does the following:

1. *Provides a sense of identity for members.* The more clearly an organization's shared perceptions and values are defined, the more strongly people can associate themselves with their organization's mission and feel a vital part of it.
2. *Generates commitment to the organization's mission.* Sometimes it's difficult for people to go beyond thinking of their own interests: How will this affect me? However, a strong, overarching culture reminds people of what their organization is all about.
3. *Clarifies and reinforces standards of behavior.* Culture guides employees' words and deeds, making it clear what they should do or say in a given situation, thereby providing stability to behavior.

WAYS IN WHICH ORGANIZATIONAL CULTURES DIFFER

At the root of any organization's culture is a set of core characteristics that are collectively valued by members of an organization. These characteristics illustrate the essential ways in which the cultures of organizations differ from one another.[3] These are as follows:

- *Sensitivity to the needs of customers and employees.* For example, several years ago, the culture at UPS was relatively rigid and inflexible with respect to its customers' needs. Today, however, its new culture places a high value on customer service and satisfaction.
- *Interest in having employees generate new ideas.* Walt Disney Company employees—or "cast members," as they are called—undergo lengthy orientation programs to ensure that they know exactly what to say and how to behave toward guests. By contrast, people working at MCI are encouraged to be unique and to bring fresh ideas to their work.
- *Value placed on taking risks.* For example, whereas Bank of America is very conservative, making only the safest investments, buyers at The Limited are discouraged from making too many "safe" choices.
- *Openness of available communication options.* In some companies, such as DuPont, employees are expected to make decisions freely and to communicate with whomever is needed to get the job done. At IBM, however, the tradition has been to work within the proper communication channels and to vest power in the hands of only a few key individuals (although this appears to be changing).
- *Friendliness and congeniality of the employees toward one another.* At some companies, such as Nokia Corporation, the employees are all highly collegial, whereas they are far more cutthroat and competitive at the toy maker Mattel, Inc.
- *Value placed on people in the organization.* Some companies consider their employees as valuable only insofar as they contribute to production, much as they view machinery. Such organizations, wherein people do not feel valued, are considered having **toxic organizational cultures**. A recent survey found that 48 percent of people believe they work in toxic cultures.[4] Organizations with toxic cultures tend to lose good employees. By contrast, organizations that treat people well—said to have **healthy organizational cultures**—tend to have very low

FIGURE 12.1 The Financial Benefits of Healthy Organizational Culture: Doing the Math

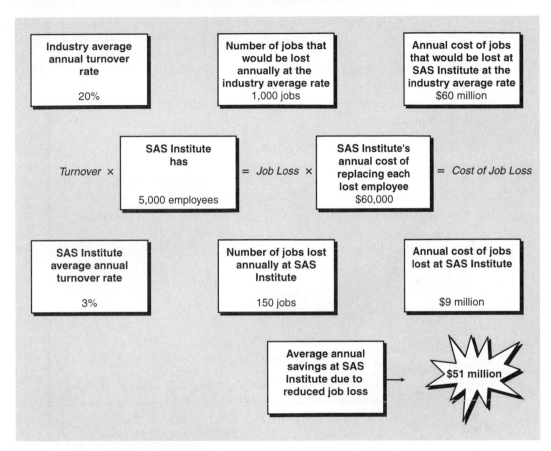

The SAS Institute is considered to have a *healthy organizational culture.* Its family-friendly policy never forces employees to choose between their work and family, and the pace of work is enjoyable. As a result, turnover is well below the industry average, which, according to human resources manager David Russo, saves the company some $51 million annually—savings that are reinvested into programs that make the organizational culture even healthier. So you can see where this figure comes from, his calculations are summarized here. (*Source:* Based on information reported in Webber, 1998; see Note 5.)

turnover. Examples of companies with healthy cultures include Hewlett-Packard, the Men's Wearhouse, and Starbucks. As summarized in Figure 12.1, using figures from the SAS Institute (a statistical software company in Cary, North Carolina), having a healthy organizational culture can pay off handsomely on the bottom line.[5]

These examples clearly illustrate different sets of core values that are reflected in the cultures of organizations.

CULTURES WITHIN ORGANIZATIONS: ONE OR MANY?

The discussion thus far has implied that each organization has only a single, uniform culture—one set of shared values and expectations. In fact, this is rarely the case. Instead, organizations, particularly large ones, typically have *several* cultures operating within them.

In general, people tend to have more attitudes and values in common with others in their own fields of work or their own company units than they do with those in other fields or other parts of the organization. These various groups may be said to have several different **subcultures**—cultures existing within parts of organizations rather than entirely through them. These typically are distinguished with respect to either functional differences (i.e., the type of work done) or geographic distances (i.e., the physical separation between people). Indeed, research suggests that several subcultures based on occupational, professional, or functional divisions usually exist within any large organization.

This is not to say, however, that there also may not be a **dominant culture,** a distinctive, overarching "personality" of an organization—the kind of culture to which we have been referring. An organization's dominant culture reflects its core values, the dominant perceptions that are generally shared throughout the organization. Typically, while members of subcultures may share additional sets of values, they generally also accept the core values of their organizations as a whole. Thus, subcultures should not be thought of as a bunch of separate cultures, but rather "mini" cultures operating within a larger, dominant culture.

The Formation and Maintenance of Organizational Culture

Now that I have described what organizational culture is and how it operates, you are prepared to consider two more issues that are important: how culture is initially created and how it is sustained—that is, what keeps it going once it is created.

HOW IS ORGANIZATIONAL CULTURE CREATED?

Having established what organizational culture is, it is natural to ask how it is created in the first place. Three major factors contribute to the emergence of organizational culture.

Company founders.   First, organizational culture may be traced, at least in part, to the founders of the company.[6] These individuals often possess dynamic personalities, strong values, and a clear vision of how the organization should operate. Because they are on the scene first and play a key role in hiring initial staff, their attitudes and values are readily transmitted to new employees. The result: These views become the accepted ones in the organization and persist as long as the founders are on the scene.

The culture at Microsoft calls for working exceptionally long hours, in large part because that's what cofounder Bill Gates has always done.

For example, the culture at Microsoft calls for working exceptionally long hours, in large part because that's what cofounder Bill

Gates has always done. Sometimes founders' values can continue to drive an organization's culture even after that individual is no longer with the organization. For example, the late Ray Kroc founded the McDonald's restaurant chain on the values of good food at a good value served in clean, family-oriented surroundings—key cultural values that persist at McDonald's today.

Experience with the environment.   Second, organizational culture often develops out of an organization's experience with the external environment. Every organization must find a niche for itself in its industry and in the marketplace. As it struggles to do so in its early days, it may find that some values and practices work better than others. For example, one company may determine that delivering defect-free products is its unique market niche; by doing so, it can build a core of customers who prefer it to competing businesses. As a result, that organization may gradually acquire a deep, shared commitment to high quality. In contrast, another company may find that selling products of moderate quality, but at attractive prices, works best. The result: A dominant value centering on *price leadership* takes shape. In these and countless other ways, an organization's culture is shaped by its interaction with the external environment.

Contact with others.   Third, organizational culture develops out of contact between groups of individuals within an organization. As this occurs, people's interpretations of events and actions are likely to be shared, promoting the development of organizational culture. In other words, organizational culture reflects the fact that people assign similar meaning to various events and actions—that they come to perceive the key aspects of the world, those relevant to the organization's work, in a similar manner (see Chapter 2).

TOOLS FOR TRANSMITTING CULTURE

How are an organization's cultural values transmitted between employees? In other words, how do people come to learn about their organization's culture? Several key mechanisms are involved: *symbols, stories, jargon, ceremonies,* and *statements of principle.*

Symbols: Objects that say more than meets the eye.   First, organizations often rely on **symbols**—material objects that connote meanings that extend beyond their intrinsic content. For example, some companies use impressive buildings to convey the organization's strength and significance, signifying that it is a large, stable place. Other companies rely on slogans to symbolize their values, including such classic examples as General Electric's "Progress is our most important product," or Ford's "Quality is job one." Corporate cars (or even jets!) also are used to convey information about certain aspects of an organization's culture, such as who wields power. Material symbols are potent tools for sending messages about organizational culture. (To demonstrate this phenomenon for yourself, try the **Group Exercise** on p. 331.)

Stories: "In the old days, we used to. . . ".   Organizations also transmit information about culture by virtue of the **stories** that are told in them, both formally and informally. Stories illustrate key aspects of an organization's culture, and telling them can effectively introduce or reaffirm those values to employees.[7] For example, employees of Nike are told tales about how the company was founded in an effort to underscore the company's abiding commitment to athletes (for some examples, see Table 12.1).[8] It

TABLE 12.1 The Nike Story: Just Telling It—And Keeping It Alive
New employees at Nike are told stories that transmit the company's underlying cultural values. The themes of some of the most important Nike stories are summarized here along with several of the ways the company helps keep its heritage alive.(*Source:* Based on information in Ransdell, 2000; see Note 8.)

New employees are told the following stories. . .

- Founder Phil Knight was a middle-distance runner who started the business by selling shoes out of his car.
- Knight's running coach and company cofounder, Bill Bowerman, developed the famous "waffle sole" by pouring rubber into the family waffle iron.
- The late Steve Prefontaine, coached by Bowerman, battled to make running a professional sport and was comitted to helping athletes.

To ensure that these tales of Nike's heritage are kept alive, the company. . .

- Takes new hires to the track where Bowerman coached and the site of Prefontaine's fatal car crash.
- Has created a "heritage wall" in its Eugene, Oregon, store.
- Requires salespeople to tell the Nike story to employees of the retail stores that sell its products.

is important to note that stories need not involve some great event, such as someone who saved the company with a single wise decision, but may be small tales that become legends because they so effectively communicate a message.

Jargon: The special language that defines a culture.   Even without telling stories, the everyday language used in companies helps sustain culture. For example, the slang or *jargon* that is used in a company helps its employees define their identities as members of an organization. For example, someone who works in a human resources department may be found talking about the FMCS (Federal Mediation and Conciliation Service), ERISA (the Employee Retirement Income Security Act), BFOQs (bona fide occupational qualifications), RMs (elections to vote out a union), and other acronyms that sound odd to the uninitiated. Over time, as organizations—or departments within them—develop unique language to describe their work, their terms, although strange to newcomers, serve as a common factor that brings together individuals belonging to a corporate culture or subculture.

Ceremonies: Special events that commemorate corporate values.   Organizations also do a great deal to sustain their cultures by conducting various types of *ceremonies*. Indeed, ceremonies may be seen as celebrations of an organization's basic values and assumptions. Just as a wedding ceremony symbolizes a couple's mutual commitment and a presidential inauguration ceremony marks the beginning of a new presidential term, various organizational ceremonies also celebrate some important accomplishment. For example, one accounting firm celebrated its move to much better facilities by throwing a party, a celebration signifying that it "has arrived" or "made it to the big time." Such ceremonies convey meaning to people inside and outside the organization. As one expert put it, "Ceremonies are to the culture what the movie is to the script . . . values that are difficult to express in any other way."[9]

Statements of principle: Defining culture in writing. A fifth way in which culture is transmitted is via the direct *statements of principle*. Some organizations have explicitly written their principles for all to see. For example, Forrest Mars, the founder of the candy company M&M Mars, developed his "Five Principles of Mars," which still guide his company today.[10] These are quality (everyone is responsible for maintaining quality), responsibility (all employees are responsible for their own actions and decisions), mutuality (creating a situation in which everyone can win), efficiency (most of the company's 41 factories operate continuously), and freedom (giving employees opportunities to shape their futures).

Some companies have chosen to make explicit the moral aspects of their cultures by publishing **codes of ethics**—explicit statements of a company's ethical values. According to Hershey Foods' chief executive officer, Richard Zimmerman, this is an effective device: "[O]ften, an individual joins a firm without recognizing the type of environment in which he will place himself and his career. The loud and clear enunciation of a company's code of conduct . . . [allows] that employee to determine whether or not he [or she] fits that particular culture."[11]

Organizational Culture: Its Consequences and Capacity to Change

By now, you probably are convinced that organizational culture plays an important role in the functioning of organizations. To make this point explicit, I now will examine the various ways in which organizational culture has been found to affect organizations and the behavior of individuals in them. Because some of these effects might be undesirable, organizations are sometimes interested in changing their cultures. Accordingly, we also will consider why and how organizational culture might be changed.

THE EFFECTS OF ORGANIZATIONAL CULTURE

Organizational culture exerts many effects on individuals and organizational processes—some dramatic and others more subtle. Culture generates strong pressures on people to go along, to think and act in ways consistent with the existing culture. Thus, if an organization's culture stresses the importance of product quality and excellent service, its customers generally will find their complaints handled politely and efficiently. If, instead, the organization's culture stresses high output at any cost, customers seeking service may find themselves on a much rockier road. An organization's culture can strongly affect everything from the way employees dress (e.g., the white shirts traditionally worn by male employees of IBM) and the amount of time allowed to elapse before meetings begin, to the speed with which people are promoted.

Turning to the impact of culture on organizational processes, research has focused on the possibility of a link between culture and performance.[12] We know, for example, that to influence performance, organizational culture must be strong. In other words, approval or disapproval must be expressed to those who act in ways consistent or inconsistent with the culture, respectively, and there must be widespread agreement on values among organizational members. Only if these conditions prevail will a link between organizational culture and performance be observed.

> *People seeking employment should examine carefully the prevailing culture of an organization before deciding to join it. If they don't, they run the risk of finding themselves in a situation where their own values and those of their company clash.*

This idea has important implications both for individuals and for organizations. First, it suggests that people seeking employment should examine carefully the prevailing culture of an organization before deciding to join it. If they don't, they run the risk of finding themselves in a situation where their own values and those of their company clash. Second, it also suggests that organizations should focus on attracting individuals whose values match their own (what is referred to as **person–organization fit**). This involves identifying key aspects of organizational culture, communicating these to prospective employees, and selecting those for whom the person–organization fit is best. Considerable effort may be involved in completing these tasks. Given that high levels of person–organization fit can contribute to commitment, satisfaction, and low rates of turnover among employees, however, the effort appears to be worthwhile.

WHY AND HOW DOES ORGANIZATIONAL CULTURE CHANGE?

My earlier comments about the relative stability of organizational culture may have left you wondering if and when organizational culture ever changes. Why isn't it simply passed from one generation of organizational members to the next in a totally static manner? The basic answer, of course, is that the world in which all organizations operate constantly changes (see Chapter 14). External events such as shifts in market conditions, new technology, altered government policies, and many other factors change over time, necessitating changes in an organization's mode of doing business—and hence, its culture.

Composition of the workforce.　Over time, the people entering an organization may differ in important ways from those already in it, and these differences may impinge on the existing culture of the organization. For example, people from different ethnic or cultural backgrounds may have contrasting views about various aspects of behavior at work. For instance, they may hold dissimilar views about style of dress, the importance of being on time (or even what constitutes "on time" behavior), the level of deference one should show to higher-status people, and even what foods should be served in the company cafeteria. In other words, as large numbers of people with different backgrounds and values enter the workplace, changes in organizational culture may be expected to follow.

Mergers and acquisitions.　Another, and even more dramatic, source of cultural change is *mergers* and *acquisitions*, events in which one organization purchases or otherwise absorbs another.[13] When this occurs, there is likely to be a careful analysis of the financial and material assets of the acquired organization. However, it is rare that any consideration is given to the acquired organization's culture. This is unfortunate, insofar as there have been several cases in which the merger of two organizations with incompatible cultures has led to serious problems referred to as **culture**

Life in companies with incompatible cultures tends to be conflict-ridden and highly disruptive, often resulting in arguments and considerable uncertainty about what to do. In some cases, organizations have even been known to disband because of extreme culture clashes.

clashes. As you might imagine, life in companies with incompatible cultures tends to be conflict-ridden and highly disruptive, often resulting in arguments and considerable uncertainty about what to do. In some cases, organizations have even been known to disband because of extreme culture clashes. For several good examples of culture clashes resulting from mergers and acquisitions, see Table 12.2.[14]

Planned organizational change. Even if an organization doesn't change by acquiring another, cultural change still may result from other planned changes, such as conscious decisions to alter the internal structure or the basic operations of an organization (see Chapter 14). Once such decisions are reached, many practices in the company that both reflect and contribute to its culture may change. A good example of this can be seen at IBM.[15] In response to staggering losses, IBM realized that one of its problems was that it was heavily bureaucratic, making it difficult for lower-level people to make on-the-spot decisions. As a result, IBM changed the nature of its corporate structure from one in which there was a steep hierarchy with many layers of management to a "delayered" one with far fewer managers. As you might imagine, the newly "right-sized" IBM developed a new corporate culture. Once known for a highly rigid, autocratic culture in which decision making was centralized in the hands of just a few, the reorganized company is now much more open and democratic in its approach than ever before.

Responding to the Internet. There can be no doubt that the Internet is a major influence on organizational culture these days. Compared to traditional businesses, where things move slowly, and people look at change skeptically, the culture of Internet businesses is agile, fast-paced, and receptive to new solutions.[16] Information sharing is key, as such organizations not only accept but also embrace the expansion of communication networks and business relationships across organizational boundaries. When traditional bricks-and-mortar businesses expand into e-commerce, changes in their organizational culture follow suit. We see this, for example, at the venerable investment firm, Merrill Lynch, which launched a Web site for trading stock in an effort to compete with brokerage firms such as E*Trade, which do business only online. The organizational culture at this venerable, traditional firm has become far more fast-paced ever since it adapted to the Internet economy.

To conclude, it is clear that although organizational culture is generally stable, it is not immutable. In fact, culture often evolves in response to outside forces (e.g., changes in workforce composition) as well as deliberate attempts to change the design of organizations (e.g., through mergers and corporate restructuring). An important aspect of culture that organizations frequently strive to change is the degree to which it approaches problems in creative and innovative ways. With this in mind, I will now turn the attention to the topics of *creativity* and *innovation* in organizations.

TABLE 12.2 Organizational Culture Clashes: Three Examples

Three major examples of culture clashes in the past few decades are summarized here, along with the cast of characters. As you read about these, think about what it must have been like to work in these companies at the time the clashes were occurring. (*Source:* Based on information from references cited in Note 14.)

Original Company and CEO at time of merger	Original company and CEO at time of merger	New Company (merger date) and original officers	Nature of Culture Conflict
Chrysler *Robert J. Eaton, CEO*	**Daimler-Benz** *Jüergen E. Schrempp, CEO*	**Daimler-Chrysler (1998)** *Robert J. Eaton, and Jüergen E. Schrempp, co-CEOs*	The so-called "merger of equals" was decidedly unequal. Executives' lifestyles were in sharp contrast. Those who came from Chrysler traveled together to meetings in minivans and flew economy class. However, Daimler-Benz officials arrived in chauffer-driven Mercedes-Benz sedans and flew first class. While spending six months working this out, executives ignored important corporate problems. Sales have slumped and many officials have left the company. In 2001, Chrysler laid off a quarter of its employees.
RJ Reynolds *Tylee Wilson, CEO*	**Nabisco** *Ross Johnson, CEO*	**RJR Nabisco (1988)** *Ross Johnson, CEO*	Nabisco executives had a fast-paced lifestyle, with perks such as corporate jets, penthouse apartments, and lavish parties. RJ Reynolds was characterized by a strong work ethic, much less autonomy for employees, and a deep commitment to its local community. A bitter feud erupted and Johnson fired RJ Reynolds executives.
HFS (franchising company) *Henry Silverman, CEO*	**CUC International (membership-club company)** *Walter Forbes, CEO*	**Cendant (1997)** *Henry Silverman, CEO; and Walter Forbes, chairman of the board*	Silverman was a control freak who insisted on seeing and knowing everything. However, Forbes saw himself as a visionary and left the details to others. Power clashes grew, eventually leading someone to blow the whistle on CUC officials for creating phony profits. The resulting scandal harmed the company greatly.

Creativity in Individuals and Teams

Although you probably have no difficulty recognizing creativity when you see it, defining creativity can be a bit more challenging. Scientists define **creativity** as the process by which individuals or teams produce novel and useful ideas.[17] With this definition to guide us, I will explain how the process of creativity operates. Specifically, I will begin by describing the components of individual and team creativity and then outline several steps you can take to enhance your own creativity.

COMPONENTS OF INDIVIDUAL AND TEAM CREATIVITY

Creativity in individuals and teams is composed of three basic components—domain-relevant skills, creativity-relevant skills, and intrinsic task motivation.

Domain-relevant skills. Whether it's the manual dexterity required to play the piano or to use a computer keyboard, or the sense of rhythm and knowledge of music needed to conduct an orchestra, specific skills and abilities are necessary to perform these tasks. In fact, any task you might undertake requires certain talents, knowledge, or skills. These skills and abilities that we already have constitute the raw materials needed for creativity to occur. After all, without the capacity to perform a certain task at even a basic level, one has no hope of demonstrating creativity on that task. For example, before he can even begin to create stunning automotive stunts, a stunt driver must have the basic skills of dexterity and eye–hand coordination required to drive a car.

Creativity-relevant skills. Beyond the basic skills, being creative also requires additional skills—special abilities that help people approach the things they do in novel ways. Specifically, when fostering creativity, it helps to do the following:

- *Break mental sets and take new perspectives.* Creativity is enhanced when people do not limit themselves to old ways of doing things. Restricting oneself to the past can inhibit creativity. Take a fresh look at even the most familiar things. This involves what is known as **divergent thinking**—the process of reframing familiar problems in unique ways. Divergent thinking is often promoted by asking people to identify as many unusual uses for common objects as possible.
- *Understand complexities.* Instead of making things overly simplistic, don't be afraid to consider complex ways in which ideas may be interrelated.
- *Keep options open and avoid premature judgments.* Creative people are willing to consider all options. To do so, they consider all the angles and avoid reaching conclusions prematurely. People are particularly good at this when they are new to an organization and, therefore, don't know enough to accept everything the way it is. With this in mind, some companies actually prefer hiring executives from outside their industry.
- *Follow creativity heuristics.* People sometimes follow certain strategies, known as **creativity heuristics,** to help them come up with creative new ideas. These are rules that people follow to help them approach tasks in novel ways. They may involve such techniques as considering the counterintuitive and using analogies.
- *Use productive forgetting.* Sometimes our creativity is inhibited by becoming fixated on certain ideas that we just can't seem to get out of our heads. With this in

mind, it helps to practice **productive forgetting**—the ability to abandon unproductive ideas and temporarily put aside stubborn problems until new approaches can be considered.

To help individuals and groups become more creative, many organizations invite employees to participate in training exercises designed to promote some of these skills. (These may include exercises similar to the one described in the **Self-Assessment Exercise** on pp. 329-331. Try the exercise described here to experience firsthand how it may help your own creative juices flow.)

Intrinsic task motivation. The first two components of creativity, domain-relevant skills and creativity-relevant skills, focus on what people are *capable* of doing. However, the third component, intrinsic task motivation, refers to what people are *willing* to do. The idea is simple: For someone to be creative, he or she must be interested in performing the task in question. In other words, there must be a high degree of **intrinsic task motivation**—the motivation to do work because it is interesting, engaging, or positively challenging. Someone who has the capacity to be creative, but who isn't motivated to do what it takes to produce creative outcomes, certainly wouldn't be considered creative. People are most likely to be highly creative when they are passionate about their work.[18]

Intrinsic task motivation tends to be high under several conditions. For example, when an individual has a *personal interest* in the task at hand, he or she will be motivated to perform it—and may go on to do so creatively. However, anyone who doesn't find a task interesting surely isn't going to perform it long enough to demonstrate any signs of creativity. Likewise, task motivation will be high whenever an individual perceives that he or she has internal reasons to be performing that task. People who come to believe that they are performing a task for some external reason—such as high pay or pressure from a boss—are unlikely to find the work inherently interesting, in and of itself, and are unlikely to show much creativity when performing it.

Putting it all together. As you might imagine, the components of creativity are important insofar as they can be used to paint a picture of when people will be creative. In this connection, scientists claim that people will be at their most creative when they have high amounts of all three of these components (see Figure 12.2).

Specifically, it has been claimed that there is a multiplicative relationship between these three components of creativity. Thus, if any one component is low, the overall level of creativity will be low. In fact, people will not be creative at all if any one of these components is at zero (i.e., it is completely missing). This makes sense if you think about it. After all, you would be unlikely to be creative at a job if you didn't have the skills needed to do it, regardless of how motivated you were to be creative and how well-practiced you were at coming up with new ideas. Likewise, creativity would be expected to be nonexistent if either creativity-relevant skills or motivation were zero. The practical implications are clear: To be as creative as possible, people must strive toward attaining

To be as creative as possible, people must strive toward attaining high levels of all three components of creativity— task skills, creative skills, and intrinsic motivation.

FIGURE 12.2 Components of Creativity

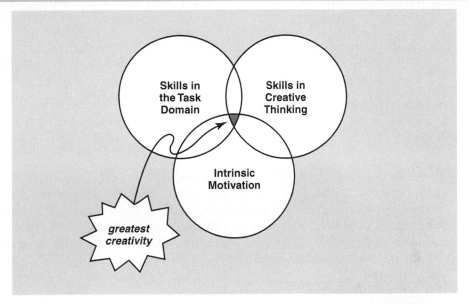

Scientists claim that people will be at their most creative when they exhibit high levels of the three factors shown here. (*Source:* Adapted from Amabile, 1988; see Note 17.)

high levels of all three components of creativity—task skills, creative skills, and intrinsic motivation.

A MODEL OF THE CREATIVE PROCESS

Although it isn't always obvious to us how people come up with creative ideas, scientists have developed a model that outlines the various stages of the creative process.[19] Specifically, this model specifies that the process of creativity occurs in the following four stages.:

1. *Prepare to be creative.* Although we often believe that our most creative ideas come "out of thin air," people are at their most creative when they have made suitable preparations. This involves gathering the appropriate information and concentrating on the problem.
2. *Allow ideas to incubate.* Because ideas take time to develop, creativity can be enhanced by putting the problem out of our conscious minds and allowing it to incubate. If you've ever been successful at coming up with a fresh approach to a problem by putting it aside and working on something else, you know what I am describing. The phrase "sleep on it" captures this stage of the process.
3. *Document insight.* At some point during the first two stages, you are likely to come up with a unique idea. However, that idea may be lost if it is not documented. With this in mind, many people carry small voice recorders that allow them to capture their ideas before they become lost in the maze of other ideas.

Likewise writers keep diaries, artists keep sketch pads, and songwriters keep tape recorders handy to capture ideas whenever inspiration strikes.

4. *Verify ideas.* Coming up with an idea is one thing, but verifying that it's any good is quite another. Assessing the usefulness of an idea requires consciously thinking about it and verifying it, such as by seeing what others have to say about it. In other words, you want to see if those ideas that came to you in a moment of inspiration in the middle of the night are still any good in the morning light.

Knowing about the creative process is particularly useful insofar as it can be applied to promoting individual and team productivity. I will now turn to the process of doing so.

Promoting Creativity in Organizations

Highly creative people are an asset to any organization. But what exactly do organizations do to promote creativity within their ranks? In general terms, the answer lies in things that we can do as individuals and that organizations can do as a whole. Specifically, two major approaches may be identified—training people to be creative and developing creative work environments.

TRAINING PEOPLE TO BE CREATIVE

It is true that some people, by nature, are more creative than others. Such individuals are inclined to approach various situations in new ways and tend not to be bogged down by previous ways of doing things.[20] However, there are still skills that anyone can develop to become more creative. Generally, training people to become more creative involves three steps.[21] These are as follows:

Encourage openness to new ideas. Many good ideas go undeveloped because they are not in keeping with the current way of doing things. Becoming more creative requires allowing oneself to be open to new ideas, or as it is often described—*thinking outside the box*. Some companies do this by sending their employees on *thinking expeditions*—trips specifically designed to put people in challenging situations in an effort to help them think differently and become more creative. According to the CEO of a company that specializes in running such expeditions for clients, these trips "push people out of their 'stupid zone'—a place of mental and physical normalcy—so that they can start to think differently," adding, "it's an accelerated unlearning experience."[22]

Take the time to understand the problem. Meaningful ideas rarely come to those who don't fully understand the problem at hand. Only when time is taken to understand the many different facets of the issue can people be equipped to develop creative solutions. Consider, for example, BrightHouse, the 17-employee Atlanta-based company that specializes in developing new ideas for its clients (among them have been Coca-Cola, Home Depot, and Georgia-Pacific).[23] For a fee of $500,000, the entire staff devotes a full 10 weeks to the issues their clients have in mind (e.g., how to improve upon billboard advertising at Turner Field, the home of baseball's Atlanta Braves).

Develop divergent thinking. As I noted earlier, divergent thinking involves taking new approaches to old problems. Teaching people various tactics for divergent thinking allows problems to incubate, setting the stage for creative new ideas to develop. One popular way of developing divergent thinking is known as **morphology.** A morphological analysis of a problem involves identifying its basic elements and combining them in systematically different ways. (For an example of this approach, and for a chance to practice it yourself, see the **Self-Assessment Exercise** on p. 329.)

DEVELOPING CREATIVE WORK ENVIRONMENTS

Thus far, I have identified ways of making people more creative as individuals. In conjunction with these approaches, it is also useful for organizations to take concrete steps to change work environments in ways that bring out people's creativity. Several such approaches may be identified.[24]

Provide autonomy. It has been established that people are especially creative when they are given the freedom to control their own behavior—that is, they have *autonomy* (see Chapter 4) and are *empowered* to make decisions (see Chapter 11). At the Japanese video game manufacturer, Nintendo, creativity is so important that no one considers it odd when designers leave work to go see a movie or a play.

Allow ideas to cross-pollinate. People who work on just one project run the risk of getting stale, whereas those who work on several are likely to come into contact with different people, and have a chance of applying an idea they picked up on one project to another project. This is done all the time at IDEO, the company described in this chapter's opening case. For example, in coming up with an idea about how to develop a more comfortable handle for a scooter, designers might use ideas they picked up while working on a project involving the design of a more comfortable computer mouse.

Make jobs intrinsically interesting. Research has shown that people are inclined to be creative when they are intrinsically interested in the work they do. After all, nobody will want to invest the effort it takes to be creative at a task that is uninteresting. With this in mind, creativity can be promoted by enhancing the degree to which tasks are intrinsically interesting to people. The essence of the idea is to turn work into play by making it interesting. For some specific suggestions on how to do this, see Table 12.3.

This approach is used routinely at Play, a marketing agency in Richmond, Virginia. Instead of coming up with ideas by sitting in boring meetings, staff members are encouraged to play (much like at IDEO, as described in this chapter's opening case). For example, to aid the process of coming up with a new marketing campaign for the Weather Channel, employees spent time in a corner office developing costumes for superheroes. According to cofounder Andy Stefanovich, the idea is simple: "When you turn work into a place that encourages people to be themselves, have fun, and take risks, you fuel and unleash their creativity. The best ideas come from playful minds. And the way to tap into that playfulness is to play—together."[25]

Set your own creative goals. Being free to do as you wish does not necessarily imply goofing off. In fact, the freedom to make your own decisions pays off most handsomely when people set their own creative goals. For example, the famous inventor Thomas A.

TABLE 12.3 Boosting Creativity by Making Jobs More Intrinsically Interesting

As summarized here, several specific features of the work environment can boost a job's intrinsic interest, hence, the degree to which people are likely to demonstrate creativity. (*Source:* Based on suggestions from Amabile, 2000; see Note 18.)

Characteristic	Description
Challenge	People are likely to be creative at tasks they find interesting because they are required to work hard at them.
Autonomy	People are likely to be interested their work, and be creative in performing it, when they are free to determine how to do it.
Work group support	Intrinsic interest in a task is enhanced, as is creativity, when others share ideas about it and have the skills needed to perform it.
Supervisory and organizational encouragement	Workers are likely to be interested in performing a job, and to do it creatively, when they believe their immediate supervisor, or the organization as a whole, encourages their efforts.
Absence of organizational impediments	People will be interested in working, and likely to be creative, when key organizational impediments are eliminated, such as political problems, negative criticism of new ideas, and pressure to maintain the status quo.

> *The famous inventor Thomas A. Edison set the goal of having a minor invention every 10 days and a major invention every 6 months. This kept Edison focused on being creative—and, with over 1,000 patients in his name, he clearly did an outstanding job of meeting his goals.*

Edison set the goal of having a minor invention every 10 days and a major invention every 6 months. This kept Edison focused on being creative—and, with over 1,000 patents in his name, he clearly did an outstanding job of meeting his goals. It is important to underscore that I'm not talking about strict external pressure to be creative, which rarely results in anything positive. However, creativity is aided when people are encouraged to set their own goals about being creative.

Support creativity at high organizational levels. Nobody in an organization is going to go out of his or her way to be creative if it is not welcomed by the bosses. Supervisors, team leaders, and top executives must encourage employees to take risks if they are to have any chance of being creative. At the same time, this involves accepting any failures that result. This idea is embraced by Livio D. DeSimone, the CEO of 3M, one of the most innovative companies in the world. "Failure is not fatal," he says, adding that, "Innovations are simply chance breakthroughs. And when you take a chance, there is always the possibility of a failure."[26] In the **Winning Practices** section on the following page, I describe the many efforts taken to promote creativity at 3M. As you read this section, you will find that this company relies upon several of the techniques described here.

WINNING PRACTICES

Scotch-Brand Creativity at 3M

3M is one of those companies whose products just cannot be avoided. Whether it's Scotch Magic Transparent Tape, Post-it Notes, Scotch-Brite Scouring Pads, Scotchgard fabric protector, or O-Cel-O Sponges, the 3M name appears everywhere around the house. And, although you might not know it, hundreds of 3M products also are widely used in hospitals, factories, and along our roadways. In fact, there are over 900 different varieties of Scotch tape alone! From its beginning about 100 years ago, 3M began producing innovative products that met customers' needs.[27] (Among the first was 3M-Ite, a cloth abrasive that was used to help sand the contoured areas of automobile bodies without giving off harmful irritants.)

If there's a problem, chances are good that 3M employees have developed a product to solve it. For example, to help address the problem of making batteries that are powerful enough to run notebook computers but small enough to be toted around easily, 3M did not develope a new battery, but a new way of making computer screens draw less energy. And, if you've broken a limb in recent years, chances are good that your orthopedic physician set your break using fiberglass-reinforced synthetic casting tape (Scotchcast Casting Tape) instead of the weaker and heavier wet plaster casts that were used for hundreds of years.

What makes 3M's engineers so highly creative? Among the answers is the company's "15 percent rule," which allows technical personnel to devote as much as 15 percent of their time to projects of their own choosing without getting approval from others. From the company's early days, it was recognized that when technical people were allowed to tinker as they wished, they came up with ideas that could not be envisioned by management. To this day, the 15 percent rule is alive and well at 3M.

Furthering its creative culture, 3M encourages cross-pollination of ideas between departments. With this in mind, the company promotes both formal and informal networking among technical personnel. For example, 3M divisions regularly hold fairs in which they show off their latest technologies to colleagues from other divisions.

Management's primary objective at 3M is to foster creativity and innovation. With this in mind, 3M has long challenged its personnel to produce new products following a "25/5 rule." That is, 25 percent of annual sales were to come from products that were around for no more than 5 years. Then, in 1992, Chairman and CEO L. D. DeSimone noted that product life cycles were shrinking and introduced a more difficult goal: From then on, 30 percent of sales were to come from products that had been around for no more than 4 years. This goal really sparked the creative fires, and it was met only two years later.

Although most companies recognize their employees' accomplishments with some form of monetary reward, 3M takes things a step further by giving a variety of special, highly coveted awards to employees who have been among the most creative. For example, 3M has established the "Carlton Society," an honorary organization that recognizes extraordinary contributions to 3M's science and technology. Among its members are those individuals who have invented such ubiquitous products as Post-it Notes, Scotch Magic Transparent Tape, and Scotchgard fabric protector. Various grants are also given to both technical and nontechnical personnel to help them develop innovations whose expenses fall outside their department's regular budgets.[28] Obviously, 3M is a company that goes out of its way to ensure that its employees are highly creative. To a large degree, this focus on creativity has been responsible for the company's century-long record of success.

Questions for Discussion

1. A few years ago, 3M quietly did away with the 30/4 rule. Why do you think this decision was made?
2. Do you think the people who work at 3M are naturally creative, or does the environment bring out whatever creativity they have, or both? Explain.
3. What other techniques might 3M use to promote creativity within its ranks?

The Process of Innovation

Now that you know about the process of creativity, you are prepared to understand situations in which people implement their creative skills for the sake of improving their organizations. This is the process of **innovation**—the successful implementation of creative ideas within an organization. To understand this process I will review the various stages through which innovation progresses. Before doing this, however, I will begin by identifying the various components of innovation.

COMPONENTS OF INNOVATION: BASIC BUILDING BLOCKS

Earlier, I depicted individual creativity as being composed of three components— motivation, resources, and skills. As it works out, these same components are involved in organizational innovation as well, albeit in somewhat different ways.

Motivation to innovate. Just as individual creativity requires that people are motivated to do what it takes to be creative, organizational innovation requires that organizations have the kind of cultures that encourage innovation. When top executives fail to promote a vision of innovation, and accept the status quo, change is unlikely. However, at companies such as Microsoft, where leaders (including cofounder, Bill Gates) envision innovation as being part of the natural order of things, it is not surprising that innovative efforts are constantly underway.

Resources to innovate. Again, a parallel to individual creativity is in order. Just as people must have certain basic skills to be creative, so too must organizations possess certain basic resources that make innovation possible. For example, to be innovative, at the very least, organizations must have what it takes in terms of human and financial resources. After all, unless the necessary skilled people and deep pockets are available to do what it takes to innovate, stagnation is likely to result.

Innovation management. Finally, just as individuals must hone special skills needed to be creative, so too must organizations develop special ways of managing people so as to encourage innovation—that is, *skills in innovation management.* Most notable in this regard is the matter of *balance.* Specifically, managers help promote innovation when they show balance with respect to three key matters: goals, reward systems, and time pressure (see Figure 12.3).

FIGURE 12.3 Skills in Innovation Management: A Careful Balancing Act

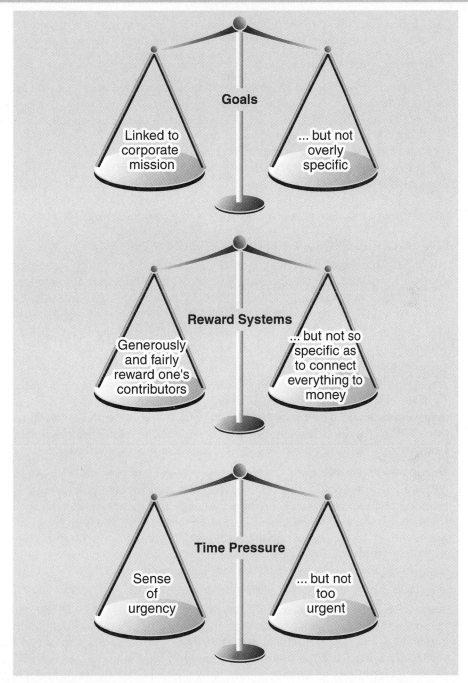

Goals

Linked to corporate mission

... but not overly specific

Reward Systems

Generously and fairly reward one's contributors

...but not so specific as to connect everything to money

Time Pressure

Sense of urgency

... but not too urgent

Managing innovation requires carefully balancing the three matters identified here. (*Source:* Based on information reported by Amabile, 1988; see Note 17.)

- Organizational innovation is promoted when *goals* are carefully linked to the corporate mission. However, they should not be so specific as to tie the hands of those who put them into practice. Innovation is unlikely when such restrictions are imposed.
- *Reward systems* should generously and fairly recognize one's contributions, but they should not be so specific as to connect literally every move to a bonus or some type of monetary reward. To do so discourages people from taking the kinds of risks that make innovation possible.
- Innovation management requires carefully balancing the *time pressures* under which employees are placed. If pressures are too great, people may be unimaginative and offer routine solutions. By the same token, if pressure is too weak, employees may have no sense of time urgency and believe that the project is too unimportant to warrant any creative attention on their part.

STAGES OF THE ORGANIZATIONAL INNOVATION PROCESS

Any CEO who snaps her fingers one day and expects her troops to be innovative on command will surely be in for disappointment. Innovation does not happen all at once. Rather, innovation occurs gradually, through a series of stages. Specifically, scientists have identified five specific stages through which the process of organizational innovation progresses.[29] I will now describe each of these five stages (see the summary in Figure 12.4):

Stage 1: Setting the agenda.   The first stage of the process of innovation begins by setting the agenda for innovation. This involves creating a *mission statement*—a document describing an organization's overall direction and general goals for accomplishing that movement. The component of innovation that is most involved here is motivation. After all, the highest-ranking officials of the organization must be highly committed to innovation before they will initiate a push toward it.

Stage 2: Setting the stage.   Once an organization's mission has been established, it is prepared to set the stage for innovation. This may involve narrowing down certain broad goals into narrower, more specific tasks and gathering the resources to meet them. It also may involve assessing the environment, both outside and inside the organization, searching for anything that may either support or inhibit later efforts to "break the rules" by being creative. Effectively setting the stage for innovation requires using the skills necessary for innovation management as well as the full use of the organization's human and financial resources.

Stage 3: Producing the ideas.   This stage of the process involves coming up with new ideas and testing them. It is in this third stage that individual and small group creativity enters the picture. As a result, all of the components of individual creativity mentioned earlier are involved. What's more, these may combine in important ways with various organizational factors. For example, an individual who has the skills and motivation to be highly creative might find his motivation waning as he attempts to introduce novel new ideas in an organization that is not committed to innovation, and that fails to make the necessary resources available. By contrast, the highly innovative nature of an organization may bring out the more creative side of an individual who may not have been especially creative.

FIGURE 12.4 The Process of Innovation

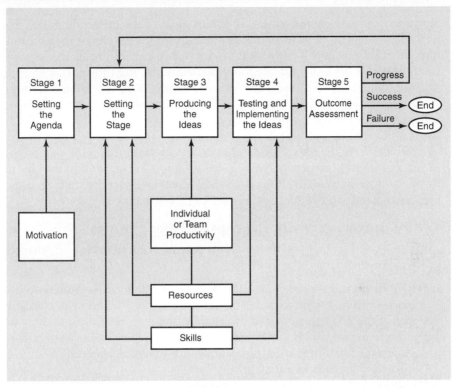

The innovation process consists of the various components, and follows the steps, shown here. (*Source:* Adapted from Amabile, 1988; see Note 17.)

Stage 4: Testing and implementing the ideas.   This is the stage where implementation occurs. Now, after an initial group of individuals has developed an idea, other parts of the organization get involved. For example, a prototype product may be developed and tested, and market research may be conducted. In short, input from the many functional areas of the organization is provided.

I note in Figure 12.4 that skills in innovation management are very important in this stage of the process. In large part this is because for good ideas to survive it is necessary for them to be "nourished" and supported throughout the organization. Even the best ideas may be "killed off" if people in some parts of the organization are not supportive. For this same reason, resources in the task domain are another important component involved in this stage. After all, unless adequate amounts

> *For good ideas to survive it is necessary for them to be "nourished" and supported throughout the organization. Even the best ideas may be "killed off" if people in some parts of the organization are not supportive.*

of money, personnel, material systems, and information are provided, the idea will be unlikely to survive.

Stage 5: Outcome assessment. The final stage of the process involves assessing the new idea. What happens to that idea depends on the results of the assessment. Three outcomes are possible. If the resulting idea (e.g., a certain product or service) has been a total success, it will be accepted and carried out in the future. This ends the process. Likewise, the process is over if the idea has been a complete failure. In this case, there is no good reason to continue. However, if the new idea shows promise and makes some progress toward the organization's objectives, but still has problems, the process starts all over again at Stage 2.

Although this five-stage process does not account for all innovations you may find in organizations, this general model does a good job of identifying the major steps through which most innovations go as they travel along their path from a specific organizational need to a product or service that meets that need.

SUMMARY: HAVE I MET THE LEARNING OBJECTIVES?

You can be certain that you have met the learning objectives for this chapter found on p. 305 if you understand the following:

1. **DEFINE organizational culture and IDENTIFY the various functions it serves in organizations.** Organizational culture is a cognitive framework consisting of assumptions and values shared by organization members. It plays three major roles in organizations: (a) It provides a sense of identity for its members, (b) it generates commitment to the organization's mission, and (c) it clarifies and reinforces standards of behavior.

2. **IDENTIFY the ways in which organizational cultures differ and the mechanisms through which organizational culture is transmitted.** Organizational cultures differ from one another with respect to: (a) sensitivity to the needs of customers and employees, (b) interest in having employees generate new ideas, (c) value placed on taking risks, (d) openness of available communication options, (e) friendliness and congeniality of the employees toward one another, and (f) the value placed on people in the organization. Organizational culture may be transmitted through the use of symbols, stories, jargon, ceremonies, and statements of principle.

3. **IDENTIFY the factors responsible for creating organizational culture and for getting it to change.** Organizational culture is created by the influence of company founders, an organization's experience with the environment, and contact between groups of people. Although organizational culture tends to be stable, it is subject to change. Among the factors most responsible for changing organizational culture are the composition of the workforce, mergers and acquisitions, planned organizational change, and responding to the Internet.

4. **DEFINE creativity and DESCRIBE the basic components of individual and team creativity.** Creativity is the process by which individuals or teams produce novel and useful ideas. Creativity in organizations is based on three fundamental components: domain-relevant skills (basic knowledge needed to perform the task at hand), creativity-relevant skills (special abilities needed to generate creative

new ideas), and intrinsic task motivation (people's willingness to perform creative acts).

5. **DESCRIBE various approaches to promoting creativity in organizations.** Organizational creativity can be promoted by: (a) training people to be creative (e.g., by encouraging openness to new ideas, taking the time to understand the problem, and developing *divergent thinking*), and (b) developing creative work environments (e.g., by providing autonomy, allowing ideas to cross-pollinate, making jobs intrinsically interesting, setting your own creative goals, and supporting creativity at high organizational levels).

6. **IDENTIFY the basic components of innovation and the various stages of the innovation process.** Innovation is composed of three components that are analogous to the three components of creativity. These are motivation to innovate, resources to innovate, and innovation management. These components are used in a process that generally proceeds in five stages: setting the agenda, setting the stage, producing the ideas, testing and implementing the ideas, and assessing the outcome.

You Be the Consultant

The president of your organization, a small manufacturing company, has been complaining that sales are stagnant. A key problem, you discover, is that the market for the products your firm makes is fully developed—and, frankly, the products themselves are not very exciting. No one seems to care about doing anything innovative. Instead, the employees seem more interested in doing things the way they have always done them. Answer the following questions based on the material in this chapter.

1. What factors do you suspect are responsible for the way the culture in this organization has been over the years?
2. What do you recommend should be done to enhance the creativity of this company's employees?
3. What could be done to help make the company's products more innovative?

SELF-ASSESSMENT EXERCISE

Morphology in Action: Using the Idea Box

One day, the marketing director of a company that makes laundry hampers was tinkering with ways of boosting sales in a stagnant, mature market.[30] To trigger his imagination, he thought explicitly about something that most of us take for granted—the basic parameters of laundry hampers. Specifically, he noted that they differed in four basic ways: the materials of which they were made, their shape, their finish, and how they are positioned. For each of these dimensions, he identified five different answers, resulting in the following chart, known as an *idea box*.

Improve Design for Laundry Hamper

	Material	Shape	Finish	Position
1	Wicker	Square	Painted	Sits on Floor
2	Plastic	Cylindrical	Painted	On Ceiling
3	Paper	Rectangle	Clear	On Wall
4	Metal	Hexagonal	Luminous	Chute to Basement
5	Net Material	Cube	Neon	On Door

Source: Reprinted with permission from *Thinkertoys* by Michael Michalko. Ten Speed Press, Berkeley, California.

Then, by randomly combining one item from each column—net material, cylindrical shape, painted finish, and positioning on a door—he came up with a completely new idea. It was a laundry hamper made to look like a basketball net: about a yard of netting attached to a cylindrical hoop, hung from a backboard attached to the back of a door.

With some quick math, you can see that this particular idea box generates 3,125 different combinations. Given that this is a far greater number of ideas than you could probably generate without the aid of the idea box, it makes sense to practice generating idea boxes for situations you face in which creative new solutions are required. Nurture your own creativity by following the four simple steps identified by creativity expert Michael Michalko.[31]

Steps for Generating an Idea Box

1. *Specify the challenge you are facing.* Although you may not be interested in developing exciting new laundry baskets, you must start at the same point indicated in our example—that is, by identifying exactly what you are attempting to do.
2. *Select the parameters of your challenge.* Material, shape, finish, and position were the parameters of the laundry basket problem. What are yours? To help determine if the parameter you are considering is important enough to add, ask yourself if the challenge would still exist without that parameter.
3. *List variations.* Our example shows five variations of each parameter, but feel free to list as many key ones as you can. After all, as your idea box grows larger, it gets increasingly difficult to spot new ideas. (For example, if your idea box had 10 parameters, each of which contained 10 variations, you'd face 10 billion potential combinations to consider—hardly a practical task!)
4. *Try different combinations.* After your idea box is completed, work your way through the box to find some of the most promising combinations. Begin by examining the entire box, and then eventually limit yourself to the most promising combinations.

Questions to Consider

1. Have you ever used the idea box, or something similar to it, before now? If so, how effectively has it worked?
2. For what kinds of challenges is the idea box most useful and least useful?

3. It has been said that generating an idea box is similar to writing a poem. How is this so?

GROUP EXERCISE

What Does Your Work Space Say About Your Organizational Culture?

Newcomers' impressions of an organization's culture depend greatly on the visual images of that organization they first see. Even without knowing anything about an organization, just seeing the workplace sends a message, intentional or unintentional, regarding what that organization is like. The following exercise is designed to demonstrate this phenomenon.

Directions

1. Each member of the class should take several photographs of his or her workplace and select the three that best capture, in his or her own mind, the essence of what that organization is like.
2. One member of the class should identify the company depicted in his or her photos, describe the type of work it does, and present the photos to the rest of the class.
3. Members of the class should then rate the organization shown in the photos using the following dimensions. Circle the number that comes closest to your feelings about the company shown.

unfamiliar	: 1 : 2 : 3 : 4 : 5 : 6 : 7 :	familiar
unsuccessful	: 1 : 2 : 3 : 4 : 5 : 6 : 7 :	successful
unfriendly	: 1 : 2 : 3 : 4 : 5 : 6 : 7 :	friendly
unproductive	: 1 : 2 : 3 : 4 : 5 : 6 : 7 :	productive
not innovative	: 1 : 2 : 3 : 4 : 5 : 6 : 7 :	innovative
uncaring	: 1 : 2 : 3 : 4 : 5 : 6 : 7 :	caring
conservative	: 1 : 2 : 3 : 4 : 5 : 6 : 7 :	risky
closed	: 1 : 2 : 3 : 4 : 5 : 6 : 7 :	open

4. Take turns sharing your individual reactions to each set of photos. Compare the responses of the student whose company pictures were examined with those of the students who were seeing the photos for the first time.
5. Repeat this process using the photos of other students' organizations.

Questions for Discussion

1. For each set of photos examined, how much agreement or disagreement was there within the class about the companies rated?
2. For each set of photos examined, how close did the descriptions of members of the class come to the photographers' assessments of their own companies? In other words, how well did the photos capture the culture of the organization as perceived by an "insider"?
3. As a whole, were people more accurate in assessing the culture of companies with which they were already familiar than those they didn't already know? If so, why do you think this occurred?

NOTES

Case Notes

Anonymous. (1999, September 13). Seriously silly. *Business Week,* p. F14. Brown, E. (1999, April 12). A day at Innovation U. *Fortune,* pp. 163–165. Garner, R. (2000, April). Innovation for fun and profit. *Upside,* pp. 88–90, 92, 94, 96.

Chapter Notes

[1] Schneider, B. (1990). *Organizational climate and culture.* San Francisco: Jossey-Bass.

[2] Schein, E. H. (1985). *Organizational culture and leadership.* San Francisco: Jossey-Bass.

[3] Martin, J. (1996) *Cultures in organizations.* New York: Oxford University Press.

[4] Toxic shock? (1999, April). *Fast Company,* p. 38.

[5] Webber, A. M. (1998, November). Danger: Toxic company. *Fast Company,* pp. 152–159.

[6] Martin, J., Sitkin, S. B., & Boehm, M. (1985). Founders and the elusiveness of a cultural legacy. In P J. Frost, L. F. Moore, M. R. Louis, C. C. Lundberg, & J. Martin (Eds.), *Organizational culture* (pp. 99–124). Beverly Hills, CA: Sage.

[7] Martin, J. (1982). Stories and scripts in organizational settings. In A. Hastorf & A. Isen (Eds.), *Cognitive social psychology* (pp. 255–306). New York: Elsevier-North Holland.

[8] Ransdell, E. (2000, January–February). The Nike story? Just tell it. *Fast Company,* pp. 44, 46.

[9] Neuhauser, P. C. (1993). *Corporate legends and lore: The power of storytelling as a management tool.* New York: McGraw-Hill (quote, p. 63).

[10] Brenner, J. G. (1999). *The emperors of chocolate: Inside the secret world of Hershey and Mars.* New York: Random House.

[11] Manley, W. W., II. (1991). *Executive's handbook of model business conduct codes.* Upper Saddle River, NJ: Prentice Hall (quote, p. 5).

[12] Weiner, Y. (1988). Forms of value systems: A focus on organizational effectiveness and cultural change and maintenance. *Academy of Management Review, 13,* 534–545.

[13] Walter, G. A. (1985). Culture collisions in mergers and acquisitions. In P. J. Frost, L. F. Moore, M. R. Louis, C. C. Lundberg, & J. Martin (Eds.), *Organizational culture* (pp. 301–314). Beverly Hills, CA: Sage.

[14] Naughton, K. (2000, December 11). A mess of a merger. *Newsweek,* pp. 54–57. Elkind, P. (1998, November 9). A merger made in hell. *Fortune,* pp. 134–138, 140, 142, 144, 146, 149, 150. Burrough, B., & Helyar, J. (1990). *Barbarians at the gate.* New York: HarperCollins. Muller, J. (1999, November 29). Lessons from a casualty of the culture wars. *Business Week,* p. 198. Mueller, J. (1999, November 15). The one-year itch at Daimler Chrysler. *Business Week,* p. 42.

[15] Carroll, P. (1993). *Big blues: The unmaking of IBM.* New York: Crown.

[16] Fischer, I., & Frontczak, D. (1999, September). Culture club. *Business 2.0,* pp. 196–198.

[17] Amabile, T. M. (1988). A model of creativity and innovation in organizations. In B. M. Staw & L. L. Cummings (Eds.), *Research in organizational behavior* (Vol. 10, pp. 123–167). Greenwich, CT: JAI Press.

[18] Amabile, T. M. (2000). Stimulate creativity by fueling passion. In E. A. Locke (Ed.), *The Blackwell handbook of principles of organizational behavior* (pp. 331–341). Oxford, England: Blackwell.

[19] Kabanoff, B., & Rossiter, J. R. (1994). Recent developments in applied creativity. In C. Cooper & I. T. Robertson (Eds.), *International review of industrial and organizational psychology* (Vol. 9, pp. 283–324). London: John Wiley.

[20] Michalko, M. (1998, May). Thinking like a genius: Eight strategies used by the supercreative, from Aristotle and Einstein and Edison. *The Futurist,* pp. 21–25.

[21] Kabanoff, B., & Bottiger, P. (1991). Effectiveness of creativity training and its reaction to selected personality factors. *Journal of Organizational Behavior, 12,* 235–248.

[22] Muoio, A. (2000, January–February). Idea summit. *Fast Company,* pp. 151–156, 160, 162, 164 (quote, p. 152).

[23] Sittenfeld, C. (1999, July–August). This old house is a home for new ideas. *Fast Company,* pp. 58, 60.

[24] Oldham, G. R., & Cummings, A. (1996). Employee creativity: Personal and contextual factors at work. *Academy of Management Journal, 39,* 607–634.

[25] Dahle, C. (2000, January–February). Mind games. *Fast Company,* pp. 169–173, 176, 178–179.

[26] Sutton, R. I., & Hargadon, A. (1996). Brainstorming groups in context: Effectiveness in a product design firm. *Administrative Science Quarterly, 41,* 685–718 (quote, p. 702).

[27] Coyne, W. E. (1997). 3M (Minnesota Mining and Manufacturing Company). In R. M. Kanter, J. Kao, & F. Wiersema (Eds.), *Innovation* (pp. 43–63). New York: Harper Business.

[28] Kanter, R. M., Kao, J., & Wiersema, F. (1997). *Innovation.* New York: Harper Business.

[29] See Note 17.

[30] Michalko, M. (1991). *Thinkertoys.* Berkeley, CA: Ten Speed Press.

[31] See Note 30.

13

Designing effective organizations

LEARNING OBJECTIVES

After reading this chapter, you will be able to:

1. DEFINE organizational structure and DISTINGUISH between five aspects of organizational structure that are represented in an organization chart.

2. DISTINGUISH between the three types of departmentalization: functional organizations, product organizations, and matrix organizations.

3. DEFINE organizational design and DISTINGUISH between classical and neoclassical approaches to organizational design.

4. DESCRIBE the contingency approach to organizational design.

5. DESCRIBE four emerging approaches to organizational design.

6. IDENTIFY two different types of interorganizational designs.

THREE GOOD REASONS WHY YOU SHOULD CARE ABOUT. . .

Designing Effective Organizations

You should care about organizational design because:

1. To understand how organizations function you must know about their structural elements, their basic building blocks.

2. The effective design of organizations can have profound effects on organizational functioning.

3. The way organizations are designed has been changing in recent years and will continue to change in years ahead.

Making the Case for... Designing Effective Organizations

VF Corporation Sews Together Its Operations

Although you may have never heard of VF Corporation, you probably are quite familiar with its products, including jeans (with such brands as Lee, Wrangler, Britannica, and Rustler) and underwear (Vanity Fair and Vassarette), as well Healthtex clothing for children and Jantzen bathing suits. For over a century, Greensboro, North Carolina-based VF did just fine. Although the company wasn't falling apart at the seams, in recent years, sales were flat and expenses were rising.

Among other problems, officials realized that the apparel company had grown to be incredibly inefficient. Each of the 17 brands, for example, operated independently, with its own purchasing, producing, and marketing. Making matters worse, each brand had its own computer system that was incompatible with the others. But lack of coordination at VF went beyond the realm of computers. People in the various divisions never consulted with one another before ordering raw materials—and worse, the various brands competed for the same customers. According to a high-ranking company official at VF, "We had all the disadvantages of a small company and none of the advantages of a big one."

When Mackey McDonald became VF's new CEO, he developed a four-pronged plan for stitching things together. First, he combined the 17 different brands into five units—jeanswear, intimates, playwear, knitwear, and international operations and marketing. Second, he relocated the company from its Wyomissing, Pennsylvania, headquarters to a new facility in Greensboro, North Carolina, which was closer to most of VF's factories. Third, he worked out a unified system for developing products, planning the manufacturing process, and distributing merchandise. At the core of McDonald's plan was a secret weapon—a highly sophisticated new information technology center, called VF Services, which interconnected the various units in a centralized computer network. The idea is not only to organize work more efficiently, but to do so in a manner that maximizes sales. Ultimately, the system McDonald envisions would be so sophisticated in its understanding of consumer purchase patterns that that it would have precisely the right items on the right store shelves at the very time consumers want to buy them.

McDonald's plan cost the company over $100 million—mostly from the complete overhaul and installation of an integrated computer system—cutting into the company's operating expenses. However, preliminary information shows that the plan seems to be working: On-floor inventory has been reduced 11 percent and product turnover has increased some 15 percent. In other words, the merchandise is moving. Will it work in the end? McDonald is optimistic, noting, "Our people designed the products and the process. That's why I think we can have success."

VF Corporation made several drastic changes to the way its various work functions were organized: Among other things, it rearranged 17 units into 5, and trimmed 17 separate systems for planning, developing, manufacturing, and distributing merchandise into a single unified plan. Although this approach seems to be working, thus far, I have said nothing in this book about the fundamental question underlying McDonald's actions: How should companies organize themselves into separate units to be most effective? This question is a venerable one in the field of business—and, as I shall explain in this chapter, a very important one.

OB researchers and theorists have provided considerable insight into the matter by studying what is called *organizational structure*—the way individuals and groups are arranged with respect to the tasks they perform—and *organizational design*—the process of coordinating these structural elements in the most effective manner.[1] As you may suspect, finding the best way to structure and design organizations is no simple matter. However, because understanding the structure and design of organizations is key to fully appreciating their functioning, organizational scientists have devoted considerable energy to this topic. I will describe these efforts in this chapter. To begin, I will identify the basic structural dimensions of organizations. Following this, I will examine how these structural elements can be most effectively combined into productive organizational designs. In so doing, I will cover some of the traditional ways of designing organizations as well as some of the rapidly developing organizational forms emerging today.

Structural Dimensions of Organizations

Think about how a simple house is constructed. It is composed of a wooden frame positioned atop a concrete slab covered by a roof and siding materials. Within this basic structure are separate systems operating to provide electricity, water, and telephone services. It is possible to extend this analogy to the structure of organizations. Let's use as an example an organization with which you are familiar—your college or university. It is probably composed of various departments working together to serve special functions. Individuals and groups are dedicated to tasks such as teaching, providing financial services, maintaining the physical facilities, and so on. Of course, within each group, even more distinctions can be made between the jobs people perform. For example, it's unlikely that the instructor for your OB course is also teaching seventeenth-century French literature.

This illustrates my main point: An organization is not a haphazard collection of people, but a meaningful combination of groups and individuals working together purposefully to meet organizational goals. The term **organizational structure** refers to the formal configuration between individuals and groups with respect to the allocation of tasks, responsibilities, and authority within organizations.[2]

Unlike the structure of a house, we cannot see the structure of an organization; it is an abstract concept. However, the connections between various clusters of functions of which an organization is composed can be represented in the form of a diagram known as an **organization chart**. Specifically, an organization chart may be considered a representation of an organization's internal structure. Organization charts are useful tools for specifying how various tasks or functions are interrelated within organizations. For example, look at the chart depicting part of a hypothetical manufacturing organization shown in Figure 13.1. Each box represents a specific job, and the lines connecting them reflect the formally prescribed lines of communication between the individuals performing those jobs (see Chapter 8). To specialists in organizational structure, however, such diagrams reveal a great deal more.

DIVISION OF LABOR

The standard organization chart reflects the fact that the many tasks to be performed within an organization are divided into specialized jobs, a process known as the **division of labor**. The more that tasks are divided into separate jobs, the more those jobs

FIGURE 13.1 Organization Chart of a Hypothetical Manufacturing Firm

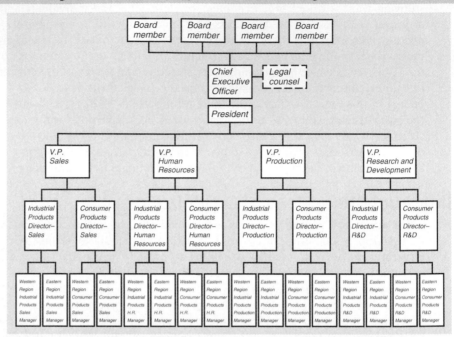

An *organization chart,* such as this one, identifies pictorially the various functions performed within an organization and the lines of authority between people performing those functions.

are *specialized* and the narrower the range of activities that job incumbents are required to perform. For example, the jobs performed by members of a pit crew for a race car are divided into highly specialized functions, such as refueling, changing tires, and so on. In theory, the fewer tasks a person performs, the better he or she may be expected to perform them, freeing others to perform the tasks that they perform best. (I say "in theory" because if specialization is too great, people may lose their motivation to work at a high level and performance may suffer; see Chapter 4.) Taken together, an entire organization is composed of people performing a collection of specialized jobs. This is probably the most obvious feature of an organization that can be observed from the organization chart.

As you might imagine, the degree to which employees perform specialized jobs is likely to depend on the size of the organization. The larger the organization, the more the opportunities for specialization are likely to exist. For example, someone in the advertising department of a large agency is likely to specialize in a certain narrowly defined task, such as writing radio jingles, whereas someone working at a smaller agency is likely to have to perform a much wider variety of tasks, including preparing copy for print ads, meeting with clients, and maybe even sending out the bills.

HIERARCHY OF AUTHORITY

Organization charts provide information about who reports to whom—what is known as **hierarchy of authority**. The organizational diagram reveals which particular lower-

FIGURE 13.2 Span of Control in Tall versus Flat Organizations

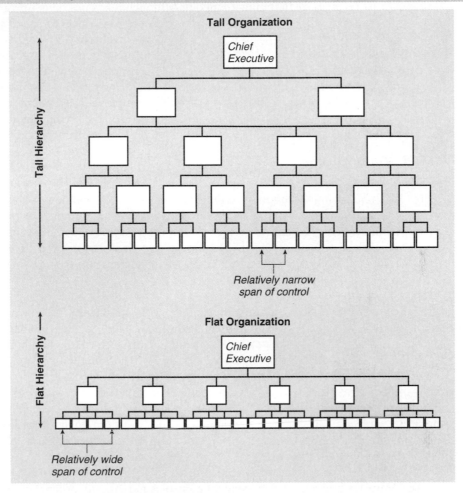

Each of the two organizations depicted here have 31 employees, but they are structured differently. In the *tall organization,* shown at the top, the hierarchy has many layers, and managers have a *narrow span of control.* However, in the *flat organization,* shown at the bottom, the hierarchy has fewer layers and managers have a *wide span of control.*

level employees are required to report to which particular individuals immediately above them. In our hypothetical example in Figure 13.1, the various regional salespeople (at the bottom of the diagram) report to their respective regional sales directors, who report to the vice president of sales, who reports to the president, who reports to the chief executive officer, who reports to the members of the board of directors. As we trace these reporting relationships, we work our way up the organization's hierarchy. In this case, the organization has five levels. Organizations may have many levels, in which case their structure is considered *tall,* or only a few, in which case their structure is considered flat (see Figure 13.2).

In recent years, a great deal has appeared in the news about organizations restructuring their workforces by flattening them out. Although it has not been uncommon for large companies to lay off people in low-level jobs, in recent years, middle managers and executives, who were long believed to be secure in their positions, found themselves unemployed as their companies "downsized," "rightsized," "delayered," or "retrenched" by eliminating entire layers of organizational structure. Even the U.S. Army has downsized by 30 percent in recent years.[3] The underlying assumption behind these changes is that fewer layers reduce waste and enable people to make better decisions (by moving them closer to the problems at hand), thereby leading to greater profitability. Although some layers of hierarchy are necessary, too many can be needlessly expensive. Moreover, as technology advances, fewer people are needed to carry out management roles.

> *In recent years, middle managers and executives, who were long believed to be secure in their positions, found themselves unemployed as their companies "downsized," "rightsized," "delayered," or "retrenched" by eliminating entire layers of organizational structure.*

SPAN OF CONTROL

Over how many individuals should a manager have responsibility? The earliest management theorists and practitioners alike (dating back to the Roman legions) addressed this question. When you look at an organization chart, the number of people formally required to report to each individual manager is immediately clear. This number constitutes what is known as a manager's **span of control**. Those responsible for many individuals are said to have a *wide* span of control, whereas those responsible for fewer are said to have a *narrow* span of control. In our organization chart (Figure 13.1), the CEO is responsible for only the actions of the president, giving this individual a narrower span of control than the president himself or herself, who has a span of control of four individuals.

When a manager's span of control is wide, the organization itself has a flat hierarchy. In contrast, when a manager's span of control is narrow, the organization itself has a tall hierarchy. This is demonstrated in Figure 13.2. The diagram at the top shows a *tall* organization—one in which there are many layers in the hierarchy, and the span of control is relatively narrow (i.e., the number of people supervised is low). By contrast, the diagram at the bottom of Figure 13.2 shows a *flat* organization—one in which there are only a few levels in the hierarchy, and the span of control is relatively wide. Although both organizations depicted here have 31 positions, these are arranged differently.

It is not possible to specify the "ideal" span of control that should be sought. Instead, it makes better sense to consider what form of organization is best suited to various purposes. For example, because supervisors in a military unit must have tight control over subordinates and get them to respond quickly and precisely, a narrow span of control is likely to be effective. As a result, military organizations tend to be extremely tall. In contrast, people working in a research and development lab must have an open exchange of ideas and typically require little managerial guidance to be successful. Units of this type tend to have very flat structures. (As you might imagine, there may be widespread differences with respect to spans of control in different types of organizations. To learn about this possibility, complete the **Group Exercise** on p. 363.)

LINE VERSUS STAFF POSITIONS

The organization chart shown in Figure 13.1 reveals an additional distinction that deserves to be highlighted—that between *line positions* and *staff positions.* People occupying **line position**s (e.g., the various vice presidents and managers) have decision-making power. However, the individual shown in the dotted box—the legal counsel—cannot make decisions, but provides advice and recommendations to be used by the line managers. For example, such an individual may help corporate officials decide whether a certain product name can be used without infringing on copyright restrictions. This individual may be said to hold a **staff position.** In many of today's organizations, human resources managers may be seen as occupying staff positions because they may provide specialized services regarding testing and interviewing procedures as well as information about the latest laws on personnel administration.

Differences between line and staff personnel are not unusual. Specifically, staff managers tend to be younger, better educated, and more committed to their fields than to their organizations. Line managers might feel more committed to their organizations not only because of the greater opportunities they have to exercise decisions but also because they are more likely to perceive themselves as part of a company rather than as an independent specialist whose identity lies primarily within his or her specialty area.

DECENTRALIZATION

During the first half of the twentieth century, as companies grew larger and larger, they shifted power and authority into the hands of a few upper-echelon administrators—executives whose decisions influenced the many people below them in the organizational hierarchy. In fact, during the 1920s Alfred P. Sloan, Jr., then the president of General Motors, introduced the notion of a "central office," the place where a few individuals made policy decisions for the entire company. Another part of Sloan's plan involved pushing decisions regarding the day-to-day operation of the company lower and lower down the organizational hierarchy, thereby allowing those individuals who were most affected to make the decisions. This process of delegating power from higher to lower levels within organizations is known as **decentralization**. It is the opposite of **centralization**, the tendency for just a few powerful individuals or groups to hold most of the decision-making power.

Many organizations have moved toward decentralization to promote managerial efficiency and to improve employee satisfaction (the result of giving people greater opportunities to take responsibility for their own actions). For example, thousands of staff jobs have been eliminated at companies such as 3M, Eastman Kodak, AT&T, and GE as these companies have decentralized.

Recent years have seen a marked trend toward increasingly greater decentralization.[4] As a result,

TABLE 13.1 Decentralization: Benefits When Low and When High

Various benefits are associated with low decentralization (high centralization) and high decentralization (low centralization) within organizations.

Low Decentralization (High Centralization)	High Decentralization (Low Centralization)
Eliminates the additional responsibility not desired by people performing routine jobs	Can eliminate levels of management, making a leaner organization
Permits crucial decisions to be made by individuals who have the "big picture"	Promotes greater opportunities for decisions to be made by people closest to problems

organization charts might show fewer staff positions, as decision-making authority is pushed farther down the hierarchy. Many organizations have moved toward decentralization to promote managerial efficiency and to improve employee satisfaction (the result of giving people greater opportunities to take responsibility for their own actions). For example, thousands of staff jobs have been eliminated at companies such as 3M, Eastman Kodak, AT&T, and GE as these companies have decentralized. In particular, people working in research and development positions are likely to enjoy the autonomy to make decisions that decentralization allows. With this in mind, many companies heavily involved in research and development—including parts of Hewlett-Packard, Intel Corporation, Philips Electronics, and AT&T's Bell Laboratories—have shifted to more decentralized designs. By contrast, people working on production jobs are likely to be less interested in taking responsibility for decisions and may enjoy not having to take such responsibility. For a summary of the relative advantages and disadvantages of centralization, see Table 13.1.

Departmentalization: Ways of Structuring Organizations

Thus far, I have been talking about "the" organization chart of an organization. Typically, such charts, like the one shown in Figure 13.1, divide organizations according to the various functions performed. However, this is only one option. Organizations can be divided up not only by function but also by product or market or a combination of both. I will now take a closer look at these various ways of breaking up organizations into coherent units—that is, the process of **departmentalization**.

FUNCTIONAL ORGANIZATIONS: DEPARTMENTALIZATION BY TASK

Because it is the form organizations usually take when they are first created, and because it is how we usually think of organizations, the **functional organization** can be considered the most basic approach to departmentalization. Essentially, functional organizations departmentalize individuals according to the functions they perform, with people who perform similar functions assigned to the same department. For example, a manufacturing company might consist of separate departments devoted to basic functions such as sales–marketing, production, human resources, and research and development (recall Figure 13.1). Even small companies such as Beauty.com have

FIGURE 13.3 Departmentalization of an Information Technology Unit

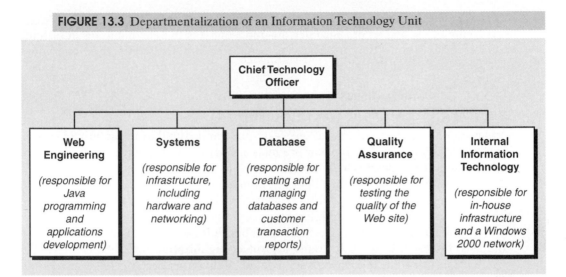

Beauty.com is an e-commerce company specializing in selling a wide range of beauty supplies. Given that information technology is a central business function of any Web-based business, it is not surprising that Beauty.com has a separate information technology unit. The head of this unit, the chief technology officer, is responsible for each of the five different departments, whose areas of responsibility are summarized here. (*Source:* Based on information reported in Goff, 2000; see Note 5.)

found it useful to departmentalize by function.[5] For example, the fifteen members of the company's information technology group are divided into the five separate departments, shown in Figure 13.3.

Naturally, as organizations grow and become more complex, additional departments are added or deleted as the need arises. Consider, for example, something that is beginning to happen at Johnson & Johnson (J&J). Although this company has long been highly decentralized, certain functions are now beginning to become centralized (e.g., the legal and human resources operations). This makes it possible for resources to be saved by avoiding duplication of effort, resulting in a higher level of efficiency. Not only does this form of organizational structure take advantage of economies of scale (by allowing employees performing the same jobs to share facilities and not duplicating functions), but it also allows people to specialize, thereby performing only those tasks at which they are most expert. The result is a highly skilled workforce—a direct benefit to the organization.

Partly offsetting these advantages, however, are several potential limitations. The most important of these stems from the fact that functional organizational structures encourage separate units to develop their own narrow perspectives and to lose sight of overall organizational goals. For example, in a manufacturing company, an engineer might see the company's problems in terms of the reliability

Functional organizational structures encourage separate units to develop their own narrow perspectives and to lose sight of overall organizational goals.

of its products and lose sight of other key considerations, such as market trends, overseas competition, and so on. Such narrow-mindedness is the inevitable result of functional specialization—the downside of people seeing the company's operations through a narrow lens.

PRODUCT ORGANIZATIONS: DEPARTMENTALIZATION BY TYPE OF OUTPUT

Organizations—at least successful ones—do not stand still; they constantly change in size and scope. As they develop new products and seek new customers, they might find that a functional structure doesn't work as well as it once did. Manufacturing a wide range of products using a variety of different methods, for example, might put a strain on a manufacturing division of a functional organization. Similarly, keeping track of the varied tax requirements for different types of business (e.g., restaurants, farms, real estate, manufacturing) might pose quite a challenge for a single financial division of a company. In response to such strains, a **product organization** might be created. This type of departmentalization creates self-contained divisions, each of which is responsible for everything to do with a certain product or group of products. For a look at the structure of a hypothetical product organization, see Figure 13.4.

When organizations are departmentalized by products, separate divisions are established, each of which is devoted to a certain product or group of products. Each unit contains all the resources needed to develop, manufacture, and sell its products. The organization is composed of separate divisions, operating independently, the heads of which report to top management. Although some functions might be centralized within the parent company (e.g., human resource management or legal staff), on a day-to-day basis each division operates autonomously as a separate company or, as accountants call them, "cost centers" of their own.

FIGURE 13.4 Structure of a Typical Product Organization

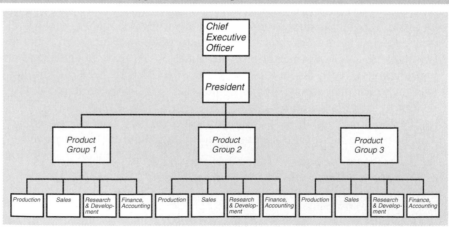

In a *product organization,* separate units are established to handle different product lines. Each of these divisions contains all the departments necessary for it to operate as an independent unit.

Consider, for example, how separate divisions of General Motors are devoted to manufacturing cars, trucks, locomotives, refrigerators, auto parts, and the like. The managers of each division can devote their energies to one particular business. Organizations may be beneficial from a marketing perspective as well. Consider, for example, Honda's 1987 introduction of its line of luxury cars, Acura. By creating a separate division for Acura, manufactured in separate plants and sold by a separate network of dealers, the company made its higher-priced cars look special, and avoided making its less expensive cars look less appealing by putting them together with superior products on the same showroom floors. Given Honda's success with this configuration, it is not surprising that Toyota and Nissan followed suit when they introduced their own luxury lines, Lexus and Infiniti, in 1989.

Product organizations also have several drawbacks. The most obvious of these is the loss of economies of scale stemming from the duplication of various departments within operating units. For example, if each unit carries out its own research and development functions, the need for costly equipment, facilities, and personnel may be multiplied. Another problem associated with product designs involves the organization's ability to attract and retain talented employees. Because each department within operating units is necessarily smaller than a single combined one would be, opportunities for advancement and career development may suffer. This, in turn, may pose a serious problem with respect to the long-term retention of talented employees. Finally, problems of coordination across product lines may arise. In fact, in extreme cases, actions taken by one operating division may have adverse effects on the outcomes of one or more others.

A clear example of such problems was provided by Hewlett-Packard, a major manufacturer of computers, printers, and scientific test equipment. During most of its history, Hewlett-Packard adopted a product design. It consisted of scores of small, largely autonomous divisions, each concerned with producing and selling certain products. As it grew, the company found itself in an increasingly untenable situation in which sales representatives from different divisions sometimes attempted to sell different lines of equipment, often to be used for the same basic purposes, to the same customers. To deal with such problems, top management at Hewlett-Packard decided to restructure the company into sectors based largely on the markets they served (such as business customers, and scientific and manufacturing customers). In short, Hewlett-Packard switched from a traditional product organization to an internal structure driven by market considerations.

MATRIX ORGANIZATIONS: DEPARTMENTALIZATION BY BOTH FUNCTION AND PRODUCT

When the aerospace industry was first developing, the U.S. government demanded that a single manager in each company be assigned to each of its projects so that it was immediately clear who was responsible for the progress of each project. In response to this requirement, TRW established a "project leader" for each project, someone who shared authority with the leaders of the existing functional departments. This temporary arrangement later evolved into what is called a matrix organization, the type of organization in which an employee is required to report to both a functional (or division) manager and the manager of a specific project (or product). In essence, TRW developed a complex type of organizational structure that combines both the function and product forms of departmentalization. To better understand matrix organizations, let's take a closer look at the organization chart shown in Figure 13.5.

FIGURE 13.5 Structure of a Typical Matrix Organization

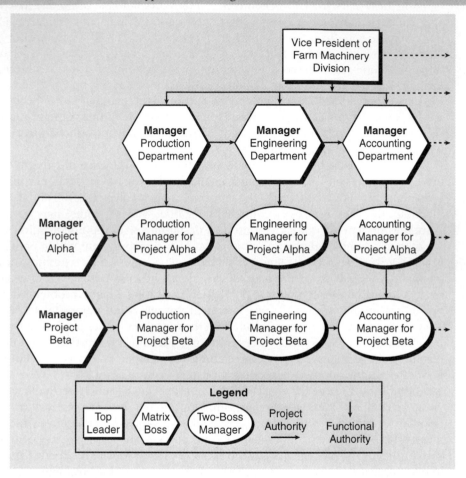

In a *matrix organization,* a product structure is superimposed on a functional structure. This results in a dual system of authority in which some managers report to two bosses—one for the specific product (or project) and one for the specific functional department involved.

Employees in matrix organizations have two bosses (or, more technically, they are under *dual authority*). One line of authority, shown by the vertical axis in Figure 13.5, is *functional,* managed by vice presidents in charge of various functional areas. The other, shown by the horizontal axis, is *product* (or it may be a specific project or temporary business), managed by specific individuals in charge of certain products (or projects).

In matrix designs, there are three major roles. First, there is the *top leader*—the individual who has authority over both lines of authority (the one based on function and the one based on product or project). It is this individual's task to enhance coordination between functional and product managers and to maintain an appropriate balance of power between them. Second, there are the *matrix bosses*—people who head functional departments or specific projects. Because neither functional managers nor project managers have complete authority over subordinates, they must work together to assure that their efforts mesh rather than conflict. In addition, they must agree on issues such as promotions and raises for specific people working under their joint authority. Finally, there are *two-boss managers*—people who must report to both product and functional managers, and attempt to balance the demands of each. Because people working in this fashion have two bosses, they must have sufficient freedom to attain their objectives. As you might imagine, a fair amount of coordination, flexibility, openness, and trust is essential for such a program to work, suggesting that not everyone adapts well to such a system.

Organizations are most likely to adopt matrix designs when they confront certain conditions. These include a complex and uncertain environment (one with frequent changes), and the need for economies of scale in the use of internal resources. Specifically, a matrix approach is often adopted by medium-size organizations with several product lines that do not possess sufficient resources to establish fully self-contained operating units. Under such conditions, a matrix design provides a useful compromise. Some companies that have adopted this structure, at least on a trial basis, are TRW Systems Group, Liberty Mutual Insurance, and Citibank.

> *A matrix approach is often adopted by medium-size organizations with several product lines that do not possess sufficient resources to establish fully self-contained operating units.*

I have noted several advantages offered by matrix designs. First, they permit flexible use of an organization's human resources. Individuals within functional departments can be assigned to specific products or projects as the need arises and then return to their regular duties when this task is completed. Second, matrix designs offer medium-size organizations an efficient means of responding quickly to a changing, unstable environment. Third, such designs often enhance communication among managers; indeed, they literally force matrix bosses to discuss and agree on many matters. Unfortunately, matrix designs can create frustration and stress caused by having to report to two different supervisors. However, in situations in which organizations must stretch their financial and human resources to meet challenges from the external environment or to take advantage of new opportunities, matrix designs can be useful.

Traditional Organizational Designs

I began this chapter by likening the structure of an organization to the structure of a house. Now I will extend that analogy for purposes of introducing the concept of *organizational design*. Just as a house is designed in a particular fashion by combining its structural elements in various ways, so too can an organization be designed by combining its basic elements in certain ways. Accordingly, **organizational design** refers to the process of coordinating the structural elements of organizations in the most appropriate manner.[6]

CLASSICAL AND NEOCLASSICAL APPROACHES:
THE QUEST FOR THE ONE BEST DESIGN

It is not difficult to realize that for organizations to function effectively, their designs must not be static, but dynamic—changing in response to various conditions (e.g., governmental regulations, competition, and so on). As obvious as this may be to us today, the earliest theorists interested in organizational design paid little attention to the need for organizations to be flexible. Instead, they approached the task of designing organizations as a search for "the one best way," seeking to establish the ideal form for all organizations under all conditions—the universal design.

In Chapter 1, I described the efforts of organizational scholars such as Max Weber and Frederick Taylor. These theorists believed that effective organizations were ones that had a formal hierarchy, a clear set of rules, specialization of labor, highly routine tasks, and a highly impersonal working environment. You may recall that Weber referred to this organizational form as a *bureaucracy*. This **classical organizational theory** has fallen into disfavor because it is insensitive to human needs and is not suited to a changing environment. Unfortunately, the "ideal" form of an organization, according to Weber, did not take into account the realities of the world within which it operates. Apparently, what is ideal is not necessarily what is realistic.

In response to these conditions, and with inspiration from the Hawthorne studies, the classical approach to the bureaucratic model gave way to more of a human relations orientation (see Chapter 1). Several other organizational theorists attempted to improve upon the classical model which is why their approach is labeled **neoclassical organizational theory.** These approaches argue that economic effectiveness is not the only goal of an industrial organization, but that employee satisfaction is also important. The key, neoclassical organizational theorists argued, was not rigidly controlling people's actions, but actively promoting their feelings of self-worth and their importance to the organization. The neoclassical approaches called for organizations to be designed with flat hierarchical structures (minimizing managerial control over subordinates) and a high degree of decentralization (encouraging employees to make their own decisions). Indeed, such design features may well serve the underlying neoclassical philosophy.

> *Like the classical approach, the neoclassical approach also may be faulted on the grounds that it promoted a single best approach to organizational design. Although the benefits of flat, decentralized designs may be many, to claim that this represents the universal or ideal form for all organizations would be naive.*

Like the classical approach, the neoclassical approach also may be faulted on the grounds that it promoted a single best approach to organizational design. Although the benefits of flat, decentralized designs may be many, to claim that this represents the universal or ideal form for all organizations would be naive. In response to this criticism, more contemporary approaches to organizational design have given up on finding the one best way to design organizations in favor of finding different designs that are appropriate for the different circumstances and contexts within which organizations operate.

THE CONTINGENCY APPROACH:
DESIGN BASED ON ENVIRONMENTAL CONDITIONS

Today, it is widely believed that the best design for an organization depends on the nature of the environment (e.g., the economy, geography, labor markets) in which the organization is operating. This is known as the **contingency approach** to organizational design. Although many features of the environment may be taken into account when considering how an organization should be designed, a key determinant appears to be how stable (unchanging) or unstable (turbulent) the environment is.

If you've ever worked at a McDonald's, you probably know how highly standardized each step of the most basic operations must be. Boxes of fries are to be stored two inches from the wall in stacks one inch apart. Making those fries is another matter—one that requires 19 distinct steps, each of which is clearly laid out in a training film shown to new employees. The process is the same, whether it's done in Moscow, Idaho, or Moscow, Russia. This is an example of a highly mechanistic task. Organizations can be highly mechanistic when conditions don't change. Although the fast-food industry has changed a great deal in recent years (with the introduction of healthier menu items and competitive pricing), making fries at McDonald's has not changed. If the environment doesn't change, a highly **mechanistic form** of organization can be very efficient.

An environment is considered stable whenever there is little or no unexpected change in product, market demands, technology, and the like. Have you ever seen an old-fashioned-looking bottle of E. E. Dickinson's witch hazel (a topical astringent used to cleanse the skin in the area of a wound)? Because the company has been making the product following the same distillation process since 1866, it is certainly operating in a relatively stable manufacturing environment. Without change, people can easily specialize. When change is inevitable, specialization is impractical.

Mechanistic organizations can be characterized in several additional ways (for a summary, see Table 13.2). Not only do mechanistic organizations allow for a high degree of specialization, but they also impose many rules. Authority is vested in a few people located at the top of a hierarchy who give direct orders to their subordinates. Mechanistic organizational designs tend to be most effective under conditions in which the external environment is stable and unchanging.

TABLE 13.2 Mechanistic versus Organic Designs

Mechanistic designs and *organic designs* differ along several key dimensions identified here. These represent extremes; many organizations fall in between.

	Structure	
Dimension	*Mechanistic*	*Organic*
Stability	Change unlikely	Change likely
Specialization	Many specialists	Many generalists
Formal rules	Rigid rules	Considerable flexibility
Authority	Centralized in a few top people	Decentralized, diffused throughout the organization

Now, think about high-technology industries, such as those dedicated to computers, aerospace products, and biotechnology. Their environmental conditions are likely to be changing all the time. These industries are so prone to change that as soon as a new way of operating could be introduced into one of them, it would have to be altered. It isn't only technology, however, that makes an environment turbulent. Turbulence also can be high in industries in which adherence to rapidly changing regulations is essential. For example, times were turbulent in the hospital industry when new Medicaid legislation was passed, and times were turbulent in the nuclear power industry when governmental regulations dictated the introduction of many new standards that had to be followed. With the dominance of foreign automobiles in the United States, the once stable American auto industry has faced turbulent times. Unfortunately, in this case, the design of the auto companies could not rapidly accommodate the changes needed for more organic forms (because the American auto industry was traditionally highly mechanistic).

The pure **organic form** of organization may be characterized in several different ways (see Table 13.2). The degree of job specialization possible is very low; instead, a broad knowledge of many different jobs is required. Very little authority is exercised from the top. Rather, self-control is expected, and an emphasis is placed on coordination between peers. As a result, decisions tend to be made in a highly democratic, participative manner. Be aware that the mechanistic and organic types of organizational structure described here are ideal forms. The mechanistic-organic distinction should be thought of as opposite poles along a continuum rather than as completely distinct options for organization. Certainly, organizations can be relatively organic or relatively mechanistic compared with others, but may not be located at either extreme. (Which particular form of organizational form do you prefer? The **Self-Assessment Exercise** on p. 362 will give you some insight into your individual preferences for mechanistic and organic organizations.)

Emerging Organizational Designs

Thus far, the organizational designs I have been describing have been around for a long time, and because they are so well known and often so effective, they are not likely to fade away anytime soon. However, during the past decade, several emerging forms of organizational design have come onto the scene. Given how popular and promising these seem to be, I will describe them here.

THE HORIZONTAL ORGANIZATION:
DESIGNING WITH PROCESS IN MIND

If the experts are right, we are in store for a new way of structuring work in tomorrow's organizations—one that means more than just tinkering with the boxes on an organization chart. Enter the **horizontal organization**—an approach advocated by many organizational experts and touted by consultants from the firm McKinsey & Company as "the first real, fundamentally different, robust alternative" to the functional organization.[7]

The essence of the idea is simple. Instead of organizing jobs in the traditional, vertical fashion, by having a long chain of groups or individuals perform parts of a task (e.g., one group that sells the advertising job, another that plans the ad campaign, and yet another that produces the ads), horizontal organizations have flattened hierarchies. That is, they arrange autonomous work teams (see Chapter 7) in parallel, each performing many different steps in the process (e.g., members of an advertising team may bring different skills and expertise to a single team responsible for all aspects of advertising). Essentially, organizations are structured around *processes* instead of tasks. Performance objectives are based on customers' needs, such as lowered cost or improved service. Once the core processes that meet these needs (e.g., order generation, new-product development) have been identified, they become the company's major components—instead of the traditional departments such as sales or manufacturing (for a summary, see Figure 13.6).

According to consultant Michael Hammer, "In the future, executive positions will not be defined in terms of collections of people, like head of the sales department, but in terms of processes, like senior-VP-of getting-stuff-to-customers, which is sales, shipping, billing. You'll no longer have a box on an organization chart. Rather you'll own part of a process map."[8] Envision it as a whole company lying on its side and organized by process. An ardent believer in this approach, Lawrence Bossidy, CEO of AlliedSignal, says, "Every business has maybe six basic processes. We'll organize around them. The people who run them will be the leaders of the business."[9] In an industrial company, for example, these processes might include things such as new-product development, flow of materials, and the order-delivery-billing cycle. Individuals will constantly move into and out of various teams as needed, drawing from a directory of broadly skilled in-house corporate experts available to lend their expertise.

The horizontal organization is already a reality in at least parts of several of today's organizations—including AT&T (network systems division), Eastman Chemical (a division of Kodak), Hallmark Cards, and Xerox. Consider, for example, General

---

FIGURE 13.6 The Horizontal Organization

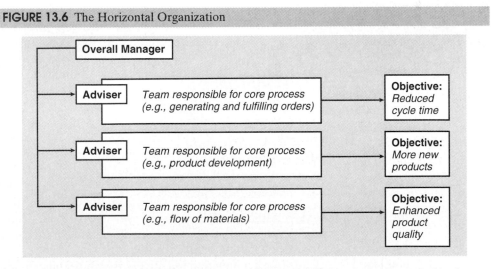

In a *horizontal organization,* teams of employees with diverse skills are created to meet objectives relating to various core processes that must be performed.

Electric's factory in Bayamón, Puerto Rico. The 172 hourly workers, 15 salaried "advisers," plus a single manager manufacture "arresters" (surge protectors that guard power stations from lightning). That's the entire workforce; there are no support staff and no supervisors—only about half as many people as you'd find in a conventional factory. Bayamón employees are formed into separate teams of approximately 10 widely skilled members who "own" such parts of the work as shipping and receiving, assembly, and so on. The teams do whatever is needed to get the job done; the advisers get involved only when needed.

Although carefully controlled studies have yet to assess the impact of this new approach, those who have used it are convinced of its effectiveness. One top McKinsey consultant, for example, claims that this new approach to organizational design can help companies cut their costs by at least one-third. Some of their clients, they boast, have done even better. Will the horizontal organization replace the traditional pyramid of the hierarchical organization? Only time will tell. Meanwhile, those who have turned to horizontal organizational structures appear to be glad they did.

THE BOUNDARYLESS ORGANIZATION: BUSINESS WITHOUT BARRIERS

You hear it all the time: Someone is asked to do something, but responds defiantly, saying, "It's not my job." As uncooperative as this may seem, such a comment may make a great deal of sense when it comes to the traditional kind of organizational structures we've been describing—ones with layers of carefully connected boxes neatly stacked atop each other in hierarchical fashion. The advantage of these types of organizations is that they clearly define the roles of managers and employees. Everyone knows precisely what he or she is supposed to do. The problem with such arrangements, however, is that they are inflexible. As a result, they do not lend themselves to the rapidly changing conditions in which today's organizations operate.

Sensitive to this limitation, Jack Welch, former CEO of General Electric, proposed the **boundaryless organization**. This is an organization in which chains of command are eliminated, spans of control are unlimited, and rigid departments give way to empowered teams. Replacing rigid distinctions between people are fluid, intentionally ambiguous, and ill-defined roles. Welch's vision was that GE would operate like a family grocery store (albeit a $60 billion one)—one in which the barriers within the company that separate employees from each other, and that separate the company from its customers and suppliers, would be eliminated.[10] Although GE has not yet become the completely boundaryless organization Welch envisioned, it has made significant strides toward breaking down boundaries, as have other organizations.[11]

For boundaryless organizations to function effectively, they must meet many of the same requirements as successful teams. For example, there must be high levels of trust between all parties concerned. Also, everyone involved must have such high levels of skill that they all can operate without much, if any, managerial guidance. Insofar as the elimination of boundaries weakens traditional managerial power bases, some executives may find it difficult to give up their authority, leading to political behavior. However, to the extent that the elimination of boundaries leverages the talents of all employees, such limitations are worth striving to overcome.

The boundaryless organizations we have been describing involve breaking down both internal and external barriers. As a result, they are sometimes referred to as *barrier-free organizations.* However, there are variations of the boundaryless organization involving only the elimination of external boundaries.[12] These include the *modular organization* (in which secondary aspects of the company's operations are outsourced) and the *virtual organization* (in which organizations combine forces with others on a temporary basis to form new organizations, usually only briefly). I will describe these below. Meanwhile, for a summary of these three related organizational designs, see Figure 13.7.

MODULAR ORGANIZATIONS

Many of today's organizations outsource noncore functions to other companies while retaining full strategic control over their core business. Such companies may be thought of as having a central hub surrounded by networks of outside specialists that can be added or subtracted as needed. As such, they are referred to as **modular organizations**.[13]

As a case in point, you surely recognize Nike and Reebok as major designers and marketers of athletic shoes. However, you probably didn't realize that Nike's production facilities are limited, and that Reebok doesn't even have any plants of its own. Both organizations contract all their manufacturing to companies in countries such as Taiwan and South Korea where labor costs are low. In so doing, not only can they avoid making major investments in facilities, but they also can concentrate on what they do best—tapping the changing tastes of their customers. While doing this, their suppliers can focus on rapidly retooling to make the new products.[14]

Smith Corona is another good example of a modular organization.[15] For 112 years, Smith Corona was a leader in the field of portable typewriters. Then, as word processing took hold, Smith Corona was forced to sell all its plants and declare bankruptcy. However, because the brand name had value, the company reemerged to sell office products (such as fax machines and phones) that are made by others. The company clearly switched from one that specialized in design and manufacture of products, to one that deals only in selling products made by others under its name. Today's Smith Corona is a modular company insofar as it focuses on its core competency of marketing, relying on other companies to handle the manufacturing.

Unlike Smith Corona, which used to handle all aspects of the office machine business itself, some companies have existed only for purposes of assembling or selling products made by others. For example, Dell and Gateway buy computer components made by other companies and perform only the final assembly themselves, putting together systems ordered by customers. Online merchants operate in much the same way. Amazon.com, for example, specializes only in having a Web presence and an order fulfillment facility. Other than a few best-sellers, it doesn't inventory any merchandise. It simply processes and fulfills orders. It is a modular company insofar as it combines

FIGURE 13.7 The Boundaryless Organization, the Modular Organization, and the Virtual Organization

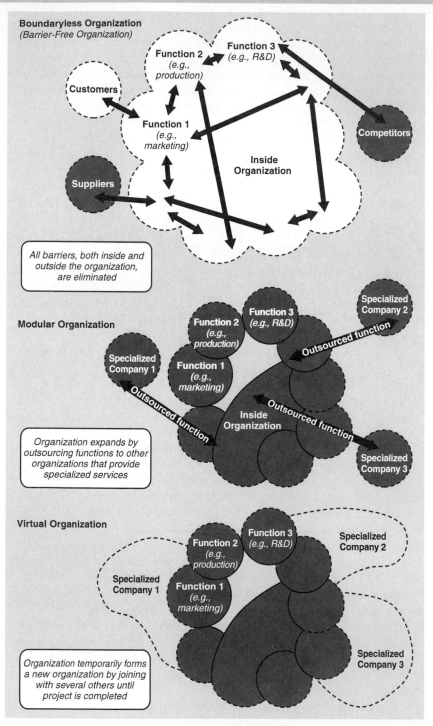

The true *boundaryless organization* is free of both internal barriers and external barriers. Variants, such as the *modular organization* and the *virtual organization,* eliminate only external barriers.

its own expertise in order fulfillment with other companies' expertise in inventory handling and shipping to serve its customers.

VIRTUAL ORGANIZATIONS

Another variation on the boundaryless organization is the **virtual organization**. Such an organization is composed of a continually evolving network of companies (e.g., suppliers and customers) that are linked together to share skills, costs, and access to markets. They form a partnership to capitalize on their existing skills while pursuing common objectives. In most cases, after these objectives have been met, the organizations disband.[16] Unlike modular organizations, which maintain close control over the companies with which they do outsourcing, virtual organizations give up some control and become part of a new organization, at least for a while.

> Corning, the giant glass and ceramics manufacturer, is a good example of a company that builds upon itself by developing partnerships with other companies (including Siemens, the German electronics firm, and Vitro, the largest glass manufacturer from Mexico). In fact, Corning officials see their company not as a single entity, but as "a network of organizations."

Corning, the giant glass and ceramics manufacturer, is a good example of a company that builds upon itself by developing partnerships with other companies (including Siemens, the German electronics firm, and Vitro, the largest glass manufacturer from Mexico). In fact, Corning officials see their company not as a single entity, but as "a network of organizations."[17] The same can be said of NEC, the large Japanese computer and electronics company, and the software giant Microsoft.[18] Both companies actively develop new organizations with which to network by providing venture capital funding for current research to staff members to develop their own companies. These new companies are referred to as **affiliate networks**—satellite organizations that are affiliated with core companies that have helped them develop. The idea behind affiliate networks is that these new firms can work with, rather than compete against, their much larger parents on emerging technology.[19]

The underlying idea of a virtual organization is that each participating company contributes only its core competencies (i.e., its areas of greatest strength). By several companies mixing and matching the best of what they can offer, a joint product is created that is better than any single company could have created alone. Virtual corporations are not unusual in the entertainment industry. Indeed, Time Warner also has become part of several multimedia ventures. By sharing risks, costs, and expertise, many of today's companies are finding the virtual organization to be a highly appealing type of organizational structure.

Interorganizational Designs: Going Beyond the Single Organization

All the organizational designs I have examined thus far have concentrated on the arrangement of units *within* an organization—what may be termed *intraorganizational*

When Should Companies Go Virtual?

More and more of today's companies are finding it useful to "go virtual," downscaling their hierarchies and networking with other companies on an ad-hoc basis. Doing so allows them to move more quickly, standing a better chance of improving in a highly competitive environment. However, virtual organizations are far from perfect. Because people from different companies do not share common values, interpersonal conflicts are likely to occur, and coordination is often challenging. This raises an important question: When should companies organize in a virtual manner?

The answer depends on how the organizations fare with respect to two considerations: the type of capabilities the company needs and the type of change that will be made.[20] Specifically, organizational changes may be either *autonomous* or *systemic*. **Autonomous change** is one that is made independently of other changes. For an example, an auto company that develops a new type of upholstery may do so without revising the rest of the car. **Systemic change** is such that change in one part of an organization requires changes in another part of that same organization. For example, Polaroid's development of instant photography required changes in both film and camera technologies.

A second key distinction involves the capabilities needed to complete the project. In some cases, outside capabilities are required. For example, in the early 1980s, IBM was able to develop its first personal computer in only 15 months because it went outside the company for expertise (e.g., buying chips from Intel and an operating system from Microsoft). Other times, capability can be found inside the company. For example, Ford traditionally develops many of the components used in its cars, making it less dependent on other companies (although it does far less of this than it used to).[21]

By combining these factors, it becomes clear when companies should "go virtual" and when they should work exclusively within their own walls. *Virtual organizations work best for companies considering autonomous changes using technologies that exist only outside their walls.* For example, Motorola has developed virtual organizations with several battery manufacturers for its cell phones and pagers. In so doing, it can focus on its core business—the delivery of wireless communication—while ensuring it has the battery power to make such devices work.

In contrast, *companies should keep their focus inward when changes are systemic in nature and involve capabilities the company either already has can create.* Under such conditions, relying on outside help may be far too risky—and unnecessary. For example, these days Intel is making extensive investments to enhance its current and future capacities.

Finally, for conditions that fall between these extremes (i.e., when systemic changes are being made using capabilities that come only from outside the company, and when autonomous changes are being made using capabilities that must be created), virtual alliances should be created with extreme caution. Clearly, the virtual organization has a key place in today's organizational world. The trick, however, lies in understanding precisely what that place is. These guiding principles represent useful guidance in that respect.

Questions for Discussion

1. Using these guidelines, what companies do you think should "go virtual"? Explain why.
2. Using these guidelines, what companies do you think should strive to be self-contained? Explain why.
3. Besides those mentioned here, what additional advantages and disadvantages are there to forming virtual organizations?

designs. However, sometimes at least some parts of different organizations must operate jointly. To coordinate their efforts on such projects, organizations must create *interorganizational designs,* plans by which two or more organizations come together. Two such designs are commonly found: *conglomerates* and *strategic alliances*.

CONGLOMERATES: DIVERSIFIED "MEGACORPORATIONS"

When an organization diversifies by adding an entirely unrelated business or product to its organizational design, it may be said to have formed a **conglomerate**. Some of the world's largest conglomerates may be found in Asia. For example, in Korea, companies such as Samsung and Hyundai produce home electronics, automobiles, textiles, and chemicals in large, unified conglomerates known as **chaebols**.[22] These are all separate companies overseen by the same parent company leadership. In Japan, the same type of arrangement is known as a **keiretsu**.[23] A good example of a keiretsu is the Matsushita Group.[24] This enormous conglomerate consists of a bank (Asahi Bank), a consumer electronics company (Panasonic), and several insurance companies (e.g., Sumitomo Life, Nippon Life). These examples are not meant to suggest that conglomerates are unique to Asia. Indeed, many large U.S.-based corporations, such as IBM and Tenneco, are also conglomerates.

Companies form conglomerates for several reasons. First, as an independent business, the parent company can enjoy the benefits of diversification. Thus, as one industry languishes, another may excel, allowing a stable economic outlook for the parent company. In addition, conglomerates may provide built-in markets and access to supplies, because companies typically support other organizations within the conglomerate. For example, General Motors cars and trucks are fitted with Delco radios, and Ford cars and trucks have engines with Autolite spark plugs. Delco and Autolite are separate companies that are owned by their respective parent companies. In this manner conglomerates can benefit by providing a network of organizations that are dependent on each other for products and services, thereby creating considerable advantages.

In recent years, however, many large conglomerates have been selling off parts of themselves in a move to concentrate on their core business.[25] For example, The Limited, the large women's clothing retailer, closed or sold off some of its specialty stores in 1998 (e.g., Cacique and Abercrombie & Fitch) so that it could focus on its core business.

STRATEGIC ALLIANCES: JOINING FORCES FOR MUTUAL BENEFIT

A **strategic alliance** is a type of organizational design in which two or more separate firms join their competitive capabilities to operate a specific business. The goal of a strategic alliance is to provide benefits to each individual organization that could not be attained if they operated separately. They are low-risk ways of diversifying (adding new business operations) and entering new markets. Some companies, such as GE and Ford have strategic alliances with many others. Some alliances last only a short time, whereas others have remained in existence for well over 20 years and are still going strong.[26] Three major types of strategic alliances may be identified.[27] As shown in Figure 13.8, these may be arranged along a continuum from those alliances that are weak and distant, at one end, to those that are strong and close, at the other end. I will now describe each.

Mutual service consortia.   At the weak end of the continuum are strategic alliances known as **mutual service consortia**. These are arrangements between two similar companies from the same or similar industries to pool their resources to receive a benefit that would be too difficult or expensive for either to obtain alone. Often, the focus is some high-tech capacity, such as an expensive piece of diagnostic equipment that might be shared by two or more local hospitals (e.g., a magneto-resonance imaging, or MRI, unit).

Value-chain partnerships.   At the opposite end of the scale are the strongest and closest type of collaborations, referred to as **value-chain partnerships**. These are alliances between companies in different industries that have complementary capabilities. Customer–supplier relationships are a prime example. In such arrangements one company buys necessary goods and services from another so that it can do business. Because each company greatly depends on the other, each party's commitment to their

FIGURE 13.8 Strategic Alliances: A Continuum of Interorganizational Relationships

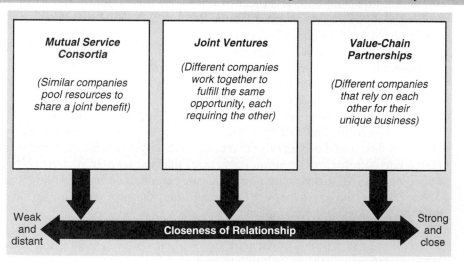

The three types of *strategic alliances* identified here may be distinguished with respect to their location along a continuum ranging from weak and distant at one end, to strong and close, at the other end.

mutual relationship is high. As noted earlier, Toyota has a network of 230 suppliers with whom it regularly does business. The relationship between Toyota and these various companies represents value-chain partnerships.

Joint ventures. Between these two extremes are **joint ventures**. These are arrangements in which companies work together to fulfill opportunities that require the capabilities of the other. For example, two companies might enter into a joint venture if one has a valuable technology and the other has the marketing knowledge to help transform that technology into a viable commercial product.

There are clear benefits to be derived from forming joint ventures. These primarily come in the form of improved technology, widened markets, and greater economies of scale (e.g., sharing functional operations across organizations). However, as you might imagine, for these benefits to be realized, a high degree of coordination and fit must exist between the parties, each delivering on its promise to the other.

> *AT&T and Olivetti tried unsuccessfully to work together on manufacturing personal computers. Strong differences in management styles and organizational culture were cited as causes.*

Not surprisingly, not all strategic alliances are successful. For example, AT&T and Olivetti tried unsuccessfully to work together on manufacturing personal computers. Strong differences in management styles and organizational culture were cited as causes (see Chapter 11). Clearly, for strategic alliances to work, the companies must be able not only to offer each other something important but also to work together to make it happen.

With an enormous market now opening its doors to Western capitalism, the idea of joint ventures with Chinese companies is very appealing to organizations in the Western world. Some companies, such as Johnson & Johnson, have enjoyed considerable success in such joint ventures. However, most are finding it difficult to make these relationships work.[28] Consider, for example, the experiences of a U.S.-based household-products company that formed a joint venture with Shanhai Jahwa Corporation, China's largest cosmetics manufacturer. The U.S. company was looking for help introducing its products in the large Chinese market by tapping into Jahwa's distribution systems. It also was hoping for what the Chinese call *guanxi*—that is, the social and political connections required to become successful in China. In turn, Jahwa officials were looking for help in upgrading their technology and boosting their capacity to compete in the international marketplace. Unfortunately, serious disagreements over directions and resources paralyzed the two companies, thereby resulting in a failed deal. Making matters worse, joint ventures are difficult to dissolve in Chinese culture because the relationship between the two companies is based on trust. Thus, walking away from such relationships comes at a considerable loss of face (i.e., esteem in the eyes of others). Not surprisingly, OB scientists are paying considerable attention to the question of how to improve joint ventures across national boundaries.[29]

SUMMARY: HAVE I MET THE LEARNING OBJECTIVES?

You can be certain that you have met the learning objectives for this chapter found on p. 335 if you understand the following:

1. **DEFINE organizational structure and DISTINGUISH between five aspects of organizational structure that are represented in an organization chart.** The formal configuration between individuals and groups with respect to the allocation of tasks, responsibilities, and authority within organizations is known as *organizational structure*. An organization chart reveals five different elements of organizational structure. These are: (a) *division of labor* (the degree to which jobs are specialized, (b) *hierarchy of authority* (a summary of reporting relationships), (c) *span of control* (the number of individuals over which a manager has responsibility), (d) *line versus staff positions* (jobs permitting direct decision-making power versus jobs in which advice is given), and (e) *decentralization* (the degree to which decisions can be made by lower-ranking employees as opposed to a few higher-ranking individuals).

2. **DISTINGUISH between the three types of departmentalization: functional organizations, product organizations, and matrix organizations.** Within organizations, groups of people can be combined into departments in various ways. The most popular approach is the *functional organization,* created by combining people in terms of the common functions they perform (e.g., sales, manufacturing). An alternative approach, to departmentalize people by virtue of the specific products for which they are responsible, is known as the *product organization*. Another form of departmentalization combines both of these approaches into a single form known as the *matrix organization*. In such organizations, people have at least two bosses; they are responsible to a superior in charge of the various functions and a superior in charge of the specific product. Employees also may have to answer to high-ranking people responsible for the entire organization, the top leaders.

3. **DEFINE organizational design and DISTINGUISH between classical and neoclassical approaches to organizational design.** The process of coordinating the structural elements of organizations in the most appropriate manner is known as *organizational design*. *Classical organizational theories* claim that a universally best way to design organizations exists, an approach based on high efficiency. *Neoclassical organizational theories* also claim that there is one best way to design organizations, although this approach emphasizes the need to pay attention to basic human needs to succeed and express oneself.

4. **DESCRIBE the contingency approach to organizational design.** The *contingency approach* to organizational design is predicated on the belief that the most appropriate way to design organizations depends on the external environments within which they operate. Specifically, a key factor has to do with the degree to which the organization is subject to change: A *stable environment* is one in which business conditions do not change, whereas a *turbulent environment* is one in which conditions change rapidly. When conditions are stable, mechanistic organizations are most effective. A *mechanistic organization* is one in which people perform specialized jobs, many rigid rules are imposed, and authority is vested in a few top-ranking officials. When conditions are turbulent, an *organic organization* is effective. In these organizations, jobs are very general, there are few rules, and decisions can be made by low-level employees. The mechanistic and organic forms are pure types, and organizations can be located in-between these two extremes.

5. **DESCRIBE four emerging approaches to organizational design.** The *horizontal organization* involves flattening organizational hierarchies and using autonomous teams working together on basic processes, rather than separate tasks. The *boundaryless organization* is an organization designed such that there are no chains of command, spans of control are unlimited, and empowered teams with ill-defined roles are used instead of rigid departments. Variations include *modular organizations* (in which secondary aspects of the company's operations are outsourced) and *virtual organizations* (in which organizations combine forces with others on a temporary basis to form new organizations).

6. **IDENTIFY two different types of interorganizational designs.** Interorganizational designs represent ways of combining more than one organization. They include the *conglomerates* (large corporations that diversify by getting involved in unrelated businesses) and the *strategic alliances* (organizations combining forces to operate a specific business). There are three types of strategic alliances: *mutual service consortia* (in which similar companies pool resources to share a joint benefit), *joint ventures* (in which different companies work together to fulfill the same opportunity, each requiring the other), and *value-chain partnerships* (in which different companies rely on each other for their unique business).

You Be the Consultant

The president of a small but rapidly growing software company asks you to consult with him about an important matter. As the company expands, several options for designing the company's operations are being considered, and your job is to help him make a decision about which route to take. Answer the following questions relevant to this situation based on the material in this chapter.

1. What would you recommend with respect to the following structural variables: division of labor (specialized or not?), hierarchy of authority (tall or flat?), span of control (wide or narrow?), and degree of centralization (highly centralized or highly decentralized?). Explain the reasons behind your recommendations.

2. How do you think the company should be departmentalized—by task (functional), by output (product), by both task and output (matrix), or by process (horizontal)? What are your reasons for these conclusions?

3. If the company were thinking about entering into a strategic alliance with another, what factors would have to be considered? What kind of company would be an effective partner in an alliance with this software firm?

SELF-ASSESSMENT EXERCISE

Which Do You Prefer—Mechanistic or Organic Organizations?

Because mechanistic and organic organizations are so different, it is reasonable to expect that people will tend to prefer one of these organizational forms over the other. This questionnaire is designed to help you identify your own preferences (and, in so doing, to help you learn about the different forms themselves).

Directions

Each of the following questions deals with your preferences for various conditions that may exist where you work. Answer each one by checking the one alternative that best describes your feelings.

1. When I have a job-related decision to make, I usually prefer to:
   ____a. make the decision myself.
   ____b. have my boss make it for me.
2. I usually find myself more interested in performing:
   ____a. a highly narrow, specialized task.
   ____b. many different types of tasks.
3. I prefer to work in places in which working conditions:
   ____a. change a great deal.
   ____b. generally remain the same.
4. When a lot of rules are imposed on me, I generally feel:
   ____a. very comfortable.
   ____b. very uncomfortable.
5. I believe that governmental regulation of industry is:
   ____a. usually best for all.
   ____b. rarely good for anyone.

Scoring

1. Give yourself 1 point each time you answered as follows: 1 = b; 2 = a; 3 = b; 4 = a; 5 = a. This score is your preference for *mechanistic organizations*.
2. Subtract this score from 5. This score is your preference for *organic organizations*.
3. Interpret your two scores as follows: Higher scores (closer to 5) reflect stronger preferences, and lower scores (closer to 0) reflect weaker preferences.

Questions for Discussion

1. How did you score? That is, which organizational form do you prefer?
2. Think back over the jobs you've had. For the most part, have these been in organizations that were mechanistic or organic?
3. Do you think you were any more committed to working in organizations whose designs matched your preferences as compared to those in which there was a mismatch?

(**GROUP EXERCISE**)

Comparing Span of Control in Organization Charts

One of the easiest things to determine about a company by looking at its organization chart is its span of control. This exercise will allow you to learn about, and compare, span of control within different companies.

Directions

1. Divide the class into four equal-size groups.
2. Assign one of the following industry types to each group: (a) manufacturing companies, (b) financial institutions, (c) public utilities, and (d) charities.
3. Within the industry assigned to each group, identify one company per student. It helps to consider larger organizations inasmuch as these are more likely to have formal organization charts. For example, if there are five students in the "financial institutions" group, name five different banks or savings and loan institutions.
4. Each student should get a copy of the organization chart (or, at least a portion of it) for the company assigned to him or her in step 3. You may be able to get this information from various companies' Websites or by consulting their annual reports (which may be found in many libraries). If all else fails, you may have to ask someone you know who works at a given company to show you its organization chart.
5. Meet as a group to discuss the spans of control of the organizations in your sample.
6. Gather as a class to compare the findings of the various groups.

Questions for Discussion

1. Were you successful in being able to collect the organization charts, or were the organizations reluctant to share them?
2. Did you find that there were differences with respect to span of control?
3. Were spans of control different at different organizational levels or for different industry groups? If so, in what ways were they similar and different?

NOTES

Case Note
Brown, E. (1998, December 7). VF Corp. changes its underware. *Fortune*, pp. 115–118.

Chapter Notes

[1] Daft, R. L. (2000). *Essentials of organization theory and design.* Cincinnati, OH: South-Western.
[2] Schminke, M., Ambrose, M. L., & Cropanzano, R. S. (2000). The effect of organizational structure on perceptions of procedural fairness. *Journal of Applied Psychology, 85*, 284–304.
[3] Cameron, K. S. (1998). Strategic organizational downsizing: An extreme case. In B. M. Staw & L. L. Cummings (Eds.) *Research in organizational behavior* (Vol. 20, pp. 141–184). Greenwich, CT: JAI Press.
[4] Kaufman, L. H. (2000). Centralized or decentralized management. *Railway Age, 201*(8), 47-52.
[5] Goff, R. (2000, May 29). Business careers. *Computerworld*, pp. 54–56.
[6] Tushman, M. L., Nadler, N. B., & Nadler, D. A. (1997). *Competing by design: The power of organizational architecture.* New York: Oxford University Press.
[7] Stewart, T. A. (1992, May 18). The search for the organization of tomorrow. *Fortune*, pp. 93–98 (quote p. 93).
[8] Byrne, J. A. (1993, December 20). The horizontal corporation. *Business Week*, pp. 76–81 (quote p. 96).
[9] See Note 8 (quote p. 96).
[10] GE: Just your average everyday $60 billion family grocery store. (1994, May 2). *Industry Week*, pp. 13–18.
[11] Ashkenas, R., Ulrich, D., Jick, T., & Kerr, S. (1998). *The boundaryless organization: Breaking the chains of organizational structure.* San Francisco: Jossey-Bass.

[12] Dees, G. D., Rasheed, A. M. A., McLaughlin, K. J., & Priem, R. L. (1995). The new corporate architecture. *Academy of Management Executive, 9,* 7–18.

[13] See Note 12.

[14] Tully, S. (1993, February 3). The modular corporation. *Fortune,* pp. 106–108, 110.

[15] Werther, W. B., Jr. (1999, March–April). Structure-driven strategy and virtual organizational design. *Business Horizons,* pp. 13–18.

[16] Byrne, J. (1993, February 8). The virtual corporation. *Business Week,* pp. 99–103.

[17] Sherman, S. (1992, September 21). Are strategic alliances working? *Fortune,* pp. 77–78 (quote p. 78).

[18] Nathan, R. (1998, July–August). NEC organizing for creativity, nimbleness. *Research Technology Management,* pp. 4–6.

[19] Moore, J. F. (1998, Winter). The rise of a new corporate form. *Washington Quarterly,* pp. 167–181.

[20] Chesborough, H. W., & Teece, D. J. (1996, January–February). When is virtual virtuous? Organizing for innovation. *Harvard Business Review, 96,* 65–73.

[21] See Note 20.

[22] Nakarmi, L., & Einhorn, B. (1993, June 7). Hyundai's gutsy gambit. *Business Week,* p. 48.

[23] Lincoln, J. R., Gerlach, M., & Ahmadjian, C. (1998). Evolving patterns of keiretsu organization and action in Japan. In Staw & Cummings (Eds.), *Research in organizational behavior* (Vol. 20, pp. 303–345).

[24] Miyashita, K., & Russell, D. (1995). *Keiretsu: Inside the Japanese conglomerates.* New York: McGraw-Hill.

[25] Lubove, S. (1992, December 7). How to grow big yet stay small. *Forbes,* pp. 64–66.

[26] Kanter, R. M. (1994, July–August). Collaborative advantage: The art of alliances. *Harvard Business Review,* pp. 96–108.

[27] See Note 27.

[28] Vanhonacker, W. (1997, March–April). Entering China: An unconventional approach. *Harvard Business Review, 97,* 130–131, 134–136, 138–140.

[29] Merchant, H. (2000). Configurations of international joint ventures. *Management International Review, 40*(2), 107–140.

14

Managing organizational change:
strategic planning and organizational development

LEARNING OBJECTIVES

After reading this chapter, you will be able to:

1. IDENTIFY the major external forces responsible for organizational change.

2. DESCRIBE what is meant by strategic planning and IDENTIFY the steps in the process of planning strategic change.

3. IDENTIFY the conditions under which organizational change occurs.

4. DESCRIBE why people are resistant to change in organizations and ways in which this resistance may be overcome.

5. DEFINE organizational development (OD) and DESCRIBE three OD techniques.

6. DESCRIBE the conditions under which OD is most effective.

THREE GOOD REASONS WHY YOU SHOULD CARE ABOUT. . .

Managing Organizational Change

You should care about managing organizational change because:

1. The success—even the mere survival—of companies depends on their ability to adapt to change.

2. Overcoming resistance to change promotes organizational effectiveness.

3. Organizational development techniques help people adapt to change.

Making the Case for... Managing Organizational Change

Making Change at the U.S. Mint

When Philip Diehl became director of the United States Mint in September 1994, he found it to be the stereotype of an old government agency—inefficient, slow, and without a clue about the standards of performance required for success in the private sector. Today, however, the U.S. Mint makes money by making money. It sells the services of its heralded police force to other government agencies, and it sells collectable coins to the public, including the popular 50 State Quarters Program. It even has a full-featured Web site where visitors can share their ideas on the design of coins and purchase such items as commemorative coins, jewelry, and gifts of all types. So successful is the Mint that it has grown to a *Fortune* 500–sized manufacturing and international marketing company with 2,200 employees and over $1 billion in annual revenue. "If this were a company," Diehl told his colleagues at a meeting, "a bunch of you would be millionaires."

During his six years at the Mint, Diehl has made big changes, "but they've been made incrementally," he cautions, adding that, "You do big things by doing lots of small things." Diehl's first order of business involved improving the Mint's relationships with its customers. Until he came along, the Mint treated its customers awfully. Orders were held an average of two months until customers' checks cleared before shipping their orders. Irate customers called, but often no one answered the phone. Not only wasn't there any sense of urgency about the problem, but many workers sensed that there wasn't even a problem at all.

To find out exactly what customers thought of the Mint and how to improve services, Diehl decided to administer a questionnaire. He found, however, that the Office of Management and Budget actively discouraged government agencies from spending money on surveys. So, if the Mint couldn't conduct a survey, Diehl decided to do his own survey. He went to coin conventions where he spoke to hobbyists and writers from coin collecting magazines, listening carefully to what they had to say. Two problems immediately came to his attention: Orders took too long to be filled, and the Mint held onto its customers' up-front payments too long.

To tackle these problems, Diel assembled a task force, which made some progress, but more was needed. So, he went public with a new customer service agenda. To the media, he announced that the Mint would process 95 percent of its orders within six weeks. Although this goal was modest, it was a reasonable beginning. Soon, employees felt a sense of urgency and developed a new sense of accountability to customers. As this goal was approached, Diehl tightened the standard to 95 percent in four weeks, ratcheting it up still further with each successive improvement in performance. Today 95 percent of the products are delivered within two weeks, and many are shipped in only one.

Soon, Mint employees developed a new sense of pride and excitement in their work, and customers became more enthusiastic about the Mint's products. Calls to the customer service center that used to be answered in 2 minutes, if at all, are now being answered in only 17.5 seconds. Similarly, returns or credits that used to take a month to process are now being handled in only 3 days. So improved are the Mint's services that it has received the highest scores of any government agency in a national poll. Its customer satisfaction scores are tied with the venerable H. J. Heinz and rank second only to Mercedes-Benz.

There can be no doubt that Diehl has overseen a dramatic change in the Mint's operations, helping it attain "mint condition" as a service provider. Of course, it's not only the Mint that has seen dramatic changes over the years. Just think about how the menus of fast-food restaurants have become more diversified, commerce over the Internet now occurs regularly, and banks are merging into "megafinancial institutions."

Although the impact of *organizational change* can be found everywhere, most people have difficulty accepting that they may have to alter their work methods. After all, if you're used to working a certain way, a sudden change can be very unsettling. Fortunately, social scientists have developed various methods, known collectively as *organizational development* techniques, that are designed to implement needed organizational change in a manner that is both acceptable to employees and that enhances the effectiveness of the organizations involved.

I will review these techniques in this chapter. Before doing so, however, I will take a closer look at the organizational change process by chronicling different forces for change acting on organizations. Then, I will explore some major issues involved in the organizational change process, such as what is changed, when change occurs, why people are resistant to change, and—importantly—how this resistance can be overcome.

Today's First Rule of Business: Change or Disappear!

A century ago, advances in machine technology made farming so highly efficient that fewer hands were needed to plant and reap the harvest. The displaced laborers fled to nearby cities, seeking jobs in newly opened factories, opportunities created by some of the same technologies that sent them from the farm. The economy shifted from agrarian to manufacturing, and the *industrial revolution* was under way. With it came drastic shifts in where people lived, how they worked, how they spent their leisure time, how much money they made, and how they spent it. Today's business analysts claim that we are currently experiencing *another* industrial revolution—one driven by a new wave of economic and technological forces. As one observer put it, "This workplace revolution . . . may be remembered as a historic event, the Western equivalent of the collapse of communism."[1]

In recent years, just about all companies, large and small, have made adjustments in the ways they operate, some more pronounced than others. Citing just a few examples, General Electric, Allied Signal, Ameritech, and Tenneco all have radically altered the way they operate: their culture, the technology they use, their structure, and the nature of their relations with employees. With so many companies making such drastic changes, the message is clear: *Either adapt to changing conditions or shut your doors.* As technology and markets change, organizations face a formidable challenge to adapt. When they fail to do so, they are forced to close their doors forever.

EXTERNAL FORCES FOR ORGANIZATIONAL CHANGE

What outside forces cause organizations to change? Although there are many different drivers of organizational change, five particular forces are sufficiently important to be described. These are the introduction of information technology, changing employee demographics, performance gaps, government regulation, and global economic competition.

Computer technology. Probably the most potent impetus for organizational change is the introduction of the computer. In offices, word processing systems have replaced typewriters; in factories, robots have replaced people performing dangerous and repetitive jobs; and in some recording studios, sophisticated synthesizer units housed in simple black boxes have replaced orchestras full of people. Although office personnel, factory workers, and musicians surely have not become extinct, computer technology has changed the way they are doing their jobs. For an overview of ways in which the introduction of high-tech devices in the workplace have helped people perform—and to better serve the needs of customers and society at large—see Table 14.1.

> *Although some jobs have been eliminated because of automation, technology generally has helped those who have become displaced find more interesting and personally fulfilling jobs. The widespread fear that many people had about "being replaced by robots" has proven to be unfounded.*

Although some jobs have been eliminated because of automation, technology generally has helped those who have become displaced find more interesting and personally fulfilling jobs. The widespread fear that many people had about "being replaced by robots" has proven to be unfounded. More typical is the situation in which people work side by side with robots, each doing what they do best. For example, although robots play a large part in the production of automobiles, such as General Motors' highly regarded Saturn, company officials acknowledge that the technology works only because of the people. Advanced technology alone won't build a successful car. In the words of Japanese industrialist Jaruo Shimada, "Only people give wisdom to the machines."[2] The idea is that people and machines are complementary aspects of any organization.

Changing employee demographics. There's no mistaking the fact that the composition of the workforce has changed in the past few years. As I noted in Chapter 5, the American workforce is now more racially and ethnically diverse than ever. It also contains more women, more foreign nationals, and more elderly people. To people concerned with the long-term operation of organizations, this is not simply a curious sociological trend, but a set of shifting conditions that forces organization officials to make various adaptations. For example, human resources specialists need to know if there will be a drop in the number of qualified applicants (suggesting the need to import employees from other locations or even to relocate the company), as well as the specific skills employees will be bringing to their jobs (suggesting the need to revise training programs) and their special needs (such as child care, or flexible working arrangements). In the words of a high-ranking executive at General Electric, the changes in workforce demographics "will turn the professional human-resources world upside down."[3]

Performance gaps. A product line that isn't moving, a vanishing profit margin, and a level of sales that isn't up to corporate expectations—these are examples of **perfor-**

TABLE 14.1 How Has Computer Technology Changed the Way We Work?		

Advances in computer technology have revolutionized many of the ways we work. Some key ways in which this has been occurring are summarized here.

Area of Change	*Old Way*	*New Technology Examples*
Use of machines	Materials were moved by hand, with the aid of mechanical devices (e.g., pulleys and chains).	**Automation** is prevalent—the process of using machines to perform tasks that might otherwise be done by people. For example, computer-controlled machines manipulate materials and perform complex functions, a process known as **industrial robotics (IR)**.
Work by handicapped employees	People with various physical or mental handicaps either were relegated to the most simple jobs, or they didn't work at all.	**Assistive technology** is widespread—devices and other solutions that help individuals with physical or mental problems perform the various actions needed to do their jobs. For example, **telephone handset amplifiers** make it possible for people with hearing impediments to use the telephone and **voice recognition systems** read to people with visual impairments.
Monitoring employees	Supervisors used to physically enter the offices of employees at work and observe them from afar.	**Computerized performance monitoring** systems are in widespread use, which allow supervisors to access their subordinates' computers for purposes of assessing how well they are performing their jobs.
Customer service	Individual service providers did things to help employees, customizing goods and services as time and skill allowed.	**Personalized service** is likely to take the form of greeting visitors to one's Web page with information customized to match the goods and services in which they expressed interest in their last visit (e.g., Amazon.com does this).
Environmental friendliness	Products at the end of their lives were buried in landfills, often polluting the earth.	**Design for disassembly (DFD)** is the process of designing and building products so that their parts can be reused several times and then disposed of at the end of the product's life without harming the environment.

mance gaps, discrepancies between real and expected levels of organizational performance. Few things force change more than sudden and unexpected information about poor performance. A recent example is General Motors' decision to phase out its Oldsmobile brand. Although the Oldsmobile was produced for over 100 years, its failure to respond to changing demands (specifically, vehicles that were appealing to younger buyers) eventually led to its demise.[4] Organizations that are best prepared to mobilize change in response to downturns are best prepared to succeed. Indeed, General Motors officials are hoping that the decision to pull the plug on the Oldsmobile brand will help the company regain its prominence in the auto industry.[5]

Government regulation.   One of the most commonly witnessed unplanned organizational changes results from government regulations. In recent years, restaurant owners in the United States had to alter the way they report the income of waiters and waitresses to the federal government for purposes of collecting income taxes. Moreover, the U.S. federal government has been involved in both imposing and eliminating regulations in industries such as commercial airlines (e.g., mandating inspection schedules, but no longer controlling fares) and banking (e.g., restricting the amount of time checks can be held before clearing, but no longer regulating interest rates). Such activities have greatly influenced the way business is conducted in these industries.

Global economic competition.   Competition from the marketplace is a key driver of organizational change. Any company that fails to keep up with the competition (with respect to price, features, services, or other key features) doesn't stand a chance of surviving. Although competition always has been crucial to organizational success, competition today comes from all over the world. As it has become increasingly less expensive to transport materials around the world, the industrialized nations have found themselves competing with each other for shares of the international marketplace in nations all over the world. This extensive globalization of the economy presents a strong need to change and to be innovative.[6]

For example, large American automobile manufacturers suffered in the 1970s and 1980s because they were unprepared to meet the world's growing demand for small high-quality cars—products their Japanese competitors were only too glad to supply to an eager marketplace. As a result, the automobile business has become truly global in scope. Instead of domination by the traditional "Big Three" auto makers (General Motors, Ford, and Chrysler), all based in the United States, today's auto market is dominated by the "Global Five" (General Motors, Ford, Daimler-Chrysler, Toyota, and Volkswagen), only two of which are headquartered in the United States, and all of which have facilities throughout the world.[7]

MAGNITUDE OF CHANGE: HOW MUCH CHANGE CONSTITUTES CHANGE?

As you might imagine, not all organizational changes are equal in magnitude. Whereas some are minor and subtle, others are far more dramatic and wide-reaching in scope and impact.

First-order change.   Change that is continuous in nature and that involves no major shifts in how an organization operates is known as **first-order change** (or **incremental change**). Changes of this type are apparent in the deliberate, incremental modifications Toyota has made in continuously improving the efficiency of its production process. Not surprisingly, employees are less threatened by incremental changes than by more monumental changes because they have time to adapt and to make appropriate adjustments.

Second-order change.   Other types of organizational change are far more complex. **Second-order change** (or **quantum change**) refers to radical change, involving major shifts in different levels of the organization and different aspects of the business.[8] For example, many large companies, such as General Electric and AlliedSignal, have radically altered the way they operate, their culture, the technology they use, their structure, and the nature of their relations with employees. Not surprisingly, quantum change often is quite jarring and highly traumatic to employees, and as such, getting them to accept such changes is often difficult.

Planning Strategic Change

Thus far, I have described unplanned organizational change. However, not all changes that are made in organizations fall into this category. Organizations also make changes that are carefully planned and deliberate. This is the idea of **strategic planning**, defined as the process of formulating, implementing, and evaluating organizational changes in ways that enable an organization to achieve its objectives.[9] In this section of the chapter, I will describe the strategic planning process.

BASIC ASSUMPTIONS ABOUT STRATEGIC PLANNING

To understand the nature of strategic plans used in organizations today, it is important to identify three fundamental assumptions about them.[10]

1. *Strategic planning is deliberate.* When organizations make strategic plans, they make conscious decisions to change fundamental aspects of themselves. These changes tend to be radical, second-order changes (e.g., changing the nature of the business) as opposed to minor, first-order changes (e.g., changing the color of the office walls) in nature.

2. *Strategic planning occurs when current objectives no longer can be met.* Generally, when a company's present strategy is bringing about the desired results, change is unlikely. However, whenever it becomes clear that current objectives no longer can be met, new strategies are formulated to turn things around.

3. *New organizational objectives require new strategic plans.* Whenever a company takes steps to move in a completely new direction, it establishes new objectives, and it designs a strategic plan to meet them. Acknowledging that the various parts of an organization are interdependent, this new strategic plan is likely to involve all functions and levels of the organization.

To illustrate how these assumptions come to life, I will now describe some examples of strategic plans for change.

ABOUT WHAT DO COMPANIES MAKE STRATEGIC PLANS?

As you might imagine, organizations can make strategic plans to change just about anything. Most of the strategic planning today, however, involves changing either a company's products and services or its organizational structure.

Products and services. Over the past few years, many well-known bricks-and-mortar retail establishments, such as Barnes & Noble, Toys "R" Us, and CompUSA, jumped on the e-commerce bandwagon after it became apparent that doing so would expand their customer base by extending their well-known names to the Web. They also made this strategic move as a hedge against losing business to companies such as Amazon.com and MicroWarehouse, whose online-only presence made serious inroads into their respective markets. Some companies have even moved in the opposite direction. For example, Gateway made a strategic move from online presence to physical presence, with its Gateway Country stores. These are all examples of strategic changes in the delivery of services. Many companies also have made strategic changes in their product offerings. For example, Sony has added several new television sets to its product line, including tiny handheld units and large, thin, widescreen plasma models in a strategic move to develop new segments of the market.

Often, plans for strategic change create considerable challenges in organizations, as they struggle with the new technologies and skills required to succeed. For example, during the early 1990s, FedEx (which was Federal Express at the time) suffered dramatic growing pains as it sought to expand its market from North America to the rest of the world. Although service suffered at first under the strain of the added business, the company's international operations have proven successful. Still, outside North America, it is not FedEx, but DHL, which has the greatest presence in the parcel delivery market, suggesting that FedEx has a long way to go. However, with its recent acquisition of RPS, FedEx's strategic plan appears to focus more on chipping away at UPS's dominance in the North American market than on global expansion. As these examples illustrate, strategic plans in products and services can be quite complex.

Organizational structure.   In addition to making strategic plans about changes in products and services, companies also make strategic plans about their organizational structures (see Chapter 13). Consider, for example, PepsiCo's strategic decision to reorganize.[11] For many years, it had a separate international food-service division, which included 62 foreign locations of its Pizza Hut and Taco Bell restaurants. Then, in 1990, because of the great profit potential from its foreign restaurants, PepsiCo officials decided to reorganize, putting these restaurants under direct control of the same executives responsible for the successful U.S. operations of Pizza Hut, Kentucky Fried Chicken, and Taco Bell. In 1997, however, PepsiCo made another strategic decision—to get out of the restaurant business altogether. It spun off these three restaurants to form a separate company, TRICON Global Restaurants.

> *In 1990, because of the great profit potential from its foreign restaurants, PepsiCo officials decided to reorganize, putting these restaurants under direct control of the same executives responsible for the successful U.S. operations of Pizza Hut, Kentucky Fried Chicken, and Taco Bell. In 1997, however, PepsiCo made another strategic decision—to get out of the restaurant business altogether. It spun off these three restaurants to form a separate company, TRICON Global Restaurants.*

These days, many organizations have made strategic changes regarding the nature of the work they will do. In fact, they have completely eliminated units that focus on noncore sectors of their business and then contracted with outside firms to perform these functions instead. This practice is known as outsourcing. For example, companies such as ServiceMaster, which provides janitorial services, and ADP, which provides payroll-processing services, allow organizations to concentrate on the business functions most central to their missions, thereby freeing them from these peripheral support functions. Companies institute strategic plans to use outsourcing when the work they want to do is so highly critical and specialized that it requires outside assistance. For example, many manufacturing companies have found it more cost-effective to outsource some of their manufacturing operations to specialized companies than to build the expensive plants and find the trained workers required to build certain products. In fact, one industry analyst has estimated that 30 percent of the largest U.S. industrial firms outsource more than half their manufacturing.[12]

THE STRATEGIC PLANNING PROCESS

The process of strategic planning typically follows 10 ordered steps, which I will now describe.[13] These steps are not immutable, and they are not always followed in perfect order. However, they do a reasonably good job of describing how companies plan change strategically. As I describe these steps, you may find it useful to examine the summary appearing in Figure 14.1.

1. *Define goals.* Strategic plans begin with clearly stated goals. Typically, these involve gaining a certain share of the market (e.g., market penetration of 40 percent) or achieving a certain financial standing (doubling profit in five years). Organizational goals also can involve society (e.g., making $1 million in charitable donations) or organizational culture (e.g., making the workplace more

FIGURE 14.1 Strategic Planning: A 10-Step Process

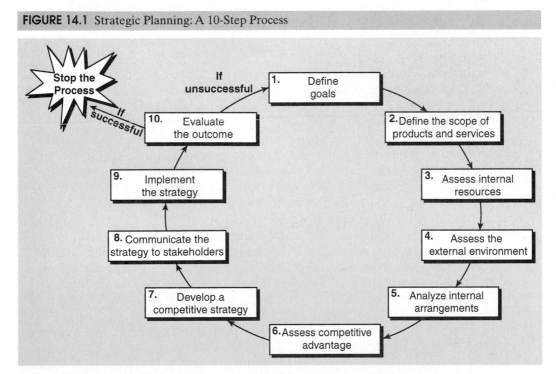

Strategic planning—the process of formulating, implementing, and evaluating decisions that enable an organization to achieve its objectives—generally follows the 10 steps summarized here. (*Source:* Based on suggestions by Christensen, 1994; see Note 13.)

pleasant for employees). It is important to note that overall organizational goals must be translated into corresponding goals to be achieved by the various individual units. For example, if a company has the goal of achieving 10 percent penetration into a market, it is important to establish clear goals for the marketing department (e.g., how to advertise so as to reach the right customers) and the production department (e.g., producing finished products at the appropriate rate to meet market demands).

2. *Define the scope of products and services.* For a strategic plan to be effective, company officials must define their organization's scope—that is, the businesses in which it already operates and the new businesses in which it aims to participate. If a company's scope is defined too broadly, it will dilute its effectiveness; if scope is defined too narrowly, it will overlook opportunities. Beech-Nut faced this issue when confronted with the fact that lowered birthrates shrunk the size of its market. In an effort to rebuild its business, Beech-Nut executives made the strategic decision to broaden its scope by developing products to feed elderly people with digestive problems.[14]

3. *Assess internal resources.* Organizations must ask themselves: What resources does the company have available to plan and to implement its strategy? The resources in question involve funds (e.g., cash to make purchases), physical assets (e.g., required space), and human assets (e.g., workers' knowledge and skills).

4. *Assess the external environment.* As I have noted throughout this book, organizations do not operate in a vacuum. Rather, they function within environments that influence their capacity to operate and to grow as desired. The extent to which the environment aids or hinders a company's growth—or even its existence—depends on several key factors. Specifically, a company has a competitive advantage over others when its resources cannot easily be imitated by others, its resources will not depreciate anytime soon, and competitors do not have better resources.[15]

5. *Analyze internal arrangements.* By "internal arrangements," I am referring to the nature of the organization itself. For example, are employees motivated to strive for corporate goals (see Chapter 4)? Does the organizational culture encourage people to be innovative and make changes (see Chapter 12)? Do people communicate with one another clearly enough to accomplish their goals (see Chapter 8)? These and other basic questions about the organization must be answered to formulate an effective strategic plan. After all, unless the organization is operating properly, even the best strategic plans are doomed to fail.

6. *Assess the competitive advantage.* One company is said to have a competitive advantage over another to the extent that customers perceive its products or services as being superior (e.g., in quality, cost, or both) to those of other companies. Superiority may be assessed in terms of factors such as quality, price, breadth of product line, reliability of performance, styling, service, and company image.

7. *Develop a competitive strategy.* A **competitive strategy** is the means by which an organization achieves its goal. Based on careful assessment of the company's standing regarding the factors described earlier (e.g., available resources, com-

TABLE 14.2	Varieties of Competitive Strategies

Some of the most popular competitive strategies used by today's organizations are summarized here.

Strategy	*Description*
Market-share increasing strategies	Developing a broader share of an existing market, such as by widening the range of products, or by forming a joint venture (see Chapter 13) with another company that already has a presence in the market of interest
Profit strategies	Attempting to derive more profit from existing businesses, such as by training employees to work more efficiently or salespeople to sell more effectively
Market concentration strategies	Withdrawing from markets where the company is less effective and concentrating resources in markets where the company is likely to be more effective
Turnaround strategies	Attempting to reverse a decline in business by moving to a new product line or by radically restructuring operations
Exit strategies	Withdrawing from a market, such as by liquidating assets

petitive advantage, and so on), a decision is made about how to achieve its goal. Some possible strategies are described in Table 14.2.

8. *Communicate the strategy to stakeholders.* The term **stakeholder** refers to an individual or group in whose interest the organization is run. The most important stakeholders include employees at all levels, boards of governors, and stockholders. It is essential to communicate a firm's strategy to stakeholders so they may contribute to its success, whether actively (e.g., employees who pitch in to help meet the goals) or passively (e.g., investors who pour money into the company to help meet goals). Unless stakeholders fully understand and accept a firm's strategy, that firm is unlikely to receive the full support needed to meet its goals.

9. *Implement the strategy.* Once a strategy has been formulated and communicated, the time has come for it to be implemented. When this occurs, some fallout is inevitable as employees scramble to adjust to new ways of doing things. As I will explain later in this chapter, people generally resist change, but as I also will describe, several steps can be taken to ensure that the individuals making the required changes will come to embrace them.

10. *Evaluate the outcome.* Finally, after a strategy has been implemented, it is crucial to determine if the goals have been met. If so, new goals may be sought; if not, different goals may be defined or different strategies may be followed to achieve success next time.

If, after reading this, you are thinking that developing a strategic plan is very difficult, and that carrying it out is even more challenging, you have reached the same conclusion as many top executives. For practice in creating your own strategic plan, see the **Self-Assessment Exercise** on p. 389.

Readiness for Change: Accepting and Resisting Organizational Change

As you might imagine, there are times when organizations are likely to change and times during which change is less likely. In general, change is likely to occur when the people involved believe that the benefits associated with making a change outweigh the costs involved. The factors contributing to the benefits of making a change are as follows:

- The amount of dissatisfaction with current conditions
- The availability of a desirable alternative
- The existence of a plan for achieving that alternative

Theorists have claimed that these three factors combine multiplicatively to determine the benefits of making a change (see Figure 14.2). Thus, if any one of these factors is zero, the benefits of making a change, and the likelihood of change itself, will be zero. If you think about it, this makes sense. After all, people are unlikely to initiate change if they are not at all dissatisfied, or if they don't have any desirable alternative in mind (or any way of attaining that alternative, if they do have one in mind). Of course, for change to occur, the expected benefits must outweigh the likely costs involved (e.g., disruption, uncertainties).

WHY IS ORGANIZATIONAL CHANGE RESISTED?

Although people may be unhappy with the current state of affairs confronting them in organizations, they may be afraid that any changes will be potentially disruptive and will only make things worse.[16] Indeed, fear of new conditions is quite real and it creates an unwillingness to accept change. Organizational scientists have recognized that **resistance to change** stems from both individual and organizational variables.

FIGURE 14.2 Organizational Change: When Will It Occur?

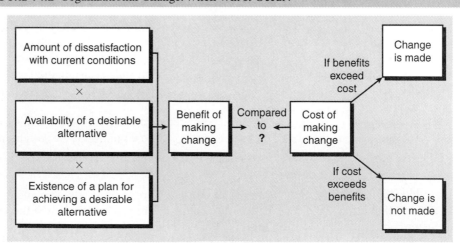

Whether an organizational change is made depends on people's beliefs regarding the relative benefits and costs of that change. These are reflected by the three considerations reviewed here.

Individual barriers to change. Researchers have noted several key factors that are known to make people resistant to change in organizations.[17] These are as follows.

- *Economic insecurity.* Because any changes on the job have the potential to threaten one's livelihood—by either loss of job or reduced pay—some resistance to change is inevitable.
- *Fear of the unknown.* Employees derive a sense of security from doing things the same way, knowing who their coworkers will be, and whom they're supposed to answer to from day to day. Disrupting these well-established, comfortable patterns creates unfamiliar conditions, a state of affairs that is often rejected.
- *Threats to social relationships.* As people continue to work within organizations, they form strong bonds with their coworkers. Many organizational changes (e.g., the reassignment of job responsibilities) threaten the integrity of friendship groups that provide valuable social rewards.
- *Habit.* Jobs that are well learned and become habitual are easy to perform. The prospect of changing the way jobs are done challenges people to develop new job skills. Doing this is clearly more difficult than continuing to perform the job as it was originally learned.
- *Failure to recognize the need for change.* Unless employees recognize and fully appreciate the need for changes in organizations, any vested interests they may have in keeping things the same may overpower their willingness to accept change.

Organizational barriers to change. Resistance to organizational change also stems from conditions associated with organizations themselves.[18] Several such factors may be identified. These are as follows:

- *Structural inertia.* Organizations are designed to promote stability. To the extent that employees are carefully selected and trained to perform certain jobs, and rewarded for doing them well, the forces acting on individuals to perform in certain ways are very powerfully determined—that is, jobs have *structural inertia.* Thus, because jobs are designed to have stability, it is often difficult to overcome the resistance created by the forces that create stability.
- *Work group inertia.* Inertia to continue performing jobs in a specified way comes not only from the jobs themselves but also from the social groups within which people work—*work group inertia.* Because of the development of strong social norms within groups (see Chapter 8), potent pressures exist to perform jobs in certain ways. Introducing change disrupts these established normative expectations, leading to formidable resistance.
- *Threats to existing balance of power.* If changes are made with respect to who's in charge, a shift in the balance of power between individuals and organizational subunits is likely to occur. Those units that now control the resources, have the expertise, and wield the power may fear losing their advantageous positions resulting from any organizational change.
- *Previously unsuccessful change efforts.* Anyone who has lived through a past disaster understandably may be reluctant to endure another attempt at the same thing. Similarly, groups or entire organizations that have been unsuccessful in introducing change in the past may be cautious about accepting further attempts at introducing change into the system.

During the 1980s and 1990s, General Electric (GE) has undergone a series of wide-spread changes in its basic strategy, organizational structure, and relationship with employees. In this process, it experienced several of the barriers just identified. For example, GE managers had mastered a set of bureaucratic traditions that kept their habits strong and their inertia moving straight ahead. The prospect of doing things differently was scary for those who were so strongly entrenched in doing things the "GE way." In particular, the company's interest in globalizing triggered many fears of the unknown. Resistance to change at GM was also strong because it threatened to strip power from those units that traditionally possessed most of it (e.g., the Power Systems and Lighting division). Changes also were highly disruptive to GE's "social architecture"; friendship groups were broken up and scattered throughout the company. In all, GE has been a living example of many different barriers to change all rolled into a single company.

HOW CAN RESISTANCE TO ORGANIZATIONAL CHANGE BE OVERCOME?

Because organizational change is inevitable, managers should be sensitive to the barriers to change so that resistance can be overcome. This, of course, is easier said than done. However, several useful approaches have been suggested, and the key ones are summarized here.[19]

1. *Shape political dynamics.* For change to be accepted, it is often useful (if not absolutely necessary) to win the support of the most powerful and influential individuals in the company. Doing so builds a critical internal mass of support for change. Demonstrating clearly that key organizational leaders endorse the change is an effective way to get others to go along with it—either because they share the leader's vision or because they fear the leader's retaliation. Either way, their support will facilitate acceptance of change.

2. *Educate the workforce.* Sometimes, people are reluctant to change because they fear what the future has in store for them. Fears about economic security, for example, may be put to rest by a few reassuring words from power holders. As part of educating employees about what organizational changes may mean for them, top management must show a considerable amount of emotional sensitivity. Doing so makes it possible for the people affected by change to help make it work. Some companies have found that simply answering the question "what's in it for me?" can help allay a lot of fears.

3. *Involve employees in the change efforts.* It is well established that people who participate in making a decision tend to be more committed to the outcomes of that decision than are those who are not involved. Accordingly, employees who are involved in responding to unplanned change, or who are made part of the team charged with planning a needed organizational change, may be expected to have very little resistance to change. Organizational changes that are "sprung" on the workforce with little or no warning might be expected to encounter resistance simply as a knee-jerk reaction until employees have a chance to assess how the change affects them. In contrast, employees who are involved in the change process are better able to understand the need for change and are therefore less likely to resist it. Says Duane Hartley, general manager of Hewlett-Packard's microwave instruments division, "I don't think people really

> *Employees who are involved in the change process are better able to understand the need for change and are therefore less likely to resist it. Says Duane Hartley, general manager of Hewlett-Packard's microwave instruments division, "I don't think people really enjoy change, but if they can participate in it and understand it, it can become a positive [experience] for them."*

enjoy change, but if they can participate in it and understand it, it can become a positive [experience] for them."[20]

4. *Reward constructive behaviors.* One rather obvious, and quite successful, mechanism for facilitating organizational change is rewarding people for behaving in the desired fashion. Changing organizational operations may necessitate changing the kinds of behaviors that need to be rewarded by the organization. This is especially critical when an organization is in the transition period of introducing the change. For example, employees who are required to learn to use new equipment should be praised for their successful efforts. Feedback on how well they are doing not only provides a great deal of useful assurance to uncertain employees but also helps shape the desired behavior.

5. *Create a "learning organization."* Although all organizations change, whether they want to or not, some do so more effectively than others. Those organizations that have developed the capacity to adapt and change continuously are known as **learning organizations**.[21] In learning organizations, people set aside old ways of thinking, freely share ideas with others, form a vision of the organization, and work together on a plan for achieving that vision. Examples of learning organizations include Ford, General Electric, Motorola, Wal-Mart, and Xerox. As you might imagine, becoming a learning organization is no simple feat. In fact, it involves implementing many of the principles of organizational behavior described in this book. Specifically, for a firm to become a continual learner, management must take the three steps outlined in Table 14.3.

Although these five suggestions may be easier to state than to implement, efforts at following them will be well rewarded. Given the many forces that make employees resistant to change, managers should keep these guidelines in mind. (For a chance to think more about resistance to organizational change and ways to overcome it, see the **Group Exercise** on p. 390.)

Organizational Development Interventions: Implementing Planned Change

Now that you appreciate the basic issues surrounding organizational change, you are prepared to understand systematic ways of implementing it—tactics collectively known as techniques of **organizational development** (**OD**). Formally, organizational development may be defined as a set of social science techniques designed to plan and implement change in work settings for purposes of enhancing the personal development of individuals and improving the effectiveness of organizational functioning. By planning organization-wide changes involving people, OD seeks to enhance organizational

TABLE 14.3 Ways to Become a Learning Organization

Learning organizations are ones that are successful at acquiring, cultivating, and applying knowledge that can be used to help it adopt to change. To become an effective learning organization, managers must follow the rules outlined here.

Rule	Description
Establish a commitment to change	Unless all employees clearly see top management as being strongly committed to changing and to improving the organization, they will be unlikely to make the changes necessary to bring about such improvements.
Adopt an informal organizational structure	Change is more readily accepted when organizational structures are flat (see Chapter 13), when cross-functional teams are created (see Chapter 9), and when formal boundaries between people are eliminated.
Develop an open organizational culture	As described in Chapter 12, managers play a key role, in forming organizational culture. To adapt effectively to changes in their environments, organizations should have cultures that embrace risk taking, openness, and growth.

performance by improving the quality of the work environment and the attitudes and well-being of employees.[22]

Over the years, many different strategies for implementing planned organizational change (referred to as **OD interventions**) have been used by specialists attempting to improve organizational functioning (referred to as **OD practitioners** or **change agents**). These are individuals, usually from outside the organization, who coordinate and facilitate an organization's change efforts. All the major methods of organizational development attempt to produce some kind of change in individual employees, work groups, or entire organizations.[23] This is the goal of the three OD interventions I will review here.

SURVEY FEEDBACK

For effective organizational change to occur, employees must understand the organization's current strengths and weaknesses. That's the underlying rationale behind the **survey feedback** method. This technique follows the three steps summarized in Figure 14.3. First, data are collected that provide information about matters of general concern to employees, such as organizational climate, leadership style, and job satisfaction. This may take the form of intensive interviews, structured questionnaires, or both. Because it is important that this information be as unbiased as possible, employees providing feedback should be assured that their responses will be kept confidential. For this reason, this process is usually conducted by outside consultants.

The second step calls for reporting the information obtained back to the employees during small group meetings. Typically, this consists of summarizing the average scores on the attitudes assessed in the survey. Profiles are created of feelings about the organization, its leadership, the work done, and related topics. Discussions also focus on why the scores are as they are, and what problems are revealed by the feedback. The final step involves analyzing problems dealing with communication, decision making, and other organizational processes to make plans for dealing with them. Such discus-

FIGURE 14.3 Survey Feedback: An Overview

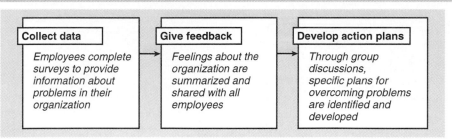

The *survey feedback* technique of OD follows the three steps outlined here: collecting data, giving feedback, and developing action plans.

sions are usually most effective when they are carefully documented and a specific plan of implementation is made, with someone put in charge of carrying it out.

Survey feedback is a widely used organizational development technique. This is not surprising in view of the advantages it offers. It is efficient, allowing a great deal of information to be collected relatively quickly. Also, it is very flexible and can be tailored to the needs of different organizations facing a variety of problems. However, the technique can be no better than the quality of the questionnaire used—it must measure the things that really matter to employees. Of course, to derive the maximum benefit from survey feedback, it must have the support of top management. The plans developed by the small discussion groups must be capable of being implemented with the full approval of the organization. When these conditions are met, survey feedback can be a very effective OD technique.

MANAGEMENT BY OBJECTIVES

In Chapter 3 I discussed the motivational benefits of setting specific goals. As you might imagine, not only individuals, but entire organizations stand to benefit from setting specific goals. For example, an organization may strive to "raise production" and "improve the quality" of its manufactured goods. These goals, well-intentioned though they may be, may not be as useful to an organization as more specific ones, such as "increase production of widgets by 15 percent" or "lower the failure rate of widgets by 25 percent." After all, as the old saying goes, "It's usually easier to get somewhere if you know where you're going." Peter Drucker, consulting for General Electric during the early 1950s, was well aware of this idea and is credited with promoting the benefits of specifying clear organizational goals—a technique known as **management by objectives (MBO)**.

The MBO process, summarized in Figure 14.4, consists of three basic steps. First, goals are selected that employees will try to attain to best serve the needs of the organization. The goals should be selected by managers and their subordinates together. The goals must be set mutually by all those involved, not simply imposed. Further, these goals should be directly measurable and have some time frame attached to them. Goals that cannot be measured (e.g., "make the company better"), or that have no time limits, are useless. It is also crucial that managers and their subordinates work together to plan ways of attaining the goals they have selected—developing what is known as an *action plan*.

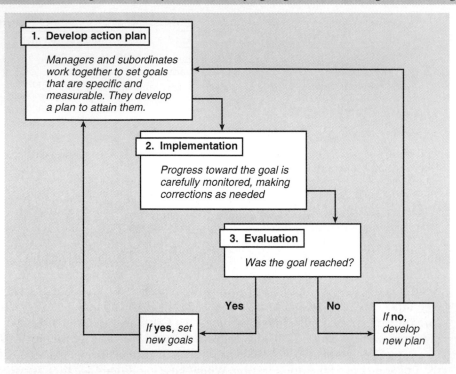

FIGURE 14.4 Management by Objectives: Developing Organizations Through Goal Setting

1. Develop action plan

Managers and subordinates work together to set goals that are specific and measurable. They develop a plan to attain them.

2. Implementation

Progress toward the goal is carefully monitored, making corrections as needed

3. Evaluation

Was the goal reached?

Yes   No

If **yes**, set new goals

If **no**, develop new plan

The OD technique known as *management by objectives* requires managers and subordinates to work together on setting and trying to achieve important organizational goals. The basic steps in the process are outlined here.

Once goals are set and action plans have been developed, the second step calls for *implementation*—carrying out the plan and regularly assessing its progress. Is the plan working? Are the goals being approximated? Are there any problems being encountered in attempting to meet the goals? Such questions need to be considered while implementing an action plan. If the plan is failing, a midcourse correction may be in order—changing the plan, the way it's carried out, or even the goal itself. Finally, after monitoring progress toward the goal, the third step may be instituted: *evaluation*—assessing goal attainment. Were the organization's goals reached? If so, what new goals should be set to improve things still further? If not, what new plans can be initiated to help meet the goals? Because the ultimate assessment of the extent to which goals are met helps determine the selection of new goals, MBO is a continuous process.

MBO represents a potentially effective source of planning and implementing strategic change for organizations. Individual efforts designed to meet organizational goals get the individual employee and the organization itself working together toward common ends. Hence, system-wide change results. Of course, for MBO to work, everyone involved has to buy into it. Because MBO programs typically require a great deal of participation by lower-level employees, top managers must be willing to accept and support the cooperation and involvement of all. Making MBO work also requires a great deal of time—anywhere from three to five years. Hence, MBO may be inappropriate in organizations that do not have the time to commit to making it work. Despite these considerations, MBO has become one of the most widely used techniques for affecting organizational change in recent years. It not only is used on an ad hoc basis by many organizations but also constitutes an ingrained element of the organizational culture in some companies, such as Hewlett-Packard and IBM.

APPRECIATIVE INQUIRY

Although survey feedback and MBO are highly regarded OD techniques, they focus on deficiencies, such as negative feedback and unmet goals. A new approach to organizational development known as *appreciative inquiry* helps organizations break out of this focus on negative dynamics by focusing on the positive and the possible.[24] Specifically, **appreciative inquiry** is an OD intervention that focuses attention away from an organization's shortcomings, and toward its capabilities and potential. It is based on the assumption that members of organizations already know the problems they face and that they stand to benefit more by focusing on what is possible.

As currently practiced, the process of appreciative inquiry follows four straightforward steps. These are as follows:[25]

1. *Discovery.* The discovery step involves identifying the positive aspects of the organization, the best of "what is." This frequently is accomplished by documenting the positive reactions of customers or people from other organizations.
2. *Dreaming.* Through the process of discovering the organization's strengths, it is possible to begin dreaming by envisioning "what might be." By discussing dreams for a theoretically ideal organization, employees are free to reveal their ideal hopes and dreams.
3. *Designing.* The designing stage involves having a dialogue in which participants discuss their ideas about "what should be." The underlying idea is that by listening to others in a highly receptive manner, it is possible to understand others' ideas and to come to a common understanding of what the future should look like.
4. *Delivering.* After having jointly discussed the ideal state of affairs, members of the organization are ready to begin instituting a plan for delivering their ideas. Specifically, this involves establishing specific objectives and directions regarding "what will be."

Because appreciative inquiry is an emerging approach to OD, it has not been widely used. However, those organizations in which it has been used have been quite pleased with the results.[26]

Special Issues in Organizational Development

No discussion of organizational development would be complete without addressing three important questions—do the techniques work, are their effects culture-dependent, and are they ethical? I will now address each of these issues.

THE EFFECTIVENESS OF ORGANIZATIONAL DEVELOPMENT: DOES IT REALLY WORK?

Thus far, I have described some of the major techniques used by OD practitioners to improve organizational functioning. As is probably clear, carrying out these techniques requires a considerable amount of time, money, and effort. Accordingly, it is appropriate to ask if this investment is worthwhile. In other words, does OD really work? Given the popularity of OD in organizations, this question is very important.

The answer is generally *yes:* Research has shown that OD interventions tend to be beneficial when it comes to improving organizational functioning.[27] I hasten to add that any conclusions about the effectiveness of OD should be qualified in several important ways. Specifically:

- OD interventions generally are more effective among blue-collar employees than among white-collar employees.
- The beneficial effects of OD can be enhanced by using a combination of several techniques instead of any single one.
- To be effective, OD techniques must have the support of top management; the more strongly OD programs are supported from the top, the more successful they are.

Despite the importance of attempting to evaluate the effectiveness of OD interventions, a great many of them go unevaluated. Although there are undoubtedly many reasons for this, one key factor is the difficulty of assessing change. Because many factors can cause people to behave differently in organizations, and because such behaviors may be difficult to measure, many OD practitioners avoid the problem of measuring change altogether. In a related vein, political pressures to justify OD programs may discourage some OD professionals from honestly and accurately assessing their effectiveness. After all, in doing so, one runs the risk of scientifically demonstrating one's wasted time and money. With an eye toward assessing the effectiveness of change efforts before they are implemented, growing numbers of organizations are turning to simulations. For a closer look at how organizational change is simulated, see the **Winning Practices** box below.

WINNING PRACTICES

Simulating Organizational Change

Toronto's Optus Corporation has a problem: It's growing too fast for its own good. In just its first 13 months, the company, which custom designs documents for financial-services companies, such as Aetna and Citibank, has boosted its employee base 500 percent and has acquired a new company every three months. Revenues jumped from $40 million in 1999 to $100 million (Canadian) in 2000. Although many executives would be envious of such a "problem," such dramatic growth has taken its toll on company officials, who wonder how they will ever be able to catch up with the deadlines without slowing down the company's growth.

To help, Chief Operating Officer John Hantho decided that the members of his senior executive team should cross the Sahara Desert—virtually, that is.[28] And so they did. With help from two facilitators from InCourage, a Canadian multimedia company, the 10-person team worked its way through *Shifting Sands*, an exercise that helps groups prepare for organizational change. The simulation consists of a full-day multimedia recreation of an actual 1977 expedition across the 1,000-mile-wide Sahara Desert. At various points along the journey, the team is challenged to make decisions that will either help members make it further across the desert or bury them in the sand. The trip across the various microclimates, ecosystems, and cultures is a metaphor for the changes confronting Optus.

As the journey begins, the travelers bid good-bye to the lives they knew in the civilized world, prompting one of the facilitators to ask what people are willing to give up as their old company evolves into something entirely new. The response that emerged from the ensuing discussion was that employees of the various companies acquired by Optus had to give up their identities and think of themselves as being part of Optus. To do this without completely giving up their previous identities, the team came up with the idea of developing a Hall of Fame, where names of the acquired companies could be put to rest in an honorable fashion.

Further into the trip, the group saw a slide showing a two-track road that ended abruptly, with nothing but desert sand beyond it. This was Optus—moving into an unknown world without signs to point the way. Slowing down to get team members' bearings made sense, but competing in the rapidly changing marketplace didn't allow them to do so. Metaphorically, they were stuck in the sand, spinning their wheels but getting nowhere. Eventually, the team found a solution: Keep the sales reps from making unrealistic promises to clients, allowing them to take on new business without getting further behind and angering clients with unfulfilled promises.

Optus officials are convinced that the simulation helped the company in two key ways. First, the simulation provided a mechanism that allowed members of the executive team to stand back and gain perspective from daily job pressures, allowing them to identify problems and ways of solving them. By testing their ideas in the simulated desert environment, they came away from the exercise with a good idea of what would work back in the office. Second, the simulation helped by building camaraderie in the executive suite, allowing the team members to reconnect. In the simulation's terms, they could recalibrate their compasses before heading into the next leg of their journey.

Questions for Discussion

1. What do you see as the major advantages of the simulation approach used by Optus?
2. What limitations of such simulations, if any, do you envision?
3. In what ways might such a simulation help you assess change in the job you do?

IS ORGANIZATIONAL DEVELOPMENT DEPENDENT ON NATIONAL CULTURE?

For organizational development to be effective, people must be willing to share their ideas candidly with others, they must be willing to accept uncertainty, and they must be willing to show concern for others, especially members of their own teams. However, not all people are willing to do these things; this pattern better characterizes the people from some countries than others. For example, this profile perfectly describes people from Scandinavian countries, suggesting that OD may be most effective in such nations. However, people from Latin American nations are much the opposite, suggesting that OD interventions will be less successful when conducted there.[29] For a summary of the extent to which the basic assumptions of OD fit with the cultural styles of people from various nations, see Figure 14.5.

Although the predominant cultural values of people from the United States place it in the middle region of the diagram in Figure 14.5, this is not to say that OD is doomed to be ineffective in American companies. Not all OD techniques are alike with respect to their underlying cultural values.[30] For example, MBO has become a very popular OD technique in the United States, in large part because it promotes the American values of willingness to take risks and working aggressively at attaining high performance. However, because MBO also encourages superiors and subordinates to negotiate freely with each other, the technique has been generally unsuccessful in France, where others' higher levels of authority are well accepted.[31] Reasoning similarly, one may expect survey feedback to be unsuccessful in the Southeast Asian nation of Brunei, where the prevailing cultural value is such that problems are unlikely to be confronted openly.[32]

These examples illustrate a key point: The effectiveness of OD techniques will depend, in part, on the extent to which the values of the technique match the underly-

FIGURE 14.5 Organizational Development: Its Fit with Cultural Values

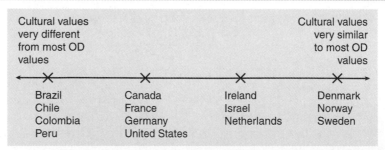

Organizational development (OD) techniques tend to be more successful when the underlying values of the technique match the cultural values of the nation in which it is used. General OD values tend to conform more to the cultural values of some nations, shown on the right (where OD is more likely to be accepted) than to others, shown on the left (where OD is less likely to be accepted). (*Source:* Based on suggestions by Jaeger, 1986; see Note 29.)

The effectiveness of OD techniques will depend, in part, on the extent to which the values of the technique match the underlying values of the national culture in which it is employed. As such, OD practitioners must fully appreciate the cultural norms of the nations in which they are operating.

ing values of the national culture in which it is employed. As such, OD practitioners must fully appreciate the cultural norms of the nations in which they are operating. Failure to do so not only may make OD interventions unsuccessful, but they may even have unintended negative consequences.

IS ORGANIZATIONAL DEVELOPMENT INHERENTLY UNETHICAL?
A DEBATE

By its very nature, OD applies powerful social science techniques in an attempt to change attitudes and behavior. From the perspective of a manager attempting to accomplish various goals, such tools are immediately recognized as very useful. However, if you think about it from the perspective of the individual being affected, several ethical issues arise.[33]

For example, it has been argued that OD techniques impose the values of the organization on the individual without taking the individual's own attitudes into account. OD is a very one-sided approach, reflecting the imposition of the more powerful organization on the less powerful individual. A related argument is that the OD process does not provide any free choice on the part of the employees. As a result, it may be seen as coercive and manipulative. When faced with a "do it, or else" situation, employees tend to have little free choice and are forced to allow themselves to be manipulated, a potentially degrading prospect.

Another issue is that the unequal power relationship between the organization and its employees makes it possible for the true intent of OD techniques to be misrepresented. As an example, imagine that an MBO technique is presented to employees as a means of allowing greater organizational participation, whereas in reality it is used as a means for holding individuals responsible for their poor performance and punishing them as a result. Although such an event might not happen, the potential for abuse of this type does exist, and the potential to misuse the technique—even if not originally intended—might later prove to be too great a temptation.

Despite these considerations, many professionals do *not* agree that OD is inherently unethical. Such a claim, it has been countered, is to say that the practice of management is itself unethical. After all, the very act of going to work for an organization requires one to submit to the organization's values and the overall values of society. One cannot help but face life situations in which others' values are imposed. This is not to say that organizations have the right to impose patently unethical values on people for making a profit (e.g., stealing from customers). Indeed, because they have the potential to abuse their power (such as in the MBO example), organizations have a special obligation to refrain from doing so.

The ethical use of OD interventions requires that they be supervised by professionals in an organization that places a high value on ethics. To the extent that top management officials embrace ethical values and behave ethically themselves, norms for behaving ethically are likely to develop in organizations.

Although abuses of organizational power sometimes occur, OD itself is not necessarily the culprit. Indeed, like any other tool (even a gun!), OD is not inherently good or evil. Instead, *whether the tool is used for good or evil will depend on the individual using it.* With this in mind, the ethical use of OD interventions requires that they be supervised by professionals in an organization that places a high value on ethics. To the extent that top management officials embrace ethical values and behave ethically themselves, norms for behaving ethically are likely to develop in organizations. When an organization has a strong ethical culture, it is unlikely that OD practitioners would even think of misusing their power to harm individuals. The need to develop such a culture has been recognized as a way for organizations to take not only moral leadership in their communities, but financial leadership as well.

SUMMARY: HAVE I MET THE LEARNING OBJECTIVES?

You can be certain that you have met the learning objectives for this chapter found on p. 365 if you understand the following:

1. **IDENTIFY the major external forces responsible for organizational change.** Organizational change is promoted by advances in computer technology, changing employee demographics, performance gaps, government regulation, and global economic competition.

2. **DESCRIBE what is meant by strategic planning and IDENTIFY the steps in the process of planning strategic change.** Strategic planning is the process of formulating, implementing, and evaluating organizational changes in ways that enable an organization to achieve its objectives. The process consists of the following 10 steps: (a) defining goals, (b) defining the scope of products or services, (c) assessing internal resources, (d) assessing the external environment, (e) analyzing internal arrangements, (f) assessing the competitive advantage, (g) developing a competitive strategy, (h) communicating the strategy to stakeholders, (i) implementing the strategy, and (j) evaluating the outcome.

3. **IDENTIFY the conditions under which organizational change occurs.** Organizational change is likely to occur when (a) people are dissatisfied with current conditions, (b) a desirable alternative is believed to be available, (c) a plan exists for achieving a desirable alternative, and (d) the benefits of making the change are believed to exceed the costs.

4. **DESCRIBE why people are resistant to change in organizations and ways in which this resistance may be overcome.** In general, people are resistant to change because of individual factors (e.g., economic insecurity, fear of the unknown) and organizational factors (e.g., the stability of work groups, threats to the existing balance of power). However, resistance to change can be overcome in several ways, including shaping political dynamics, educating the workforce

about the effects of the changes, involving employees in change efforts, rewarding constructive behaviors, and creating a learning organization.

5. **DEFINE organizational development (OD) and DESCRIBE three OD techniques.** *Organizational development* is a set of techniques for systematically planning organizational change for purposes of enhancing personal and organizational outcomes. *Survey feedback* is an OD technique in which questionnaires or interviews are used as the basis for identifying organizational problems, which then are addressed in planning sessions. *Management by objectives* (*MBO*) focuses on attempts by managers and their subordinates to work together at setting important organizational goals and developing a plan to meet those goals. *Appreciative inquiry* is a new OD technique that focuses attention away from an organization's shortcomings, and toward its capabilities and its potential. It is based on the assumption that members of organizations already know the problems they face and that they stand to benefit more by focusing on what is possible.

6. **DESCRIBE the conditions under which OD is most effective.** OD techniques are generally effective, although they tend to be most effective among blue-collar workers, when several different techniques are used at once, when they have the support of top management, and when the values underlying the technique match the values of the people in the country in which the intervention is carried out.

You Be the Consultant

Things have been rough for the former employees at Small Town S&L ever since their institution was bought by First National Mega Bank. First National's procedures were more formal and nowhere as casual as those at Small Town. The CEO of First National is concerned about the employees' adjustment to the change and calls upon you for help. Answer the following questions relevant to this situation based on the material in this chapter.

1. Besides new operating procedures, what other planned and unplanned changes would you suspect as being responsible for the employees' negative responses?
2. What barriers to change are likely to be encountered in this situation, and what steps would you propose to overcome them?
3. Do you think that an OD intervention would help in this case? If so, which one (or ones) do you propose, and why?

SELF-ASSESSMENT EXERCISE

Developing a Strategic Plan

Developing a strategic plan is not easy. In fact, doing it right requires a great deal of information—and a great deal of practice. This exercise will give you a feel for some of the challenges involved in developing such a plan.

Directions

1. Suppose you are the president of a small software-development firm that for years has sold a utility that added functionality to the operating system used in most computers. Now you suddenly face a serious problem: Microsoft has changed its operating system, and your product no longer serves any purpose.
2. Using the 10 steps outlined in Figure 14.1, develop a strategic plan to keep your company alive. Make any assumptions you need to develop your plan, but state these in the process of describing it.

Questions for Discussion

1. How easy or difficult was it to develop this plan? What would have made the process easier?
2. Which step do you imagine would be the easiest to implement? Which step do you think would be the most difficult?
3. What special challenges, if any, would the employees of your company face as they implemented this plan? How would you overcome these challenges?

Recognizing Impediments to Change—And How to Overcome Them

One of the most fundamental steps when it comes to confronting the reality of organizational change involves recognizing the barriers to change. Then, once these impediments have been identified, consideration can be given to ways of overcoming them. This exercise is designed to help you practice thinking along these lines while working in groups.

Directions

1. Divide the class into groups of approximately six and gather each group around a circle.
2. Each group should consider each of the following situations.

   Situation A: A highly sophisticated e-mail system is being introduced at a large university. It will replace the practice of transmitting memos on paper.

   Situation B: A very popular employee who's been with the company for many years is retiring. He will be replaced by a completely new employee from the outside.

3. For each situation, discuss three major impediments to change.
4. Identify a way of overcoming each of these impediments.
5. Someone from the group should record the answers and present them to the class for a discussion session.

Questions for Discussion

1. For each of the situations, were the impediments to change similar or different?
2. For each of the situations, were the ways of overcoming the impediments similar or different?
3. How might the nature of the situation confronted dictate the types of change barriers confronted and the ease with which these may be overcome?

NOTES

Case Note
Muoio, A. (1999, December). Mint condition. *Fast Company,* pp. 330–332, 335–338, 342, 344, 346, 348.

Chapter Notes

1 Sherman, S. (1993, December 13). How will we live with the tumult? *Fortune,* pp. 123–125.

2 Neff, R. (1987, April 20). Getting man and machine to live happily ever after. *Business Week,* pp. 61–63.

3 Stewart, T. A. (1993, December 13). Welcome to the revolution. *Fortune,* pp. 66–68, 70, 72, 76, 78.

4 Kiley, D. (2000, December 13). GM waves goodbye to its Oldsmobile brand. *USA Today,* pp. 1B, 3B.

5 Freeland, R. F. (2001). *The struggle for control of the modern corporation: Organizational change at General Motors.* New York: Cambridge University Press.

6 Guillen, M. F. (2001). *The limits of convergence: Globalization and organizational change in Argentina, South Korea, and Spain.* Princeton, NJ: Princeton University Press.

7 Howes, F. (1998, December 21). Future hinges on global teams. *Detroit News,* p. C1.

8 Chaize, J. (2000). *Quantum leap: Tools for managing companies in the new economy.* New York: St. Martin's Press.

9 Dudik, E. M. (2000). *Strategic renaissance: New thinking and innovative tools to create great corporate strategies using insights from history and science.* New York: AMACOM.

10 Meade, R. (1998). *International management (2nd ed.).* Malden, MA: Blackwell.

11 McCarty, M. (1990, October 30). PepsiCo to consolidate its restaurants, combining U.S. and foreign operations. *Wall Street Journal,* p. A4.

12 See Note 3.

13 Christensen, H. K. (1994). Corporate strategy: Managing a set of businesses. In I. L. Flahey & R. M. Randall (Eds.), *The portable MBA in strategy* (pp. 53–83). New York: John Wiley.

14 Markides, C. (1997, spring). Strategic innovation. *Sloan Management Review,* pp. 9–23.

15 Collis, D. J., & Montgomery, C. A. (1995, July–August). Competing on resources: Strategy in the 1990s. *Harvard Business Review, 73,* 118–128.

16 Duck, J. D. (2001). *The change monster: The human forces that fuel or foil corporate transformation and change.* New York: Crown.

17 Nadler, D. A. (1987). The effective management of organizational change. In J. W. Lorsch (Ed.), *Handbook of organizational behavior* (pp. 358–369). Upper Saddle River, NJ: Prentice Hall.

18 Katz, D., & Kahn, R. L. (1978). *The social psychology of organizations (2nd ed.).* New York: John Wiley.

19 See Note 17.

20 Huey, J. (1993, April 5). Managing in the midst of chaos. *Fortune,* pp. 38–41, 44, 46, 48.

21 Senge, P. M. (1990). *The fifth discipline.* New York: Doubleday.

22 Anderson, L. S. A., & Anderson, D. W. (2001). *Beyond change management: Strategies for leading conscious transformation.* San Francisco: Jossey-Bass.

23 Harigopal, K. (2001). *Management of organizational change: Leveraging transformation.* Newbury Park, CA: Sage.

24 Watkins, J. M., & Mohr, B. J. (2001). *Appreciative injury: Change at the speed of imagination.* New York: John Wiley.

25 Whitney, D., & Sachau, C. (1998, Spring). Appreciative inquiry: An innovative process for organization change. *Employment Relations Today, 25,* 11–21.

26 Bushe, G. R., & Coetzer, G. (1995). Appreciative inquiry as a team-developed intervention: A controlled experiment. *Journal of 'Applied Behavioral Science, 31,* 13–30.

27 Porras, J. I., & Robertson, P. J. (1992). Organization development: Theory, practice, and research. In M. D. Dunnette & L. Hough (Eds.), *Handbook of industrial and organizational psychology (2nd ed.).* (Vol. 3, pp. 719–822). Palo Alto, CA: Consulting Psychologists Press.

[28] Blau, R. (1999, December). The practice of change. *Fast Company,* pp. 408–410, 412–416, 418–423.

[29] Jaeger, A. M. (1986). Organizational development and national culture: Where's the fit? *Academy of Management Review, 11,* 178–190.

[30] Kedia, B. L., & Bhagat, R. S. (1998). Cultural constraints on transfer of technology across nations: Implications for research in international and comparative management. *Academy of Management Review, 13,* 559–571.

[31] Trepo, G. (1973, autumn). Management style *à la française. European Business, 39,* 71–79.

[32] Blunt, P. (1988). Cultural consequences for organization change in a Southeast Asian state: Brunei. *Academy of Management Executive, 2,* 235–240.

[33] White, L. P., & Wotten, K. C. (1983). Ethical dilemmas in various stages of organizational development. *Academy of Management Review, 8,* 690–697.

Index

Bold entry indicates figure

A

Abrashoff, D. Michael, 297
Absence control programs, 72
Absenteeism, 127
Achievement motivation, 56–58; *see also* Job
    performance
Achievement-oriented, and path-goal theory, 292
Action plan, 381
Ad hoc committees; *see* Formal organizational
    group
ADA; *see* Americans with Disabilities Act
Additive tasks, 230
Affective commitment, 132; *see also*
    Organizational commitment
Affiliate networks, 355
Affirmative action plans, 119
  and mentoring, 178
  myth vs. fact, **120**
Affirmative action; *see* Affirmative action plans
Agreeableness, **54;** *see also* Personality
Allied-Signal, 351
Allstate Insurance Company, 122
Amazon.com, 353
American Express, 295
American Society for Training and
    Development, 40
Americans with Disabilities Act (ADA), 116
Ampex Corporation, 241
Anticipatory socialization; *see* Socialization
Appreciative inquiry, 383
Arousal, 83
Asia, and decision making, 256
Attribution
  of causality, 31
  correspondent inferences, 29–30; *see also*
    Social perception; Kelley's theory
  fundamental attribution error, 32
  Kelley's theory, 30–31, **31**

Authority, hierarchy of, 338–339
Automated decision conference, 273
Autonomy and independence, 180; *see also*
    Career anchors
  and creativity, 321
Autonomous change, 356
Avoidance; *see* Negative reinforcement

B

B.F. Goodrich, 257
Barnes&Noble.com, 298
Bank of America, 308
Bargaining, 156–158
Barnard, Seph, 52
Barrier-free organizations; *see* Boundaryless
    organizations
Bausch & Lomb, 240
Bay of Pigs, 270
Beauty.com, 342–343
Behavior
  causes of, 30
  external, 30–31
  internal, 30–31
  and overcoming change barriers, 379
Bestfoods, 295
Bethune, Gordon, 36
BFOQs; *see* Bona Fide Occupational
    Qualifications
Bijur, Peter I, 112
Black & Decker, 242
Bona Fide Occupational Qualifications
    (BFOQs), 312
Born leaders; *see* Leadership
Bossidy, Lawrence, 351
Bottom-line mentality, 258
Boundaryless organizations; *see* Organizations
Bounded discretion; *see* Ethics
Bounded rationality, 263